PREFACE

AT one time it was thought possible for the present work to be undertaken conjointly by the Rev. M. C. F. Morris, author of *Yorkshire Folk-Talk*, and myself. Such collaboration, though pleasing to both, was found to be quite impracticable. Many of my patrons and friends having urged me to undertake the work single-handed, I have ventured to do so. I have aimed at no higher standard than the chatty style which I have adopted in drawing-rooms and on the platform. If friends and critics prove but half as kind and considerate in this new venture as they have hitherto done, I have little to fear. My main object has been simply to place on record, in, I hope, a readable form, some of the wit, character, customs, and folklore of the North Riding which I have thought to be sufficiently interesting and worthy of being saved from that long list of things forgotten.

The chapter on some characteristic sayings of both the North and East Ridings, kindly contributed by the Rev. M. C. F. Morris, will add greatly to the value and interest of the work. I may here mention that he is in no way answerable for any other single sentence throughout the work. I feel it to be my duty to make this quite clear, for, as a humorist, I have ventured to include certain items which the reverend gentleman most probably would have run his pen through, had either the MS. or proof-sheets passed through his hands.

The Glossary, though far from containing all the words of our North Riding folk-speech, is as complete as it has been possible for me to make it.

My thanks are due to Mr. Atkinson and to Mr. Morris, whose glossaries I have frequently consulted, and in no less a degree to my friend Dr. Johnson of Lancaster for his MS. notes, so generously lent me.

I have done my best, and if my literary repast is not set before my readers with the usual glitter of silver and cut glass, I would humbly remind them that the fare has been fairly stalked and prepared with all due care as to accuracy, and cooked and served

Wit, Character, Folklore And Customs Of The North Riding Of Yorkshire: With A Glossary Of Over Four Thousand Words And Idioms Now In Use

Richard Blakeborough

Wit

Character, Folklore & Customs

OF THE

NORTH RIDING OF YORKSHIRE

WITH

A GLOSSARY OF OVER 4,000 WORDS AND IDIOMS NOW IN USE

BY

RICHARD BLAKEBOROUGH

(SOCIETY HUMORIST)

LATE HON. CURATOR OF THE R.S.S.; AUTHOR OF 'MORE THAN A DREAM,'
'T' HUNT O' YATTON BRIGG,' THE COMEDIES 'TOMBOY,' 'AUNTIE,' ETC.

London
HENRY FROWDE
OXFORD UNIVERSITY PRESS WAREHOUSE
AMEN CORNER, E.C.
1898

THIS WORK

IS DEDICATED TO

THE

REV. E. S. CARTER, M.A.

OF YORK

AND

J. G. WILSON, M.A.

OF DURHAM

AS A MEMENTO OF SINCERE GRATITUDE

FOR MANY ACTS OF FRIENDSHIP

SHOWN TO

THE AUTHOR

with the best of everything my literary kitchen possesses.

Many stories illustrative of Yorkshire character and humour are given, mostly gathered from original sources covering a period of many years, and in the main are true. None of them, I believe, have hitherto been published, and very few contained in these pages have I given publicly.

The stories afford numerous examples of the idiom and dialect as spoken in the North Riding, but mainly (as to dialect) in that of Cleveland. The reason for specializing that district is given elsewhere.

To the scores of happy hours spent with both old and young by their own firesides, I owe the contents of this book. Nearly all it contains they have given me: to them I return my warmest thanks.

One other word—should a copy of this work find its way into other lands, and be read by any of my Yorkshire colonial cousins, to them I sincerely offer the grip of friendship. And should any of our Yorkshire words have gained a footing on other soil, I shall be grateful for a list of the same.

To many of my subscribers I owe a lasting debt of gratitude for that kindness and cordiality which at once made me one of their house party when staying with them as Society Humorist, and also for the kind letters of encouragement they were so good as to send me in the early stage of my work, and to one and all I now offer my most sincere thanks for their cordial replies in answer to my circular.

In conclusion, should this work bring conviction that the Riding ought to have a Folklore and Dialectical Society identified with itself, I shall not have written in vain, and it would have my hearty if humble support. No time should be lost. Bear in mind, each aged person who passes from amongst us is another valuable volume removed from the shelves of an ever-decreasing library. I shall be glad to receive the names of any of my readers willing to help me in forming a North Riding Folklore and Dialectical Society.

THE AUTHOR.

24 TRENT STREET,
    STOCKTON-ON-TEES,
        September 27, 1898.

CONTENTS

LIST OF SUBSCRIBERS

A.

ALLISON, Dr. T., 9 Picton Place, Newcastle.
ALLISON, F., Church Green, Guisborough.
ANDERSON, TEMPEST, M.D., J.P., St. Agnes-gate, York.
ANDERSON, Major F. H., Fulford, York.
ANDERSON, W., Rimswell, Thornaby-on-Tees.
ARGLES, C. G., St. Clement's Vicarage, York.
ASHTON, The Right Hon. Lord, Rylands, Lancaster.

B.

BACKHOUSE, C. H., J.P., Darlington.
BARKER, E., Cleveland House, West Hartlepool.
BARKER, G., Tancred Grange, Scorton.
BARLING, Dr. A. S., Dalton Square, Lancaster.
BARRACLOUGH, W., Swainby.
BAYNES, Alderman JNO., J.P., Ripon.
BEATTY, Dr. H. J., Van Mildert House, Stockton-on-Tees.
BECK, Mrs., Carthorpe House, Bedale.
BECKETT, E. W., M.P., 17 Stratton St., Piccadilly, W.
BELL, HUGH, J.P., Red Barnes, Redcar.
BELL BROS., Ltd., Middlesborough.
BERESFORD PIERSE, Mrs., The Hall, Bedale.
BEST, Mrs., 31 Lyddon Terrace, Leeds.
BETHELL, Miss L., Newton Kyme, Tadcaster (2 copies).
BEVERLEY, The Right Rev. Lord Bishop of, Bolton Percy.
BIRCH, Mrs., Middleham, R.S.O.

BIRD, Col. C. H., Crookhey Hall, Garstang, Lancashire.
BLACKETT, Capt. C. M., Newsham Hall, Darlington.
BLAIR, Gen., V.C., C.B., Thorpe Hall, Wycliffe, Darlington.
BLANDFORD, Dr. J. M., Norton, Stockton-on-Tees.
BOHR, VON, Mill Hill, Brandsby.
BOWES-WILSON, T., Enterpen Hutton, Rudby (2 copies).
BOWSTEAD-WARWICK, P., Settlebeck, Sedbergh.
BRAMLEY, W., Church St., Guisborough.
BRIGGS, Rev. A. C., Moor Allerton.
BROOKSBANK, E. C., Helaugh Old Hall, Tadcaster.
BROWN, F., J.P., Norton, Stockton-on-Tees (2 copies).
BROWN, W. T., Yew Court, Scarborough.
BUCHANNAN, G., Whitby, Yorkshire.
BURRA, R., The Hall, Gate, Sedbergh.
BURRELL, Miss, Fairthorn, Botley, Hants.
BURTON, Rev. B. C., The Rectory, Cherry Burton, Beverley.
BURTON, D. F., The Hall, Cherry Burton, Beverley (2 copies).
BUTCHER, J. S., M.P., 22 Collingham Place, S.W.

C.

CADLE, C. E., 5 North Bailey, Durham.
CARLISLE, The Right Hon. Lady, Naworth Castle.
CARPENTER, Admiral the Hon. W. C., Kipling Hall, North-
    allerton.
CARTER, Rev. E. S., St. Michael's-le-Belfry, York.
CARTER, T., J.P., Richmond, Yorkshire.
CAYLEY, DIGBY, J.P., Brompton, R.S.O. (4 copies).
CHALONER, Mrs., Long Hull, Guisborough.
CHAPMAN, Mrs., The Cliff, Leyburn.
CHARLTON, W., North Eastern Bank, Durham.
CLARKE, A. F., The Ven. Archdeacon of Lancaster (2 copies).
CLEGG, J., 1 Spring Bank, Preston.
COBB, C., Clifton, York.
COLLIER, Rev. CARUS, Great Ayton.
COLLINSON, S., Royal Hotel, Scorton.
COLLISON, W., 79 Fenchurch St., London.
COMERLINE, Rev. A. S., York.

CONING, T., 28 Bankment, York.
COPER, Rev. J. M. A., Robin Hood's Bay.
CORNEY, Miss, Newton Hall, Great Ayton.
CRADDOCK, C., J.P., Grove House, Wakefield.
CRUSHER, T., Forest Farm, Scorton.

D.

DALE, Sir DAVID, Bart., West Lodge, Darlington.
DALTRY, The Rev. VERNON G., The Rectory, Yarm.
DAWNAY, Col., The Hon., Benningbrough Hall.
DENT, Miss I., Ribston Hall, Wetherby.
DERBY, Right Hon. Earl, K.G., Knowsley, Prescot.
DIXON, DAVID, Brotton Hall.
DIXON, D. D., Coquetdale House, Rothbury.
DIXON, Sir RAYLTON, Kt., Gunnegate Hall, Cleveland.
DURHAM, The Right Rev. the Lord Bishop of.

E.

EAVES, Mrs., The Vicarage, Lyminge.
ECCLES, E. E., Fenton House, Lancaster.
EDMUNDSON, C. F. P., Nutwith House, Masham.
ELLERTON, Dr. J., Grove Hill, Middlesborough.
ELLIOTT, C., The Lodge, Scorton.
EMMERSON, J. J., Easby Hall, Great Ayton (4 copies).

F.

FALLOW, T. M., Coatham House, Redcar.
FAWCET, Miss, North Bailey, Durham.
FIFE, Capt., Langton Hall, Northallerton.
FLINTOFF, C., The Grange, Scorton.
FORBES, C. M., 14 New St., York (2 copies).
FOSTER, MARTIN, Claremont, Norton.
FOWLER, Rev. J. C., Whorlton, Northallerton.
FRY, J., Cleveland Lodge, Great Ayton.

G.

GADDESDEN, Mrs., Hunmanby Hall, East Yorkshire (2 copies).
GALLIMORE, J. S., Escrick, York.
GAUSSEN, Rev., The Vicarage, Malton.

b

GILPIN BROWN, Mrs., Sedbury Park, Richmond, Yorkshire (6 copies).
GISBORNE FAWCETT, T., Yarm (2 copies).
GRAVELY, A. C., Hutton Grange, Guisborough.
GRAY, The Right Hon. Lady Mayoress, York (2 copies).
GREENBANK, THOS., Bank of Liverpool, Sedbergh.
GREENWOOD, Capt., Swartcliff Hall, Leeds.
GREGSON, B. P., The Hall, Caton, Lancaster (2 copies).

H.

HALES, Rev., Aysgarth School, Jervaulx (2 copies).
HAMILTON RUSSELL, The Hon. CONSTANCE, Brancepeth Castle.
HARRISON, W., North Road, Ripon.
HARTLEY, Mrs., The Rectory, Burneston.
HAWKE, The Right Hon. Lady, Wighill Park, Tadcaster.
HAWKINS, C., Sowerby, Thirsk.
HEAD, Mrs. J., Hartburn Hall (2 copies).
HEAVISIDES, J., Stockton-on-Tees.
HEDLAM, Rev. A. W., Gainford (2 copies).
HEPPENSTALL, Rev. F. W., East Layton (2 copies).
HESLOP, R. O., 12 Arkenside Hill, Newcastle.
HILL, Miss, Romanby.
HILL, J., Newport, Middlesborough.
HINCKS, Capt. J. C., Terrace House, Richmond (2 copies).
HORSFALL, E. F. WILSON, Potto Grange (2 copies).
HOWARD, Rev. R. G., Hovingham.
HUDDART, Rev. G., Kirklington.
HULTON, ——, Bolton-le-Moors, Lancaster.
HUTTON DARCY, Miss E., Aldborough Hall, Masham.
HULL, The Right Rev. Lord Bishop of.
HUNTER, Rev. C., Seaton Carew.
HUNTER, Rev. F. W., Wath.

I.

INGLEBY, Sir H., Bart., Ripley Castle.
IRWIN, Rev. J., Hurworth.
IRVIN, Major, Ragworth, Norton.

J.

JAMES, Rev. F. G., The Rectory, Marske.
JEFFERSON, J., Dunnington Priory, York.
JOHNSON, Dr., Dallas Road, Lancaster.
JOHNSTONE, The Hon. Miss, Hackness Hall (8 copies).
JOHNSTONE, The Rev., Hackness Hall.
JONES, ED., Manor House, Scorton.

K.

KEARSLEY, Col. G., Prospect House, Ripon.
KENNEDY, Mrs., Wetherby.
KING, F. E., Edgley, Leyburn.
KIRK, W., Norton.
KITCHIN, A. E., The Firs, Great Ayton.
KITCHIN, H., The Grange, Great Ayton (2 copies).
KNIGHT, Rev. J. G. P., Eastgate, Darlington.

L.

LANGLEY, W. C., J.P., Stockton-on-Tees.
LASCELLES, The Hon. G. E., Sion Hill, Thirsk (2 copies).
LEADMAN, Dr. ALEX. D. H., Pocklington.
LEE, J. B., The Worshipful the Mayor, Ripon.
LEGARD, J. H., Welham, Malton.
LESLEY, Mrs. A., The Hall, Little Habton.
LEVETT, Rev. T. P., Richmond, Yorkshire.
LOCKWOOD, P. H., Sedbergh.
LODGE, Col., The Rookeries, Bishopdale.
LONDESBOROUGH, The Right Hon. Lord, Londesborough Park.
LONGBOTHAM, Dr. G. F., Birtley.
LOVEJOY, Rev. H. T., Hamsterley, Bishop Auckland.

M.

MACCARTIE, Rev. J., Wilton.
MASON, O. MATTHEWS, The Hall, Crayke.
MATTHEWS, F. W., The Bank, Leyburn.
MAULE-COLE, Rev. E., Wetwang.
MAYNARD, A. C. HUTTON, Pickhill House, Pickhill (2 copies).

M^cCRIRICK, Rev. T. W., Stockton-on-Tees.
M^cKAY, W., Haldthorpe House, Scarborough.
MELROSE, J., Clifton Croft, York.
METCALFE, R. M. D., Leyburn.
MICKLE, Dr. G., Kirklington (2 copies).
MIDDLETON, Lady, The Right Hon. JULIA, Setterington House
   (4 copies).
MILNER, Mrs., The Mount, York (2 copies).
MITCHELL, Rev. A. P., The Rectory, Brotton (2 copies).
MITTAN, Rev. H., Sherburn House, Durham.
MOORSOM, M. MAUDE, Harewood, Leeds.
MORGAN, Rev. F. H., The Rectory, Guisborough.
MORRIS, Rev. M. C. F., The Rectory, Nunburnholme.

N.

NELSON, Alderman THOS., J.P., Newstadt, Norton.

O.

ORD, CHAS., Guisborough.
ORNSBY, J. A., 5 North Bailey, Durham.
ORTON, Mrs. E. S., Westgate, Guisborough.
OXFORD, The Right Rev. the Lord Bishop of.

P.

PAGE, J. W., J.P., Norton, Stockton-on-Tees (2 copies).
PEARSON, H., Whitby.
PEASE, A. E., M.P., Pinchingthorpe Hall (2 copies).
PEASE, Mrs. G., Woodside, Darlington.
PEASE, HOWARD, Arcott Hall, Dudley, Northumberland.
PEASE, Sir JOSEPH W., Bart., M.P., Hutton Hall (2 copies).
PEASE, PIKE, Undercliff, Great Ayton.
PECKSTONE, J., Stockton-on-Tees.
PEEL, The Right Hon. Lady, Potterton Hall, Barnoldswick.
PEGLER, T. B., Sholebrook Avenue, Leeds.
PEIRSON, Rev. W. B., Rothwell, Leeds.
PLATNAUER, H. M., St. Olive's Road, York (2 copies).
PLEWS, W. J., Southend End, Northallerton.

POLLEXFEN, Rev. H., Stanwick, Darlington.
PORTER, CHAS., Mill Vale, Great Ayton.
PRINCE, E., Woodhouse Moor, Leeds (2 copies).
PROUD, J., The Hall, East Layton.
PURVIS, R., 6 Westoe Crescent, South Shields.

R.

RAW, Rev. G., 250 Hawthorne Road, Bootle.
REYNARD, Capt., Camp Hill, Bedale.
RICHARDSON, W., Guisborough.
RICHMOND, The Right Rev. Lord Bishop of (4 copies).
RIDDELL, E. C., J.P., The Hall, Leyburn.
RIDDELL, Sir J., Bart., The Hall, Hepple, Rothbury.
RIPLEY, Rev. THOS., Kirklington.
RIPON, The Most Noble the Marchioness of.
RIPON, The Right Rev. Lord Bishop of.
RIPON, The Very Rev. the Dean of (2 copies).
ROBINSON, F. J. H., Easingwold.
ROBINSON, Rev. STEWART, The Rectory, Richmond, Yorkshire.
ROBINSON, Rev. W., The Rectory, Tadcaster.
ROPNER, G., J.P., The Grove, Richmond, Yorkshire.
ROPNER, Col. R., J.P., Preston Hall, Egglescliffe.
ROWCLIFFE, H. S., Guisborough.
ROWSELL, Rev. Canon, Topcliffe.
RUDD, A. G., The Worshipful the Mayor, Stockton-on-Tees.

S.

SALMAN, Rev. J. S., The Vicarage, Lastingham.
SCOTT, Rev. ERRINGTON, The Vicarage, Norton.
SEDGWICK, Miss, The Hall, Sedbergh.
SHAND, Dr., Fountain Street, Guisborough.
SHARP, F. J., Skelton, near Boroughbridge.
SHEFFIELD, The Right Hon. Lady, Yeadon Manor, Henley-on-
    Thames (2 copies).
SISSONS, D. W., North Ferriby, Brough.
SISSONS, W., Nunthorpe, Jesmond Park.
SLINGSBY, W., Red House, Moor Monkton, York.

SMITH ALDERSON, G. A., J.P., D.L., Scarborough.
SMITH, E. J., The Bank, Bridlington (4 copies).
SMITH, T. RUDOLPH, 25 Bridge Road, Stockton-on-Tees.
SOMERSON, J., Pocklington.
SPRENT, Dr. W. S., Slingsby.
STANBRIDGE, T., The Hall, Harlsey.
STANNYFORTH, Capt. E., J.P., The Hall, Kirkhammerton.
STARKIE, Miss S., Scarthwaite, Lancashire.
STAVELEY, Miss, Old Slenningford Hall, Ripon.
STIRLING-NEWALL, Mrs., The Hall, Birtley, Durham.
STOBART, ——, The Hall, Spellow Hill (2 copies).
STOBART, Col. W., Pepper Arden.
STOREY, Sir THOS., D.L., Lancaster (2 copies).
ST. QUINTIN, W. H., J.P., Scampston Hall (2 copies).
STRICKLAND, Sir C., Bart., Boynton Hall (2 copies).
STRICKLAND CONSTABLE, Mrs., The Hall, Wassand (2 copies).
SUDLOW, THOS., Stockton-on-Tees.

T.

TATTERSAL, O., Green Royd, Ripon (2 copies).
TAYLOR, J., Brotton Grange, Brotton.
TEMPLE, Miss M., Saltergill, Yarm.
TETTLEY, A., The Right Hon. Lady Mayoress, Leeds (2 copies).
THOMSON, J. S., New Buildings, Thirsk (2 copies).
TINDAL, Miss, Kirby Misperton Hall, Pickering.
TOMLINSON, Miss, Heysham House, Lancaster.
TOMLINSON, Rev. W., Vicarage, North Cave.
TREVOR, W. C., Overbeck, Guisborough.

V.

VIE, E. J., Paradise Row, Stockton-on-Tees (2 copies).

W.

WADE, E. W., 5 Clyde Terrace, Hull.
WADE-DALTON, Col. HAMLET COOTE, C.B., Hawxwell Hall.
WAKEFIELD, The Right Rev. Lord Bishop of.

WALDY, Rev. A. G., Horsley Vicarage, Derby.

WALKER, Capt. GERALD, Hill House, Richmond, Yorkshire.

WALKER, Sir J., Bart., 41 Belgrave Square, S.W.

WARD, Rev. H., The Rectory, Amotherby.

WATSON, FRED. BYERS, Stockton-on-Tees.

WATSON, THOMAS, M.D., Argyle House, Stockton-on-Tees (2 copies).

WEST, Mrs., Stoneybrough, Thirsk.

WHITE, Col. W. A., J.P., Clifton Green, York.

WILLAN, Rev. A., The Vicarage, Copmanthorpe.

WILLIAMSON, T., J.P., Fairfield, Ripon.

WILSON, Miss A., Hutton House, Hutton Rudby.

WILSON, Mrs. A., Rockhurst, York (2 copies).

WILSON, I., Nunthorpe Hall.

WILSON, Rev. J. ALDER, Craythorne Rectory, Yarm

WILSON, J. G., 12 South Bailey, Durham (2 copies).

WILSON, P., Bedale.

WILTON, R., The Rev. Canon, Londesborough.

WIMBUSH, Rev. S., The Rectory, Terrington.

WITHINGTON, Rev. R., Rectory, Great Ayton.

WOOD, F. MAURICE DALE, Swainby, Northallerton.

WOOD, Rev. F., The Rectory, Nunthorpe.

WRIGHT, Professor J., M.A., Langdale House, Oxford (2 copies).

WYNDHAM, Mrs., 31 Cambridge Street, Hyde Park, S.W.

WYNNE FINCH, Mrs., Manor House, Stokesley.

Y.

YEOMAN, Miss C., Prior House, Richmond, Yorkshire.

YORK, His Grace the Archbishop of.

Z.

ZETLAND, The Right Hon. Lord, Aske Hall, Richmond, Yorkshire.

THE YORKSHIRE FOLK-SPEECH IS NOT
A DIALECT, BUT A LANGUAGE.

To those unacquainted with our folk-speech, the following list will be helpful when reading. A glossary of words now in use in the North Riding will be found at the end of the volume.

Ah	= *I.*		't	= *it.*
Ah's	= (*I is*) *I am.*		t'	= *the.*
Ah s'	= *I shall.*		ta	= *thou* or *you.*
'an	= *than.*		ti	= *to.*
'at	= *that, which, who.*		ti t'	= *to the.*
i'	= *in,* 'iv' before a vowel.		ti 't	= *to it.*
i' 't	= *in it.*		till	= *to.*
i' t'	= *in the.*		tiv, used before a vowel = *to.*	
'll	= *will.*		wa	= *we.*
ma	= *me.*		wi'	= *with,* as a rule 'wiv'
mah	= *my.*			before a vowel.
na	= *nor, no, than.*		ya	= *you.*
o'	= *on,* also *of.*		yer	= *your.*
ov	= *of.*		yah, adj., personal numeral = *one.*	
's	= *is, has,* or *as.*		yan, adj. = *one*	
s'	= *shall.*		ya'd	= *you had* or *you would.*

CHAPTER I

YORKSHIRE STORIES OF WIT AND CHARACTER.

'EDDICATION an' self-binnders is gahin ti to'n t' wo'lld upsahd doon,' said an honest Yorkshireman to me the other day. 'Are things in general really much different now from what they were, say, fifty years ago?' I asked. To which I received this laconic reply, 'Nowt's t' saam[1].' Nothing could have been more forcible: the words meant much, and the tone in which they were uttered meant even more.

Unfortunately this 'tone,' which is the very soul of the dialect, can never be rendered in print. How poor and meaningless in the mouth of a stranger sound the words, 'Cu' thi waays, honey,' but from the lips of a Yorkshire mother to her bairn they carry with them the sound of tenderest love and solicitude. They ring with music, but it is music which is only tuneful to the Yorkshire ear.

But to return to our friend. Now, though he said 'Nowt's t' saam' in somewhat a depreciatory manner, he was fully aware of the value of education and the utility of the various mechanical appliances which

---

[1] 'Nothing is the same.'

B

have of late years revolutionized agricultural labour. There is a species, shall I say of conservatism? deeply ingrafted in the Yorkshireman's character. It is a natural cautiousness which ever keeps this conservatism to the forefront in everything connected with his daily life. He does not, nor ever has, taken kindly to novelties. He views with suspicion all things which he considers innovations, i.e. which have a tendency to alter the general rut in which his father travelled before him. To him the old way is good, and he is loth to leave it. No matter whether it be temporal or spiritual, he hangs on long and hard to the old and beaten track. *Errare est humanum* fully applies to the Yorkshireman; he makes mistakes, but never owing to his having been too precipitate. He is naturally cautious and eminently practical. 'Ah leyke ti ken hoo tweea an' tweea's gahin ti mak fowr, an' 'at fowr penn'oth o' stuff's wo'th fow'pence, afoor Ah ware mah brass on owt,' said an old Tyke one day. This caution and practical turn in our character, and which is carried into all things, naturally leads those who are strangers to form the opinion that we are dull and slow of comprehension, but to those who can read between the lines this verdict is very speedily reversed; for should it be necessary to *spend* only words, 'which costs nowt, bud deean't want wasting foor all that,' then it will be readily conceded that the Yorkshireman's brain can grasp a question and turn on steam so as to give an answer as quickly and as much to the point as the best of them.

It may not be couched in the politest of language;

nay, most likely it will be very plain-spoken, even to bluntness ; but it will be just what the speaker thinks, devoid of all the silken trimmings of conventionalism.

Many of the answers given to inquisitive questioners often seem irrelevant ; they need as it were some sidelight to point the application, and generally it is necessary one should have a considerable knowledge of the dialect and idiom before its terseness can be fully appreciated.

Nevertheless, when properly approached our people are communicative, and express their opinion freely and always *ad rem*.

But once having weighed any matter over, the opinion so formed is, as it were, engraved on a rock of adamant. Perhaps one or two illustrations will show the different phases of character referred to in a clearer light than pages of written explanation.

The new vicar (not a Yorkshireman) of a country parish decided that his congregation should stand up when he and the choir processed from the vestry. ' Tha'll nut deea 't,' said the churchwarden when the question was mooted; 't' au'd fau'k nivver did seea, an' t' young uns weean't.' The tone in which this was uttered would have been conclusive to any Yorkshireman.

' I think I can make them,' said the vicar. ' Mak 'em!' with great unction; ' did ya saay mak 'em ? Noo ya mebbe mud 'tice 'em—yan nivver knaws what'll happen—bud Ah's mairna sartin sewer 'at ya'll nivver mak 'em ; an' tha'll tak a gay bit o' 'ticing, if Ah knaw owt.'

' Oh, leave it to me, I'll manage it,' said the vicar

confidently. 'Whya noo, gan on wi' ya; bud deean't forgit 'at a hoss sumtahms tumm'ls ower t' raal 'at it's loup'd afoor,' was the parting advice of the worthy churchwarden.

The following Sunday evening the vicar told his congregation that he wished them to stand as the choir came from the vestry, but next Sunday morning found his congregation stolidly seated as heretofore.

'Ah tell'd ya tha wadn't deea 't,' chuckled the churchwarden.

'But they will,' replied the vicar. 'Bud tha weean't,' put in the churchwarden; and then he added as a clincher, 'Acoz tha've made up tha mahnds aboot it, an' ya weean't shift 'em when yance tha've deean that.'

'You wait until evening,' said the vicar, 'and I shall make them stand.' And he did. Coming to the doorway of the vestry, he gave out the hymn, the organ commenced to play, up rose the congregation, and out marched the choir and vicar.

'Ah'll watch him fra deeaing that onny mair,' muttered one old dame loud enough for half the church to hear.

'Did I not say they would rise? And I'll do that every Sunday,' said the vicar, as he and the warden walked home.

'Whya, Ah deean't knaw saa mich aboot that. It's nut awlus seeaf ti ride wiv a curb an' spurs. Ya'll 'a'e ti tak care noo; wa deean't tak kindly ti being tricked, Ah can tell ya; bud wa s' see at eftther.'

Next Sunday morning out stepped the vicar, gave out the hymn, and then waited in the vestry until the organ and congregation were in full swing; then, and not until then, did he and the choir march out, and to his no little surprise he found the whole congregation lustily singing, but seated to a man.

As an example of their plain-speaking, as well as their objection to fall in with a new order of things, perhaps the following is fairly to the point.

The wife of the Vicar of——, having engaged a new maid, concluded various instructions by saying, 'Should any ladies call during the afternoon, and I ring, you must bring in the small tea-tray and a kettle of boiling water.' The first two days passed over without a hitch, but when the bell rang on the third afternoon, instead of tea-tray and kettle a head was thrust through the half-open door, and Mary said, 'Here Ah saay, cum ootsahd; Ah want ya a minit.' On the hostess retiring, Mary was heard to say, 'Noo then! is this new-fengled gahin-on gahin ti happen ivvery daay? Baith them an' yow owt ti knaw 'at it's maist inconvenient leeaving yan's reg'lar wark ti mak tea at this tahm o' t' daay. Ya'll 'a'e ti gan back an' saay 'at wa s'aan't be yabble ti mannish owt for 'em this eftthermeean; Ah's up ti t' elbows i' muck.'

The Archdeacon of —— gave me the following story, which is too good to hide its head. The bishop had been preaching a restoration sermon in one of our villages. After the sermon his lordship and the archdeacon overtook the village blacksmith, a well-known character. 'Well, John, and how have

you enjoyed the sermon?' inquired the archdeacon.
'Whya, nowt bud weel. Ah s'u'd think, sir' (turning
to the bishop), 'wiv a bit mair practis ya'll mannish
cannily. I' t' main what ya sed war varra good;
a larl bit ti low i' t' voice for me, bud ya'll mend
o' that. Noo, Ah yance did hear a young chap, an'
he war nobbut a young un an' all. Ah think 'at he
war iv a grosser's shop, bud Ah's nut sartin; bud
that's nowt. He yance preeached i' t' Methody
chapel, an' theer's nut a wo'd of a lee aboot it, what
Ah saay is trew; ya c'u'd hear him slap t' Bahble
an' shoot hauf t' waay doon t' village. Aye, ya c'u'd
stan' ootsahd an' smeeak ya're pipe an' get all t' good
fra what he war saaying; *bud, then, he war a
preeacher.*' I can well imagine the tone that last
'bud, then, he war a preeacher' would be uttered in.

The younger fry are just as open as the older folk.
I remember a lady telling me she had called at a farm-
house. Evidently she had been seen approaching.
It would seem the doll and other litter of the wee
daughter had been quickly bundled out of sight, and
all things, as far as possible, put in order. For the
moment the amusement of the little one was put an
end to, and this did not escape the notice of the
child. She, Yorkshire-like, formed her own opinion
upon the proceeding, and only waited for a suitable
moment to very plainly express the same. Resting
her elbows on the lady's knees, with her chubby little
face in her hands, she said, when a lull in the conversation gave her a chance to speak, 'Ah saay,
missus, hoo pleasant it wad 'a'e been if you'd nivver
'a'e cum'd.'

The cautiousness of the Yorkshireman is so evident in all matters, it is so pronounced, that to give examples is almost to lay oneself open to the charge 'ov telling a chap summat he knaws.' Nevertheless I give you one, not so much because it is exactly Q.E.D., but because it is one of the best expositions of Socialism I have ever heard. It seems that some Socialist won one man over to his views, and this man met a friend of his. 'Whya, noo then,' began the friend; 'what tha tell ma 'at thoo's to'n'd ti be a Socialist, is 't reet?' 'Aye, it's reet; an' it's a gran' thing an' all. Thoo owt ti join uz.' 'Owt Ah? What is 't 'at ya're efter?' 'Whya, thoo knaws it's lyke this; ther's a lot o' fau'k living i' gert hooses, an' tha're eating an' drinking all t' daay lang an' guzzling t' neet thruff, sum on 'em, an' it's gahin ti be stopped. Ivverything's gahin ti be shared up, an' all on uz get what's wer awn; neeabody nowt na mair 'an onnybody else, dizn't ta see.' 'Whya, nut fur sartin,' said his friend. 'Diz ta meean 'at thoo'll share up an' all?' 'Aye, ivverybody will.' 'What, is 't gahin ti be a soart o' brotherly luv'? Ivverybody wi' nowt neea mair na onnybody else.' 'Aye, that's it; brotherly luv'. Ivverybody all t' seeam, neeabody nowt neea different neeawaays ti neeabody i' neea road.' 'It soonds grand; bud diz ta meean ti saay if thoo 'ed tweea hosses an' Ah 'edn't a hoss 'at thoo'd gi'e ma yan?' 'Iv a minit Ah wad. If Ah'd tweea an' thoo 'edn't yan Ah s'u'd gi'e tha yan leyke all that,' said he, slapping his friend on the back. 'Aye, an' if ta 'ed tweea coos, an' Ah wanted a coo, wad ta gi'e uz a coo?' 'Just t' seeam. If thoo 'edn't a coo, an' Ah 'ed tweea, Ah s'u'd tell tha ti tak yan awaay wi tha. Noo thoo understands what wa're efter.' 'An' if thoo'd tweea pigs, an' Ah 'edn't a pig, an' Ah ass'd tha fur a pig, wad ta gi'e ma yan?' 'Naay noo,' said the Socialist; 'thoo's cumin' teea clooase hand noo; thoo knaws 'at Ah 'ev tweea pigs.'

Possibly not a little surprised was the angler who, when fishing in one of the small streams of the upper reaches of the Ure, said jokingly to an old chap who had been watching his vain attempts to land several fish, 'I think I need a hanger on; what do you say?' The old chap had been thoroughly disgusted with the way in which the fish had been played. It was no case for joking; it was a downright sin for such a man to be allowed to fish. So the answer, as may be expected, was more to the point than polite. 'What thoo wants,' said the old chap with a grunt of disgust, 'is nut a hinger on, bud a flinger oot. If it's fish 'at thoo's efter, thoo'll 'a'e ti lig t' rod doon an' set ti wark wi t' net; thoo mebbins mud 'a'e t' luck ti catch yan o' them 'at thoo's hauf killed. Thoo's naa fisher; thoo's nowt bud a spoil watter, that's what thoo is.' Thus relieving himself, Old Willie walked away.

One of my sketches, given at a Primrose League meeting, gave great offence to the coachman of a noble lord. Entertainers, by the way, do not hold any social position in the eyes of such. Some time afterwards I was asked to go as entertaining guest on his lordship's son's attaining his majority. A day or two before my arrival my host asked his coachman if he had not been to the entertainment which I had given.

'Aye,' said the old chap, 'bud I wadn't gan agaan. He's up ti nowt, isn't yon youth; he'll nivver git on. He's gitten impedence foor owt, he spares nowt na neeabody, he taks sarvants an' t' quality off all alike; Ah reckon nowt on him at all.'

'I am sorry to hear that,' said his master.

'Whya, Ah's seear ya've gitten neea call ti be, he's nut wo'th it. Ya mun excuse me, my lord, bud what mud ya be sorry foor?' 'Well, because he is coming here.' 'Cumin' here!' said the coachman, amazed; 'what ivver foor?' 'To entertain my guests.' 'What! deea ya meean when t' young lord cums at age?' he asked, his amazement increasing. 'Yes,' said his lordship, greatly amused. 'Oha! an' wheer will ya put him up? 'coz Ah can tell ya 'at t' sarvants weean't want ti 'ev him amangst them, tha neeawaays setten up wiv him.' 'But he won't be with the servants.' 'Then wheer will he be?' 'With us, of course.' 'Deea ya meean ti saay 'at he'll dine wi' yow an' t' quality?' asked the old chap, fairly amazed now. 'Certainly.' For a moment the old fellow hesitated; he was bewildered by such a piece of folly. And then he spoke his mind. 'Well!' he gasped, 'ya mun excuse me, my lord, bud Ah think 'at yer gahin ti mak a varra common do on 't.' Nice for me, wasn't it?

However boorish and brusque strangers may dub us, it is admitted on all hands that the Yorkshireman is fairly 'cute: he always has an eye to the main chance. And although others who are glibber of tongue may to a certain extent fairly 'mazzle' him with their verbosity, yet any such may certainly claim to having done the 'hat trick' if in the end they manage to outwit the Tyke. 'He ommaist 'wildered ma wiv his slather, bud Ah pairted wi' nowt,' said an old man who had been tackled by a book agent.

'Did ta bet owt at t' races?' asked one Tyke of another. 'Neea, Ah didn't. It war leyke this, thoo knaws. T' chaps 'at Ah seed stanning o' t' top o' steeals an' sitting unner gert um'erellas all seeam'd ti 'ev gawd rings an' cheeans on, an' tha war varra weel dhriss'd an' all, whahl monny ov 'em 'at war 'livering ther brass up war oot at t' teeas an' doon at t' heels. Seea Ah sed tiv mysen, " T' steeal an' t' um'erella chaps leeak ez if tha war 'evving t' best o' t' bargain all t' waay thruff,' an' seea neean on 'em gat onny o' mah brass. Dizn't ta think 'at Ah war i' t' reet on 't?'

Cautiousness and 'cuteness is fairly well set forth in the following story. Old Jobson wished to gain some legal information, ' bud he didn't want ti pay owt for 't.' Meeting the legal light one day, he began, ' Ah saay, if Ah wor ti ax ya summat aboot summat, s'u'd Ah 'a'e ti pay summat? It's aboot yon pathwaay o' mahn 'at Ah want ti knaw summat.' 'Certainly; I don't give advice free,' replied the lawyer. 'Whya then, Ah weean't ax ya nowt; things may bahd ez they are, whahl yow want a larl piece o' knowledge fra me, an' then wa'll see if wa caan't mak a swap on 't. Nowther t' field na t' path'll shift,' said Jobson as he walked away. And so matters rested for some months, in fact until the lawyer's horse (a very valuable one) was suddenly taken ill. Jobson was at once sent for, he being an expert in all horse ailments. The old farmer, after a careful examination of his patient, declared he knew what was amiss and what was needed to effect a cure. 'Then I will send my man for what you need at once,' said the owner.

'Aye, bud wait a bit; deean't ya aim 'at tahm's cum'd when wa s'all 'a'e ti swap wer knowledge?' said the farmer, with a twinkle in his eye. The solicitor burst out laughing; he saw the joke and admitted the validity of the claim. The old chap saved the horse, and the pathway was satisfactorily arranged.

The Yorkshireman always sees that he gets value for his money, at least he always tries to do so.

The village orchestral society were rehearsing for a public performance which was to be given the following week. The squire and a musical friend had just dropped in towards its conclusion. The friend, speaking at the conclusion with the conductor, said, 'You have a remarkably good band; you only lack one slight addition to make it one of the best for the size of your village I have ever listened to. Will you allow me to suggest that you get a horn? you lack only that.' 'Oha, an' what's a horn?' inquired the conductor. Having had the matter fully explained, he asked what a horn could be bought for. But the gentleman pointed out there was hardly time to procure a horn and teach a man how to play it before the entertainment came off. 'Whya then,' asked the conductor, 'deea yer knaw a chap 'at c'u'd cum an' play t' horn foor uz, an' what wad he cum foor?' 'I know a first-class player, and I think he would come for five pounds.' 'Fahve pund!' gasped the conductor. 'Whya, Ah c'u'd git a whoale band foor that!' 'Never mind the money, John,' said the squire; 'I'll see about that.' 'Oha, whya, if it's gahin ti be leyke that, let's 'a'e t' chap wi' t' horn.' And so the matter was settled. On the night of the performance the man with the horn put in an appearance, and all went well for about ten minutes, when the conductor stopped the band, and turning to the horn-player, he said, 'Noo then, thee wi' t' horn, thoo isn't playing.' 'No,' said he; 'I have forty-five bars rest here.' Whereupon the conductor electrified every one by saying, 'Mebbe thoo thinks seea, bud leeaks ta here, wa've paid thee fahve pund foor t' neet an' thoo'll 'a'e ti puff all t' waay thruff.'

Scores of stories could be given illustrating the aptitude our country-people exhibit in extricating themselves when placed in an awkward corner.

The dear old lady who was my study for Mrs. Waddleton asked me to paint her a picture— 'seea ez Ah s'all 'a'e summat ti leeak at 'at ya've deean yersel when ya've geean,' said she. I readily promised to do so, and in due course sent her a little snow scene.

A few days afterwards she saw me passing. 'Noo then,' she shouted, 'cum in wi' ya. Ah've gitten 't heng'd up, an', mah wo'd, bud it leeaks grand, dizn't it?' 'I am glad you like it,' said I, as I gazed at my work of art nestling amongst coloured grasses and peacock feathers; 'and very nicely you have arranged everything. But perhaps it would be better if you hung it the right way up.' Her face was a picture. The dear old soul felt that she had blundered; she was fearful lest I should feel hurt.

But her native wit saved her. 'Wrang sahd up,

is 't? Aa, bud, Ah saay, ya mun be a clivver penter seea ez ti pent a picter 'at leeaks reet onny road up.' Then, after a moment's consideration, she added, ' But mebbies Ah'd best to'n 't t'other road roond; sum fau'k mud think 'at yan didn't knaw t' reet end ov a picter if yan let it bahd ez 'tis.'

Sir C—— and Mr. W——, a solicitor, once overtook Abe Braithwaite, a well-known character in Bedale, on the way to the meet. ' Good morning,' said Sir C——; ' shall we have a find, Abe?' ' Nut i' yon cover; bud Ah cud gi'e ya a wrinkle.' ' Well, let's have it,' said Sir C——. ' Whya, deean't weeast mich tahm yonder, bud gan ti t' far cover, an' ya'll finnd yan theer, hard eneeaf.' ' All right, Abe, I'll bear in mind what you say,' said Sir C—— as the two rode off. ' Ah saay,' shouted Abe after the retreating horsemen, ' if ya'd ass'd advice frev him 'at's wi' ya he'd 'a'e wanted six an' eightpence, bud Ah nivver charge nowt na mair 'an a bob mysen.' And he got it.

A story just strikes me which illustrates several points already mentioned. A young fellow who was supposed to be learning land agency bought a horse at an adjacent fair, and was most systematically swindled. The said horse was being looked over by one of the village Tykes. Now for many reasons the fellow did not wish to offend the purchaser, but it was really impossible to say one thing in its favour. ' Well, Tom, what is the verdict?' asked the embryo agent. And then came the answer, which was worthy of a Grecian lawyer: ' Whya noo, that gertly depends. Ya weean't 'a'e bowt it owther ti

show or hunt, noo 'a'e ya?' 'Oh no, just to knock
about on.' 'Oha, whya then, 't'll deea grandly ti
knock aboot on,' said Tom. 'All the same you
think they've swindled me, now don't you?' 'Whya,
it's mebbins mair 'an Ah'd 'a'e gi'en for 't mysen,
but 't'll deea grandly ti knock aboot on.' At this
juncture they were joined by the village ostler, one
who was never overnice in his remarks. 'Now,
Jack, what do you think of my bargain?' 'What
div Ah think on 't? Whya, Ah wadn't be seen
takking it ti t' kennels' (i. e. taking it to feed the dogs);
and then, thinking he had been a little too severe,
he added, 'Bud Ah'll tell ya what, 't'll deea foor yer
ti larn what a hoss s'u'd be, foor it's getten neean o'
t' points 'at a hoss owt ti 'ev, an' ommaist ivvery yan
'at it s'u'dn't; 't'll deea foor yer ti study 't up.'

The Tyke has a habit of answering you in a kind of
metaphor, which, as before remarked, is almost unin-
telligible unless something of dialect and idiom has
been mastered. As a case in point, I remember
after the last general election saying to an old fellow,
'Now, John! what do you think of this complete
change in the country?' Now, John did not know
which side I favoured, neither did he wish me to learn
for which party he had voted, and, further, he was
determined not to say anything which would either
give offence to me or expose his own hand. The
question for a moment was a difficult one to answer,
but the answer came pat enough: 'Whya, Parliment's
varra mich leyke t' land—ya mun chaange t' crops
noos an' agaan, or it's ti neea good. Ah s' 'a'e ti be
gahin noo; good daay ti ya.' He had answered me,

fully answered me. He had let nothing escape him. I was none the wiser as to what his own opinions were, and I might just as well have saved myself the trouble of asking.

The inspectors of our Board schools can recount many true and curious anecdotes of our country scholars; but it should be borne in mind by the department that, although the Yorkshire country-people and their bairns are bilingual, it is only their mother tongue and ordinary English which up to the present they have mastered. The southern twang, pronunciation, and slang is to them as a mystic rune. North-country men, if you please, to examine North-country boys and girls. Very often the questions, as put by South-country inspectors, might just as well be asked in Sanskrit, and very naturally they remain unanswered, whilst the class is voted as hopeless dunces, when the fault really lies at the door of the questioner. At one school in Wensleydale a South-country inspector, when examining a class on the Bible, put this question, 'Neow tell me something abeout Mouses.' 'Cats kill 'em,' was the prompt reply. Another one said to a promising standard in mental arithmetic, 'Three packets of pins at a penny each, five hanks of tape penny each, nine reels of thread penny each, five boxes of hair-pins penny each, and six ounces of worsted at three halfpence per ounce. How much does the parcel come to? Quick!' But the speed with which the question had been asked, the twang, and the unfamiliar sound of many of the words, left the standard almost in absolute ignorance of the question. One thing, and of only one thing, were they clear upon—that they were being

asked something about *thread*, *worsted*, and *hair-pins*.
But as the inspector uttered that 'Quick!' he fixed his
eyes on one lad, and the effect of that glance was
mesmeric.   The lad immediately answered, ' Pleease,
sur, wa ar'n't lasses.'

But it is not the South-country man alone who
receives unlooked for answers from the practical
bairns of our dales.   After a somewhat lengthy
and highflown picture-painting on faith, the teacher,
wishing to see if the children had grasped her foolish
poetical outburst, said to one of the boys, whose
mother, by the way, was a widow and desperately
poor, ' Now, Tommy, if I were to say to you, " There
will be a rich plum pudding for your dinner," and
you believed me, what would that be ? ' ' It 'ud
be a gert tak in, for wa nivver 'a'e nowt na better
'an a suet dumpling at oor hoos,' was the unexpected
reply.

Again, an inspector asked one of the boys in Bilsdale,
or rather commenced to ask, a question in mental
arithmetic : said he, ' If you had in your hand five
apples, two oranges, and three pears, and I was to
take——' But he got no further ; the practical bairn
stopped him by saying, ' Pleease, sur, Ah c'u'dn't ho'd
'em all i' yah han'.'

To conclude this chapter, just one more example.
Said an inspector to a little girl, ' If I knitted twelve
stitches in a minute, how many stitches should I have
on my needle at the end of five minutes ? ' ' Ya wadn't
a'e neean, 'coz ya deean't knit stitches ; ya're nut
gahin ti catch me i' that waay.'   He ought to have
said ' loops.'

CHAPTER II

WIT AND CHARACTER

OUR country-people possess in a very marked degree the faculty of explaining away anything which for special reasons they do not care to admit. Very often they do this in a marvellously subtle way. Sometimes so fine is the point upon which they turn an argument, that that which was to be demonstrated is entirely lost sight of, whilst new issues are introduced in such a seemingly natural way that in the end you find yourself contending for some point in which you have no earthly interest, and which has no connexion with the original argument, but which, owing to this strategical shifting, has put them on sure ground, leaving you at a hopeless disadvantage. Equally conspicuous is their pride and independency; no matter how poor they may be they strongly object to being patronized.

'Ah weean't let onnybody clap me on t' back. Ah paay fer what Ah git, an' that's good eneeaf; he's nowt na better 'an what Ah is,' said a man one day, who had been spoken to, with the kindest intention, but in that unfortunate way which some of the best-intentioned people have of being familiar, but faintly colouring the same with just a slight whiff of patronizing superiority. And the Yorkshireman won't stand it.

C

Don't misunderstand me: although no respecter of person he is quite willing to pay deference to those whom he considers his superiors and who are worthy of it; but he is the one who acts as judge in such a case. If you are a stranger, you will have to earn this deference by good behaviour on your part, or it is quite possible, if you act otherwise, you will be the recipient of some very plain Yorkshire, whether you understand it or not. And also bear in mind the Tyke is always equal to giving an answer, and in his own peculiar way very smart at repartee.

A good example of one of the peculiarities mentioned is made evident in the following story. Master and man were returning from a coursing match, at which the master's dog had been badly beaten. The man knew it was a great disappointment, and as a faithful servant he felt keenly the adverse result of the day's outing. 'I felt sure our dog would win,' said the master, and then waited for his man to reply. Now, Tom would not say how much inferior their dog really was to the winner; in fact, he would only admit that to himself. So he held his peace. A moment later the master tackled him again, and this time with a question direct. 'You saw the course, Tom; how do you account for it?' 'Whya, sur,' began Tom, 'dogs is queer things, an' hares is queer things; in fact, theer's nowt na queerer 'an what hares offen is. Noo, they're varra flighty things is hares, an' Ah've offens thowt 'at sumtahms tha tak mair ti yah dog na what tha deea ti t' tother. An' ya knaw leyke, when tha finnd oot 'at theer's nowt else for 't bud what they 'a'e ti be killed, tha let t' dog deea't 'at they've ta'en t' maist fancy tull. Ah caann't mak 't oot onny other road, an' that mun be it.'

Years ago, when guides showed tourists and others round Fountains Abbey, giving at the same time their version of the history of the ruins—much of which it must be said was the outcome of their own imagination, and, though deeply interesting, was opposed to all the canons of archaeology—several members of the Royal Archaeological Society and a party of ladies and gentlemen were relegated to the care of 'Scott,' an old guide and a well-known Yorkshire character of those days. As they went through the ruins the old fellow gave his version, only a moment afterwards to hear quite a different explanation given by some member of the R.A.S. At last Scott could 'bahd it na langer.' 'Ah saay,' questioned he, 'war you here when t' Abbey war built?' 'No, neither were you, my friend,' replied the gentleman. 'Mebbe nut, bud Ah've been here a seet langer 'an what you 'ev, for all that; sum fau'k think tha knaw sa mich,' he was heard to mutter. By-and-by the round was completed, and then it was that old Scott fired off his last shot. 'Noo then,' said he, 'cum on all t' lot on ya, an' Ah'll tak ya ti summat 'at neean on ya can owther gainsaay or alter; noo then, cum on,' and he marched them under the echo. 'Noo then, gentlemen, ya can't dispute owt 'at's sed here; gan on, sum on ya, shoot summat.' One of the party, who had already had more than one wordy battle with the old fellow, shouted, 'Any one seen an old fool knocking about this morning?' At which

there was a general laugh. But before the repeat
had died away, the old fellow shouted in a voice which
made the echo ring again, ' Neea, bud theear's onny
amount o' young uns under t' echo.' And I think
he scored.

Another good story: in fact many hail from
Great Ayton. When the Grange was being built,
artists and other workmen from town and elsewhere were requisitioned to beautify the place. Many
of these travelled gentlemen, on their first arrival,
considered the Yattoners fair game for their sport
and wit, but very often they found out, when too
late to save themselves, that they had pressed the
wrong button. During their stay a small wild-beast
show opened on the green. In front of the monkeys'
cage stood a Yattoner, greatly amused with their
antics. ' Admiring your relations ? ' inquired one
of the foreign masons as he passed. ' They're neea
relations o' mahn ; neean ov oor family's owt akin
ti yours,' was the instant reply. ' Why don't you
wash your brains ? there's plenty of water in the beck,'
said another of the foreign fraternity. ' Ther mebbins
is what 'ud wesh mahn, bud you'd 'a'e ti wait whahl
a fresh cam doon.' ' Go home,' said another of
them, ' and tell your father you are the biggest fool he
has ever seen.' ' He'd leather ma for telling a lee if
Ah did ; ya're forgitting 'at ya lodge wiv uz ; ' and then
he dodged a lump of wood which came that way.

Old Bessy kept the village store, and in her way
was quite a character ; so was her shop for the matter
of that. I never was in such a shop in my life. Anything, everything, and all on the top of something

else. In fact it was as one of the natives put it,
'Owt 'at Bessy 'ezn't 's nut wo'th assing for.' The
one big house in the place for a short time was rented
by a gentleman whose family made up for any de-
ficiency in pedigree by all-round rudeness to every one
with whom they came in contact. On one occasion
a daughter of the said house flounced into Bessy's
shop and asked for something which it was most
unlikely would be kept in a shop of that kind. 'Naay,'
said Bessy, 'Ah 'a'en't gitten nowt o' that soart;
Ah deean't knaw what t' stuff is ya're assing for.'
'It is just useless my trying to buy anything in
a pottering little shop like this. You keep nothing
but a lot of old rubbish. You never have anything
I want,' was the young lady's rude reply. 'Why noo,
Ah'll tell ya what, t' next tahm 'at Ah gan ti Ripon,
Ah'll see if Ah can't get a box o' good behav'o'r ; you
mun cum in then, an' Ah'll gi'e ya good weight, for ya
want it mair na onnybody else. Noo deean't forgit
ti cum in,' were the last words the young lady heard
as she hurried out.

His Honour Judge ——— for some little time had
a house in a Cleveland village, and whilst there he
did a bit of 'hoss swapping' with one of the farmers.
Unfortunately his Honour's horse did not turn out
well. Meeting the farmer one day, he said, 'Robert,
you took me in with that horse, it has turned out
very badly.' 'Hez 't, noo? Whya, that's a bad job ;
bud you maun't gan blethering aboot 'at Ah've ta'en
ya in, or else fau'k'll get it i' ther heeads 'at ya're
nobbut a varra poor judge.'

Quite likely enough, if you get into conversation

with the old people, they will give you their opinion
upon most things, and that too very often without
your asking for it.   There will be no beating about
the bush, no attempt to smooth away rough corners;
the Yorkshireman detests putty and varnish.   What
he has to say, like his hitting, comes straight from the
shoulder.

The hounds were in full cry.   A lady and gentleman
on approaching a closed gate against which a farmer's
man was leaning, the gentleman called out, 'Hi there!
open the gate, look sharp!' but the man stood stolidly
looking at the hounds.   'Why don't you open the gate,
you fool?' shouted the horseman angrily.   Turning
slowly round, the yokel said very quietly, 'Ah deean't
call ti mahnd 'at ivver Ah 'ed a God's-penny fra you.
If ya'll nobbut stan' back Ah've na doot t' lady'll
show ya t' road ower.   Ah can see 'at ya're a bit caff-
hearted.'   Springing to the ground the horseman
found the gate was locked.   'Why, it's locked,' said
he, turning to the lady.   'Ah c'u'd 'a'e tell'd ya that
lang sin,' said the yokel.   'Well, I think you might
have done so,' said the lady, kindly.   'We have lost
a lot of time.'   'If you'd cum'd byv yersen, miss,
Ah'd 'a'e brokken t' gate doon for ya.   Bud yah feeal
losses his wits when he's called yan byv another,'
was the compliment and retort all in one.

On another occasion, the horseman forgetting to
pay the usual toll, the gate-opener greatly amused
every one by saying, as he touched his cap, 'Noo,
mebbe ya 'evn't gitten neea small chaange on ya,
bud Ah'll tell ya hoo wa can mannish 't: Ah've gitten
nahnpence, if you've a bob?'

A good story is told by a Cleveland vicar. The day on which he arrived in his new parish he had to transact some little matter with the sexton. On inquiry he was informed this worthy was to be found in the far pasture. Thither he went, finding the old man busy mowing. 'Well, my man!' began the vicar. 'Noo then,' said Old Willie, going on with his mowing. 'I wish to have a word or two with you,' said the vicar, not very pleased with his off-hand reception. He was not Yorkshire, and didn't understand their ways then.

'All reet, gan on wi' tha.' This without stopping the swing of his scythe.

'I think you don't know who I am. I am your new vicar.' Doubtless at the time the vicar imagined the effect of this startling announcement would be such that Old Willie's scythe would fall from his hands, and most abject apologies be poured forth. But no, Willie just remarked, 'Oh, are ya? Whya, ya maun't stan theer ; ya'll 'a'e ti shift yersen, or Ah s'all mow yer legs off t' next swathe Ah tak.' And the vicar moved.

Our country-people have a way of summing up and giving a verdict quite on lines of their own. But it must be borne in mind that what is taken in a figurative sense by those of a wider experience, is often accepted literally by those whose lives for the most part have been bounded by their own homestead and dale. When the last historical pageant was held at Ripon, trips brought the dales-people from all parts. And although I do not think any of them went so far as to imagine the various characters

impersonated had been dug up and set in motion for
their amusement and edification, I am sure in the
main they were greatly mystified as to how they had
all been gathered together. On the last day, when
possibly fifteen thousand people were present, a group
of ladies and gentlemen were standing near the east
window of the Abbey—near by were two or three
monks conversing with several knights in chain
armour, and on their right stood King Charles
surrounded by the ladies of his court. A gentleman
standing hard by said to his lady companion, 'It is
really a splendid spectacle, and gives one a perfect
picture of what it must have been in days past.'
'You'll excuse me, sir,' said a dame who had overheard
his remark, 'bud is this leyke what it used ti be?'
'Yes, my good woman, exactly,' the gentleman
answered. 'Whya then, Ah can weel understan' hoo
it war 'at tha pulled t' pleeace doon' (meaning the
Abbey), 'for it's a giddy gahin-on is this. Bud Ah
will saay,' pointing to the ladies of King Charles'
Court, ''at Ah nivver seed a finer set o' lasses i' all
mah leyfe. An' Ah've na doot 'at that accoonts for 't.'

The last clause, I imagine, referred to the ruinous
state of the Abbey.

The same peculiar trait was fully exemplified during
an Art exhibition at York. Several of the pictures
were offered for sale, the price being given in the
catalogue. Whilst a couple were gazing in wonder-
ment at one picture, the woman was overheard to say,
'Ah nivver thowt 'at fraams cost seea mich brass.
Sitha, mun, that yan's ower a hunderd pund; it mun
be t' fraam, thoo knaws, fer t' picter's nobbut hauf

deean; t' chap 'at's pented it 'ezn't 'ed tahm ti finish 't, fer neean on 'em's gitten ther cleeas on.'

Some few years ago there was an excursion started from Whitby *via* Battersby, its destination being Wensleydale. Many who availed themselves of the trip alighted at Aysgarth. One batch in charge of the curate wended their way to the force, which owing to recent rains was seen at its best. 'By gum,' said one, 'bud ther's a seet o' watter cuming ower yonder.' 'Ah'll tell ya what,' said another, giving a huge wink, 'they weean't be yabble ti keep that gam up lang; tha'll be letting 't all off afoor t' tothers cum up, if they deean't mahnd.' The curate was shocked; his poetical soul was pained at such, as he imagined, crass ignorance, so he endeavoured to lift them from out of themselves. After quite a rhetorical outburst bearing on the grandeur of the scene, he wound up with, 'Is it not marvellous, magnificent, overwhelming, to behold it thundering, rumbling, tumbling over?' Poetry of that kind makes the speaker breathless, and he paused. Then, turning to one of the party, he said, 'What do you think, John, eh?' 'Aye, ya're all reet about its thunnering, tumm'ling, an' rumm'ling, bud for t' leyfe o' mah Ah deean't see owt 'at ther is ti ho'd it back,' was the laconic reply.

I remember on one occasion, when being driven to the station by a real old Yorkshire coachman—I had been one of a house party for three days as society humorist—the old fellow giving me a huge dig with his elbows, and saying, 'Ah saay, is yon all you deea fer a living?' 'That is all,' I replied. 'Well, by goa! bud ya git yer living easy, you deea.' 'I don't know;

if you had all the knocking about that I have perhaps you would not think it quite so easy,' said I.
'Whya, Ah deean't knaw; what ya'll 'ev yer expenses
paid, 'evn't ya?' 'Certainly,' I answered. 'Aye; an'
ya git fed fer nowt, deean't ya?' 'Of course,' I replied,
greatly amused. 'Whya then,' said he, 'Ah'll tell
ya what: ya travel fer nowt, yer sheltered fer nowt, fed
fer nowt, an' ya deea nowt; Ah leeak upon ya ez
nowt i' t' wo.lld else bud a aristocratic pauper.' 'Wait
a moment,' said I; 'don't you think brains count for
something in a matter of this kind?' And then,
with that ineffable scorn which I think only the
Yorkshireman of that type can assume, he said,
'Braans! braans!! braans!!! Ugh, Ah've ez monny
brains ez you 'ev if they war nobbut scraped oot.'

'Which waay did ta vote?' asked one. 'Whya noo,
it war leyke this waay: Ah went an' heeard all 'at
t' blew chap 'ed ti saay, an' he made it oot ez cleear
ez t' neease on yer feeace 'at t' yallers war up ti neea
good; an' efter that Ah went ti lissen ti t' yaller chap,
an' he sed 'at t' blews war warse 'an nowt at all. Seea
Ah thowt ti mysen, 'at if them 'at's my betters dizn't
knaw what's what, it's nut for sike o' me ti saay; seea
when t' voting daay cam Ah stopped at yam an' sell'd
t' pig.'

A classical curate was seized with an inordinate
yearning to improve and elevate the 'thought tone' (I
quote his words) of certain Cleveland farmers. Now, as
a body of men, the Cleveland farmers, as I know them,
are about as shrewd, practical, and thoroughly business-
like as you will find anywhere in Yorkshire, and that
is saying a deal; still I am bound to admit, though

I know little of 'thought tone' myself, they know less. There is no money in it. Make it clear that an income of two hundred a year can be squeezed out of 'thought tone,' and Yorkshire will supply the world with any amount, in tins, condensed, and hermetically sealed. At present it is not quoted on 'Change. But to my story. The curate made a dead set at one farmer in particular, giving him, on one occasion, a graphic account of the siege of Troy. 'One general, sir,' said he, 'though sorely wounded, commanded his armour-bearer to strap on his armour, and this having been done he placed himself in the forefront of the battle' (here much dramatic action and tone was indulged in by the curate, and the hearth-rug greatly disarranged) —'in the forefront, sir, and single-handed he engaged three of the Trojans' (seizing the poker and swinging it round his head). 'He slew two of them, but the third pierced him to the heart, and he sank lifeless upon his vanquished foes. 'Twas a brave deed, and a noble death, the death of a hero. What do you think, sir?' Breathless, and with dampened brow, he waited for an outburst of tone, which he fully expected would rush forth as waters from the burst bank of a reservoir. The farmer just removed his pipe and placidly remarked, 'Too bou'd, sir, too bou'd.' The curate sank into a chair aghast. Was the man human, or was he beyond hope! 'Is that all?' he gasped; 'has no other thought struck you whilst I recounted my story?' 'Whya,' said the farmer, 'Ah did yance ower aim 'at ya'd be fetching t' clock doon wi' t' poker, bud fort'natly ya didn't.' The curate fled.

CHAPTER III

WIT AND CHARACTER—*continued*.

OUR country-people, as has been incidentally re-marked, are very proud and independent, but I venture to say both their pride and independency are cast in a right groove, and may certainly be classed amongst the chief elements which have made the Yorkshireman the self-reliant mortal which he certainly is. I have already said that he is eminently practical, and I now add hard to convince. Often, I admit, his mode of arguing would puzzle a Philadelphian lawyer, but after all it is argument, if you are only Yorkshire scholar enough to understand his way of handling a subject. The country-people are hard to convince, and no respecters of person.

Mary W—— had for many years received a dole of ten shillings every Christmas for coals, but having obtained regular work at the Hall, the vicar rightly decided that five shillings in future would meet her circumstances, the more so as there were many other deserving cases. At the time appointed he left five shillings with Mary's daughter, the mother being out at the time. On her return she was told of the vicar's call, and of the five shillings which he had left. 'And what did you do, Mary?' asked a lady, some short time afterwards. 'Deea! deea! Whya, Ah 'ed t' fahve shillin' seal'd an' posted back agaan tiv him, afore he left t' village. Ah'm nut that poor 'at Ah want for fahve shillin'; an' if Ah can't be treated like a lady wi' ten shillin', Ah weean't be maad a pauper on; neea, nut if t' archbishop war ti cum wiv it hissel.'

Chatting one day with a very old friend of mine, the Vicar of ——, he gave me the following:—' In my younger days,' said he, 'I was brought up amongst the South-country peasantry, and for some time after I came into the North Riding I was greatly surprised at the small amount of deference paid to me as their pastor. So marked was this, that I determined if possible to discover the reason; so one day I entered into conversation with a blunt but honest old stone-breaker I found hard at work by the roadside. "Now, Willie," said I, "you are hard at it." "Aye," said he, "Ah've gitten ti arn my bit; ya've nivver 'ed ti deea a stroak foor yours." Not heeding his remark—which, by the way, a South-country man of like position would never dared have uttered—I asked: "How is it, Willie, that none of the villagers ever touch their caps or the women curtsy when they meet me?" I know it was a bit snobbish to ask such a question, but I had good reason for so doing: I wished to find out if I was in any way remiss. "Touch wer caps an' co'tsey!" said he, still continuing to break his stones. "Wa've neea call ti deea owther t' ane or tither; wa knaw varra larl aboot ya ez yit." "But I am your pastor," I urged, feeling at that time that was all-sufficient. "That coonts fer larl," said the old fellow. "Ther's good uns

an' bad uns ov all soarts. Ah tell ya 'at wa knaw varra
larl aboot ya ez yit. Wa s'all finnd oot efter a bit what
soart o' stuff yer maad on, bud ya'll 'a'e ti treead yer
teeas cannily, or wa s'aan't tak ti ya at all." All this,'
said my old friend, 'at that time was a complete
revelation to me. Up to then I had been used, anyway before my face, to something approaching ser-
vility, and here was a stone-breaker plainly telling me
I should have to be very careful, and doing so without
so much as ceasing his work.' Let me add, the stone-
breaker has been laid to rest now many a year, and
the flock has fully recognized the vicar as their
shepherd, and as one worthy both of their love and
respect; and in their way they give the one and show
the other in a marked degree. It takes a little time
to get at the bottom of our people, but the trying to
do so always brings a plenteous reward.

Mr. Pawson by nature was bumptious. He was
distinctly of the genus *novus homo*. He came to
the village as a stranger, and built himself a house,
and from the day he came to reside therein, figura-
tively speaking, he began to push the villagers about.
'He'll stritch t' lastic' (elastic) 'whahl it flees back an'
smacks him i' t' feeace,' said one. And he did. It
happened this way. One day, turning to a small pig-
jobber, he said, 'Jackson, tell one of your lads to
take my dog back to the house; and, Jackson, he had
better call at the saddler's and take some repairs along
at the same time.' Now, as has been already remarked,
this addressing the country folk by their surname is
deeply resented; and in the case of Mr. P. there was
almost open rebellion. Jackson, however, was in no

way dependent on the self-elected squire; so, winking to the bystanders, he said, 'All reet; bud Ah saay, Mr. Pawson, Ah think 'at ya owt ti saay Mister when ya speeak ti ma. Ya knaw fau'k's saying 'at maist leyklings wa s'all seean be related, ez mah au'dest lad's gitten his e'e on that eldest lass o' yours.' The roar of laughter which followed was— well, I pity Mr. Pawson.

A lady of ample means, whose one desire was to do good to others, found the people very difficult to approach when she first came amongst them. As a fact, she knew nothing of the idiosyncrasy of the Yorkshire people. Said she one day to an old Yorkshire dame whom she had weeding her garden : 'Bessy, how is it the people do not take kindly to me ? I am most wishful to help them, and to make them my friends, but they won't let me; how is it ?' 'Whya, ya see wa're a larl bit different mebbe ti t' fau'k 'at you'll 'a'e been amang, afoor ya cam inti these pairts; Ah've allus fun' ya varra canny ti deea wi' mysen, Ah will saay that.' 'Yes, but how is it the other cottagers do not seem pleased to see me when I call ?' 'Whya, mebbins Ah c'u'd tell ya, bud Ah deean't knaw 'at Ah s'u'd be deeaing mysen onny good if Ah did,' said Bessy, cautiously. 'But I should be greatly obliged to you if you would.' 'Aye, ya saay seea noo, bud ya'd leyklings git yer back up if Ah tell'd ya.' 'No, indeed I won't; I am really wishful to know.' 'Oha, whya noo, when ya gi'e ma yer wo'd on 't, Ah s' 'a'e ti gi'e ya a bit ov an inkling. Noo, it's leyke this, mum : wa deean't tak kindly ti fau'k 'at tak liberties wiv uz. Noo, Ah

deean't want ti saay owt 'at'll vex ya, bud neea doot,
bidoot meeaning it, ya tak a gert deal upon yersen.'
'In what way?' asked the lady, being quite unaware
of ever having done anything of the kind. 'Whya
noo, for yah thing, ya nivver knock at neeabody's
deear; ya just lift t' sneck an' cross t' deearstan ez
if t' pleeace belang'd ti ya. An' Ah'll tell ya anuther
thing whahl Ah's aboot it: ya ass.[1] a seet ti monny
quessions for yan 'at isn't varra weel knawn ti yan.
Ya s'u'dn't deea seea. Ya wadn't be sae setten up
noo, if yan ov uz cam an' walked wersens inti your
parlour, bidoot knocking or owt, an' started ti ass ya
quessions aboot all manner o' macks an' mander o'
things, noo wad ya? Noo, wa ar'n't aboon awning
wer betters; bud, mahnd ya, wer betters 'ez ti wait
whahl wa deea't, an' they 'ev ti let uz deea't i' wer
awn waay an' all, an' ther's nowt aboot that,' concluded Bessy. Let me add, the lady took the hint,
and in time learnt to love the plain-spoken people
she had come to live amongst; and they gave their
love in return tenfold, which, if rugged and rough at
the edges, only enables you to get a firmer grip of it.

Just a few illustrations proving the practical side of
our character.

In the village schoolroom a lecturer very learnedly
and emphatically discoursed on the human eye.
Amongst other things he declared the eye could
quell the most savage beast. 'Ah saay,' said a
sturdy farmer at the close of the lecture, 'deea ya
ho'd ti be trew all 'at ya've been telling uz aboot
wer e'es?' On assuring him every word was quite

[1] Ask.

true, the lecturer was somewhat staggered by the farmer's desire for a practical proof. 'Whya then,' said he, 'Ah'll tell ya what, Ah deean't believe owt 'at ya've tell'd uz; an' mair 'an that, if you'll cum up ti mah hoos ti morn at morn, Ah'll gi'e ya a chance ti tell mah 'at Ah's wrang. Noo, leeak here, if you'll gan inti mah paddock, Ah'll gie ya leave ti e'e mah bull ez mich ez ivver ya leyke, an' if he dizn't shift ya afoor ya can count fo'tty, Ah'll gi'e ya leave ti tak him yam wi' ya. Bud you'll be shifted.' A friend calling to see one who was seriously ill, said just before parting, 'Whya noo, thoo maun't gi'e waay; thoo mun keep thi pluck up, or else it'll be owered wi' tha.' 'Aye, mun!' said the invalid, 'bud it's hard ti keep yan's pluck up, when yan feels all ov a shutther. Ah'll tell tha what, if summat dizn't sthraangely alter, Ah's foor off, an' ther's nowt can ho'd ma back.' 'Oha well,' said the visitor, 'thoo owt ti knaw t' best; bud whativver thoo diz, thoo maun't dee iv a horry' (hurry). 'It's fowr mile ti t' chetch, an' thoo's na leet weight, an Ah s'u'd be bidden, an' 'a'e ti len' a han' ti hug tha. Liggin i' bed a bit taks yan doon a lot; thoo mun try ti hing on a week or tweea, hooivver.'

Old I—— of Masham, a well-known jobber in days past, was once asked for a loan. But I will give the . story as given to me years ago by William Scorrer, than whom a finer specimen of the old school of Yorkshiremen never lived, and to whom I am indebted for many of the best stories and other information in this book. Could you but have heard the old man tell them—old! why, he never looked old, and he was nearly

D

eighty when I knew him—but you never will hear
him ; he has stepped over the line. His style, raciness,
and everything which goes to make a Yorkshire story
worth listening to, were lost when the grave closed
over his last remains. At least, that is to my way
of thinking. I know scores of people who can tell
a Yorkshire story, and tell it admirably, perfect as
to dialect, and humorously, too ; but still, there always
lacks that something—I mean crispness ; no, sparkle
is the word—which the old chap always managed to
give just at the right moment. ' Requiescat in pace.'

Pardon me, I will to the story. Old I—— was at
Northallerton Market, when another jobber rushed up
to him. ' Ah saay,' said he, ' c'u'd ta mannish ti len'
uz fahve pund. Ah finnd mysel that sho't, an' Ah s'all
loss a grand bargain if Ah caan't leet on sumbody 'at
'll len' uz 't. ' Whya, thoo knaws, Bill,' said I——, ' Ah
deean't ho'd wi' lennin' ; ta knaws it offens maks frien's
leeak shy at yan anuther ; bud if so be 'at thoo's gahin
ti miss a bargain, whya, Ah mun stritch a point foor
yance, bud, mahnd tha, thoo 'ezn't ti mak a common
practis on 't. Noo, when diz ta think 'at thoo'll be
yabble ti pay 't back ? An' what 'ez ta gitten, 'at thoo's
gahin ti 'liver up ez security ? ' ' Whya, Ah'll let tha
'a'e my watch, an' Ah'll gi'e tha mah wo'd—— '

' Nivver mahnd thi wo'd, let's leeak at t' watch.
Ah tell tha what,' said I——, when he had the watch in
his hand, ' thoo mebbins sets gert store byv it thisen,
bud tha'd bunch tha oot ov a pawn shop if thoo war
brazzen'd eneeaf ti ass a pund for 't. When can ti let
mah 'ev it back ? ' ' Ah'll gi'e tha 't at Bedale next
Tuesday.' ' Whya noo, Ah'll trust tha for yance,

bud it's mair 'an what thi awn feyther 'ud deea. Noo thoo maun't tak ma in; Ah s'all leeak for tha ti' pay't back when Ah see tha at Bedale.' To Bill's credit, the money was paid the week following. But a fortnight afterwards he again begged for a loan, this time for fifteen pounds. 'Neea!' said I——, 'thoo teeak mah in yance; Ah'll nut trust tha na mair.' 'Teeak tha in! Didn't Ah pay tha back hard eneeaf at Bedale, when Ah tell'd tha Ah wad?' 'Aye, thoo paid ma back all reet, bud Ah nivver thowt 'at thoo wad; naay, thoo's ta'en ma in yance, Ah weean't be on agaan.'

That by nature the Tyke is tenacious of his opinion, and hard to convince, may be taken as an axiom. I have referred to this before, but this is a convenient opportunity to produce proofs of the same.

For years, old Sykes and Hobson, though neighbours, had been on unfriendly terms. Years back, Sykes had found on several occasions a certain gate thrown off its hinges. Whether he held any proof, history does not recount, but he blamed Hobson for doing it. Hobson, however, stoutly denied all knowledge of the affair. Anyway, for long they remained about as unfriendly as they well could; until one day, Hobson, at the risk of his life, rescued Sykes' lad from drowning. On hearing of the rescue, Sykes hurried away to thank Hobson. They met in one of the latter's fields. 'Whya, noo then,' began Sykes, 'Ah've cum'd ti shak tha byv t' han'; thoo's saved my bairn, an' Ah's behodden ti tha foor awlus. Noo wa s'all 'a'e ti let bygones be bygones, an' start afresh. Thoo knaws wa used ti hit it off all reet yance ower;

D 2

noo, what diz ta saay?' 'Wha, mun, ther's my hand on 't, an' Ah's mair 'an glad 'at wa've hap't t' au'd sore up at last; an' ez thoo sez, wa mun start afresh, just ez if nivver nowt 'ed cum'd atween uz.' So they shook hands, and talked farming for an hour or so, until it was time for Sykes to return. Shaking Hobson by the hand, he said, 'Noo thoo knaws Ah s'all nivver be yabble ti mak it up ti tha for saving t' lad, an' Ah's reet glad 'at Ah can gan yam an' tell t' missus 'at thee an' me's kind agaan, an' Ah whoap 'at wa s'all awlus keep seea. Bud mahnd tha, Ah still ho'd ti 't 'at it war thoo 'at flang t' yat offen t' creeaks,' i.e. 'But bear in mind, I still think it was you who flung the gate off the hinges.'

Old Hall, a well-known character in one of our dales, was the doctor for miles round, and proud was the village wherein he actually resided. He was more than doctor, he was the vet. as well; he read the lessons in church; in fact, he was the father of the village. He was consulted, and his advice acted upon in all things which are incident to a village community. And then he died, and a new doctor took his place—top hat, frock-coat, and everything. Some little time after his arrival, Wilson's cow died, and the death of the said cow was fully discussed the day following, in the blacksmith's shop. 'What did ta gi'e it?' asked one. 'Nowt. Hoo mud Ah knaw what ti git for 't?' 'Did ta gan for t' doctor?' asked another. 'Aye, an' he war neean sae setten up, at being fetched oot o' bed i' t' middle o' t' neet.' 'Warn't he! What did he saay?' 'He tell'd ma 'at he warn't a coo doctor, an' knew nowt aboot 'em.'

'Did he saay that?' asked the smith slowly, resting on his hammer, as he waited for an answer. 'Aye, an' he tell'd ma ti gan yam an' nivver wakken him up na mair on sike an earand.' 'Wha, then,' said the smith very deliberately, 'he's nut a Hall! an' he mud just ez weel teeam his stuff oot, an' quit his bottles foor au'd glass. Foor Ah meean ti saay 'at a chap 'at dizn't knaw nowt aboot t' innards' (the inside) 'of a coo, an' hosses, an' pigs, an' sike leyke, isn't gahin ti practis on onny ov uz, 'coz if he 'ezn't gitten them off, he caan't knaw nowt aboot oor innards, foor wa're a seet mair intrickiter' (intricate) 'na onny o' t' dumb critters. He's nut a Hall, an' he's na ewse tiv uz.' The oracle having spoken, it was agreed on all hands that it was so. And from that moment the influence of that man as a doctor ceased.

Here is another, which brings out a trait I purpose touching upon afterwards. Incidentally, I may mention, a bargain is a bargain, and must be maintained and carried out as originally agreed upon. The story, however, I give as an illustration of how hard it is to convince our people that their preconceived notion on any subject is wrong.

It was quite four miles from a certain house to the village, and as the gardener was often required to go thither for one thing or another, his master bought him a bicycle, thinking to make the journey easier for him. A few days after the machine had been presented, John said, 'Noo, sir, Ah wanted ti 'ev a wo'd wi' ya. Noo, when Ah cam, Ah cam for ti be t' gardener, an' ti deea onny odd jobs 'at wanted deeaing.

Bud, ya knaw, Ah s'all want a bit mair a week if Ah've ti larn ti mannish yon thing'—jerking his thumb over his shoulder in the direction of the tool-house, where the byke was kept. 'Ya knaw, sir, ther warn't nivver nowt at no tahm owt sed aboot a bisittle, an' Ah s' want a bit mair afoor Ah tattle yon thing. Noo, hoo mich is 't ti be?' The master pointed out that it was for his (the gardener's) own comfort, and to lighten the journey to and from the village, he had been induced to buy the bicycle. 'Whya, noo, Ah deean't knaw sae mich aboot that,' said John; 'it soonds weel eneeaf t' waay 'at you put it; ther's nowt aboot that, bud Ah've leeaked fother inti 't 'an what yow 'ev. Noo, leeak here, it taks me nigh on ti tweea hoors an' a hauf ti gan an' cum walking; noo, hoo lang is 't gahin ti tak ma ti deea 't o' yon thing?' 'When you get used to it, you will run there and back easily in an hour.' 'Oha, s'all Ah! Then that'll be leyke an hoor an' a hauf ti t' good.' 'Yes, you will save quite that.' 'Then when Ah git back, s'all Ah 'a'e ti sit ma doon an' deea nowt for t' hoor an' t' hauf?' 'Sit down and do nothing! Certainly not; you will go on with your work.' 'Aye, Ah thowt seea; an' that's what maks ma saay 'at ya'll 'a'e ti gi'e ma a larl bit mair, ez Ah's gahin ti put sa monny mair hoors' wark in i' t' week. Ya see, you reckon yah waay, an' Ah reckon another, an' Ah think Ah's i' t' reet on 't.'

Those who have given the slightest attention to the various traits which are so interesting in the character of our people, will not have failed to notice one which is very pronounced. I mean the objection they have to showing, and the cleverness they display in hiding, their ignorance on any matter. If in speaking to our country people you use a word which they do not understand, they never let you know that they do not catch your meaning: they wait until you say 'summat else,' in the hope that they may gather therefrom what you mean; and if you do not happen to say anything which throws light upon the unknown word, well, there the matter ends, and as a rule it does not trouble them for one moment. A farm labourer fell off a bicycle, and sprained his arm very severely; the doctor, a young locum, and a trifle pedantic, gave him a bottle of lotion, saying, as he did so, 'Your arm will be all right in a few days: you have strained your biceps, you must rub it well with this lotion.' 'What diz ta think on him?' asked one, who had been waiting outside. " Whya, he's nowt bud a fondheead, is yon. What diz ta think? He sez 'at Ah've spraaned my airm, an' he's gi'en ma a bottle o' stuff ti rub t' bisittle wiv; let's gan ti t' bone-setter.' A lady visiting a poor young fellow who was seriously ill, and very feverish, said to the mother, 'Your son is very ill, I fear.' 'He is that, mum; he's nut foor lang doon here. Hooivver, wa've deean t' best 'at lay i' wer power, an' yan isn't yabble ti deea na mair 'an that. Bud Ah's pleeased ti saay 'at wa've gitten eneeaf saved up ti put him deeacently by, an' that's a blessing. It'll be a beautiful funeral, mum, an' wa've let him saay whau's ti be bidden; an' Ah deean't think he's forgitten yan ov his au'd frien's—bud he awlus was thowtful.' 'That is very nice,' said the lady, for she understood something of the people and their ways. 'I will send you a couple of ice wafers,' said she, thinking they would be nice for him to cool his lips with. ' I think your son will like them, he seems so feverish.' Next day, when she inquired how the patient was, the poor mother said, with tears in her eyes, ' Thank ya, mum, Ah think he's warse.' ' Did he like the wafers?' she inquired, adding, ' you can have more.' ' Well, mum,' said the mother, ' Ah c'u'dn't saay foor sartin whether he liked 'em or nut. Ya see, ez seean ez ya sent 'em, Ah put him t' white yan on his chist; bud he 'pleeaned 'at it felt varra cau'd, an' seea Ah teeak it off, an' put t' pink un on a plate i' front o' t' fire ti warm. Bud Ah think t' cat must 'a'e gitten 't, foor it war gone when Ah went for 't. So ya see, iv a waay, he 'adn't a fair go wiv 'em. Bud you needn't send na mair, he's gahin fast noo.'

A gentleman said to a Yorkshire dame, ' Your little chap looks very robust.' ' Aye, an' your larl chap leeaks t' saame,' said she; not in the least knowing what ' robust' meant. ' Nay, nay,' said the gentleman; ' I only wish he was'—glancing at the very weakly child he held by the hand. The dame perceived she had made a mistake, so added, ' Whya he seean wad be '; and then, not quite certain of her ground, or where ' robust ' was going to land her, continued, ' bud then yan nivver knaws.' When the gentleman had left the group, one of the bystanders said, ' Dolly, what diz ro-bust meean?' ' Deean't ass me, Ah've na mair idea na t' man i' t' meean,' said she. ' Then what maad ta saay 'at his bairn leeaked t' saame ez what he sed thahn did?' ' Whya, Ah thowt 'at if he war calling mah bairn naames, Ah'd let him 'ev

ez good ez he sent; whahl, if he war sayin' summat
i' praise on 't, Ah sud be deeaing t' saame byv his.'

On another occasion, a village dame entered the
doctor's visiting-room. 'Noo, then,' she commenced,
'gie ma summat, an' leeak sharp aboot it, fer Ah is
badly; Ah can nowther bahd ti sit doon, stan' up,
ner nowt.' 'What is the matter with you?' inquired
the doctor.' 'Naay, what; it's neea ewse assing me,
Ah've cumd to see you aboot that.' 'Well, but what
ails you?' 'Aals ma! Ah've gitten galloping paans all
reet roond aboot ivverywheear; Ah is badly.' 'But
what have you been doing to get them?' 'Whya, Ah
can think o' nowt bud, t' daay afoor yesterdaay, Ah
war weshin', an' Ah mun 'a'e kept a damp ap'on on,
an' Ah aim 'at it's gi'en ma cau'd all reet roond aboot
ivverywheer.' 'Now I know what's the matter with
you. Here's a bottle for you; take it home, and you
had better drink a teaspoonful every ten minutes, and
it will be best if you take it in a recumbent position,'
said he, handing Martha the bottle. Now, 'recumbent
position' was quite outside Martha's vocabulary; she
had not the least idea what he meant, but she was not
going to expose her ignorance by asking. So off home
she set, saying to herself as she went along, "Re-cum-
bunt po-zition;" noo what diz that mean?' However,
Yorkshire like, she hit upon a plan of getting to know,
without exposing her own ignorance. Calling on
a neighbour as she passed by, she shouted, ''Liza
Jane, Ah've been ti t' doctor, an' he's gi'en ma a
bottle o' stuff, an' Ah 'ev ti tak a speeanful on 't ivvery
ten minits; bud he sez 'at Ah 'ev ti tak it in a recumbunt po-zition. Bud thoo knaws Ah 'evn't gitten

yan, an' Ah thowt mebbe 'at thoo'd be seea good ez ti let ma 'a'e t' len' o' thahn; will ta?' Liza Jane knew no more what 'recumbunt pozition' meant than Martha, but she was not going to give herself away, so she replied, 'Ah wad 'a'e deean sa wi' t' gertest o' pleasure i' t' wo'lld, nobbut Ah lent mahn yisterday. Bud ez thoo gans up t' village, call in at t' shop an' buy yan for thisen, an' then thoo'll 'ev it at heeam when thoo wants it; an' if tha 'evn't gitten yan, buy a mug —it'll deea just t' seeam.'

One more. Bessy having explained to the doctor that her husband was suffering from a fearful pain in the head, was ordered to apply the half-dozen leeches which he gave her. Now, had the doctor said, 'stick 'em on,' or 'clap 'em on,' Bessy would have known what she had to do with them. However, she had half a dozen leeches to do something with, so she went home and did her level best. A couple of days after, the doctor, seeing Bessy, asked her how John was. 'Oh, he's all reet noo. Them things capped him; tha did, hooivver.' 'You managed all right, did you, Bessy?' asked he. 'Whya, Ah caan't saay 'at wa mannished sa weel wi' t' fo'st un 'at Ah gav' him; he chow'd on wi' 't, bud he c'u'd catch ho'd on 't neea road, soa Ah boil'd him t' rest, an' he sluthered 'em doon neycely.'

CHAPTER IV

WIT AND CHARACTER—*continued*

THERE are many other side-lights to our character, only a few of which it will be possible to notice. But every story is pictured in such varying light and shade as to afford those who can fully appreciate them many varied traits of our character. And one word, if you please, with reference to these stories. Nearly all have the merit of being in essence true. They have been gathered from various sources, but in the main first hand. Many of the characters were known personally to the writer ; and although in a few instances the origin and authenticity are doubtful, they are included because they so fully illustrate that which was to be demonstrated, and because they are so true to life, and just what would really have happened under like circumstances.

There is one special gift which the Yorkshireman possesses in a high degree, i.e. the humorous. It is a humorousness, too, which often (given that you understand and appreciate the dialect) sparkles with genuine wit. I plead guilty to the fact that much of the wit of our country-people is, as it were, given with the back of the hand. Still, it is none the less witty, for all that. And if the same sounds rough and unmusical to you,

kindly bear in mind that the Chinese consider our
best music little else than a tumult of discordant
sound. It is generally the last few words uttered
which contain the bud, blossom, and fruit all in one. I
remember once being completely shut up by a Yorkshire lad, and he only uttered two words; but the tone
and the look were the very cream of sarcastic jeering.
This was how it came about. The lad was driving
home some ducks from the pond. 'You have a lot of
fine ducks, my boy,'. said I. And then, thinking to
buy a couple, I asked, 'How often do you kill them?'
'Nobbut yance,' was the laconic reply.

'T' law's nowt bud a takin all t' waay thruff,' said one.
'When me an' Tom went afoor wer betters aboot that
hedge, Ah'd Jackson ti talk foor me, an' he 'ed Smith
ti talk foor him. An' ti lissen ti them tweea black-
guarding yan anuther when t' case war on, yan mud
'a'e thowt 'at tha war i' arnist, an' 'at tha nivver wad 'a'e
spokken civil t' ane tither agaan; bud bless mah leyfe,
when t' case war adjourned ti t' next court daay, an'
when me an' Tom, scooling at yan anuther leyke all
that, went inti t' Black Lion ti 'ev a glass o' yal, if
wa didn't finnd them tweea takking wine an' 'ranging ti
gan fishing tigither t' next daay. "Tom," sez Ah, "if
this is t' waay tha mak t' feeal o' yan, seeaner thee an'
me haps t' business up an' t' better it'll be foor baith
on uz." An' he sez ti me, "Gi'e uz thi han' on 't,"
an' Ah did. An' then Ah shoots oot, "Hil Ah'll tell
ya what, you tweea 'ed best 'range to gan fishing foor
awlus; bud mahnd ya, nowther me ner Tom's gahin
ti finnd t' bait for owther on ya!"

Sally Ridge was a terror to all those she took a

dislike to. She usually played some prank to the detriment of those who, for the time being, were out of favour. On one occasion, however, she went a trifle too far; she broke the back of a duck with a stone. This got poor Sally into fearfully hot water, and there was every likelihood of her being summoned; however, the writer interceded on her behalf, and on Sally faithfully promising never to stone a duck again, she was pardoned. Within an hour afterwards, I surprised her gaily pitching stones amongst the feathered swimmers. 'Didn't you promise me faithfully not to throw stones at the ducks again, Sally?' I asked, taking hold of her, and adding, 'it is wicked of you to break your word in this way.' 'Ah 'evn't brokken my wo'd,' replied Sally, trying to free herself. 'But you have; you promised not to throw stones at the ducks again,' I repeated. 'An' Ah isn't; Ah's thrawing at yon geese, an' it's nut mah fau't if t' silly au'd ducks git thersens i' t' road. Leave lowse, Ah nivver sed nowt ti naebody aboot geese.'

Three visitors hired a boat at Staithes for an hour's fishing, having a man each to attend to their lines. On returning to land, the fishermen were paid half a crown for the sail. The visitors had not got far away, when one of the fishermen ran after them. 'Ah saay, mister,' said he, turning the half-crown over in his hand, 'ya see ther's three on uz, an' nut being schollars, wa're bet ti knaw hoo ti share 't oot; bud Ah'll tell ya what wa deea knaw,' he added, with a merry twinkle in his eye, 'if ya war ti gi'e uz anuther sixpence, wa s'u'd 'ev a bob apiece.' And they got it.

An old keeper was told off to hand the gun for

a very poor shot. After blazing away at several coveys, he turned to the old chap, saying, 'I am afraid you will think me a very bad shot!' 'Nut Ah. Ah think 'at Ah nivver seed naebody shut better an' hit warse i' mah leyfe.' 'And yet I have made many a good bag before to-day,' said the sportsman, just a wee bit nettled. 'Aye, bud oor bo'ds flee, tha deean't sit ti be shutten at,' was the quiet rejoinder.

Lady —— said to one of her under-gardeners, 'Thomas, the maids tell me that you often say very nasty things about women; do you ever do the same of the men?' And then her ladyship looked him squarely in the face, but Thomas was equal to the occasion. 'Neea, my lady, that Ah deean't, acoz i' that case it 'ud be trew, ya knaw.'

Tommy had been fishing on Sunday; he had been caught red-handed by the Chapel minister. The good man read Tommy a long lesson on the enormity of his sin, concluding by asking what Tommy had to say for himself. 'It's nut a real rod!' ventured Tommy. 'That does not matter,' said his judge; 'the sin is just the same, and the Lord never prospers those who break the sabbath.' 'Wha, then,' promptly replied Tommy, 'it mun 'a'e been Au'd Scrat' (i.e. Satan) ''at's egg'd 'em on ti bite ti-daay, foor Ah nivver catched sa monny afoor'—holding up a bottle fairly alive with sticklebacks and minnows.

Whether I am succeeding or not is for others to judge, but what I am striving to do is to paint the various points in our character faithfully. I am neither hiding nor glossing. Our brusquerie and doggedness, our tenacity of opinion and keenness to acquire the all-needful, our pride and independency, as also our want of that respect for those who may consider themselves our superiors, have been as fully and as truthfully set forth as space would admit of.

On the other hand, our people are warm-hearted, hospitable to a degree, and exhibit a deep sense of gratitude for favours received, such as would never be credited by those who judge us by our rugged exterior. But it is there, for all that. Let me give you two or three stories quite true, which prove to some extent what I have just asserted.

A woman possessed an old, carved corner cupboard, not really worth much, but it had been her mother's, and she prized it greatly—in fact, far above its market value. The village doctor had often tried to buy it, but without success. Her husband falling seriously ill, the doctor was called in, and though there was no hope of a long bill being paid, he was most assiduous in his attendance day and night. When recovering, the patient, fully aware that he had been fairly snatched from the grave, said to his wife one night, when she was sitting by the bedside, 'Fanny, thoo'll 'a'e ti let t' doctor 'ev t' cupboard.' He well knew what a wrench this would be, and was no little surprised when his wife replied, 'Bless tha, mun, ez seean ez ivver thoo gat a to'n foor t' better, Ah 'ed t' cupboard rovven doon, an' sent Bob wi' 't. Doctor didn't want ti 'a'e 't, an' sent it back, bud Ah sent Bob wiv it agaan, an' tell'd him ti saay 'at if he sent it back onny mair Ah'd mak firewood on 't.

Thoo's wo'th mair 'an all t' cupboards i' t' wo'lld ti me, an' it war t' only road ther war o' paying him.'

Again. An old dame having been ill for a long time, recovered, much to the surprise of every one. During her long illness a certain lady often visited her, and sent her many little comforts. Some months after the old dame's recovery, she presented her bene-factress with an elaborate clip-hearthrug. For this the lady wished to pay her, but that the old dame almost indignantly refused. 'Neea, mum,' said she, with tears in her eyes; 'Ah've 'ed ommaist ivvery bit o' t' stuff gi'en ma 'at Ah've maad t' clips on, an' if ivvery prod 'at Ah've gi'en an' ivvery clip 'at Ah've cutten war a gowden guinea, it wadn't mak up foor hauf your kindness ti me.' Oh no, they do not lack gratitude.

The vicar's bride had a remark made to her by one of the oldest men in the village, which seemed to her to have a nasty application, but in its idiomatic sense it was quite innocent of any such construction; and the remark as addressed to the lady was certainly given in its idiomatic form. By-and-by she learnt she had been a little hasty in condemning the old fellow. However, to make up for any unkindness on her part, she engaged the old man as a sort of anything-you-like about the vicarage. It was not long ere the old chap won a very warm place in the lady's heart. This was after the arrival of the baby. Every night, when his work was done, he would say, 'Noo then what, Ah've deean; bud Ah mun 'ev a leeak at t' baa'n afoor Ah gan.' One evening, after this same formula had been gone through,

he said, 'Noo, Ah'll tell ya what ; t' baa'n's nut sa
varra weel ti-neet, an' Ah knaw a seet mair aboot
babbies 'an what you deea. Noo you mun put 't iv
a hot bath, an' then hap 't up an' keep 't varra warm.
Noo you mun deea ez Ah've tell'd ya.' With this
admonition he left the vicarage, and, though turned
seventy-eight years of age, set off at once to
trudge seven miles for a doctor, landing back again
about midnight. The doctor assured the delighted
mother that, having followed the old man's advice,
and with the remedies he had brought, a severe fit
of croup had been staved off. Oh yes, these blunt
country-people have feelings. And they are grateful.

Gratitude shows itself in different ways, sometimes
in a form of self-sacrifice, as in the following, which
occurred not so very long ago. Said a vicar to one
of his parishioners—who, by-the-way, was a notorious
poacher—' I am very pleased to see you coming to
church so regularly; very pleased, indeed, William ;
and I trust that it may lead you to see the
error of your past life.' ' Well, Ah wadn't gan sa
far ez ti saay 'at owt o' that soart's leykley ti
happen, bud Ah s' cum ti t' chetch, for all that.'
' And may I ask the reason for this sudden change
in your life ? ' inquired the parson. ' Whya noo,
it war i' this waay. Me an' Luke an' tweea or
three uthers war talking ya ower yah neet i' t' Swan,
an' Luke sed 'at he didn't ho'd wi' neea parsons
'at hunted, an' Ah sed 'at a parson war nowt neea
different ti neeabody else, when he'd ta'en t' white
goon off, an' 'at it maad neea odds whether ya
hunted or whether ya didn't. Bud t' main on 'em

E

seeamed ti ho'd 'at ya warn't i' t' reet on 't hunting.
And seea Ah thowt ti mysen, t' parson's offens
deean me a good to'n, an' if ther's gahin to be
sike a lot o' narrer-mahnded fau'k i' t' village—an'
being a bit of a sportsman mysen, ya knaw—wha,
Ah sez, noo Ah'll gan ti chetch if it's foor nowt
else bud ti back ya up a bit, an' sa Ah cums.'

The hospitality of the Yorkshire people is so well
known, and so generally admitted by all those who
have been recipients of the same, that I purpose just
leaving it as an established fact. Still, there is one
curious offshoot from this generous branch, which
needs *en passant* a moment's consideration.

I once heard a South-country man say, ' Yorkshire
people give you more than you want at their table,
and then beg from you on the doorstep.' And
to those who know nothing of our ways, usages,
and customs, such would almost seem to be the
case. Of course, as put by the South-country man,
the statement, if complete, would stamp Yorkshire
and its people as being rather more than contemptible.
But such is not the case, and when the reason for
the remark was perfectly sifted, the notion which
had got such a firm hold of the speaker was found
to have been based on a want of knowledge of the
elementary rules which govern the unwritten law
of bargaining. Why, pages could be written on
bargaining, and stories told by the score.

But when a bargain has been concluded, the money
paid, the receipt given, a substantial meal partaken of,
with grog, &c., ad lib., it becomes quite easy to understand the South-country man's surprise, on leaving

the house, to be asked 'ti gi'e summat back foor luck.' To him, not knowing our ways, the trans-action was completed; with us it was not, and therein lies the difference. It does strike one as peculiar to find such marked generosity, when run on certain lines, only to be confronted the next step with some little action which at first sight looks very much like meanness. But all this misconception vanishes if we bear in mind that *hospitality* and *business* are never made to clash; they, as it were, occupy separate rooms.

I have a story in my mind which illustrates fully these peculiarities, as well as others already mentioned. As it was given to me by his lordship, so briefly let me give it to you.

One day two of a shooting party, his lordship and the Hon. G——, decided to give their guns a rest, and visit an ancient church some six miles distant. They were strongly advised to take a keeper with them, but feeling quite sure they could find their way, started by themselves. Possibly they might have succeeded, had not a sea fret and heavy fog wrapped the whole moor in a shroud. They were lost, and they knew it. Fortunately, when quite worn out, they discovered a farm-house; and on inquiry they were told that they had wandered much out of their way, being then quite ten miles from the shooting-box. Too tired to walk back, they asked the farmer if he could possibly drive them. 'Whya, Ah c'u'd,' said he, 'bud it's a langish waay, an' mah meer's a bit tired; Ah'd ommaist rayther set ya ti wheer you c'u'dn't loss yersels.' They, however, declared they were too tired to think of walking, and offered him half a sovereign as an inducement. Then the bargaining propensity came to the surface 'Haaf a sover'ign!' said he. 'Neea, what ya'll 'a'e ti mak it fifteen bob.' To which they assented. During this bargaining, the good wife was spreading the table with abundance of food. 'Noo then,' said the good man, 'ya mun .reeach teea an' mak yersens at heeam. Ya're welcome ti t' best o' what wa've gitten; deean't be neyce aboot it, ther's plenty mair wheer that's cum'd fra; Ah'll cum roond wi' t' meer efter a bit.' When they were ready for departure, one of them inquired how much they were indebted for their splendid repast. To which the farmer, in characteristic fashion, made answer: 'What wa've gi'en ya, wa've gi'en ya, an' ya're welcome ti 't; drhaaving ya ti t' shutting-box war a bargain, an' anuther thing altigither, an' ther's nowt aboot that.' And not a penny piece could either be prevailed upon to receive for their hospitality.

Just one other story, which illustrates the same propensity for bargaining. A hamper containing a dead 'pricky-back otch'n,' with one shilling carriage to pay, was delivered to one Pettigrew; by some means he found out that the hamper had been the property of a friend of his, named Tom Scott. But Scott declared on his word of honour that he was innocent of the whole transaction. Unfortunately, Pettigrew did not believe him, in consequence of which a coolness sprang up, which lasted for two years. At the expiration of that time, Pettigrew met Scott one market-day. 'Whya, noo then,' said he, 'they tell ma 'at thoo's

gahin ti wed mah cousin Martha; is 't trew?' 'Aye,
it's trew hard eneeaf, Ah is, hooivver,' acknowledged
Scott. 'Whya, then thoo knaws thee an' me owtn't
ti be at loggerheeads when t' ane's gahin ti be
related ti t' ither; owt wa, noo?' 'Neea, bud thoo
knaws 'at it's neea fau't o' mahn; Ah've nowt agaan
tha, thoo knaws,' said Scott.

'Wha, bud Ah'd gert call ti blaam tha; thoo'll awn
ti t' hamper, weean't ta?' 'Aye, Ah nivver, 'at Ah
mahnd on, ivver tried ti disawn 't. What mud Ah
foor? Sumboddy stowl 't; Ah c'u'dn't help that,
onny road, c'u'd Ah?'

'Then thoo'd nowt i' t' wo'lld ti deea wi' t' pricky-
back otch'n?' 'Ah've tell'd tha ower an' up agaan
i' tahms back 'at Ah'd nivver nowt i' noa waay
whatsoivver owt ti deea wi' t' otch'n,' said Scott,
emphatically.

'Whya, thoo knaws 'at Ah 'ed a shilling ti pay
for 't cuming; what's gahin ti be deean aboot that,
then?' 'Whya, thoo dizn't leeak ti me for 't, diz
ta?' 'Whya, Ah war that oot o' pocket, an' it war
thi hamper 'at it cam in hard eneeaf.' 'Aye, an'
Ah'll tell tha what, thoo's nivver let ma 'a'e 't back
agaan; bud nivver mahnd, thoo mun keep t' hamper,
an' wa'll lap t' job up that waay,' magnanimously
offered Scott.

'Ah see 'at Ah's boun ti be oot o' pocket wi' t'
otch'n,' persisted Pettigrew, 'bud Ah'll tell tha what,
thoo mun stan' uz a glass foor friendship's sake.'
'Whya, noo then, ez Ah's gahin ti wed thi cusin
Martha, cu' thi waays.' And so the matter was settled.

CHAPTER V

WIT AND CHARACTER—*continued*

I PURPOSE devoting this chapter to stories which in themselves are good examples, embracing, as they do, many phases of Yorkshire character. With the exception of the first two or three, they will be given regardless of classification. But these two or three do need just a word. Our country-people, in their own way, hold in sincere veneration all spiritual teaching; but don't look for too much. Bear in mind, superstition dies hard, and in judging them on this head, it is well to keep to the forefront the fact that in religion, as well as in everything else, they cling to much which their grandmothers believed before them, just as they speak of their parents as 't' au'd fau'k,' without in the least being disrespectful. So, without the least intention of being irreverent, the Deity is often addressed and spoken of in a manner which would shock the ears of many. 'Ah wadn't 'a'e deean that if Ah'd been Him,' said an old dame, after hearing how the Israelites had been punished by God's vengeance. 'He owt ti 'a'e letten 'em off that tahm,' was her concluding remark. It was her opinion, and she freely gave it. The Deity being spoken of as ' Him ' and ' He,' was as natural

to the old lady as it would have been for us to say
'the Lord.' Anyway, for real piety, I for one make
my bow to the old dame.

Again, they have a way of materializing the most
spiritual things. To them, heaven is nothing more
than a big, beautiful city, which they have to try their
best to get into, and having managed to do so, they
are safe for ever. Doubtlessly they picture it sunnier,
purer, and altogether more delightful than any place
they have ever seen or heard of. But to them it is
just a city. Certainly this applies more especially to
the older people in our dales; the rising generation
are learning different, but it will be long before they
altogether leave the old and beaten track. And may
it be so, for, after all, their religion is to them a
very real and tangible thing. It is something which
in these days of higher criticism many of us are
letting slip from us. When reading the following
stories, it should be borne in mind why they are
given, and just what I wish to illustrate.

A clergyman having asked an old dying woman
if she were quite happy, received this reply : ' Neea,
that Ah isn't. Ah's boun to dee, an' Ah s' gan ti
heaven, an' it's that what's boddering ma. Nut gahin
ti heaven—Ah deean't meean that—bud t' music,' said
she, emphatically. ' Ya see, Ah've nivver larnt nowt
o' music ; Ah knaw nowt aboot it, an' if tha start
ma off wiv owther a harp or a dulcima, Ah s'all
mak nowt bud a laughing-stock o' mysel, for Ah
can nowther tune ner scrat on 'em. Noo, if 't c'u'd be
'ranged foor ma ti tak care o' yan o' t' angel babbies,
Ah s'u'd be ez reet ez ninepins, foor Ah allus did git

on wi' childer, an' Ah'd fetch it up a pattern, an' Ah'd promise nivver ti slap it; onny road, Ah s'all mak nowt ow 't wiv a dulcima.'

The village artist was dying; he had painted three out of the four village signs, he had executed the scrollwork for every church decoration for years past, and there was in his house an imitation marble mantelpiece, which he had yearned to show every one. The clergyman was about to leave him, but before doing so, asked if he should pray. 'Aye, aye,' said the dying man, 'and ez mebbe this'll be t' last tahm 'at ya will pray foor ma, Ah s'u'd be glad if ya'd mention 'at Ah's a good hand at decorating; it'll mebbe help yan a bit.'

Old Matthew was a well-known character. For years both he and his old dame lived in a little cottage near Newton-under-Rosebery. When on his death-bed, a lady, after reading to him, said, 'And after all I have read and told you, Matthew, heaven is more beautiful than you can possibly imagine; you might lie and call to mind all the beautiful things you have either seen or dreamt of, and even then you would not have the least idea what heaven is like.' To say the least, she was somewhat surprised when the old man, gently patting her hand, said in a whisper, 'Ya mebbe deean't knaw 'at Ah yance seed Leeds pantomine; that gave yan a inkling.' N.B.—The Yorkshire people always pronounce 'pantomime' as spelt above.

Old Bessy, who lived in an old house near Kildale, was very near the borderland. The clergyman found her quite happy and reconciled, and on leaving her (he was going away for some time), said, 'Well, good-bye, Bessy; I may never see you on earth again, but I shall hope to meet you in heaven.' 'Aye, an' Ah s' leeak oot for ya cuming; an' deean't forgit 'at neean on uz is nowt na different up yonder, so you maun't git yer back up if Ah just shak ya byv t' han', an' saay, famil'ar leyke, 'at Ah's glad ti see 'at ya've mannished it.'

The rest of this chapter is merely a collection of Yorkshire stories, which I think should not be lost, and which I leave to the perspicuity of my readers, who doubtless, without any hints from me, will grasp the many different phases of character contained therein.

The tire had come off the cart wheel, and the Tyke was in a bit of a fix; shortly afterwards a cyclist drew up, and dismounting, remarked, 'Punctchard. Can I lend you my pump?' and then burst out laughing at the man's dilemma and his own wit. 'Punctchard? neea, Ah isn't punctchard,' retorted the Tyke, in fairly good imitation of the would-be wit. 'An' thoo can stick ti thi pump; bud Ah deean't knaw what thoo wants it fer, fer thoo'd be all t' better if thoo war punctchard thisen a larl bit; it 'ud let sum o' thi gas oot, foor thoo's ommaist brussen wi' 't.' And then he set to work to replace the tyre, as though no cyclist had appeared upon the scene.

Several rustics were admiring two brand-new machines, whilst the owners (a lady and gentleman) regaled themselves in the village pub. When about to start on their journey again, the young fellow, taking stock of the group, and, as he thought, seeing good material for a joke, said, 'Admiring our machines?' and then, nudging his fair companion, continued, ' These are the very latest; they can either be used as cycles, musical boxes, or garden mowers. I only have to turn a screw, that's all. Clever, aren't they?' 'Aye!' said one of the group, looking as if he had swallowed every word just uttered. ' It's wunnerful what they've gitten 'em ti deea noo; my weyfe's gitten yan 'at gans wiv a can an' milks t' coos all byv itsen.' Then those two proceeded on their journey.

There had been a terrific thunderstorm, lasting most of the night. Talking the matter over next day, one said, ' Did ta ivver hear owt ti cum up tul 't?' ' Naay, it gav mah a to'n yance or twice. What diz ta mak on't?' ' It's t' aliments' (elements), 'thoo knaws; it's t' aliments.' 'Aye, thoo's reet, it'll be t' aliments; bud, Ah saay, it sets yan on ti think.' 'It diz, an' all; just eftther that despert lood crack cam, Ah thowt ti mysen, it's gahin ti be all owered wiv uz; an' foor a larl bit Ah wished 'at Ah'd ta'en Tom's bid foor t' colt.'

A delightful gathering had taken place at the rectory, followed by a most sumptuous tea. The people had come to celebrate the home-coming of the rector and his bride (a very dear South-country lady). After tea, the bride, speaking to an old fellow, said, ' I hope you have enjoyed yourself?' To which kind inquiry he promptly replied, ' Whya noo, Ah've been at monny a warse do ner this—Ah 'ev that.' This really was the very highest praise he could possibly have given. The bride, somewhat annoyed at what she considered the ingratitude of the man, turned to an old dame she saw walking down the drive. 'Have you tired yourself?' she kindly inquired. 'Tired mysen? Neea, Ah've nut tired mysen. Ah 'edn't need git mysen tew'd at a do leyke this. Ah's nut tired, bud Ah's gahin yam. Ah wad 'a'e stopped on ti t' end, bud ther's that monny flees aboot t' pleeace, whahl yan dizn't knaw what ti deea wi' yan's sen, an' sae Ah's foor off.' The only thing which had been made at all clear to the bride was that the old lady complained of being troubled with fleas, which she found too many for her. 'Fleas!' said she; 'I feel sure you are mistaken.' To which the old lady made this reply: 'Noa, Ah's nut; but Ah deean't meean fleas 'at's fleas, bud flees 'at flee' (flies that fly), leaving the rector's wife more bewildered than ever.

A new-comer related to those assembled in the village bar a most marvellous story of an accident from which his son had just recovered. If anything, it erred on the side of being just a trifle too marvellous. Several said, 'How wonderful!' but there was one man sitting in the far corner, and spake he never a word. 'Perhaps you doubt my story?' ventured the narrator. 'Nut Ah. Ah've neea call ti doot owt 'at ya've tell'd uz, foor yance yan o' mah lads swaller'd a pin, an' ya can tak mah wo'd for 't, bud i' less 'an a month eftther it cam oot o' t' back ov his brother's neck. That'll match your taal onny daay.'

The following conversation between two old mothers was overheard by a clergyman who happened to be travelling in the same compartment of the train. Said one to the other, 'Whya, noo then, wa've gitten him

sahded by.' 'Aye, wa 'ev,' sighed the other; 'Ah've
knawn him ivver sin he war a lad.' 'Thoo 'ez, an' what
thoo knaws 'at Ah went ti skeeal wiv him?' 'Aye,
thoo did,' said her friend; 'Ah'd forgitten that. Ah
saay, Mary, what a beautiful corpse he maad—sae still
an' sae quiet, bud they maistly are.' 'Aye, aye,' said
Mary, slowly adding, 'bud what a tea it war; Ah've
nivver been at sike an a-sitting doon i' mah leyfe;
ther war nowt bud tea-cakes, an' badly buttered at
that. Noo Ah've sahded fahve o' my awn, bud
thank the Lord Ah buried 'em all wi' ham,' which
was a sign not only of great respectability, but as
having shown proper respect to the dead.

Taking my seat in a third-class carriage at Malton,
two men and a woman joined me, and much edified
by their conversation I was. They commenced discussing the merits of an entertainment which had
been given the night previous in one of the villages in
the neighbourhood. I gathered from their remarks
that Lady M—— and the Hon. Mrs. B—— had
taken an active part in organizing the same. However,
for the moment, Lady M—— was very freely discussed.
The woman had possession of the carriage, and almost
without drawing breath said, 'Noo, sha's a grand
un, is t' au'd leddy; sha's gam foor owt. Mah songs,
Ah nivver cam across t' leykes on her onnywheear
else; bud ther isn't sike anuther onnywheear aboot
here, an' Ah knaw summat aboot t' maist on
'em. Sha's nut yan o' theease twopenny-haupenny
upstarts 'at dizn't knaw what's matter wiv 'em hauf
ther tahm. Aye, sha's a grand un, is t' au'd leddy.'
'Aye, sha is,' joined in one of the men, as the woman

ceased for want of breath. 'An' Ah'll tell ya what, that au'dist lad ov hers isn't a bad un, an' Ah meean ti saay 'at his lordship can rear poultry 'at neean on 'em can touch aboot here; noo, he can. He's a rare han' wi' bo'ds, is his lordship.' 'Him rear poultry!' burst in the woman. 'Him rear poultry!' she repeated, with ineffable scorn; and then, slowly and emphatically (you, who are Yorkshire people, know exactly what I mean), she added, 'Ah meean ti saay 'at t' au'd leddy can mak a hen lay mair eggs 'an onny man, woman, or bairn i' this country-sahd; an' Ah'll tell ya what, if tha deean't gi'e her yan o' t' best harps ti plaay on when sha dees an' gans ti heaven, Ah'll 'a'e nowt ti deea wi' 't.'

A vicar once asked his sexton what he thought of the previous Sunday's preacher. The pulpit had been occupied on that occasion by a clergyman whose oratorical powers are pretty widely known, but whose sermon had been quite over the heads of his congregation on that particular day. The reply the vicar got was certainly to the point. 'Whya, Ah wadn't saay bud what mebbe you mud larn summat fra what he tell'd uz, acoz ther's neea doot 'at he war varra far larnt; bud ez foor me, an' t' likes o' me, wa'd reyther sit an' lissen ti t' saam au'd ditties fra you 'at wa've heeard ower an' up agaan. Aye, that wa wad; ya see, wa knaw what's cuming.'

A neighbour's third wife lay dead. Said a dame to the husband, 'Mary's gone! Dear me, hoo sum fau'k diz 'ev bad luck; thoo'll 'a'e ti gan ti t' burying, hooivver.' 'Naay,' said the husband, 'Ah deean't think

'at Ah s'all gan this tahm; Ah went ti t' tother tweea—
they'll 'a'e ti mannish bidoot ma this tahm.' ' Naay,
what, thoo'll 'a'e ti gan, hooivver; it'll nivver deea
eftther seeing t' other tweea sahded by, nut ti gan ti t'
tho'd un. Whativver maks tha think 'at thoo weean't
gan ? ' ' Whya, thoo sees, it's ez thoo sez, Ah've seen
tweea on 'em sahded by, an' Ah think 'at it leeaks a
bit greedy ti gan ti t' tho'd un. Thoo sees, up ti noo
Ah've nivver been yabble ti return t' compliment,
an' Ah deean't leyke ti put on a chap, an' Ah s'aan't
gan.'

A good dame found her husband lying on the
chamber floor. ' Whativver is ta deeaing, ligging on t'
cham'er fleear foor ? ' ' Aa, lass,' the old chap groaned,
' Ah thowt Ah war boun ti dee ; Ah did, hooivver. If
ivver Ah's ta'en leyke that agaan, Ah s'aan't cum
round na mair; thoo'll finnd ma deead wheear Ah
tumm'ls.' ' Whya, let's get tha inti bed, an' Ah'll
fetch tha a basin o' gruel up ; an' Ah'll put t' au'd
stick byv t' sahd o' t' bed, an' thoo mun think on 'at
thoo mun thump on t' fleear if thoo's ta'en queer agaan ;
whativver thoo diz, noo, thoo maun't dee unbeknawn.
It's varra inconsiderate o' fau'k ti tak thersens off i'
that waay,' said the wife, bustling about. ' Bud thoo
knaws yan caan't help 't,' said the old chap. ' Whya,
thoo mun deea thi best, an' bear i' mahnd what a ti-
deea ther wad 'a'e been if Ah'd happened ti finnd tha
deead on t' fleear. Crowner wad 'ev 'ed ti cum'd, an'
all t' jury chaps gahin in an' oot ez if t' pleeace warn't
yan's awn, an' leykly eneeaf afoor yan 'ed gitten tidied
up, an' then Ah s'u'd 'a'e 'ed t' bobby fussing aboot an'
assing all manner o' quessions, an' Ah deean't knaw

what else. Noo, thoo mauh't let ma in foor a gahin-on
leyke that. Ah've putten tha t' stick handy, seea
mahnd thoo dizn't drop off bidoot gi'ing yan warning.
It weean't tew tha mich ti thump on t' fleear, an' then
Ah'll be up iv a crack. Noo, deean't forgit thoo
'ezn't ti dee bidoot thumping.'

Old Sally was dying. On being asked by the vicar
if she felt quite happy, the old lady said, with great
unction, 'Oh yes, Ah s'all seean be iv Jacob's
bosom.' 'Abraham's bosom, Sally,' corrected the
vicar. 'Aye, well, mebbe it is, bud if you'd been
unmarried for sixty-fahve year, leyke what Ah 'ev, ya
wudn't be particular wheeas bosom it war, seea lang.
ez ya gat inti sumbody's.'

A good story is told in Gloucestershire, which is
a fair example that Yorkshiremen are credited with
being able to take care of themselves by those of
other counties. An ostler at one of the inns in
that county in a general way managed to draw
a tip from all who put up, even from one or two
chaps who were well known as being very greedy.
Said a gentleman one day to the ostler, who had
just led out of the yard the horse and trap of one
of these penurious old chaps, 'Did you manage to
drag a tip out of him?' 'Aye,' said the ostler, 'he
awlus gi'es ma summat, bud it ommaist brecks his
heart ivvery tahm he gans away.' 'Yorkshire, are
you not?' questioned the gentleman. 'Aye, Ah's
Yorkshire hard eneeaf,' was the characteristic reply.
'Why,' said the questioner, with a smile, 'I am
a bit surprised, seeing that you have been here so
long, that the whole place doesn't belong to you.'

To which, with a twinkle in his eye, the ostler replied, 'It mebbe wad 'a'e deean afoor noo, if my maister 'edn't been Yorkshire an' all.'

A story is told of two Yorkshire Tykes bargaining— of course this was a case of ' when Greek meets Greek.' Said one, ' Whya, noo then, John, what diz ta think if wa mak a unseen swap on 't ? Thoo 'ezn't seen mah meer, an' Ah 'evn't seen tha cob; bud Ah knaw 'at thoo awlus leyked t' meer, an' Ah've awlus 'ed a bit ov a leaning ti t' cob, an' wa've knawn t' ane t' ither foor a lang whahl—noo, what diz ta saay ? ' ' Whya noo, ez thoo sez wa've knawn t' ane t' ither ivver sen wa war lads, an' ez thoo 'ezn't seen t' cob an' Ah 'evn't seen t' meer, whya, thoo mun ho'd the han' oot.' And so the bargain was struck. Then said one to the other, ' Whya, it's owered noo. Ther's neea backing oot fra t' bargain noo, bud Ah aim 'at thoo war a larl bit ti keen. Thoo sees it's leyke this: t' meer's geean that deead laam, 'at Ah deean't think 'at sha'll ivver gan agaan.' ' Oha, why, nivver mahnd,' said the other; ' t' cob's deead altigither, an' flayed.'

In the preceding five chapters, I have striven to give you some insight into the character of our people. This, however, has not been my only aim. I have endeavoured—and shall continue to do so—to put the dialect in such a way as to be easily mastered by my readers, even should they be strangers to our county.

Please bear in mind that the North and East Ridings dialectically are the same. Certainly some few words have been retained or dropped, as the case may be, in each Riding, but the pronunciation is identical, or at least almost so. These remarks, however, do not hold good when applied to the West Riding. Ripon (my native place) and Leeds are not very far distant, only twenty-six miles. Ripon, although in the West Riding, is to all intents dialectically in the North, but by the time you have travelled the twenty-six miles all is changed—you have as it were crossed the line.

F

CHAPTER VI

CUSTOMS OF THE YEAR AND FOLKLORE

CUSTOM and folklore are so interwoven that it is
quite impossible to write of them separately. The
North Riding to-day is *par excellence* the home
of both. This is easily accounted for. Many of the
dales are far removed from the varied influences of
the outer world; they are little communities; they
belong to themselves. Many of the older people
have never seen a locomotive. It is in and about
such places the student may gather a rich harvest
of folklore, always remembering that any given area is
not the whole of the riding, much less of Yorkshire.
I mention this because a custom, superstition, or
peculiarity of dialect, which may still flourish in one
dale, may be quite unknown in some other part of
the riding. Bear in mind the riding, within a very few
miles, stretches from the North Sea to St. George's
Channel; so it will be readily conceived that over
such an extensive area, much of which is sparsely
populated and not easy of access, custom and superstition still go hand in hand.

Our greatest observance of custom is, as it should
be, in connexion with Christmas-tide; indeed preparation for the same really commences some weeks in

advance. There is the pudding to make and partly boil; all the ingredients for the plum-cake to order; the mincemeat to prepare for the mince-pies; the goose to choose from some neighbouring farmer's stock; the cheese to buy and the wheat to have the hullins beaten off, and to cree, for the all-important frumenty; the yule-cakes or pepper-cake to make; the hollin to gather; the mistletoe and Santa Claus presents to buy for the little folk's stockings; the old yule log and a new one to see after, as well as the yule candles. Even long before these various duties have been taken in hand, children nightly sing their Christmas carols on our doorstep, reminding us the great event of the year is fast approaching, when peace and good will should be extended to all men. The 'vessel-cups' (i.e. wassail-cup) still come round, with their doll in a box, decked out as the Virgin Mary, lying in pink cotton-wool and evergreens. Some of these vessel-cups are in their way quite little works of art. I remember (up to the time I left Guisborough five years ago) Lavinia Leather travelled every year all the way from the other side of Leeds, to sing the vessel-cup throughout that part of Cleveland. As my wife had known the old body for many years, we always had a call. There was no mistaking the advent of Christmas, when, after unceremoniously opening the door, the old lady commenced saying,—

> God bless t' maaster of this hoos,
> An' t' mis-ter-ess also,
> An' all yer lahtle bonny bairns
> 'At round yer table go!

Fer it is at this tahm
Straangers travel far an' near.
Seea Ah wish ya a merry Kessamas
An' a happy New 'Ear.

But the days speed on, until there comes a night
when the charred remains of last year's yule log
glow with heat intense beneath the one of that
year's cutting; for the new log must always rest
upon and be lighted by the old one, which has been
carefully stored away for this, the night of nights—
Christmas Eve. The lads have kissed the lasses
under the mistletoe, fashioned out of two hoops
bedecked with holly, oranges, and apples, and with
a bunch of the mystic white berries glistening beneath.
Every picture-frame, ornament, and everywhere,
where a sprig of holly would remain, has had the
dark green leaves and red berries thrust into or
behind it. The old folk clasp each other's hands,
knowingly nodding their heads the while, 'for they
remember,' and, remembering, note the flashing eyes
and whispered nothings, sweet and low, of those whose
horizon for the present is illumined with love, with
never a cloud in sight. Shrieks of laughter loud and
hilarious from the younger branches ring from base-
ment to roof, almost deafening the 'au'd fau'k,' but
a smile lights up their wrinkled faces as they remember. By-and-by, the magic words uttered by
the maid, 'T' frummety's riddy,' results in a rush
for the dining-room or kitchen, as the case may
be. But first the yule candle must be lighted by
the master of the house. This must be done from
a piece of the candle saved from the year previous;

it too must be lighted from the blaze of the yule log, and on no account must anything be lighted from it. That would be as unlucky as giving or receiving a light on Christmas Day. Next, a cross must be scraped on the top of the uncut cheese, and then, after having wished the guests assembled 'A merry Christmas,' the frumenty may be attacked. And very palatable is the creed-wheat when boiled in milk, thickened with 'lithing,' seasoned with nutmeg and cloves, and sweetened with treacle. After this there are the yule-cakes, one for each person, with a dice of cheese and a glass of mulled ale or hot elder-berry wine.

By-and-by the younger ones are packed off to bed, and with us, as the world over, their stockings are hung at the bed-foot to await the mysterious visit of Santa Claus. It may be the sword-dancers are announced ; if so, their quaint performance is gone through, they are served with 'summat to keep 'em warm' and a few coppers, and they depart for pastures new [1]. Some maiden mayhap has retired to her chamber with a leaf and a berry plucked from the mistletoe under which she has been saluted. Having locked her door, the berry must be swallowed, whilst on the leaf she will prick the initials of him her heart loves best ; this she will stitch in the inside of her corset, so that it rest near her heart, and thus bind his love to her so long as there it remains.

In the early hours of the morning the waits will arrive, and tunefully or otherwise sing 'Christians,

[1] Before retiring to rest the older and more superstitious look round to see if there is a shadowless head thrown on the wall; should any one cast such a shadow, it is held they will die ere next Christmas Eve comes round.

awake,' and, unless precautions are taken to stuff the
bell with paper and fasten down the knocker, there
will be no sleep after five o'clock; for the children, in
their eagerness to catch the early worm, follow one
another without a moment's rest, singing loudly
through your keyhole one or other of their Christmas greetings, as—

> I wish ya a merry Kessamas
> An' a happy New 'Ear,
> A poss (purse) full o' money
> An' a barrel full o' beer,
> A good fat pig
> 'At'll sarve ya thruff t' year,
> An' pleease will ya gi'e ma
> My Kessamas box.

Gentle and simple herald Christmas morn[1] with
kindly greetings, 'A merry Christmas to you,' as they
pass.   And oh the parties, night after night, the
games, postman's knock, hunting the slipper, spinning
the trencher, cushion dance, forfeits, &c.!   Aye, but
we knew how to enjoy ourselves when I was a lad,
and in many of our dales to-day Christmas is Christmas still, with all the old observances treasured; aye,
and the old old games too.   Amidst such scenes
one is apt to forget that the hair is turning grey at
the sides, and easy to brush on the crown.

The Christmas dinner with its sirloin, turkey, or
goose, followed by the rich plum-pudding and mince-
pies, in a greater or less degree, is indulged in by all.
Go where you may on and after Christmas Day, either

---

[1] In many of our dales on Christmas morn, no one will leave the
house until some one brings luck in by crossing the threshold with
a bit of green in their hand.

plum or pepper cake (a rich kind of gingerbread), or spice-cake (a cheaper form of plum-cake) and cheese, will be found upon the sideboard or table. 'Ya mun 'ev a bit o' keeak an' cheese, hooivver,' say the country folk almost before you are seated. And be it remembered, for every cake and cheese you taste one more happy month is added to your life.

On St. Stephen's Eve maybe some will pay a visit to the 'coo byre' in the hope of seeing the oxen kneel, for the quaint notion still lives that on this eve the oxen kneel in their stalls in commemoration of the martyr's death.

On New Year's Eve it is customary to eat the remains of the frumenty left from Christmas Eve. This being finished, none other will be made until the festive season comes round again. The older people always watch the old year out and the new year in, which is made known by the ringing of the church bells, and the loud knocking at your door of the 'first foot or lucky bird.' This happens immediately on the last stroke of twelve. This first foot to cross your threshold—for none must go out until the first foot has come in—must be a man or boy with dark hair. Such only can bring luck to the household; for should he have light hair, he would not be admitted, for he could only bring dire and disastrous results.

The same clamorous singing as on Christmas Day commences just as early on New Year's morn, greetings for the new year are as freely given, and the festive season itself lasts pretty well on towards the middle of the month.

The dumb-cake is yet made—of which more hereafter—whilst other rites, ceremonies, and charms are still indulged in by the buxom lasses of the riding.

By due observance of certain ritual performed on the eve of St. Agnes, a maiden might have a vision of her future spouse.

Very often, however, difficulties of no light kind had to be overcome, before the ritual could be carried out in its entirety. And in some cases, to my thinking, the maiden would need nerves of iron, and the supple limbs of an acrobat, before she would be able to accomplish the demands made upon her.

Take for example the following, which was given to me by an old lady in Rosedale :—At midnight on the eve of St. Agnes, a maiden must pluck from the grave of a bachelor a blade of grass, walk backward from the grave to the church gate, and then hurry to her bed-chamber. Safely there, she had to lock her door, hanging the key on a nail outside the window, then undress herself; but—and here comes the difficulty—her various garments had to be removed in the same order as they had been put on, that is, that which she had donned first must be taken off first. This must have been a feat requiring great agility and no little patience, exceeding by a long way the task of skinning an eel in the dark. No doubt everything would be worn very loosely that day, and any undue exertion must have rendered such a maid liable any moment to assume the condition of a statue. Of one thing I am absolutely certain: did the maid accomplish the feat so far as her skirts and other items of her apparel are concerned, she would have to sleep with her boots on, for her stockings would present a problem which jeers at the senile efforts of the Sphinx. But, having performed the said ritual so far, it only remained for her to wrap the blade of grass in a clean sheet of paper, place it under her pillow, leave a burning candle near the window, and retire to rest, when presently she would see the man who was to be her husband open the window, look in, throw the key into the room, close the window, and depart. Where the chamber was on the ground floor, or ladders were handy, I can well understand this ritual would often succeed.

Maidens, however, may have a vision of their future lord and master (?) without the necessity of almost dislocating their joints. For I find at the present time it is only needful, on the day of the eve of St. Agnes, to fast from the time of rising, only eating a little stale bread and drinking parsley tea. On retiring to rest, remake your bed, putting thereon clean sheets and pillow-cases, remembering to repeat as you lay on each cover the following :—

> St. Agnes, I pray unto thee,
> I, a maid, would married be,
> So thou my husband show to me.

Retire to rest, sleeping by yourself, and you will see the man you will marry in a dream. Should you awake, my advice is—having seen the future husband, get up and have a good supper ; parsley tea and stale bread for a day is not satisfying. There are other forms of the same charm, differing only in minor details.

The making of the dumb-cake, however, differs only in one particular throughout the riding. Some hold that those engaged in its preparation must stand on something upon which they have never stood before, no two persons standing on a similar thing, e.g. a box-lid, a newspaper, &c. Others altogether ignore this canon in the ritual. Therefore I must leave my fair readers to decide which formula they will adopt, in case they decide to make a dumb-cake for themselves. As to the actual preparation, it must be begun after eleven o'clock p.m. on the eve of St. Agnes, and either three, five, or seven maidens may take part. In the making of a dumb-cake, each must take a handful of flour and lay it on a sheet of clean paper (this must be pretty large), bearing in mind that from the moment the first hand is dipped in the flour, not a word must be uttered whilst the cake-makers remain in that room, or the spell will be broken.

Having each laid a handful of flour on the sheet of paper, all add a small pinch of salt, water being also added, all taking part in working the same into dough, every one kneading and assisting in rolling the same into a thin cake, sufficiently large for each to mark her initials in fairly large letters thereon. All must now lend a hand in lifting it on to a tin, and in carrying it to the fire, in front of which it must be laid. Having seated themselves as far from the fire as possible, each will in turn rise, cross the room, and turn the cake round once—not over, as it must be left the inscribed side uppermost. All this having been accomplished before twelve strikes, remain quietly seated; for, a few minutes after midnight, the husband of the maiden who is to be married first will appear and touch her initials, often leaving his fingermark upon the same. So there can be no doubt about it.

Should you have no opportunity of joining others in the preparation of a dumb-cake, you may, if so inclined, on the Friday evening following that of St. Agnes (some say any Friday but Good Friday), have a vision of your future husband by a strict observance of the following :—

Make a flat dough cake about the size of a crown piece ; on this prick the initials of the one you secretly love. Next procure three small keys, all different, and make an impression of each on the underside of the cake. On retiring to rest, thread the three keys on the garter of your left leg, wrapping the same about the little cake ; stitch this ball to the inside of your night-dress so that it will rest in the centre of your bosom, and you will then dream, either of the man you love, or some other swain. If not of the one you love, then your affections for the present are misplaced.

The days in Holy Week are familiarly known as Collop Monday, Pancake Tuesday, Frutas or Fritters Wednesday, Bloody Thorsday,

> An' Lang Friday 'at's nivver deean,
> Seea lig i' bed whahl Seterdaay neean.

The usual menu for the week is still pretty much as it was. Collops of bacon and fried eggs on Monday. Pancakes served with either treacle or lemon-juice and sugar on Tuesday. Frutas, or fritters, made from a light kind of tea-cake paste, only much richer in fruit and fried either in lard or butter, on Wednesday ; and, with many of humble degree, black puddings on Thursday. Whilst on Friday, fast is kept on any frutas which may have been spared from Wednesday's feast, and there always is a very considerable helping left over.

Paste-egg or Troll-egg [1] Day, is now celebrated on Easter Monday, but in days past Easter Day and Paste-egg Day were one. At the present time the last five Sundays of Lent and Easter Day are still called Tid, Mid, Miseray, Carlin', and Paum, an' Paste-egg Day. There is some uncertainty as to what Tid and Mid mean, but there can be no doubt that Miseray is a corruption of Miserere, the commencement of one of the psalms ordered to be read during Lent. The whole of the names, however, take us back to mediaeval times, and though some are inclined to think that Tid means 'Te Deum' and Mid 'Mid Lent,' it seems to me careful research will in time give a more plausible solution. Carling Sunday is still observed in many places, grey peas fried with bacon or in butter being a well-known dish on that day, many even carrying a goodly store about in paper bags. At Great Ayton, and in many parts of Cleveland, Carling Sunday is still fully observed. The same is equally true of Palm Sunday, or, as it is called, ' Paum Sunda,' catkins, or lambs' tails, as they are universally designated, being carried in the hand, thrust in the buttonhole, or worn in the hat, whilst many a mantel-piece and ornament is often tastefully decorated with the same. From noon on Easter Day to noon the following day, an old custom which is now only kept up in remote villages, but which was quite general throughout the riding when I was a lad,

[1] Also called Pace-egg. The Danish word is Paaskeaeg.

was that of one or more young fellows seizing a female and forcibly pulling off her shoe, sometimes both, laces being no protection. These were held in bondage until a fine was paid. This very rough proceeding was formerly known as ' buckle-snatching,' the old name for the theft during the days when buckles were worn. However, if the lads had their good time from the Sunday to Monday's noon, the lasses did not fail to retaliate from that time until noon on Tuesday. From any hidden corner or doorway, out they rushed, and rarely failed to snatch either a hat, whip, stick, handkerchief, or something, they were not particular what, or to scratching either, generally managing to recuperate themselves for any losses of the day previous. On Easter Monday the bairns hie themselves to some field and roll or troll their hard-boiled eggs dyed in many colours; this lasts until the egg is broken, when the youngsters feed upon the contents. Many of the lads, however, have a much speedier method of either adding to their store of food or losing their egg. They jaup or jarp them together, i.e. one lad strikes his egg against that of his opponent, when one or both are broken; if only one, it is forfeited and becomes the property of the conqueror. Shuttlecock and battledoor is now greatly *en evidence* with the girls, and knur and spell with the lads. One might well, and with profit, write a chapter on the sequence of games, but such comes hardly within the scope of this work. But here and there a few will be noted when they have attached to them special peculiarities.

There is an old custom, almost dead now. It is

only in hidden and unfrequented spots that it still survives—I mean 'the wading of the sun.' It was common enough thirty years ago. The *modus operandi* was as follows :—As the sun rose on Easter morn, a bucket of water was placed in such a position that the sun was reflected in it. If the sun waded, i. e. glimmered in the water, it would rain that day; but if it kept fine in the morning and rained in the afternoon, then the spring would be fine and the autumn wet, and vice versa. On this morning too the flight of the crows was carefully observed; if they settled near home, instead of flying far afield to feed, the farmer shook his head, for they plainly told him, by so doing, that grub and other pests would sorely afflict his crops that year.

Friday is looked upon as an unlucky day to commence or conclude any undertaking. It is considered unlucky for the first lamb to be dropped on a Friday, to begin sowing or reaping, or to lead the last load on that day. Should the weather be very threatening, instead of finishing leading on the Friday, one stook is very often left, and not brought in until the following day.

Of St. Valentine's Day we might truly write, 'Poor St. Valentine! for with thee it is Ichabod.' No longer do we find shop windows filled with works of art, wrought in silver, lace, and gold; no longer within a coral bower, hung with icicles and rosebuds, is the maiden's hand clasped or waist encircled; no longer does a pathway of powdered fish-scales lead direct to the little church seen in the far distance, whilst the overfed cupid, who managed to sit on the edge of a very thin cloud, must have fallen off and decamped with the couple of skewered hearts which were usually floating at their own sweet will 'mid heaven. Hearts are at a discount now. Fifty years ago, love-making was a very real and somewhat pedantic proceeding; in these days, when time is money, the whole thing has been curtailed. It is—cut the dialogue and come to the bank book.

Why, there was a time, and only a few years ago, when as many pounds were spent on these love tokens as pennies now.

There may be, here and there, a maiden left who, before retiring to rest, splits a holly twig and binds within the split part a small slip of paper, upon which she has written, with her heart's blood, the name of him she loveth best, and who places the same under her pillow, so that she may dream her fate. There may be, but I doubt it. Their grandmothers did, though.

Valentine's Day may be dead, but April Fools' Day is still with us. 'Makking t' feeal o' yan' is yet common. The last sell I heard of was sending a lad from one place to another for a bucket of steam. I wonder how long ago it is since the first boy was sent for 'a penn'orth o' strap oil' or 'a pint ov pigeon's milk,' &c., &c.

On Good Friday it is considered impious to dig or plough.

> On Good Friday rist thi pleeaf;
> Start nowt, end nowt, that's eneeaf.

Perhaps one of the oldest customs is that in connexion with St. Mark's Eve. The belief is still held that those who watch the church porch at the hour

of midnight on that eve, will see pass in front of
them and enter the church the spirits of all those
friends who will die during the coming year. With
some it is held to be a *sine qua non* that the
watcher must sit within the porch; whilst others hold
four cross roads to be equally efficacious, always
provided that the body of one who had committed
suicide, with the orthodox stake driven through the
chest, had been buried there, that being the end of
suicides in the good old days.

It should be borne in mind that there are two slight
penalties attached to this porch or cross-road watching.

Firstly, should the watcher fall asleep, there is
every probability of its being the sleep of death.
Should he, however, manage to awaken from such a
lethargic slumber, it doesn't amount to much, as he
will assuredly die within the next twelve months.
Secondly, whoever tries this game once must continue
to do so ever afterwards. There is no escape; the
spell upon them is said to be too strong to withstand.

Said an old fellow at Carthorpe, 'Ah nivver
watched mysen, bud one James Haw used ti watch
t' deead gan in an' cum oot o' Bon'iston Chetch ivvery
St. Mark Eve ez it cam roond. He 'ed teea; he war
forced tul 't, he c'u'dn't help hissen; he'd deean it
yance, an' 'ed ti gan on wi' 't. Aye, an' he seed t'
sperrits ov all them 'at war gahin ti dee that year,
all on 'em dhrissed i' ther natt'ral cleeas, or else hoo
mud he 'a'e kenn'd whau tha war? They all passed
cleease tiv him, bud neean on 'em ivver gav' him a nod,
na nowt o' that soart. Bud,' added he, almost in
a whisper, 'them 'at duz it yance awlus 'ev ti deea 't;

tha cann't ho'd thersens back, they're forced ti gan
ivvery tahm St. Mark's Eve cums roond.   Mun ! it's
a despert thing ti 'a'e ti deea, 'coz ya 'a'e ti gan,
whahl at t' last end ya see. yersen pass yersen,
an' then ya knaw 'at' yer tahm's cum'd an' 'at ya'll
be laid i' t' cau'd grund afoor that daay cum twelve-
month.'

There was another method of divination very
commonly resorted to, known by the name of 'caff
riddling' (chaff riddling).   The rite was carried out
as follows :—At midnight, with the barn doors thrown
wide open, a quantity of chaff had to be riddled,
those taking part in the ceremony riddling in turn ;
should a coffin pass the door whilst any one was working the sieve, that person would die within the year.
A story is still current in Malton of a woman who
tried the above divination.   It would seem, some
little time after she had commenced to riddle, two
men passed the open doors carrying a coffin, and on
those who were with her rushing outside to see where
they went, neither men nor coffin were anywhere to
be seen.   Only the woman saw the coffin.   It is on
record that she died within the year.   The occurrence took place about forty years ago.

Perhaps we are a trifle more superstitious than some
other counties, but it must be borne in mind that
a wealth of folklore adds great respectability to a
genealogy which dates back to times so far remote,
that the rites and ceremonies of the religion from
which it sprang must now be sought for in the myth-
history of other lands.

In connexion with Royal Oak Day took place the

G

locking out of the schoolmaster by the scholars, loudly singing, whilst they held the fortress—

> It's Royal Oak daay,
> T' twenty-nahnth o' Maay,
> An' if ya deean't gi'e uz hollida
> Wa'll all run awaay.

The above was sung, to the entire satisfaction of the lads, a couple of years ago at Great Ayton.   On this day it is customary for every one to display a twig of oak ; should any one be so remiss as to walk abroad without sporting an oak-leaf or two, it is quite probable some urchin may give the delinquent a sharp reminder by switching him over the hand with a nettle.   And woe betide the lad who is so fool-hardy as to venture forth oakless, for in addition to being stung with nettles, he may have to submit to being rubbed over with chalk until he looks very like a miller.   It may be mentioned that Royal Oak Day is often called Chalky-back Day.

There are several charms and ceremonies peculiar to Midsummer Eve, the careful observance of which enables a maiden to learn something of what fate may have in store for her.   Does she doubt the constancy of her lover, she can satisfy herself once for all, no matter what other folk may say, and in spite of any-thing she may have seen or imagined herself, by observing the following rite.   Certainly the carrying out of the ceremony is a wee bit troublesome, but of what account is trouble when such vital points are at issue as the unmasking of perfidy or the establishment of truth and love?   To perform the rite the maiden must proceed as follows :—Pull three hairs from the tail of a perfectly black cat, also three from a red cow ; gather three leaves of the deadly nightshade, and, having killed a white pigeon, smear each leaf with blood from its heart. Now make three flat parcels, each containing a cat's hair, a cow's hair, and a leaf. Next stew the pigeon, saving the gravy. Now make a savoury dish, adding thereto the gravy. The suspected one must be asked to supper on Midsummer Eve, the damsel being careful to place under the table-cloth the three parcels, in such manner that one will lie under his plate, one under the dish containing the gravy, and the third under her own plate. During supper, should her lover find the least fault with any person or thing, he is faithless. If the maiden is very deeply in love, I should advise her to do most of the talking ; let it be only a one-course supper, and hurry through with it. The above charm is rarely resorted to now ; the several difficulties which have to be overcome before it can be successfully carried out, have almost laid it on one side. But I well remember its being tried years ago by one of our servants, and I have been informed that it was resorted to, inside of the last five years, at a farm-house near Swainby.

Here is another one for the same eve, which is much more widely known, and believed in yet by many. Three maids, unseen by and unknown to any other but themselves, must each gather a sprig of rosemary, and between the hours of eleven and twelve p.m. retire to an upper chamber, lock the door, and from the moment the key is turned not a word must be spoken. Near one end of the room a basin half full of water must be placed, in which each maiden has dropped a handful of red-rose leaves; the three sprigs of rosemary must now be laid on the rose leaves; next, fix a line across the room, over which each must throw—not fasten in any way—a chemise of her own make, but which she has never worn. Having thus arranged matters, they must seat themselves as far from the basin as possible, when they will be shortly rewarded, for a few moments after twelve o'clock the husband of each will appear. There can be no doubt about this, because each apparition will seize a sprig of rosemary and sprinkle the chemise of the girl he loves. Nothing could be more convincing than this; now, could there be?

If not yet fully satisfied, they may make another attempt on the eve of St. Mary Magdalene. For this they will have to prepare the following decoction :— Take a wineglassful each of rum, gin, and red wine, a teaspoonful of honey, treacle, and sugar, and the same of vinegar, lemon-juice, and sour oranges; these must be mixed together in some utensil purchased that day, and for which each must pay an equal share. When mixing the ingredients, the following rule must be observed: the first maiden must pour in the spirits and wine, the second the sweets, and the third the sours; this must be done at the hour of midnight. Let each now take a sprig of rosemary, dip it in the liquor, and then carefully stitch the same securely to the bosom of her nightdress; bear in mind you are an old maid for ever if you and your sprig part company during the night. Each in turn must now drink a tablespoonful of the mixture, until every drop is consumed, then jump into bed, all three together, and on falling asleep, each maiden will have a dream, the meaning of which cannot be misunderstood. This seems to be quite certain, and there is another thing equally assured·—one and all will awake with such a splitting headache in the morning, that they will forswear improvised cold punch for ever afterwards.

It is not within the scope of this work to take note of purely local customs, deeply interesting though they be. Therefore the Vardy dinner at Helmsley, the procession of the Lord Mayor and Lady Mayoress of York at Kilburn, the race up the hill at Askrigg, or the May-pole dances at several other places, and the like, must be passed over.

The mell supper, though lacking much of its pristine glory, is still with us. Mr. Robinson of Carthorpe, and many others in the riding, still keep to the good old ways. The mell supper, i.e. a supper and a dance after the ingathering of the harvest, is exceedingly common, but with its older observances, or at least as many of them as are remembered, is only adhered to here and there. Still, at the present day, something of the old-time doings are to be met with. The last sheaf at Carthorpe, as in Jutland, is called the 'widow,' and the last load is always led triumphantly home with songs of joy.

In many places it is common for the last few sheaves to be bound together, these being decorated with ribbons and handkerchiefs—the women racing for the ribbons, and the men contending for the handkerchiefs. This, of course, is a survival of the time when the sheaves themselves were run for; and in the days when an additional bushel of grain was a thing greatly to be desired, the prize would be not a little coveted. Here and there the mell doll is still made; certainly it is not now bedecked with all the gaudy trappings it was adorned with in days of yore, but often some skilful hand will plait the straw into fantastical shapes, exhibiting considerable artistic taste and skill. When completed, whether it be in the form of a doll[1] or that of some other device, it still goes by the name of ' t' mell doll,' and is placed in the centre of the barn, round which, by-and-by, the guests will trip on the light fantastic toe.

One characteristic of the mell supper, so far as I know, is now a thing of the past, i.e. the guisers. These were a kind of sword-dancers, who twenty years ago generally came as unbidden guests after the dancing had commenced; as a rule they were accorded a hearty welcome, as they added greatly to the merriment of the evening's revel, for as the cake and ale went round, the excitement increased, songs and shouting became general, and the dancing something after the nature of a stampede, till at last the uproar was general. It is at such times when age forgets its years, and the young let slip the tether of their youthful spirits, and romp—aye, romp; for the ale is good, the lasses are bonny, ' slim o' waist and leet o' foot.' It is Yorkshire, all Yorkshire.

The fifth of November, with its bonfires and Guy Fawkes, is as religiously observed in the riding as in any other part of the country. Over a wide area it is the festive occasion on which every good wife bakes

---

[1] The small stack often seen in our churches at a harvest thanksgiving is a survival of the mell doll.

a store of parkin, its general form being that of a flat cake of gingerbread, the recipe varying according to the means of the house.

In the days when there were no county police, if not wise enough to securely lock up your yard broom, of a certainty it would be stolen ; and if ever you did see it again, it would be on the evening of the fifth, soaked with tar, in the hands of some fellow rushing like a mad thing along the street with your property blazing in front of him.   I have known of scores of brooms which were stolen—aye, and stolen them myself—but I do not recollect an instance of the thief being prosecuted. No, if you did not secure your broom, it went, and that was very much the end of it. There was more fun running with a stolen besom than a bought one.

Quite an interesting collection of doggerel verses might be given, which the lads in various parts sing when dragging their load of sticks and thorns to the site of the bonfire. I give one, which an old inhabitant of Great Ayton tells me was sung when his grandfather was a boy.

> Au'd Grimey sits upon yon hill
> Ez black ez onny au'd craw ;
> He's gitten on his lang grey coat
> Wi' buttons doon afoor-oor-oor,
> Wi' buttons doon afoor-oor-oor,
> Wi' buttons doon afoor-oor-oor,
> He's gitten on his lang grey coat
> Wi' buttons doon afoor.

Within a week, the young carol-singers will be on your doorstep night after night, reminding you that Christmas is drawing nigh.

A very old custom, but which has now been pretty nigh stamped out by the county policeman, is that of 'Riding the Stang.' It is not dead yet, though ; I witnessed the stang being ridden as recently as 1891 in Guisborough, and in many of the villages in Wensleydale it is to this day resorted to when considered needful.

The stang is held in wholesome dread by a certain class of evil-doers. Wife-beaters and immoral characters chiefly had and have the benefit of the stang [1]. Whatever their discovered sin might be, was fully set forth in the stang doggerel. One or two points have to be, or at least are, most carefully observed : (1) The real name of the culprit must not be mentioned. (2) The stang must be ridden in three separate parishes each night ; and in many places, to make the proceedings quite legal, it was considered a *sine qua non* that the stang-master must knock at the door of the man or woman they were holding up to ridicule, and ask for a pocket-piece, i.e. fourpence.

The whole proceeding was carried out as follows :— An effigy made of straw and old clothes, representing the culprit, was bound to a pole [2] and set in an upright position in the centre of either a handcart or a small pony cart, in which was seated the stang-master ; and following behind were gathered all the ragamuffins of the village, armed with pan lids, tin cans, tin whistles, or anything which could be made to produce a discordant sound. Being ready, the cart

---

[1] The stang was ridden at Thoralby, Wensleydale, as recently as October, 1896.

[2] The pole was a stang or cow-staff.

was drawn in front of the culprit's house, and after a fearful hubbub, the stang-master cried out, in a sing-song voice,—

Ah tinkle, Ah tinkle, Ah tinkle tang,
It's nut foor your part ner mah part
'At Ah rahd the stang,
Bud foor yan Bill Switch whau his weyfe did bang,
Ah tinkle, Ah tinkle, Ah tinkle tang.
He banged her, he banged her, he banged her indeed,
He banged her, he banged her, afoor sha steead need;
Upstairs aback o' t' bed
He sairly brayed her whahl sha bled,
Oot o' t' hoos on ti t' green,
Sikan a seet ez nivver war seen,
Ez neean c'u'd think, ez neean c'u'd dream.
Sae Ah gat ma a few cumarades
Ti traal ma aboot;
Sae it's hip hip hurrah, lads,
Set up a gert shoot,
An' blaw all yer whistles,
Screeam, rattle, an' bang
All 'at ivver ya've gitten,
Foor Ah ride the stang.

Then, for a few moments, there arose a tumult of sound, to which the wildest ravings of bedlam would seem insignificant.

This performance lasts three nights, and on the third the effigy is burnt in front of the culprit's house.

Another very old custom, which is now rarely seen, is that of bottle breaking. When a house was ready for the thatch, in later days the tiles, a bottle was suspended by a ribbon from the ridge beam. Stones were then shied at it, and the one who was lucky enough to smash the bottle claimed the ribbon. If in days past this custom had anything of an occult nature attached to it, it has long ago been forgotten. In its last days it degenerated into what was considered to be a valid excuse for spending the rest of the day in the village pub. *O tempora, O mores !*

The daily life of the Guisboreans does not seem to have altered much from the time of Edward VI to the end of last century. In a letter among the Cottonian MSS., the writer, addressing Sir Thomas Chaloner, says, 'The people bread here (Guisborough) live very longe, if they be a while absent they growe sicklye ; they are altogether given to pleasure, scarce any good husband amongst them ; Day and Nighte feastinge, making Matches for Horse Races, Dog runninge, or runninge on Foote,' &c. The above was written about 1550, and we find in 1784 that things were still pretty lively, as the contents of the small hand-bill [1] (see next page) fully testify. The contents of another, setting forth the varied attractions of 'Staithes Feast,' are also characteristic of the time.

---

[1] The original was most kindly lent to me by the Lady of the Manor, Mrs. Chaloner.

Gisbrough Races.

Saturday, Auguſt 14, 1784.

A MATCH between Sir William Foulis's Afs Colt, Turkey Nab, and Mr. Chaloner's Afs Colt, Sturdy; Catch-weights, 1l. 1s. play or pay, the laſt Comer-in to Win. Change of Jockeys, croſſing, joſtling, and kicking.

A PURSE of SILVER to be run for by Men in Sacks. Croſſing and joſtling.

LADIES' PLATE.

A SHIFT to be run for by Ladies. No croſſing-and-joſtling. No Lady to enter who has won more than one Shift. A Pair of Cotton Stockings for the ſecond Lady; and a Pair of Garters for the third. Free for all Weights and Ages.

₊ After the Races, A Soap-tail'd PIG will be turn'd out. Whoever throws him over his Shoulder by the Tail is to have him for his own Property.

†₊† Smoking, Cudgel-playing, and other Entertainments.

JOHN HALE, Steward.

‡†‡ An Ordinary at the Cock at Gifbrough at Half paſt Two o'Clock. The Race to begin at Five o'Clock.

Staithes Feast.

—WILL BE HELDE ON—

TUESDAY, JUNE 20, 1797.

When the prizes As ADVERTIZED BELOW will be offered to ALL those skilled in such matters, as well as DIVERS others not herin stated.

TO WIT.

*** A fish skin purse contayninge SILVER will be run or rolled for in sacks a man and a boy in each sack. 25 YRDS. ERIC STAUMER Esq. will adjudge.

††† A 50 YRDS race. To be run for, A HOOD and CLOAK, each, for maidens runninge in pairs, the right legge of the one to be fast bound below the knee and at the ancle, to ye left legge of the other [1]. } T. METCALFE will BIND ye LEGGES AND ADJUDGE.

*** A CROWN peice for A MAN and WIFE race, ye wife to be hugged either on the backe, in arms, or by any other device, so as she be lifted clean from ye ground, HUSBANDS with light wives to be put backe. No WHEELBARROWS allowed. MR. MAT PETCH will ADJUDGE.

The choyce of a sark or petticote offered to the best performance of skille in a SKEP and POLE tryal [2]. Only

---

[1] A three-legged race. In this there was nothing unseemly, for a long way into this century the skirts worn came but little below the knee. Bear in mind, both in launching and beaching their husband's or father's boat, the women and girls of to-day often rush up to the waist in the sea to lend a helping hand.

[2] Some explanation is needed to make this task understandable. A large basket (probably a wide creel) had a strong pole thrust through the wicker-work or handles improvised for the occasion; each end of the pole was then rested upon

for married women. One clean turn to be mayde.
THOS. HILTUNE Esq. will adjudge.

††† A CŌBLE RACE for 1.l. 1.s.

*** A LYKE SUM will be gyven to the owners of the best kept
cŌBLE. To be equally divided. W. Hymers Esq. WILL
adjudge.

†₊† 2. new CROWN pieces will be gyven to yᵉ maid under
18 yeares who shalle fyrst cleanly bayte 100 hooks. Mᴿ·
W. PICKLES will adjudge.

*** LYKEWISE, Genning throw a BARFAN, SMOAKING, and
other pastimes for yᵉ entertainment of all commers
will in nowise be found lacking.

ALL friends and nighbours are dilligently invited.
This was wrote by I. STOREY, schoolmaster.

N.B. This hand-bill was not printed, but most
carefully and neatly written.

––––––––––––

some suitable support, leaving the basket free to swing
about a foot from the ground. On each support and near
to the pole a shell or other light object was placed. The
thing to be done would not be easy of accomplishment.
Those contending for the prize had in turn to seat themselves astride of the pole with both feet inside the basket;
thus seated, and firmly grasping the pole with one hand,
they had to knock off the shell with a stick (which in the
meantime they used to steady themselves with), then turn
round, reseat themselves, knock off the other shell, and
then get out without overbalancing. You try it, but have
something soft to fall upon. It is marvellous how soon it is
the next person's turn.

CHAPTER VII

CUSTOMS OF COURTSHIP, MARRIAGE, BIRTH, AND DEATH

Superstition.

THE old customs and superstitions connected with marriage festivities are perhaps more closely observed here and there in the North Riding than in any other part of Yorkshire. In some parts of Cleveland, I doubt if the bride and bridegroom would consider themselves properly wedded if there were no race for a ribbon or handkerchief. And certainly it would be a most unlucky omen, should any one but the bride cut the first piece from the bride's cake. But I anticipate—let us commence at the beginning. Very rarely, I imagine, is it that an orthodox proposal is ever made by a Yorkshire lad to the lass of his choice. No, they just 'keep cump'ny t' ane wi' t' t'other.' 'Keeping company' is the Yorkshire idiom for courting; and during that happy time, in days past, were a young fellow ever caught kissing his lady-love whilst a roof was over their heads (i. e. in any one's house), he was liable—if he did not instantly throw on the table kiss-money—to be 'pitchered[1]' on the spot, i. e. either have a hole burnt through his coat or his buttons cut off. This violent attack on the person of arson and robbery was usually effected by a bevy of damsels.

[1] Thirty years ago it was common.

In time, if all went well, the twain decided to become one; to this end the 'spurrings' were put in, i.e. the banns were published. This having been accomplished, the couple were said to be 'hanging in the bell-ropes'—no maiden would ever think of attending church during the time she was hanging in the bell-ropes, or to use another expression, 'whilst she was suffering from a broken leg after having tumm'l'd ower t' bauk.'

The wedding day having arrived, the happy couple, accompanied by their friends, either proceed two and two, or hire a cab.

Of course the bride is properly garnished for the occasion, and very nice and blushy she looks—that goes without saying. But whatever her toilet may be, one thing is certain—not a speck of blue or green will be found anywhere about her, both colours being considered very unlucky; neither will the wedding take place on a Friday.

Deean't o' Friday buy yer ring,
O' Friday deean't put t' spurrings in,
Deean't wed o' Friday. Think on o' this,
Nowther blue ner green mun match her dhriss.

If during the ceremony the sun is obscured for a short time, and then bursts forth shining on the couple, happy will such a bride be.   For

Blessed is t' bride 'at t' sun shines on,
An' blessed is t' deead 'at t' rain rains on.

Years ago, it was the custom, in many parts of Cleveland, for the bride and bridegroom to leap over a form on leaving the church porch. On this feat being accomplished, a gun was fired, this often being charged with feathers. At Guisborough the firing of guns was continued throughout the whole route. And in many parts of Cleveland, meeting the bridal procession with hot pots was common; these were bowls filled with a kind of steaming punch, and as the bridal party were expected to drink from every hot pot, one can well imagine and understand the revelry which so often took place, especially when the hot pots were numerous. Afterwards, these pots were carried from door to door, a plate covered with a saucer being also presented; a gift of money was slipped under the saucer, given to enable the hot pot to be replenished. In the Staithes district, if a guest stepped in any kind of filth on his or her way to the house, on no account would it be wiped off, it being considered very unlucky to do so. I believe, at that time, sanded floors and not carpets were the rule.

On passing through the church gates, the bridegroom usually threw a handful of coppers amongst the crowd. A man now headed the procession, carrying under his arm a young cockerel, which he made continually to 'skrike oot'; this could only be silenced by the payment of bride's money. On arriving at the bride's home, she was met on the doorstep, and presented with a small cake on a plate. A little of this she would eat, throwing the remainder over her head, typical of the hope that they might always have plenty and something to spare. She then handed the plate to her husband; this he threw over his head, their future happiness depending upon its being broken [1].

---

[1] The details of the plate-throwing vary slightly in different localities.

The race for the bride's garter was a common custom in former times, its possession being held in high esteem, and valued as a potent love charm.

Now, however, the custom has almost fallen into disuse, though within the last five years the ceremony was fully carried out. At one time it was not only a recognized custom, but in most cases special preparation was made for its due observance, the maidens spending no little time and skill in the working of their bridal garters.

Immediately after the plate had been broken, the bride's attempt to cross the threshold was hindered by the kneeling figure of the winner of the race, claiming the privilege of removing the prize. The bride then raised her skirt whilst he removed the valued trophy [1].

As it was the correct thing in those good old days for ladies to raise the skirt quite as high when dancing, and as elaborately worked stockings were worn to be looked at, nothing was thought of lifting the skirt, and nothing would in these days if some lady of title revived the custom. From an old rhyme, I give the following lines :—

T' BRAHDAL BANDS.

Blushing, theer oor Peggy sits
      Stitching, fahn stitching,
Luv knots roond her brahdal bands,
      Witching, bewitching.

[1] In some parts it was customary for the winner, after having removed the garter, to enter the bridal chamber, turn down the bed clothes, and offer to the bride a hot pot as she entered to remove her bridal attire, and then salute her; did he omit the latter, he forfeited the garter.

H

T' brahd's maids all mun deea a stitch,
   Stitching, fahn stitching,
An' tha mun binnd it roond her leg[1],
   Witching, bewitching.

Bud sum bauf[2] swain 'at's soond o' puff[3],
   Stitching, fahn stitching,
'Ll claim his reet ti tak' it off,
   Witching, bewitching.

An' he aroond his awn luv's leg,
   Stitching, fahn stitching,
'Ll lap it roond ti binnd his luv,
   Witching, bewitching.

Whahl sha sweet maid'll wear his troth,
   Stitching, fahn stitching,
Mahnding each tahm sha taks it off,
   Witching, bewitching,

That daay when sha will 'a'e ti wear,
   Stitching, fahn stitching,
Nut yan, bud tweea, a brahdal pair,
   Witching, bewitching.

Oh, happy day! when sha s'all stitch,
   Stitching, fahn stitching,
Her brahdal bands, the wearing which
   Mak maids bewitching.

It may be remembered that knights often bound the garter of their lady-love about their sword-hilts.

The following lines evidently were written when the bridal garter was held in greater favour than the ribbon :—

---

[1] I gather from a diary, dated 1625, which has been kindly sent to me as I am correcting my proof sheets, that originally it was the bridegroom's duty to tie on the bridal garters.
[2] Lusty.   [3] Sound of wind.

SONG.

Drink to the Bridal Garter.

Nance is wed ti morn at morn,
    High doon a derry O,
Monny a lad's this daay's forlorn,
    High doon a derry O;
Bud cheer up, lads, yer glasses fill,
Fer ivvery Jack ther is a Jill.
Sup off, my bucks, an' divn't spill,
    An' maay Ah win her garter O.

Neea prude is Nance; tha saay sha's maad,
    High doon a derry O,
Her brahdal bands ov gowden braad,
    High doon a derry O.
Noo fer a ribbon Ah weean't run,
It gi'es neea luck, an' stops wer fun,
Sike nimmy nammy waays 'ez sum;
    Cum drink ti t' brahdal garter O.

Here's health an' luck ti t' brahd 'at darr,
    High doon a derry O,
Her brahdal bands baith stitch an' wear,
    High doon a derry O;
Ti them 'at ho'ds a ribbon up
Neean on uz here'll draan a cup,
Sike healths wa 'evn't tahm ti sup,
    Ov slipshod, undarned stockings O.

T' brahd 'at darn't her skets pull up,
    High doon a derry O,
Maist leykly is a mucky slut,
    High doon a derry O.
Yan best can tell a lass's waays
Byv what sha wears, 'an what sha saays;
A ribbon gi'en o' wedding days
    Screens mucky undarned stockings O.

H 2

Maay ivvery bonny blushing brahd,
        High doon a derry O,
'Ev nowther muck ner hoals ti hide,
        High doon a derry O,
An' maay sha on her brahdal daay
Pull up her skets, an' smiling saay,
'Mah garter's thahn, tak it, Ah praay,
        An' gi'e 't ti thi true lovey O.'

Afoor wa pairt fill up each glass,
        High doon a derry O,
Let each yan drink tiv his awn lass,
        High doon a derry O,
Ti Bessy, Sally, Sue, an' Peg,
Ti Martha, Mary, Maud, an' Meg;
An' here 's ti ivvery shap'ly leg
        Roond which a brahdal band diz go.

Originally the ceremony of removing the bridal garter was, as has been said, carried out in a perfectly decorous manner; in time, however, it degenerated into actually stealing the garter by force. This unseemly proceeding possibly arose from the strong opposition and resentment which was felt, and for long demonstrated, whenever the ribbon supplanted the garter.

Why, as recently as 1820, Lady —— [1], a great stickler after old customs, on stepping from her bridal coach, inquired who had won the race. 'Ah did, my lady,' answered one of the stable lads. Ascending the steps, her ladyship stepped half over the threshold, calling out to the lad, 'Come, Tom, and claim your prize,' adding, as she raised her silken gown, 'I intend to be properly married and have the luck I am entitled to.' Then turning to

[1] The story was given me by an eye-witness.

the young fellow, smiling, she added, 'Take it off, Tom, and give it to your sweetheart, and may it bring luck to both of you.'

In Great Ayton the ribbon seems to have supplanted the garter in the early part of this century. In fact it is only the old folks who remember, and can tell you anything concerning the gay and festive doings of those days. But the older custom held its own for long afterwards, and that, too, within a very few miles. But intercommunication between villages has never been a strong feature. Even to-day there is a species of rivalry existing between Stokesley and Great Ayton people, but this is common to all adjacent villages.

It only adds one more proof in support of what has already been said, that the customs, superstitions, and dialect of any given locality, or even that of a whole dale, cannot, and must not, be taken as being that of the whole of the North Riding, much less of Yorkshire.

A case in point may here be mentioned. In days past it was usual in Great Ayton to discharge firearms over the bridal party as they processed both *to and from the church.* This, however, was by no means the custom throughout Cleveland[1]. Neither was the firing of the stithy, which I am told was never omitted ; i.e. a charge of powder poured into a hole in the anvil, upon which a heavy weight was laid ; this, when fired, went off with the report of a cannon. In many places the latter was only resorted to when either objectionable people were united or in the

[1] Only when returning were the guns discharged as a rule.

case of a forced marriage. In Great Ayton it was done in honour of the occasion.

Much variation exists as to the exact time when the ribbon is to be run for. In some places it is the custom for the racers to stand at the church door, and start off on a signal being given that the ring has been slipped on the bride's finger. In other localities the race takes place the moment the bride and bridegroom leave the church porch, the one arriving first at the bride's door being the winner.

In other localities it does not take place until after the wedding feast, and again, often not until evening.

In many places it is customary for the bride to stand as the winning post, holding the ribbon in her hand, the winner not only claiming the prize, but a kiss also. It may be mentioned here that the best man generally claims the first kiss at the conclusion of the ceremony. At Great Ayton and many other places sixty years ago, before the bride left the altar steps the sexton removed her shoe, which was ransomed by the bridegroom. It was, and is still, considered most lucky to rub shoulders with the bridegroom. And until somewhat recently the parson officiating was always expected to kiss the bride. Before railways were so general, and when, as often happened, the honeymoon had to be spent amongst friends within driving distance, or at the bride's home, 'throwing the stocking' at the bride and bridegroom after they had retired to rest was never omitted.

It is a bad omen should the bridal party meet a coffin, or should a cripple cross their path. Had they to pass over a stream, it was usual for both to throw something over their shoulder into the stream, saying as they did so, 'Bad luck cleave to you,' being very careful not to set eyes on the object again. On an occasion of this kind, should the man wish to be master in his own house, he had better see that he cross the centre of the bridge a little in advance of his bride, or that lady will gain an advantage she will be careful not to undervalue—the husband will have to do the wife's bidding. It is also considered unlucky to remove the wedding ring before the birth of the first child. Should a bride unfortunately do so, be sure it is the husband who replaces it; on no account must she let another man do so, unless she wishes speedily to become a widow. Before·the bride and bridegroom left for their own home, it was common for a kettleful of boiling water to be poured on the front step, upon which the bride stepped, being careful to wet both her shoes. The due observance of this custom ensured another happy marriage being arranged amongst the company there assembled.

When the time arrives for the happy couple to take their departure, either for their own home or the honeymoon, great care must be observed that the husband steps over the threshold in front of his bride, otherwise she will take the lead in all things through life. It would be a great advantage to a lot of men if the wife did step a little in advance. They must also be very careful not to make their exit with the back and front door open at the same time; and on entering their new home, a man must receive them, never a woman, neither must they enter an empty house, as it would result in a lack of friends. The belief in open doors, &c., applies to all occasions when leaving or returning home after having spent the night under a strange roof. As the bride leaves the paternal roof, some swain will endeavour to seize her foot. This doubtless is a surviving relic of the time when it was deemed a post of honour to assist the bride into the saddle. It ensures little separation through life if the happy pair, on rising from their bridal couch, take each other by the hand, and slip out of bed, so that their feet touch the floor together; then, still keeping hold of hands, they must cross the room and step outside, as equally as possible.

Whilst the immediate friends enjoyed themselves as guests at the bride's house, many of their well-wishers adjourned to the nearest hostel and drank their healths with many a glass and catch-song.

One, a kind of catch-verse, was very common a few years ago. Each time it was sung the glasses were drained, some one else being called upon to repeat the song. This had to be done at once, and in the reverse way to the former vocalist, i. e. if the last singer toasted the bridegroom, the next must commence with the bride; did he make a mistake, he had to pay for glasses round.

The Verse.

The brahdgroom's health we all will sing,
In spite of Turk or Spanish king,
The brahd's good health we will not pass,
But put them both into one glass.
See, see, see that he drink it all,
See, see, see that he let none fall,
For if he do, he shall drink two,
And so shall the rest of the company do.

Another catch-rhyme must have resulted in innumerable glasses having to be paid for each time it was sung. It was quite an action song, each taking a line in turn, every glass being raised at the commencement of each line, and then replaced, forming a ring round the bride's garter, which lay in the centre of the table, or a borrowed one doing duty for the time. As each glass had to be lifted on the word DRINK, and tapped against that of its right and left hand neighbour at CHINK, then set on the table again without spilling, some one would have to pay for glasses round. The verse ran :—

> Wa lift each glass ti t' brahdgroom's health,
> > DRINK, DRINK, DRINK.
> T' yan 'at slaps pays fer t' next roond,
> > CHINK, CHINK, CHINK.
> An' here's ti t' brahd, good luck ti t' lass,
> > Drink, Drink, Drink.
> Wa thruff her band noo pass each glass [1],
> > Wink, Wink, Wink.
> Wer liquor will all t' better seeam,
> > Chink, Chink, Chink,
> When wa call ti mahnd wheer it hez been,
> > Drink, Drink, Drink.
> Bud him 'at trimm'ls, smiles, or slaps (spills),
> > Chink, Chink, Chink,
> Pays fer wer glasses gahin ti t' taps,
> > Drink, Drink, Drink.

Quite a collection of these catch-songs might be made ; they are all quaint, and if they point to days when things were a trifle different, we must bear in mind that a hundred years hence we shall be pretty severely criticized.

[1] Each in turn slipped the garter over his glass on to his wrist. The garters were nearly a yard long ; as used above, the ends were tied together to form a loop.

Birth.

The future of a child greatly depends upon which day it is born.

A Munday's bairn will grow up fair,
A Tuesday's yan i' grace thruff prayer,
A Wednesday's bairn 'ez monny a paain,
A Tho'sday's bairn ween't bahd at heeam.
A Friday's bairn is good an' sweet,
A Settherday's warks frea morn ti neet,
Bud a Sunday's bairn thruff leyfe is blist
An' seear i' t' end wi' t' Saints ti rist.

From the day of its birth to that of its baptism, pepper cake, cheese and wine, or some other cordial, are offered to all those who cross the threshold. No one would think of refusing to ' tak a bite an' sup,' to wish the little stranger all the happiness and good luck possible. In many places, the doctor cuts the cake and cheese immediately after the happy event is over, giving a piece to every one present; neither cake nor cheese must have been previously cut into, and what is cut must be divided into just so many pieces as there are friends present, neither more nor less. Should it unfortunately happen the pieces exceed in number that of the guests, it would portend that troubles in this life will be too many to contend against; but should there be not enough pieces to go all round, then the child in after years will lack many of those comforts, the possession of which make life a blessing.

When possible, a new arrival, before being laid by its mother's side, or even touched by her, is placed in the arms of a maiden. To a boy, this early contact,

with our highest ideal of earthly purity, gives to him
a nobleness of character which in after years will help
the world to be better, whilst in the case of a girl she
will grow up to be modest and pure in all things. The
idea is pretty.

In Cleveland, and some of the dales westward, the
notion still prevails that a child should always go up
in the world before it goes down; so when it happens
that a child is born in the topmost story, in which case
it is impossible to carry it into a higher room, the
nurse will stand upon the bed with the child in her arms,
holding it above the mother, that being a higher
position than it held at its birth. After this ceremony
it may be safely taken to the lower regions. Were
this rite omitted, and the child allowed to descend
before it had gone up, failure in life would most likely
be the lot of such a one—the tendency of such always
being downhill. These little ceremonies, anyway,
point a splendid moral. One cannot begin to be
good and diligent too early in life.

When a child is born with a mask or caul over its
head, good luck will follow it all the days of its life,
always provided the caul is properly preserved.
There is some rite in the preservation of such, the
details of which I have not been able to obtain.
Speaking to one old dame, she said to me that she
did not rightly know what they did in such cases,
none of her children having been fortunate enough to
be so distinguished at their birth. This much, however, she did know, that some just dried such a covering by laying it between two layers of muslin, but—
and to give her own words—' Ther's other some 'at

'ev a straange carrying on wi' sike leyke; they lap it roond t' Bahble an' deea summat, bud Ah deean't knaw what, bud Ah can git ti knaw foor ya.' That cannot be now ; she has crossed the borderland. That such cauls or masks were held in high esteem at one time, is proved by the high prices paid for them, not because they had belonged to people of note or high degree, but because they possessed the power to ward off many evils which might assail the possessor. Sailors even to-day set great store by them : they act as a charm, saving the possessor from drowning in case of a wreck. These veils were much prized by witches, and great was the evil they could work should such ever come into their possession, hence the necessity of using all precautions against their loss.

An old body, Ann Caygill by name—I think she was a native of Bedale—told me the following story. She was seventy-five years of age, and the event took place some twenty years before she was born, but as the individual affected told the story to Ann herself, I have it pretty much from its original source. Jane Herd at her birth had a mask covering both head and face, which, as quite natural in those days, her mother carefully preserved. It turned out to be one of extraordinary power. If Jane laid it on the Bible and wished to see any one, they were bound to put in an appearance. And many other wonders she could work with her caul. Jane, it seems, was a pious girl, and never used it for an evil purpose, though, said my informant, she might have done had she been so minded. One day when Jane was using her mask

for some rightful purpose, a puff of wind blew it
through the open window. Jane of course rushed
into the street to recover her treasure, but it was
gone, and could not be found; being of such an
exceedingly light nature, the wind had carried it no
one knew whither.

And from that day Jane's life became a burden. Her
lover grew cold—the wedding day had been arranged,
but he declined to carry out his promise—a nasty
lump came on her neck, and a fearful pain and swelling attacked her right knee, which made her walk very
lame, and indeed she became a perfect wreck. At
last things got into such a parlous state with her, that
people began to suspect some evil-minded person had
found her mask, and was working her evil with it. It
was then remembered, when Jane had rushed into
the street to recover her lost treasure, that the only
person visible at the time was one Molly Cass [1],
a witch of considerable local repute in those days. But
Molly at the time had been so far distant from Jane's
cottage, that she was not even questioned. In the
end, Jane had resort to the wise man, or rather men,
of that day—Master Sadler and Thomas Spence [2],
both of Bedale. These two worthies, after many
questions, made a sign round the lump as well as
round her knee, telling Jane to collect certain things—
what these were could not be called to mind—and
bring them next day near midnight. These several
things having been collected and duly delivered to the
charmers, were mixed together, with other ingredients,

[1] A native of Exelby.
[2] It would seem these two often worked their charms in company.

and the whole boiled on a wickenwood fire, and
stirred by Jane with a wickenwood stick; near the
end of this boiling, a great smoke arose from the pan,
which Jane was told to inhale. She did so, but it
nearly choked her, still she kept on swallowing
mouthful after mouthful, until she had done so nine
times; she was then told to cease stirring, but to retain
the stick in one hand, the other being laid on the
Bible. She had then to repeat the following question:
' Has ——' (here mentioning the name of any one she
suspected) 'gotten mah caul?' Then Master Sadler,
after a moment's pause, said, ' No, she is free.' Master
Spence then joined in with ' By the power of the Holy
Writ and the charm of Hagothet and Arcon [1], mention
the name of some other person thou doubtest.' This
formula was gone through until the name of Molly
Cass was mentioned. Even as the witch's name was
uttered, the pan boiled over, filling the room with such
a fearful stench, that all three had to hurry into the
yard. So quickly was this accomplished, that they surprised the old witch scrambling off a settle, upon
which she had been standing to enable her to peep
through a small hole in the shutters. She was instantly
seized and thrust into the room, and kept there until
so nearly suffocated, that she confessed she had the caul
on her person, and promised then and there to deliver
it up. On being brought out of the room more dead
than alive, she further confessed that she had been forced
to run all the way from Leeming—the current belief,

---

[1] I have no knowledge as to the meaning of these two words; their
real pronunciation may have been lost, or perhaps they are simply
cant words.

however, was that she had come astride of a besom—
the moment they had put the pan on the wickenwood
fire. She begged to be forgiven, but as a punishment
she was locked up in a stable, a wicken peg having been
driven into the door to prevent her from escaping ; and
next day, for the diversion of the Bedale inhabitants,
she was hurried to the mill dam and duly ducked
nine times.

'A FRAGMENT,'

On the Witch Molly Cass.

. . . .

Foor seear sha war a queer au'd lass,
Ez meean ez muck, ez bou'd ez brass;
Ah meean t' au'd witch, au'd Molly Cass,
'At lived nigh t' mill at Leeming.
Noo fooak will clack, Ah've heeard 'em saay
At t' dark o' neet, when pass't that waay,
Tha fan' it ommaist leet ez daay,
Sike leets war awlus gleaming;
An' sum held ti 't 'at mair 'an yance
Wiv her feet fra t' grund they'd seean her prance,
Loup hoos heigh up, wi' t' Divil dance.

. . . .

The above would, I believe, be written about the
year 1810 by one who wrote under the signature
of R. H.[1] At that time Molly must have been dead
some twenty years, but her deeds would still be
remembered by many. Mr. W. Hird, from whom
I had the above fragment, told me he used to know
the whole piece, which was of considerable length.

But to return to recent times, still keeping to Bedale.
I remember a shopkeeper's wife saying to me, ' That

[1] My own opinion is that ' R. H.' was William Hird's father, though
he never admitted it.

girl has been lucky, but then she had a veil on when she was born, so one need not wonder.'

The case is a simple one, I know, but a straw shows which way the wind blows, and here was the belief still flourishing in the potency of the caul. This happened about twenty years ago. One has no need to go that far back; so recently as four years ago, a man, a native of Great Ayton, said to me, pointing to a girl, 'Ah've putten that lass's muther intiv a straange stew. Ah've stown' (stolen) 't' lass's mask, an' her muther's ommaist to'n'd t' hoos upsahd doon latin' on 't, bud Ah s'all let her 'ev 't back agaan; Ah wadn't keep 't foor nowt;' and then he added, 'An' Ah wadn't wark neeabody onny ill wi' 't.' Here again you have the old belief showing itself as strongly as in days past.

But to return to the baby. The baby's nails must not be cut during infancy; should they grow inconveniently long, they may be bitten off by the mother, for if they were cut, the child would grow up light-fingered, i. e. a thief. When the child has celebrated its first birthday, they may be properly cut; but here again certain days must be avoided—Fridays and Sundays are considered to be very unlucky. It is a common saying—

> Better t' baan 'ed ne'er been born,
> 'An cut its naals on a Sunday morn.

There is no virtue attached to the pieces of the nails when cut, but the first pieces bitten off should be carefully preserved, until there is a scrap from every nail on both hands; these must be wrapped together and buried under an ash-tree, and the child,

if not freed from the diseases incident to the young,
will only have them in a slight degree.

The old rhyme says—

> Cut 'em o' Munday, cut 'em foor health;
> Cut 'em o' Tuesday, cut 'em foor wealth;
> Cut 'em o' Wednesday, cut 'em foor news;
> Cut 'em o' Thorsday, ya cut foor new shoes;
> Cut 'em o' Friday, ya cut 'em foor sorrow;
> Cut 'em o' Seterday, t' bairn nivver need borrow;
> Cut 'em o' Sunday, 't 'ed better be deead,
> Foor ill-luck an' evil 'll lig on its heead.

Again :—

> Sunday clipt, Sunday shorn,
> Better t' bairn 'ed nivver been born.

Before the baby is nine days old it is wise to decide
upon its name, and once having done this, *so let
it be.* If either parent should happen to say, 'We
will call it So-and-so,' do not alter after having so
declared, for if so the child will grow up a liar, and
probably have to assume several aliases before death.
But the worst of all is to decide upon a name before
the child is born, and then afterwards change to some
other. Singular to say, in Cleveland you are told that
such a proceeding 'can end i' nowt bud harm'; but you
are not informed either precisely what form the harm
will take, or why. There is a legend lingering still in
Wensleydale, to the effect that once a soul was permitted to view the body it would shortly tenant. The
mother happened to say whilst the soul was near,
'When my baby is born, if a boy, we shall have him
christened——,' mentioning the name they had decided

I

upon. The soul knew it would be a boy, and on its return to spirit-land gave a full description of the body it was going to have for its companion on earth, mentioning at the same time the name by which it would be known. What then was its dismay to discover, on being carried to the font, that it was being christened by some other name. For a time it was sorely troubled. What must it do? What could it do? In the end it felt there was only one way open: it must hurry back to soul-land and clear itself from an apparent untruth, but in order to do this it must free itself from the body; but if ever the soul and body part company they never meet again. So the baby died, and the soul went back to spirit-land.

The above was given to me years ago by an old Yorkshire dame, who during her girlhood, if not a native, lived for many years in the village of West Burton. In the dales of Cleveland and Wensleydale, to guard her babe from the influence of evil spirits and bad wishes, the mother used to place a Bible under the pillow of the sleeping child, until such time as the infant had been christened, that being considered sufficient protection against all evil spirits. And in the days of witchcraft, in many houses where the first cradle would shortly be tenanted, it was most carefully kept wrong side up until the child was laid in it. This was done so that no other living thing in that house should sleep in it before the coming owner. Otherwise the cradle would be forestalled, and in after years the occupant might have reason to doubt the fidelity of his wife, or vice versa.

In such fear was this forestalling of the cradle held,

that one was rarely purchased until absolutely
needed. A cradle should always be paid for before
it crosses the threshold. It is said that the child
who sleeps in an unpaid-for cradle will end its days
lacking the means to pay for its own coffin, or, as
others put it, be too poor to pay for its lodgings on
the earth or in it. Should the baby when grown
older say 'Papa' before he or she utters 'Mamma,'
then be assured the next little stranger will be a
boy; however, should it say 'Mamma' first, then
it will be a girl ; and should it say 'Papa' and a girl
is born, then be quite sure that it said 'Mamma' some
little time before, when no one was near. This last
bit is mine ; I like to help even a superstition out
of a difficulty.

If baby's first tooth appears in the upper jaw, it
is not considered a good sign ; there is a fear of the
child dying in infancy. Sometimes they don't.

Should the baby be born with a mole on its chin,
success is strongly foreshadowed ; the same on the left
thigh is considered quite the reverse. One on the
right temple gives wealth and high position, and one
placed at the outside corner of either eye denotes
a sudden death. Whilst

A dimple on the chin brings a fortune in,
A dimple on the cheek leaves the fortune for to seek.

No woman ever dreamt of crossing any threshold
but her own until after she had been churched, as in
doing so she carried ill-luck into every house she
entered.

At the baptism, should a boy and a girl be presented
at the same time, the boy must always be christened

first, as otherwise he will play second fiddle to his
wife, and when come to man's estate be for ever beard-
less and effeminate ; and worse than this, the baby
girl when grown up will assuredly possess more hair
on her face than is usually considered needful, and
more than beauty demands.   She will also be manly
and masculine in her ways and habits.

When the new baby is taken round for inspection, the
lady of the house, after passing various eulogiums on
and over the small being, pins to its garments a small
packet to help the future Lord Chancellor on his way
through life.   This packet contains three things—an
egg, a silver coin, and a pinch of salt : the salt, so that it
may never lack the savour of life, whatever that may
be ; the egg assures it food, raiment, and a roof over
its head ; and the coin starts it off with a banking
account.   If these well-wishers were to add a fourth
gift, in the form of a small cane, sufficiently hypnotized
so that the young mother would be compelled to use
it when needed, what a lot of really fine bairns there
would be.   Unfortunately superstition has never been
run on practical lines.

Death.

A lack of the needful may compel the parties
concerned to wed without the smallest attempt at
rural ostentation, but not so in the case of a funeral.
Every sacrifice is made to honour the dead.   They
like it to be said that their loved ones were decently
buried.   They themselves feel proud to say, ' Aye,
he's geean ; wa've gitten him sahded by ' (buried),
' an' it war a beautiful funeral ; Ah will say that.'

In these days one can scarcely conceive the needless waste of money, and by those too who can ill afford it, which is so lavishly squandered on funeral folly. It was even worse a few years ago.

Had it been possible for the moment to put on one side the solemn fact that some dearly loved one was being borne to his or her last long rest, funerals, as I remember them years ago in Ripon, were more like circus processions than anything else. Happily many of the old notions are being laid aside by the rising generation. Yet often to-day in country places, as far as circumstances will admit, the old order of things is most rigidly observed.

Two years ago I witnessed a country funeral, almost in all the pristine glory of my youthful days. One thing it lacked, the hearse and horses with their sombre nodding plumes. This, be it remembered, was the funeral of a widow's son, her finances at the time being in anything but a flourishing condition. Two mutes stood guarding the open door. A silk scarf about three yards long was given to each bearer and mourner to fasten round his hat, and a pair of black kid gloves to every one bidden. I cannot say how much port wine was drunk, what it cost per bottle, or the weight of finger biscuits consumed, but as these were freely handed to every one assembled inside and outside the house, who could roll a pocket handkerchief into a ball, and assume a funereal aspect of countenance, considerable expense must have been incurred with these two items alone. After the return from the graveside, there was the funeral feast. Those who have never seen what provision is made for an affair of this kind can form but a very poor idea of the actual amount of food provided for and consumed by those who follow as mourners to the graveside. Refreshment is necessary for those who have driven, it may be, a long distance to pay their last respect to the departed one, but in the case of those who live near by, surely it does not need a moment's thought for them to decide upon the more seemly course to pursue. The old days of the funeral arvel, when almost the whole country-side were bidden, not only to the funeral, but to the funeral feast, have passed away, or nearly so. Even to-day, in many of our dales, the neighbours are still bidden. This bidding, and the very name of it, are both of Scandinavian origin. The order of men carrying men, and women women, is still observed. The same also with the sex of the young; only, in the case of a young maiden, the girls who act as bearers are dressed in white, and the carrying of a garland in front of the coffin is not even yet extinct. At one time these garlands [1] were after the funeral hung up in the church, and I believe in some of our dale churches in Cleveland these emblems of purity are to be seen hanging yet.

In the case of women who died in childbirth, a white sheet was thrown over the coffin. The bearing of the coffin either by towels (staves are things of

[1] The garland consisted of two hoops intertwined, decorated with white paper flowers and ribbons, in the centre of which was a white glove, often home-made, of paper or fine linen, upon which was written or worked in some fine stitch the initials or name in full and age of the deceased. According to locality this garland was either carried in front of the coffin by one of the deceased's dearest companions, or laid upon it. This custom might well have been retained.

the past now) or on the shoulders is equally common
in various parts of the riding.

Should the family of the departed one possess
a hive, the announcement of a death must at once be
made to the bees, and the hive be draped in black.
The bees must also have given to them a portion of
everything, to the minutest detail, which is offered to
the bidden guests, including wine, spirits, tobacco, and
pipes ; nothing must be omitted, for in some undefined way bees watch over the welfare of those to
whom they belong, and it would be unwise to offend
them. It is held that if the first swarm following
a death, no matter how long the interval, is easy to
hive, success is guaranteed for the next business
transaction, but should the swarm settle on a dead
bough, it foretells death to another of the family in
the near future; while should the swarm fly away
and be lost, then great care must be exercised in all
undertakings, until such times as a swarm has been
successfully hived.

It is not so very long ago since every funeral at
Guisborough[1] was headed by the sexton singing a
hymn from the house to the church gates, but this
singing by friends is common to-day.

The superstitions connected with the dying and
the dead are many and varied. Few country people
doubt the existence of a power by which the living
can (as they put it) hold back the dying. It is not
an uncommon thing to hear some one say, 'Sha
wad 'a'e deed last neet, nobbut Mary wadn't let her
gan,' or ' Mary wadn't gi'e her up,' or ' Mary ho'ds on

[1] And many other places in Cleveland.

tiv her seea.' It is, as it were, the last link of the
chain connecting life with the earthly side of eternity,
the snapping of which would for ever free the soul,
but which the dying person is unable to break, because some one refuses to be reconciled ; they cannot
bear to part with them, and in this way hold them
back. Again, the soul cannot free itself if the dying
person has been laid on a bed containing pigeon
feathers, or the feathers of wild birds even. Instances
are on record of pigeon feathers having been placed
in a small bag, and thrust under dying persons to
hold them back, until the arrival of some loved one ;
but the meeting having taken place, the feathers
were withdrawn, and death allowed to enter.

On the other hand, when something unaccountable
has seemed to prevent a person *in extremis* from
passing into the other world, pigeon feathers have
often been suspected. Under such circumstances the
invalid has been lifted out of bed, and either laid
upon another one, or seated in a chair. And as a rule
death speedily followed either treatment, the patient
passing away in an incredibly short space of time,
which of course clearly proved that such feathers had
inadvertently been mixed with those in the bed.

When the signs of death are observed the windows
and door are thrown wide open, and a silence as still
as death itself is maintained, so that nothing shall
either hinder the dark angel from setting his seal on
their loved one, or impede the soul's flight over the
borderland into that of the great unknown.

Much of what is done may be rooted in the rankest
superstition, or in many cases long-forgotten pagan rites,

and one feels inclined to smile ; but, after a moment's
consideration, one is forcibly reminded that it is equally
deeply rooted in the old belief, which embraces in its
faith a devil, a fiery hell, Jonah, whale, and everything.
As things go nowadays, theorists are not leaving us
much to believe or be superstitious about.

The death-watch, with its ' tick-a-tick,' has blanched
the cheek of many an otherwise brave Yorkshire man
and woman.   Tell them it is only the head of a small
beetle called *Atropos* tapping against the wood as it
eats its way out, and they will jeer at you.   They
know, as their fore-elders did before them, that it is
the sign of death ; if not for some one in that house,
assuredly so for some one in the village, and by-and-
by some one dies, and wise heads are shaken—they
knew.

Every care is taken that nothing animate shall pass
over the corpse.   I never heard of any domestic pet
having been killed which so offended, though such at
one time would have been the case a little further north.

The belief still lingers that the passing bell possesses
the power to drive away all evil spirits, and so prevent
them from troubling the soul in its upward flight, for
even to-day a sexton, on being asked to 'put the bell
in,' is also often urged to do so as speedily as possible.

It is looked upon as a kindly action, when standing
by the corpse of some dear one, if the visitor gently
touch the same.   In some undefined way, this solemn
contact of the living with the dead, makes known to
the sorrowing ones that nothing but sympathy is felt.
By this act all past injuries or misunderstandings, if
such existed, are blotted out, forgiven, forgotten.

So soon as the vital spark has left its earthly house, the fire, if such be burning in the room, is immediately extinguished [1], and it is not an uncommon thing for the looking-glass to be either draped entirely, turned with its face to the wall, or removed from the room. The omens denoting the near approach of death are many—a white dove fluttering near the window, the rapid flight of birds over the house, and in some instances the actual appearance, to some dearly loved one, of the wraith of the person about to die. Many instances of the latter could be given.

I cannot say when or where the Lyke Wake dirge was sung for the last time in the North Riding, but I remember once talking to an old chap who remembered it being sung over the corpse of a distant relation of his, a native of Kildale. This would be about 1800, and he told me that Lyke Wakes were of rare occurrence then, and only heard of in out-of-the-way places. Doubtless this was so, but a superstition closely connected with the Lyke Wake is still with us. Old people will tell you that after death the soul passes over Whinny Moor, a place full of whins and brambles ; and according as the soul when a tenant of the body administered to the wants of others, so would its passage over the dreaded moor be made easy. It seems, according to the old belief, every one ought to give at least one pair of new shoes to some poor person, and as often as means would allow, feed and clothe the needy. Whether these

---

[1] The author is quite aware some other writers state that the fire is never allowed to die out whilst the corpse is in the room. He never knew or heard of such a custom, though possibly such may exist.

rules were faithfully carried out or not, the soul on approaching Whinny Moor would be met by an old man carrying a huge bundle of boots ; and if amongst these could be found a pair which the bare-footed soul had given away during life, the old man gave them to the soul to protect its feet whilst crossing the thorny moor.

THE LYKE WAKE DIRGE.

This yah neet, this yah neet,
        Ivvery neet an' awl (all),
Fire an' fleet an' cann'l leet,
        An' Christ tak up thi sowl.

When thoo fra hither gans awaay,
        Ivvery neet an' awl,
Ti Whinny Moor thoo cum'st at last,
        An' Christ tak up thi sowl.

If ivver tho gav' owther hosen or shoon,
        Ivvery neet an' awl,
Clap tha doon an' put 'em on,
        An' Christ tak up thi sowl.

Bud if hosen or shoon thoo nivver ga' neean,
        Ivvery neet an' awl,
T' whinnies 'll prick tha sair ti t' beean,
        An' Christ tak up thi sowl.

Fra Whinny Moor that thoo mayst pass,
        Ivvery neet an' awl,
Ti t' Brigg o' Dreead thoo'll cum at last,
        An' Christ tak up thi sowl.

If ivver thoo gav' o' thi siller an' gawd,
        Ivvery neet an' awl,
At t' Brigg o' Dreead thoo'll finnd footho'd,
        An' Christ tak up thi sowl.

Bud if o' siller an' gawd thoo nivver ga' neean,
　　　Ivvery neet an' awl,
Thoo'll doon, doon tumm'l tiwards Hell fleeams,
　　　An' Christ tak up thi sowl.

Fra t' Brigg o' Dreead 'at thoo mayst pass,
　　　Ivvery neet an' awl,
Ti t' fleeams o' Hell thoo'll cum at last,
　　　An' Christ tak up thi sowl.

If ivver thoo gav' owther bite or sup,
　　　Ivvery neet an' awl,
T' fleeams 'll nivver catch tha up,
　　　An' Christ tak up thi sowl.

Bud if bite or sup thoo nivver ga' neean,
　　　Ivvery neet an' awl,
T' fleeams 'll bo'n tha sair ti t' beean,
　　　An' Christ tak up thi sowl.

Although there is a place called Whinny Moor, as used in the Lyke Wake song it is mythical, simply representing a wearying hindersome tract of land through which the soul must perforce pass, the ease or difficulty of such passage being lesser or greater according to the good deeds done and alms bestowed during life. There are other versions of the song; the one here given is as it was dictated to me. How the original from which it was taken was worded, I cannot say. There is another version in the North Riding which seems to have been written according to the tenets of Rome; at least I imagine so, as purgatory takes the place of hellish flames, as given above. It may be mentioned that the influence of the Reformation never reached many of the dales in Cleveland and those further westward. Hence the more com-

monly known version is in the phraseology of the
predominant belief of that time.

Evidently the version given is one of a much later
date, and must have been sung by a Protestant.

As to the ' Brigg o' Dreead,' I dare say but little ;
' Fools only rush gaily in where angels fear to tread.'
However, I may venture this far ; just as Whinny Moor
had to be passed, so the ' Brigg o' Dreead ' had to be
crossed. Upon one point all authorities agree. Wher-
ever it was, or whatever its form, the Brigg was the real
crux. Whether we incline to the theory that it was as
narrow as a thread, shaky as an aspen leaf, or slippery
as a glacier side, it had to be crossed. This accomplished, the soul was fairly safe. But did it slip or
stumble whilst crossing, then the length of time
occupied in its fearful descent, the depth to which it
fell, together with all the concomitant evils belonging
thereto, depended solely upon the amount of good
and evil with which it had been accredited during its
earthly pilgrimage.

CHAPTER VIII

OMENS, CHARMS, RECIPES

QUITE a volume might be written on the above; their number and variety is legion. Therefore in brief only will it be possible to treat many of our omens, &c. To some few of the more striking a few details will be given.

Many of the omens, charms, &c., quoted are in no sense peculiar either to our riding or county. They are with us, they are duly observed, and the belief in them is not wholly dead yet.

To break a looking-glass foreshadows an early death, or great evil in the near future, and for any one (if they have not previously seen or spoken to the person that day) to look over his or her shoulder, so that their reflection is seen in the glass, foretells an untimely death to one or both. Should a hen crow, the reward for its exhibiting such marvellous vocal powers would be immediate death. The old song says (date, the early seventies)—

> Than awn a crawing hen,
> Ah seeaner wad t' au'd divil meet,
> > Hickity O, pickity O, pompolorum jig,

Or breed a whistling lass,
Ah seeaner wad t' au'd divil treeat,
    Hickity O, pickity O, pompolorum jig.
Nowt bud ill-luck 'll fester wheear
Ther craws an' whistles sike a pair;
Maáy hens an' wimin breed neea mair,
    Pompolorum jig.

A dog howling under your window three nights in succession portends evil or death in the near future. A picture falling, if the glass be broken, speaks clearly of a death in the family at no very distant date; the glass being intact, implies that misfortune of some kind is hanging overhead, but possibly everything may come right in the end.

A strange cat coming to your house, if black, should never be driven away; if you do so, you simply drive luck from your door.

If you are unmarried, be very careful to keep in mind the fact that, having attended three funerals, you must at least be present during part of a wedding service before standing at the graveside of a fourth, or you will die single, unless you are exceedingly rash, and get married in spite of everything.

If you accidentally break anything, it is a good plan to let two other articles of little or no value slip from your hand. This will save you from breaking two other things of value, because you are bound to smash three, and it is really an advantage to be allowed to choose two of them yourself.

Yes, things go by threes. If one death takes place in a street, it won't be long ere the bell tolls for two others—so say they.

If the youngest daughter in a family is married

first, the eldest had better unravel one of her garters, knitting the same, mixed with other wool, into something a man can wear. This she must present to the one she has a special regard for, and it most likely will incline his heart towards her. Garters, by-the-way, are rather out of it now; they once were articles in great request, to work charms and spells with, but that was in the days when either a long band with a buckle, or a knitted affair about an inch wide and a yard long, was universally worn. In these days of patent things and other inventions, some of which do not encircle the leg at all, the girls are debarred from resorting to many of the old-time spells. In days past, so long as a fellow wore one of his lady love's garters round his neck, he was bound to be true to her and she to him. Did a fellow try the same thing now, he would strangle himself. The old-time garters, by-the-way, had other uses; the Bible, a key, and a garter often playing the part of a private detective, or infallibly making known to some doubting maiden the name of the man she would marry. The *modus operandi* was as follows :—In the case of an undetected thief, a key was placed within the Bible; this was bound securely within by winding a garter round it, the whole being suspended from a nail. The name of the supposed thief was now mentioned three times—in some districts seven—and if the key turned round, the thief was discovered.

Very similar were the rites used for the discovery of a future husband. In this case, however, the maiden wishing to know her fate, had to use one of her own garters, and it was also needful that the Bible should be opened at Ruth i. 16, 17. Some part of the key resting on the verses named, the Bible was then closed, and the key as before bound fast with the garter. The questioner and some other person now seated themselves opposite each other, each placing an elbow on a table and resting the open part of the key on their index fingers. All being thus arranged, the names of several of their male acquaintances were mentioned, the key turning on the name of the future husband being uttered. Not long ago the writer helped a maiden through the ceremony. The above, and the two following, are still commonly resorted to.

There is no difficulty in obtaining information touching the time you will be married. Simply let an anxious maiden take a looking-glass, and an apron which she has never worn or held between herself and the light, into the garden when the moon is at full; she must be careful not to look upon the queen of night until the rites are concluded. Keeping her back, then, to the moon, let her stand upon something she has never stood upon before—a newspaper, an old box, anything—and drawing the apron over the glass, hold it so that the moon shines upon it; let her now count the number of moons she sees reflected through the apron, and so many years will it be before the happy day arrives. I may mention, if such a one is in any violent hurry to get married, it is best to choose the apron of some light material, and to draw it tightly over the glass ; careful attention to these small details has a marvellous tendency to lessen the number of moons.

K

Throughout Cleveland the maidens have recourse to the following method of divination for the discovery whether they are to be married or die old maids. From a stream running southward a maiden fills a clean glass with water, and having borrowed an old wedding ring, or one worn by a widow—the ring must grace maternity—she suspends it over the glass of water hanging by a single hair drawn from her own head, her elbow resting on the table and the hair being laid over the ball of the thumb. Should the ring hit the side of the glass, her fate is sealed—she will die an old maid ; if, however, it spins round quickly, she will have to wait a year ; if slowly, she will be wedded more than once.

It is commonly held that if you can find a four-leaved clover, and then walk backward upstairs to bed, sleeping with the leaf under your pillow, you will dream of the man you will marry.

It is considered most unlucky to see the new moon for the first time through glass. To break the spell cast upon you by such an unfortunate occurrence, make the sign of the cross on the doorstep, and jump backwards over it into the house.

Should a hairy worm cross your path, pick it up, throw it over your shoulder, and wish.

If you tread on an ordinary road beetle, rain will presently fall.

Whenever you hear a cuckoo, turn the money over in your pocket for luck.

To see a single magpie is very unlucky ; two together is the reverse.

To see a single owl is also unlucky ; but to hear one

hoot, and then see it, foretells that you will have timely warning of some impending evil.

Wet your finger and cross your left shoe and wish every time you see a piebald horse.

Should two persons utter the same words at the same time, they must link their little fingers together and wish, keeping their wish secret.

The deciduous teeth of a male child, which have not touched the ground, if kept about the person are a specific against all manner of evil.

To ensure the child having a good and sound set of teeth, those which fall out of themselves, or which the child itself pulls out, should be dipped in salt and thrown into the fire.

A tooth found in a churchyard is believed to charm away the toothache if rubbed on the cheek.

And lastly, children's teeth must either be carefully preserved or utterly destroyed by fire with salt, as should one accidentally be swept away and fall into the ground, or be buried by some evil-minded person, the child will not live long, the first rites of ashes to ashes having been consummated.

No luck will follow a declaration of love if made on St. Dunstan's Day.

To be wed on St. Thomas's Day makes a bride a widow ere long.

A young woman, a native of Great Ayton, assured me the following was a certain charm for obtaining a sight of one's future spouse. The individual desirous of obtaining such a vision must make a cake of the following ingredients:—flour, a small pinch of graveyard mould taken from nine different graves, sufficient water from nine distinct sources, a pinch of salt, and a drop or two of blood from her third finger. The resulting dough had to be baked at midnight on the eve before that of St. Agnes, and whilst warm placed under the pillow; if found whole in the morning, well and good; if not, the charm could not be carried to its conclusion until the following year. The cake, if whole, had to be carried on the eve of St. Agnes and laid where four cross roads meet. All being accomplished, just before midnight the future husband or wife would come along, halt, look at the cake, and then vanish. Although the night might be pitch-dark, the apparition, it seems, would be quite visible. Immediately the spirit form vanished, the watcher must regain possession of the cake at once, or the water elves would seize it and work all manner of evil. These water elves keep cropping up, but little of their doings and nothing of their appearance seems to be known amongst our people. It is a bit of lost myth.

During harvest time you may easily discover how long you are destined to wait before being led to the altar. When the moon is at full, pluck three ripe ears of barley, which must be carefully wrapped up together with something belonging to him you love best. The parcel must be laid under your pillow, and on arising in the morning, open it, and if all the grains have remained *in situ*, then you will be wed that year; but if any have broken away, count how many—they tell how many years you will remain single.

If a young fellow is in love, and the girl's heart

does not incline towards him, there is a charm which will cast a spell about her from which she cannot escape. There is a difficulty, and rather a grave one, but love surmounts all things, so they say. He must cut off a willow knot and chew it. So far, it is quite a simple affair; given time, a love-lorn swain might manage to masticate the whole tree. But now comes the difficulty—having chewed the said knot, he must secrete the same in the bed of the girl he loves. Once she falls asleep with that chewed knot as her companion, she will be bound to yield to his importunities. Should, however, the knot be so placed that it causes the fair sleeper such inconvenience that she is compelled to find the cause, and having done so, throws it away, that young man may consider his case as hopeless.

If you can, within three days after becoming engaged, seize a snail by its horns and throw it over your left shoulder, you will to a very considerable extent reduce the roughness of the road which true love is said to journey along.

And remember it is unlucky to say good-night three times to the girl you love, without returning to the house and starting the whole thing over again, but one doesn't mind that. When parting with friends for any length of time, never say good-bye without adding that you hope to see them again, and never watch the parting ones out of sight—it is most unlucky.

The various nostrums administered, and the methods employed in days past for the cure of all the diseases man is heir to, one cannot help but think, if carefully observed, would usually have terminated in a funeral feast. The rank filth our forefathers had prepared for them, and doubtless were induced to swallow, has left behind the unsolvable mystery of accounting for the fact that specimens of the Anglo-Saxon race are still extant. Putting on one side for the moment the wretched stuff they had to swallow, let us turn to a few things usually employed to effect a cure.

If any one was seized with a colic, and colic water was not handy, all that was necessary was for some one to slip out and catch either a carp or a pike, slit the fish open whilst alive, and clap it on the stomach of the sufferer—and lo! a cure. This sounds all very nice, but it has often taken me three days to catch a pike, and carp, by-the-way, are not very widely distributed ; and as colic water required for the making thereof nearly every flower which blooms in our woods and gardens, and of two or three others which never do so in ' perfidious Albion '—and when actually all things had been obtained, it could not be properly prepared under nine months—possibly there may have been some other remedy I have not heard of, and which could be applied during the time the pike was being captured, otherwise the patient would often have a lengthy squirm of it.

For pains in the joints, a toad tied belly downwards over the affected part would enable the patient to walk as well as ever. Now this is something sensible ; just you find a poor body suffering from pains in the joints, and then produce a toad, and you will work a miracle. Long before you can tie it belly downwards anywhere, the patient, if a female, will be beating her best running record; if a male, his joints will be right in an instant, and you will have to take the toad outside, minus dignity.

An old lady tells me she has known a drink made from the following ingredients do a power of good in case of fever :—a handful of dandelion, agrimony, verjuice, rue, powdered crab's eyes and claws, and yarrow from off a grave. These had to be boiled for some hours, and taken when the moon was on the wane. Doubtless there was another recipe equally efficacious for those who unfortunately were struck down with fever when the moon was on the rise.

The tongue of a still-born calf, if dried and worn so that it touched the spine, would prevent fits of almost any kind.

Wart-charmers are not defunct yet. I know several who, after pronouncing an inaudible incantation, rub the wart with a special stone, and then you are assured the wart or warts will die. Frog spit rubbed on a wart ·is said to be a certain cure. If you rub your wart with a black snail, sticking the snail on a thorn where you will never see it again, the wart, as the snail dies, will disappear. If you yearn to afflict any one with warts, let them wash in water in which eggs have been boiled. This belief is quite common to-day. A plate of salt, upon which a dead man's hand has rested overnight, used to be considered good for chilblains.

Master Sadler of Bedale, in the year 1773, undertook the cure of ague in quite a simple way. After the patient had answered a few searching questions touching his past private life—which information doubtless he would much rather have kept to himself—his name was chalked at the back of the hob, an incantation pronounced, and he went home whole. I am inclined to the belief that many in these days would have to take the ague back with them. The ague is bad enough, but for a fellow to systematically trot out one's past doings would be infinitely worse. That was a hundred years ago; but only the other day I was told that if a field-mouse was skinned and made into a small pie and eaten, and the warm skin bound hair-side against the throat, and kept there for nine days, the worst whooping cough ''at ivver was' would be cured.

Speaking of whooping cough, I remember a lady at Guisborough, only a few years ago, taking both her boys to the gasworks for them to inhale the fumes from the gas-tank. It nearly poisoned the whole three, but the cough survived it nicely. However, that and the field-mouse were infinitely preferable to the recipe I had from an old dame, who assured me 'no cough o' no kind whatsoever could stan' agaan it.' It was this: equal quantities of hare's dung and owl's pellets—the latter are the disgorged remains of feathers, bones, &c., which the owl objects to digest. Well, having carefully mixed these two ingredients with dill-water, clay, and the blood of a white duck, the resulting filth had to be made into pills the size of a nut, three of which had to be taken fasting on going to bed. This was to be continued until the cough was cured or the patient buried. A much simpler method is to catch a frog, open its mouth and cough into it three times, throw the poor brute over your left shoulder, and the

patient will be cured at once. If not, depend upon it
there is some very good reason why the charm has
failed. One woman I knew, used to take her little
girl and hold her over an old well when a bad fit of
coughing seized the child. She declared, if at the time
either a frog or a toad happened to be at the bottom
of the well with its mouth open, the child would be
cured instantly. I offered to catch her a frog and
open its mouth for the child to cough into; this she
objected to, because, as she said, the frog might spit
at it and injure it for life. This belief in the poison-
ous and spitting power of frogs is still retained by
the good people of Great Ayton, and also of many
other places. I remember an old angler once saying
to me, 'Ya see, the Lord gav' t' fishes understan'ing;
tha knaw 'at frogs is venomous, an' tha're a gran'
bait foor pike, bud neea pike'll tak ho'd if ya deean't
run t' heuk thruff baith ther lips, seea ez tha can't spit
at 'em.' 'But,' said I, 'how do the pike catch them when
they are swimming in a natural state?' 'Easy eneeaf,'
answered he; 'tha tak hodden 'em fra behint, an' tha
can't spit backkards waay ower ther heeads, ya knaw.'

Still another plan may be tried to ease the little
sufferers. If they be passed nine times under the belly
and over the back of either a piebald pony or an ass
(the latter preferred), the cough will be immediately
charmed away, whilst a touch on the larynx from
the hand of a seventh son of a seventh son is held
to be a certain cure. And a hairy caterpillar or small
wood-lizard tied round the child's neck, having been
stitched in a small bag, was, and I believe is yet,
looked upon as a sovereign remedy.

Snail soup is drunk even to-day for the cure of consumption. And the skin of an eel (if skinned when alive), placed in a silken bag and worn so as to rest on the chest, is believed to cut phlegm when nothing else will.

To cure the 'water-springs,' an old name for acidity or heartburn, old people tell me the following is an infallible cure if taken in time—a very wise proviso— burnt oyster, cockle, and mussel shells ground to powder, equal parts, and mixed in worm-water. This latter was prepared by gathering a handful of worms from the churchyard and boiling them. The burnt shells might do good; ordinary water and chalk would have been equally efficacious, had they but known it.

But nearly every disease or complaint had its cure in days past, and, in a more or less degree, all were nasty.

For the moment let us return to wart-charmers. There is room here for both speculation and research. They did cure warts, of that there is not the least shadow of a doubt. The amount of evidence on record is such that contradiction and disbelief amounts to crass folly, and shows an ignorance of well-authenti- cated facts. A man I know, whose hand was covered with warts—warts which simply jeered at caustic and all such applications—at last went to the charmer. What did the man do? He simply asked the old chap if he believed he could remove them. Having answered in the affirmative, the charmer just rubbed his hand over the whole lot, muttered some words, and told the warty one to go home—in a

fortnight's time he was wartless.   Hundreds of cases
could be given.   Absolute faith that they would disappear, may have exercised some mental action over
the physical, and the trick was done.   In this way,
if we admit some hypnotic power which they uncon-
sciously used, we may account for many of the wonders
which these charmers and wise men worked in days
past, often bringing about results at which possibly
no one was more surprised than the wise men themselves ; but they, like many of to-day, had the sense
to hold their peace, and that has often dressed many
a conjuring trick with all trappings of philosophy.

It is held to-day, when any one is bitten by a dog,
that the only certain remedy against hydrophobia
is to have the brute killed at once.   For, say they,
should the dog in years to come go mad, all those
bitten by it will go mad at the same time.

The wearing of silver rings made from a single
coin presented at Holy Communion, was once held as
a sovereign remedy and preventive against epileptic
fits.

The cures for children and others afflicted with
worms are many and curious.   A few of the more
striking will be noticed.   A bunch of fine yarrow,
gathered from off a maiden's grave, had to be boiled
in water, and a wineglassful of the liquor, with
the addition of as much finely powdered glass as
would lie on a groat, had to be taken fasting for
six alternate mornings, bearing in mind that each
morning the patient was not fattening himself on
corpse yarrow and broken window-panes ; he had also
to swallow a stiff glass of salts and senna, which

not only made every kind of worm quit its hold of
his inside, but left him in a condition almost, if
not quite, ready for the worms to commence their
attack from the outside. Worms, however, are seized
with such a sudden fear when a live trout is brought
near them, that they die right off. Hence it is not
an uncommon thing for a father to procure a live
trout, and lay the same on the stomach of a wormy
one. And then, what with the fish kicking and the
bairn screaming, the poor worms have no chance, and
they know it, and throw up the sponge accordingly.

In days past cramp seems to have awakened people
three or four times a week. But sleeping with your
stockings on, with a piece of sulphur in each, or the
skin of a mole bound round the left thigh, or even
crossing your shoes on retiring to rest, would drive
the cramp away. Cramp, it would seem, was formerly
looked upon as having a very close connexion with
the devil, and was often the result of an evil wish,
spell, or witch-work. In cases when it arose from
any of the latter, something more potent than
sulphur and the crossing of shoes had to be resorted
to. A silken thread which had been passed round
a coffin, care having been taken to thread the silk
through the handles, would, if worn round the leg,
just below the knee-joint, securely guard the wearer
against wicked spells of that nature.

The skin of an eel, if tied round the leg, prevents
cramp whilst bathing.

Rings fashioned from any metal accidentally turned
up whilst digging a grave, were until quite recently
in great repute, especial virtue being attached to

one made from a coffin handle. Such rings acted as a charm against almost every kind of evil spell.

Years ago it was commonly believed that there was some kind of sympathy existing between the cause and the injury itself. An illustration of this has been given in the case of a dog-bite, but it had a much wider application; e.g. should any one be injured by a nail, or anything else, the nail, &c., was carefully cleaned, polished, wrapped up, and put away each time after dressing the wound.

I remember a case in point within the last ten years. A plough lad was hurt by the colter, the cutting iron of the plough; the ploughing was stopped, the colter removed, and sent to the blacksmith, with orders to remove all dirt and rust, and to polish all parts to which blood was adhering; and during the recovery, each time the wound was dressed, the colter was cleaned and polished with equal care.

Flint arrow-heads were for ages looked upon as elf-stones, and are to-day worn as charms against unseen evils. They also possess healing power in certain diseases. So, too, do the belemnites—a fossilized portion of an extinct cuttle-fish. These, in the hand of a skilled person, work wonders in the case of sore eyes and ringworm. Unfortunately, though belemnites are common enough, the skilled hands are rare, and so their virtue in thousands of instances lies dormant. These belemnites are supposed to fall from the clouds during a thunderstorm; the same is said of rounded pieces of quartz or flints, one and all being called thunder-bolts, or 'thunner-steeans.'

When a boy, I was an ardent archaeologist. I remember on one occasion having been told that chipped flints were to be found in a field near Blois Hall[1]. Hurrying thither the first whole holiday, I was fortunate enough on that occasion to find a flint arrow-head—the only one I ever did find. This I showed to an old fellow who was hedging; without hesitation he pronounced it to be an elf-stone, declaring that the elves were evil spirits, who in days past used to throw them at the kie—I had up to that time always been told they were shot at cattle—but my informant stuck to throwing. I well remember that he also said the elves got them out of whirlpools, where they were originally made by the water spirits, but he could not say what the water spirits used them for, though he knew of several instances in which both cattle and horses had been injured by the elves throwing their elf-stones at them. He further informed me that when the elves got them from the whirlpools, they had much longer shanks than was on the one I had found: this was so that better aim might be taken with them. 'But,' said he, 'tha're nivver fund wi' lang shanks on, acoz t' fairies awlus brak 'em off, seea ez t' elves wadn't be yabble ti potch 'em at t' beasts neea mair;' and he had been told that fairies often wore them as ornaments. Sore eyes could be cured by the touch from an elf-stone, if a fairy had ever worn it, and they were also a potent love-charm if worn so that they rested near the heart.

Speaking of fairies, I know an old lady who still fully believes in their existence. She assures me they

[1] In the North Riding, about three miles from Ripon.

have most beautiful houses at a great depth below the surface. It seems no one ever finds them, because the little folk possess the magical power of transporting them to a distance in an instant, should there be the least likelihood of their being disturbed ; owing to this, ' Nobody nivver cums across 'em when well-sinking, mining, or owt o' that soart.'

The old body told me the following story : —

In the days when tailors went out to work, she remembered one who came to work for her aunt being lost for a long time in a big field, and unable to find his way out, and all because he had said, ' If ever he saw a fairy he would catch her, and take her home, and put her in a bottle and keep her there.' So it happened, when he left the house to go home, and just when he entered the long pasture, he dropped his scissors, and for long he could not find them, and when he did place his hand on them, his sleeve-board was snatched from him. He heard it drop quite close to him, but when he stooped to pick it up, a pork pie which the farmer's wife had given him mysteriously disappeared; how, he did not know. However, a little way off, he saw a most beautiful damsel carrying a light; he implored her to come to his aid, and as the damsel and the light would not come to him, like Mahomet he went after them. This proved a most bootless errand, for the damsel and light led him on and on, hither and thither, now shining quite close at hand, then disappearing, and at last vanishing altogether, leaving the tailor utterly lost; and for long the poor fellow wandered about, until his cries for help were fortunately heard, 'bud nut afoor he'd hed aboon tweea hours on 't.'

That he had been under a fairy charm, and that she (the fairy) had been making sport of him, was evident to all. Never again did that man say he would bottle a fairy—at least, I imagine so. When a sleeve-board, a pair of scissors, and a pork pie are snatched from you, and you see a beautiful damsel carrying a light of some kind, which she snuffs out every time she is going to be caught, only to light up again some yards ahead, and then finally disappear altogether—well! even a tailor can draw his own conclusions after a game of that kind.

The other day I met an old lady in the train—a Mrs. Peary, of Sand Hill Farm, near Picton. Although the old lady told me she was turned seventy-three, she was as active as a woman of forty, and boasted she could do the work of two lasses yet. I soon discovered she possessed a fund of both witch and other lore. Next day I paid a visit to Sand Hill, and had a couple of hours' chat, or rather, I asked a few leading questions, and then made notes as quickly as I could.

For many years she lived in Bilsdale, her native place. Now, the dale in question is only a few miles distant from the borders of Cleveland, and yet she had never heard of many of the customs so common to that division of the North Riding. 'Mell suppers,' she told me, were kept up in Bilsdale in all their pristine glory so lately as twenty years ago—guisers, mell doll, and everything. She did not know the word 'spurrings,' meaning putting the banns in. The common expression in her part was, and still is, 'So-and-so 'ev tumm'l'd ower t' bauk an' brokken ther legs.' I fail to see the application.

Again, though it was the custom for the brides-maids to undress the bride, and see her comfortably into bed, she never remembered a case of stocking throwing, though she had heard of it, or of any attempt to keep the bridegroom amongst the revellers all night. Running for the bride's garter was common in her mother's time, but mostly a ribbon in her own. She had never heard of the custom of letting a child go up before it went down, or that it was unlucky to mention what name the child should be christened before its birth.

I mention these facts because it bears out a previous statement, that it is inadvisable to draw conclusions as to the non-existence of customs or superstitions on evidence of a purely local character.

Although much of what the old lady told me was general throughout the riding, the following was new to me.

For whooping cough I was assured that nothing was better than to walk along a road until you found nine frogs; these had to be carried home and made into soup. The patient on no account must see the frogs, or be told of what the soup was composed— a most wise precaution—but on his or her finishing the whole nine, soup and all, they would be found to be quite recovered. It's marvellous!

Those who suffered from a weak bladder had a remedy at hand: they simply had to stand astride at the head of an open grave, after the coffin had been lowered, but before being filled in, and then walk backwards to the foot of the same. It seems simple enough, but when you come to look at it, nine people out of ten, in endeavouring to perform the feat, would assuredly have surprised the onlookers by turning a somersault and landing flat on their backs upon the coffin below.

Again, count your warts, then unknown to any one take a small pebble from as many different graves, put the lot in a small bag, throw it over your left shoulder, and the warts will all disappear in a few days. My old friend would not commence or conclude any business on a Friday, and to break a clock-face was equally as unlucky as breaking a looking-glass. Neither did she ever allow a candle to die out; to do such a thing was, to her way of thinking, equal to passing sentence of death on some one of the household. The cutting of the pepper-cake by the doctor, on the birth of each grandchild, is still rigidly adhered to by the old lady. Being farmers, one ceremony they still observed, which was quite new to me. On the birth of a calf it was always carried rear first to the stall in which it was to lie, a little salt and water was given it to drink, and no one ever allowed to stride over it, as that would mean death or ill-luck to it; but generally 'an ower-stridden cauf deed,' said she[1].

It is a bad sign, when starting on a journey,

---

[1] *The Gospelles of Distaues*, published by Wynkyn de Worde about 1530, contains the following :—'If it happen that somebody stride over a little childe, know ye for certain that it shall never grow more, but if (unless) they stride backward over it again. Gloss ; Certainly, said Sebylle, of such thing cometh dwarfs and little women.'

should the first person you meet be a woman. In such fear was this held until quite recently, that the fishermen near Staithes would not have gone to sea that day; neither was it a good omen for a four-footed animal to cross their path when going to their boat, or at any time.

If whilst a fisherman was baiting his nets any one mentioned anything in connexion with a pig, or Dakky, as it was called, the worst of luck would be looked for, and in many cases the fisherman would have ceased to bait his lines for a time.

Again, no fisherwife would dream of winding wool by candle-light—to do such a wicked thing would be tantamount to winding the husband overboard.

Some years ago a young fisherman paid a visit to some relations inland; during his stay he fell in love with a maiden whom in time he took home as his bride. She, new to their ways and beliefs, simply laughed at their superstitions. It happened one night, when her husband was away on a voyage, that a fisherwife looked in for a bit of friendly gossip, and discovered the young wife by candle-light about to wind some wool. She implored her not to do so, telling her of the dreadful and sure result of such wicked folly; others, too, who had also dropped in, joined in declaring what a fearful and certain risk she ran, but it was all of no avail. With a laugh at such nonsense the winder laid the wool over a chair-back, daring them to wait and watch her wind it; but not a woman would stay in the house—they dare not. They fled, and the wool was wound. Three times did the ball slip from her hand. When the good wives heard of it, they shook their heads—it was a bad omen, so said they. When the husband returned hearty and well from his voyage, the young wife laughed at them more than ever, but they shook their heads. The ball had slipped from her hand thrice; he might go and return again, it was the third journey they feared. When he was told what his wife had done, his face blanched—if she had no fear, he had. He had been taught the belief all his life, she only, in a way, for five minutes. One more voyage would he make, and then the sea should know him no more; he would not, dare not chance a third voyage. Again he returned safely to his wife, but, as he had said, that was his last voyage. The two set up a little shop, and for three or four years all went well. Then there came a great storm. Volunteers were needed for the lifeboat—few able-bodied men were in the village at the time. For the moment everything was forgotten; Jack jumped in, and off they went, the women helping to launch the brave crew. The wrecked ones were saved, but in getting the last half-drowned wretch into the boat, Jack overbalanced and fell into the foaming sea; nothing could save him, and his body was found lying peacefully on the beach next morning. And then they remembered. Aye, and so should we, had we been taught the same belief when round our mother's knee. The neighbours were kind—they were more than that, they gave to the sorrowing one all their sympathy—but, in spite of their kindness, the widow felt that they held her guilty of her husband's death. So the little shop was closed, and she went forth from amongst them, and the village knew her no more.

There is a superstition in Cleveland that you must not eat a 'cock's egg,' i.e. a small egg, the last one a hen lays before sitting. When such are found, the contents are blown from the shell and burnt—the merest speck of the contents even adhering to the clothes has a baneful influence. The devil is said to superintend the laying of this last egg.

It is considered advisable that a new broom should sweep something into the house before it is used in the contrary direction, otherwise you sweep good luck away from your threshold.

I am told years ago it was considered 'a ventersome thing ti deea' for any one to speak disparagingly of their broom; the reason given being that no one was ever certain as to whether or no it had been witch-ridden. For should it have happened that a passing witch had one night borrowed their broom for a ride, it became witch-ridden, and was ever afterwards jealously watched over by the witch, and any indignity offered to her steed was sure to be resented.

It is looked upon as a most unwise thing for any one to give salt out of the house. In days past it was supposed to give witches power over the giver. Cases could be mentioned in which the work of the wise man was totally frustrated by such a proceeding.

It is most unlucky to give any one either a knife or any sharp instrument: such folly severs love, and breeds suspicion in the breasts of those who hitherto have held you in sincere regard. You may buy such a present by giving something in return for it, and such payment may be of the most trivial kind—a pin, a bit of paper, or anything.

When you discover your shoe-lace is loose, walk nine paces before tying it, otherwise you will tie ill-luck to you for that day.

Should a mouse run across the room, throw something at it, or, anyway, in the direction in which it ran. It may happen to have escaped from a witch's cat, and you will please either the cat or the witch, or both, by making some kind of pretence to stop it.

It is lucky, and acts as a charm, if you spit on, or place in your mouth, the first money you receive each day. This is common to-day, but I doubt if those who do so know its origin.

Years ago witches were supposed to watch over or, as my informant put it, 'eye-spell' the first money paid, and often used to spirit it away. This they were unable to do after it had been placed in the mouth. It has now degenerated into what is vulgarly called 'spitting on 't fer luck.' It is quite commonly done in our markets to-day.

A weasel crossing your path is most unlucky: it speaks of treachery. This evil omen may be counteracted by the performance of a very mean trick: drop a coin on the road where you saw the weasel cross, and the evil which was yours by right, will cling to those who are unlucky enough to find it. If there is a tramp behind you, when you see a coin lying, leave it for him; he won't mind about the ill-luck.

Always pass an old shoe so as to have it on your

right hand; and don't move it, lest you should help some unknown person on in the world, which would only be done to the detriment of yourself, for just as much as you advanced them, to that extent you would be the loser. An old hat you may kick about as much as you have a mind, always being careful to see some one has not placed a big stone underneath it—in that case it is always unlucky to kick a hat.

When a child was born, and it proved either unhealthy or deformed, it was generally supposed some evil-disposed person must have pricked its name with pins on a pincushion. When such a discovery was made by an expectant wife, nothing was said to the person working the evil, but the cushion was stolen, the pins withdrawn one by one, and stuck into the heart of a calf. This had to be buried in the churchyard, care being taken to bury it sufficiently deep, so that the dogs would not scratch it up. All this had to be done before the child was born, and by the mother. Such a discovery was made, and a heart stuck with pins and buried, within the last twenty years.

Sores or other evil diseases caused by witchcraft could be speedily cured if attended to when the moon was on the wane. I do not know in what form the application was used, but here are the ingredients as given to me by an old fellow who, though he had never used it, had heard ' 'at nowt cud cum up tiv it.'

> Tak' tweea 'at's red an' yan 'at's blake (yellow)
> O' poison berries three,
> Three fresh-cull'd blooms o' Devil's glut,
> An' a sprig o' rosemary;

Tak' henbane, bullace, bumm'lkite,
An' t' fluff frev a deead bulrush;
Nahn berries shak' fra t' rowan-tree,
An' nahn fra botterey bush.

To this day there are fisher lasses who wear their chemises wrong side out when their sailor lads are away at sea, and stormy weather threatens.

A friend of mine within the last five years heard a fisher lass say to a group of her friends, 'Ah deeant leyke t' leeak o' yon cloods, an' t' wind's gittin up; let's gan yam an' to'n wer sarks,' and every one of those who had a loved one on the water promptly did so.

Again, does a maiden fear that her lover is growing cold, she turns her chemise, so as to win back his cooling affections. This, like most other old beliefs, is dying out now. It is rather an undertaking, as fashion goes, for a lass to undress and dress again nowadays.

.   .   .   Her Jack war on t' sea,
An' t' tuckkins marked her swelling breast,
Fer her sark war to'n'd aboot.

.   .   .   .

CHAPTER IX

WITCHCRAFT

WITCH-LORE runs so very much in the same groove, that one fairly good example throws light on many points of interest. It was either the evil eye, or the working of some spell, injury to cattle, or surreptitiously riding horses during the midnight hour, an amusement which it would seem witches' were very prone to indulge in. Then followed a visit to the wise man, during which he did something, usually winding up on his part with an incantation, or the working of some anti-witch spell by the injured ones on their own account at home.

These charms for destroying the power of witches were numerous; in fact a careless inquirer would be led to the conclusion that every dale of any size possessed its own peculiar charm, but after a little careful research and comparison, such an opinion will be found to be untenable. The difference exists only in detail, nearly all springing from one or two common roots. When and how it came about these varied alterations crept in, is somewhat of a mystery, because one would naturally suppose, where such a vital point was at issue, every word and detail as to manipulation would be most carefully handed

down. The only solution I can offer—and I do so
in all humility—is that these charms had their birth
in remote ages. Afterwards local circumstances may
have placed almost insuperable difficulties in the way
of certain details being carried out; others would
then be substituted as nearly approaching to the
original as possible, probably by order of the priest
or wise man. Add to this the fact that a fable told
through long ages in different districts always uncon-
sciously takes a local colouring, and you have a partial
solution. Still, if the details differ, they do not run
on widely diverging lines; in general they manage
to keep fairly parallel, the main essentials being
always kept well in sight. Whether animate or
inanimate, the *thing* had to be injured, and then
something burnt; midnight was always the time
chosen for the final part of the ceremony, seclusion,
as far as possible, and absolute silence being
necessary. Many of these rites and ceremonies,
especially in connexion with witchcraft, consisting as
they do of blood, death, and burning by fire, seem
to be all that is left us of what may have been in
remote ages a propitiatory sacrifice to some pagan
god.

Chatting with an old mother one day, she remarked, ' Aye, things is altered noo. T' young uns
to'n up ther neeases' (noses) 'at ommaist ivvery thing
'at yan yance thowt an' did; tha deea nowt bud mak
gam o' yan if yan diz tell 'em owt, seea Ah nivver
tells 'em nowt.' This statement explains much; the
old people nowadays do keep their mouths shut.
It often happens that after an hour's chat with some

grey-headed occupant of the big armchair, you gain more information about the doings of days past than the rest of the household could have given you, were they even willing to do so, because in many cases they have little interest in things which 'happen'd afoor their tahm.' But, bear in mind, the unsealing of aged lips can only be accomplished when properly approached, and a bond of mutual sympathy has been established; then the lips and hearts will pour forth such a wealth of bygone lore, that you will hardly be able to jot down your notes fast enough.

But to return to my old lady. 'Why,' said I, 'when you were a girl there would be witches, or was that before your time?' For the benefit of my readers I will give the rest of the story literally, but in standard English. 'No,' said she, 'that it is not. There was one Dolly Makin; I once saw her myself, but she will be dead now, for she was over a hundred then; but my aunt once had a strange bout with her.' 'And where did Dolly live?' I asked, for I had years before heard of this same Dolly Makin. 'Nay, that's mair 'an Ah can tell ya,' said she. 'And what did she do to your aunt?' I inquired. 'Nothing; she only tried to. It was like this. There was one Tom Pickles wanted to keep company with my aunt, but he found out that she had a liking for one William Purkis. It was always thought, when Tommy found this out, that he went to the witch and gave her something to work a spell on my aunt. Anyhow, one night when she had just finished milking, a fortune-teller came up and took hold of her hand, and told her a long story about the carryings-on of William

Purkis and another lass, and she advised my aunt to
take up with Tommy, telling her that things looked
very black for her if she did anything else. But my
aunt said that she would wed who she liked, and
it would not be Tommy. At that the fortune-teller
struck the cow with her stick; the cow lashed out
and knocked the milk-pail over; my aunt flung the
milk-stool at the fortune-teller's head, but she ducked,
and it missed her, and next moment they were one
grappling with the other like all that. My aunt, however, was a well-built, strong lass, and after they had
fought for a long time, neither gaining an advantage,
the fortune-teller screamed out that my aunt had
something about her that belonged to the unburied
dead, or otherwise she would have mastered her, and
had her in her power for ever. "But," said she, as
she walked away, "I have not done with you yet;" and
then my aunt saw it was the old witch. My aunt
did not know what the witch meant by saying she
had something about her that belonged to the unburied dead; but news came next morning that her
uncle had died the day before, and it happened that
a brooch she was wearing had a bit of his hair
in it. It was that which had saved her. It would
have been useless trying to overtake the witch when
she left her, even on horseback, for she once went
from the top of Ingleborough to the top of Whernside
at one stride.' 'But,' I ventured to say, 'it is a long
way, that.' I was not quite sure of the distance, but
I knew I was within bounds when I added, 'It will
be quite nine miles.' For a moment the old lady
hesitated; even to her, after making all allowance for

the witch's marvellous power, it did seem a pro-
digious stride. 'Well,' she said, with a sigh of relief, as
an idea struck her, 'maybe I am wrong ; it would be
a leap ;' or, as she put it, 'mebbe Ah's wrang ; sha wad
loup it.' Again I pointed out that it was an enormous
leap. 'Deean't ya want her ti 'a'e deean't?' (i. e.
'Don't you want her to have done it?') she questioned,
losing her temper. And then I had to smooth her
ruffled feelings. I knew I was precious near treading
on her pet corn, but I wished to see how, as I knew,
she would explain away the difficulty. 'Whya, noo,
ez you saay it's a gertish loup,' she admitted, and
then added, 'maist leykly sha wad deea't iv a hitch,
strhad, an' a jump; onny road, sha did it.' That
being settled, I asked what took place when she
herself saw the witch. 'Nowt, bud summat might
'a'e deean.' And then she explained that one evening, a few months before she was married, she and
her sweetheart were walking to Feetham Holme,
. when they saw an old lady sitting on a great stone
It seems she looked *that sackless*, that her sweetheart burst out laughing. The moment he did that,
the old lady sprang to her feet, and almost shrieked,
'Ya aren't wed yet,' and then disappeared. A
moment afterwards, however, a black cat sprang
across their path, which was a most unlucky omen.
My informant could not say what it was, but something told her that the black cat was none other
than the old witch. She mentioned none of her
fears to her future husband, but the next day she
paid a visit to the wise man of Reeth. To him she
unburdened herself of all her fears, inquiring what

would have to be done to break any spell Dolly
might work to prevent her marriage. It seems
there were only two things the wise man knew of
equal to the occasion. One was to tear a piece of
cloth from the garment of a man hanging from a
gibbet, cut it into nine pieces, and burn them
at dead of night, with every door and window
not only closed but securely fastened. This she had
declared to be quite impossible. Her next chance was
to hear the last words of a man just before he was
hanged, write the same on nine pieces of paper,
stick a pin through each piece, and then burn them
at midnight, doors and windows as before. This
she thought might be managed. From a copy of
the *Yorkshire Gazette* which came into the dale every
week, she learnt that a man was to be hanged at York ;
so to Settle she went, and thence by the carrier
to her destination. She had a cousin living in York,
with whom she stayed until after the eventful day.
She managed to hear the last words, and carried out
all other injunctions, and so, as she said, ' Dolly nivver
c'u'd deea nowt nowther ti me ner onny o' my bairns.'

It is a well-known fact that witches have a decided
aversion to a stone with a hole through it. So
one hanging in the house goes a long way towards
keeping them outside ; and an old horse-shoe, which
has been picked up and nailed on the door, has even
greater power. Again, any girl, whilst a maiden, who
was so fortunate as to find three horse-shoes in one
year, if she threw them over her left shoulder, and
walked round them three times, being careful to
preserve all three, not only she, but when married

her children, could never be witch-held. This, be it observed, only protected the person, it did not extend to property of any kind.

Dolly Ayre, the Carthorpe witch, died within the ken of many now living. Richard Kirby, an old inhabitant of Carthorpe, gave me the following only a short time ago. I must really give it in his words. Filling his pipe, he began, 'Aye! Ah ken'd her weel; she yance witched sum coos ov au'd Tommy's, an' sha wadn't tak 't off.' I inquired what it was she would not take off, and was promptly informed it was ' summat sha'd deean tiv 'em: a spell o' sum soart 'at sha'd warked on 'em.' Old Tommy, it seems, hurried off to the wise man, Sammy Banks o' Mickly, who, after Tommy's story had been told, 'did summat, an' Tommy did summat, an' atween 'em tha baith did summat else 'at completely flustrated Au'd Dolly intiv a cocked hat, bud nut afoor sha'd mannished ti spell t' leyfe oot o' yan o' t' coos—ya see, iv a waay, sha 'ed t' fost ho'd.' On asking what they had done to master Dolly, he replied, with a shake of his head, 'Naay, noo, Ah deean't knaw; that war kept a dark secret. All 'at ivver war knawn, war 'at Tommy 'ed driven a peg o' wickenwood inti summat, an' 'at he'd thrussen summat thruff t' au'd witch's latch slit, but what it war no man nivver knew, bud it mun 'a'e been summat varra larl, or else he c'u'dn't 'a'e thrussen 't thruff, an' he bo'nt ' (burnt) ' summat at midneet 'at stank warse 'an nowt. Aye! an' noo ther war yance a queer thing happen'd at Ness, near Pick-hill.' A man, it seems, took a farm over the head of the then tenant. The man who had been so shabbily treated had once done a great kindness to Dolly, though, according to my informant, it was a most risky thing to offer a kindness to a witch, as they might take offence even at that. However, in the case mentioned, the kindness had been graciously accepted. When the new-comers arrived with their goods and chattels, they found written in blood-red writing on every door and shutter, these words, BAD LUCK; there was also something written underneath, which no man could make out. 'Aye,' said the old man, in words which there was no gainsaying, 'an' afoor they'd gitten hauf ther sticks in, doon cam a lahtle bit ov a shelf they'd putten sum pans on, an' it tumm'l'd reet on t' top o' yan o' ther bairns, an' killed it wheer it stood, an' ther's neea gitting ower that; noo, is theer?'

In this same Carthorpe, years ago, one of the houses was suspected of being witch-held, and everything about the place witch-stricken, and for some time neither land nor beast throve. It happened that one who possessed the power of smelling witches slept for a night under this particular roof. In the morning he said they were quite mistaken in supposing the house was witch-held, declaring that it was haunted. He advised them to prevail upon the parson to shout it down. The then Rector of Burneston, having been seen, kindly undertook the shouting down of the said spirit. To this end he partook of a good meal, rested for an hour, and then betook himself to the farmer's well. There he read something out of the Prayer Book, which 'incanted t' spirit up ti t' wellsahd,' and then the parson called out, 'For ever and for ay,' to which the spirit replied, 'For a year and a day.' Then the parson at it again, and the spirit did the same, 'and they baith went at it leyke all that foor ower tweea hoors, bud t' parson gat t' last wo'd acoz t' spirit c'u'dn't ho'd oot neea langer, an' seea t' parson wan t' battle i' t' end, an' cungled it doon; an' seea that spirit nivver na mair, at noa tahm, ivver agaan c'u'd cum oot o' t' bad pleeace ti wark ill agaan neeabody [1].'

For some unexplained reason, witches held in great aversion posthumous children, more especially male children. In fact their malevolence was often made manifest prior to the child's birth. An old dame gave me the following as having occurred years ago at Kirby Hill, near Boroughbridge. A young couple, recently married, met the witch (Sally Carey) near the Devil's Arrows. What they had done to gain Sally's displeasure, legend does not say, but as they passed the old lady she shook her stick, and almost screamed, 'Ya want a lad, bud Ah'll mak it a lass'; and sure enough, when the baby arrived, it was a girl. They had hoped it would be a boy, for much future fortune depended upon their having a son and heir. Still they hoped, should they be blest with a further addition, that the next arrival would be a boy. Three or four months after the birth of their daughter, the husband was thrown off his horse and killed.

Some time after the sad event, and late in the evening, Sally knocked at the widow's door; on its being opened, the old hag screamed, brandishing her stick in the widow's face, 'It shan't be a lad this tahm,

---

[1] Richard Kirby, who gave me the above and several other stories concerning witches, still lives in Carthorpe, near Bedale.

M

nowther.' So terrified was her victim that she fainted, and was found some time afterwards in a doubled-up position and unable to rise. By-and-by, when sufficiently recovered, her friends strongly urged her to pay a visit to the wise man of Aldborough. At last she was prevailed upon to do so, when a supreme effort on his part was made to break the witch's power. Much of what the wise man did, the old lady had forgotten. All she remembered was that at midnight, with closed doors and windows, a black cat and a black cock bird were roasted to a cinder, on a fire made from boughs of the rowan-tree; a long incantation was also pronounced, of which she could not call to mind a single word, for as she put it, 'wa war all ti freetened.' The 'all' consisted of the widow, my informant—then a maiden—and a mother of seven sons, the trio being necessary for the working of the charm. When the baby was born, it was a boy, but a cripple. Once again the wise man was visited. This time the almost heart-broken mother was assured that, if she remained unwedded for seven years, her son would outlive his weakness, his back would grow straight, and all would be well. This demand was readily complied with. 'But,' added the old dame, 't' au'd witch tried all maks an' manders o' waays ti git her ti wed. Ah nivver knaw'd a lass seea pesthered wi' chaps iv all mah leyfe. Sha' (the witch) 'war awlus sending some good leyke leeaking chap for ti 'tice her, bud sha kept single, and bested t' au'd witch i' t' end, fer t' bairn grew up ti be ez straight an' strang a chap ez yan need wish ti clap yan's e'es on. Ah mahnd him weel, an' ther's nowt aboot that.'

Only the other day I met an old fellow who firmly believed not only in the power of witches, but that they existed at the present day. He held that the evil eye accounted for many mishaps, which 'fooak c'u'dn't account for nooadays neea road at all.' Of witches he had known several, but of fairies he could only speak from hearsay. 'Nobbut sum fooak,' explained he, 'war yabble ti see t' fairies'; he had never possessed that power; but he continued, 'Ah've knawn fooak 'at 'ez seean 'em monny a tahm, bud that's years sen noo.' He had come to the conclusion that as people had got so into the way of saying there were no such things, 'tha 'ed all ta'en t' hig, an' takken thersens fo'ther up t' dale; bud tha cum back sum-tahms ti t' au'd spots, acoz yan offens sees t' rings wheear tha've danced owerneet. Onnybody can see t' rings fer thersens if tha nobbut tak ther een aboot wiv 'em; bud,' said he, emphatically, 'Ah think 'at tha mun awlus keep ther heeadgear on noo.' I was given to understand that so long as a fairy kept its cap or bonnet on it was invisible, but this, I think, is a bit of lore gone wrong; he ought to have said, so long as they keep their invisible caps on, &c. This old chap gave me a bit of lore which was quite new to me.

We all know that witches kept a black cat, and as a rule it was a Thomas cat; but if, to work something especially evil, a witch took to keeping a black tabby, she was, by some higher power, compelled to keep that tabby until it had kittens. When this interest-ing event was about to come off, the said tabby was securely locked up and guarded until the expected

increase arrived; immediately this happened, the whole
lot were drowned. The reason for this hurried departure of mother cat and kitten babies from the land
of the living was made quite clear. For had the
witch a son when the kittens were born, and any person
managed to steal one of the said kittens, the witch
from that moment became a 'bustard,' being bereft
of all power to work evil; but if up to that time she
had only given birth to girls, she remained a bustard
only until a son was born; then all power was restored
to her. My informant remembers a witch who was
made a bustard of, and who never again regained
power to work evil, being too old at the time to dream
of having a son.

Perhaps the most widely adopted anti-witch charm
was that of sticking a beast's heart full of pins and roasting the same at midnight, being careful to observe the
rule of closed doors and windows, absolute silence, and
the refusal to admit any one during the performance of
the rite; this, however, will be referred to by-and-by.

I think it must be put on record that witches
sometimes did good even if they committed evil to
bring it about. To do this, I shall have to step just
over the boundary of the North into the West Riding.
There was a widow residing in the village of Aldfield,
whose son, her only support, lay at death's door: he,
so I was informed, was afflicted with a disease which
was consuming his vitals. After the matter had been
fully discussed by the neighbours, the consuming of
his vitals was pronounced to be the result of a bad
wish, the evil eye, or a witch spell, and, according to
their verdict, one Nanny Appleby was suspected of

being the spell-worker. Nanny lived somewhere on the other side of Dalla Moor. This must have been before the days of the wise man of Mickley, or assuredly thither the widow would have gone. It seems that the poor mother screwed up courage to seek Nanny out herself, hoping to appease her—an almost hopeless task. Anyway, early one morning off she set; fortunately she met the old witch before she had completed half her journey.

On being questioned, Nanny swore she was innocent, but declared she knew what ailed the lad, and offered to go back with her and cure him. In much fear and trembling, the widow returned with Nanny, to the astonishment of the whole village. After having been left alone with the young fellow for some little time, Nanny told the weeping mother that her lad was possessed of a devil, which she promised to drive out. By what means she managed to induce the devil to let go his hold ' of the vitals ' is not known; but a terrific fight took place, furniture was smashed and pots were broken, amidst yells Satanic, and Nanny came off victorious. Having got the devil out of the young fellow, the next thing was, what must be done with the little imp? Nanny, however, seems to have been equal to the occasion. Of course such a doubtful customer could not be allowed to roam about at his own sweet will; oh dear no, Nanny would not grant a favour of that kind. The spirit was commanded to enter the body of a certain Tom Moss. Probably she had a spite against Tom; anyway the order seems to have been most promptly obeyed, for within a month

Tom was found drowned in Grantley Lake. The invalid recovered, and so there is no doubt about anything.

The following witch story unfortunately is wanting in one or two points of interest. I am unable to give the witch's name, or with certainty her dwelling-place. One or two things, however, tend to the belief that she was the Ayton witch, who flourished about 1750–80. If in this I am correct, she was known as Au'd Nanny; and though a native of Stokesley, she lived for many years in a tumble-down old cottage in the far corner of the green near the mill at Great Ayton.

Though doubtless a terror in her day, nearly all her deeds, like herself, have passed away. Two or three stories are yet told concerning Au'd Nanny, but they are unauthenticated and of doubtful origin. They seem to me most like latter-day ghost stories told to terrify children, with Nanny's name tacked on to them. They preserve her memory and christian name, and that is all.

One story, however, I had from an old lady whose grandmother once had an encounter with Au'd Nanny. As the story was told to me in that matter-of-fact way which leaves small room for imagination to exploit itself, I have no doubt it was repeated, for my benefit, as her mother or grandmother had told it her years before. The main interest of the story lies in the fact that it contains a witch's curse, and sets forth the proposition that a witch had the power not only of assuming the form of one recently dead, but could even inhabit the body itself.

To divest the story of much repetition and redundancy, it will be better to keep mainly to ordinary English.

It seems that her grandmother lived at Stokesley, and had a cousin living at Kildale, to whom she was deeply attached. This cousin's name was Martha Sokeld. One day Martha was taken very ill, and sent for her cousin Mary Langstaff to come at once and nurse her. Mary sent word back she would be along directly; so after she had cleaned up and 'putten things ti reets,' she put on her hood and shawl and set off to walk to Kildale—' an' it's a goodish step an' all, Ah can tell ya; an' ther's nowt aboot that.' Well, when Mary had walked above halfway, she saw an old woman 'hoppling alang t' road.' It seems there was something about the old lady which struck Mary as curious—'sha didn't leyke t' leeak on her.' What it was which made her feel certain the old body approaching was none other than 't' au'd witch[1],' she never could tell, but such became her conviction. So, to avoid the necessity of speaking to her, she stooped down and commenced to cull flowers from the hedge side. But on the old witch drawing near, she called out in a creaking voice, ' Thoo's neea call ti hing thi heead doon i' that waay. Ah ken tha, Mary Langstaff, reet weel; aye, ez weel ez if thoo ow'd ma summat. Noo, 't wadn't 'a'e cossen[2] tha mich ti 'a'e passed t' tahm o' daay wi' ma; bud sitha, Ah s'an't forgit ti-daay, an' Ah knaw all 'at thoo off'ns sez aboot ma an' all; but Ah'll paay tha

---

[1] Nanny must have been disguised in some way, at least one would think so, otherwise Mrs. Langstaff would have recognized her at once, both being natives of that part.

[2] Inconvenienced, literally ' cost.'

oot for 't, Ah'll paay tha oot for 't.' She then banged
the ground three times with her stick, and when my
informant's grandmother looked up, the witch had
disappeared. The reason why the witch did not do
her an injury at that time was easily accounted for—
she happened to be wearing in her bosom a bunch of
wicken-tree, i. e. mountain ash, berries.

On arriving at her cousin's, she found her almost
recovered. She stayed with her a few days and
then returned to Stokesley—this was on a Monday
afternoon. Much to her surprise, who should walk in
on Wednesday evening but Martha Sokeld. Martha
told her she had had another bad bout, and felt
she was not going to last long, but before she died
she would like to see her sister who lived at Northallerton. She had got a ride so far on the way that
afternoon, and then, after a night's rest, she thought she
would be able to go by the carrier to Northallerton.
Just then she felt very tired, and thought if Mary
would go over to Hannah's and get her to put some
things together which she wished to send to her sister,
she could manage to get a nap lying on the settle.
She was most pressing that Mary should not hurry
back, but stop a good hour, giving as an excuse—she
did not wish to be 'wakken'd efter sha 'ed yance
gitten ti sleep.' Mary went to Hannah's, but there
was a something that made her feel very uneasy—she
did not know what it was; 'an' i' t' end it gat sike
a grip on her, 'at sha left an' set off yam agaan.'
So that she should not awaken her cousin if she
had fallen asleep, she approached the house very
quietly; and peeping between the shutters (they did

not fit very closely), she beheld a sight which made her 'oppen wide baith e'es'—her cousin, instead of being asleep, was sitting in front of a blazing fire, dropping things into a pan ' an' saying ower an' up agaain '—

> Fire cum,
> Fire gan,
> Curling smeeak
> Keep oot o' t' pan.
> Here's a teead, theer's a frog,
> An' t' heart frev a crimson ask;
> Here's a teeath fra t' heead
> O' yan at's deead,
> 'At nivver gat thruff his task[1];
> Here's pricked i' blood a maiden's prayer
> 'At t' e'e o' man maunt see;
> It's pricked reet thruff a yet warm mask,
> Lapt aboot a breet green ask,
> An' it's all foor him an' thee.
> It boils, thoo'll drink,
> He'll speeak, tho'll think,
> It boils, thoo'll see,
> He'll speeak, thoo'll dee.

Something seemed to say to Mary, ' Sha's working a curse on thee an' Tom ' (Tom was her sweetheart). 'Thoo mun deea summat, or sha'll mak mischief atween ya.' So Mary opened the door and walked boldly in. She then told the witch—for by this time she had no doubt her visitor was such—that she had heard all she had said, and seen all she had done. She then took hold of the Bible, and said, ' Ya mun deea yer warst; Ah ho'd byv this,' meaning the Bible. No sooner had she said that she had heard and seen all, and declared that she held by the Bible, and dared her to do her

---

[1] Never accomplished his life's work, i.e. committed suicide.

worst, than the witch turned the pan wrong side up
on the fire, and shrieking out, 'Thoo's 'scaped ma this
tahm, bud Ah'll mell on tha yet,' disappeared. Early
next morning a man rode over from Kildale, with the
news that Martha Sokeld was nowhere to be found,
and it was' not until three days afterwards that her
dead body was discovered on the moor head. The
conclusion come to at that time (and which my informant thought most probable) was that the witch had
lured Martha on to the moor and then spelled the soul
out of her, taking possession of the body herself, and
so deceived her grandmother. However, her grandmother lived until she was eighty-five, having brought
up a large family ; and so, as the old lady put it, 'Efter
that t' au'd witch 'ed nivver been yabble ti deea owt
tiv her ; sha aiblins off'ns aim'd ti deea, bud it seeams
'at it nivver cam tiv a heead.'

The following further information regarding Molly
Cass, the Leeming witch, of whom mention has been
made, was given to me by Abe Braithwaite, a noted
character of Bedale twenty-five years ago. Molly,
although a native of Exelby, lived for many years
in a cottage close to Leeming Mill : some declare in
a disused part of the mill itself. Be that as it may,
one night whilst the miller, two others, and Abe's
grandfather were playing cards in the mill, George
Winterfield (one of the players) had the nine of hearts
dealt to him eight times in succession. As the ninth
deal was proceeding, one of the players laid a guinea on
the table, offering to wager Winterfield that amount to
a shilling, that the nine of hearts did not fall to his
hand that deal. 'Put thi brass i' thi pocket,' said

Au'd Molly, popping her head just inside the door;
'thi brass is nut foor him, an' his brass is nut foor thee.
Put thi brass i' thi pocket, an' leeak sharp aboot it.'
So terrified was the owner of the guinea of gaining
the ill-will of Molly, that he pocketed his guinea
at once. When the last card of the deal fell, and
whilst the cards still lay on the table, Molly said,
'Thoo's gitten 't again, George; tak thi han' up and
see,' and such turned out to be the case. 'Aye,
thoo's gitten it hard eneeaf, an' thoo's had it eight
times alriddy; t' au'd un's[1] i' tha noo, an' he'll nut
leeav tha whahl he's gitten tha altogither. Thoo hed
thi chance, an' thoo wadn't tak 't, seea Ah've potched
it inti t' Swale' (the name of the river hard by), 'an'
thoo'll 'a'e ti gan theer ti late it. T' Swale's waiting ti
be thi brahdal bed. Thoo'd better gan noo; think on
t' langer thoo waits, an' t' langer thoo'll stay[2].' On
hearing this, George, turning as white as chalk, arose,
saying, 'Ah'll wed her; Ah'll mak an honest woman
on her, if thoo'll nobbut gi'e ma anuther chance; Ah've
rewd all 'at Ah've deean.' To which Molly replied,
'Ah's nut off'ns i' t' mahnd o' gi'ing onnybody yah
chance, let aleean tweea; thoo sez 'at thoo'll tak her ti
thi bed, Ah've sed 'at thoo s'all gan tiv hers. Noo,
then, gan thi waays; thi brahd's waiting foor tha, sha's
ligging asleep on a bed o' bulls an' segs. Oh, what a
brahdal bed! Oh, what a brahdal bed!' she screamed,
banging to the door.

Winterfield left the company, saying he would go

[1] 'T' au'd un,' or the old one = the devil.
[2] Possibly this meant the longer he waited there, the longer he
would rema'n in the river.

at once to his old sweetheart and promise to marry her. The night was intensely dark, and whether he missed his way and slipped into the beck, which was much swollen at the time, and his body drifted into the Swale, or whether it was as Molly shouted to him as he left, 'Good-neet, George, all roads leead ti t' Swale ti-neet,' it is impossible to say. One thing, however, is certain—though he joined his old sweetheart, he never saw her again. It was as a corpse the current carried him along, and left his body late that night by the side of her, who, only a few hours before, in a fit of desperation and despair, had confided to the silent waters the whole of her sin and shame. Both bodies were found quite close together, tightly held by the 'bulls and segs,' in the back-water where the beck joins the Swale. I well remember, when fishing near the spot late in the evening for eels, an old lady remarking on what she considered my temerity, for she fully believed that any one who ventured near at midnight would see the dead body of a girl, and presently that of a man, float by, both being quite visible until they joined each other in the high seaves and bulrushes.

· CHAPTER X

WITCHCRAFT—*continued*

So far as we have gone, it will be evident to those who read a little between the lines, that mixed up with fact, imagination, and exaggeration, there exists a very considerable amount of respectable myth. But to which of the ancient myths we owe many of the stories told in connexion with our local witches, is often somewhat difficult to determine; but certain it is that nearly all of them possessed the power, so common to those of an earlier date, of changing themselves into some animal, the hare and cat being the favourite forms which they assumed when hard pressed. Very similar stories exhibiting this power are told of the following well-known local witches, all of whom flourished during the present century :— Peggy Flaunders, of Marske-by-the-Sea ; Bessy Slack, of West Burton, Wensleydale; Nanny Pearson, of Goatland; the Guisborough witch, Ann Grear; Nan Hardwicke, of Spittal Houses ; Au'd Nanny, of Great Ayton ; Nanny Howe, of Kildale; and Nanny Newgill, of Broughton and Stokesley. Then there was Dolly Makin and Au'd Mother Stebbins, who seem to have had no regular place of abode, but tramped the country with a few small wares.

Of these and others, pretty much the same stories are told, differing only in slight details. These also bear a very strong resemblance to others current in different parts of Europe, but of much earlier times. Then, too, we have their malicious attacks on the dairy, either in the form of spoiling or purloining the produce, or in surreptitiously milking the cows, though the latter was more prevalent further north, and often practised by the German witches. But in the exercise of the evil eye, and in the committal of all manner of evil acts, our North Riding witches held a position second to none.

Again, the methods used to overcome their power and break their spells, as has been said, runs very much on the same lines throughout Europe.

Peggy Flaunders died in 1835, at the age of eighty-five, and was buried in the churchyard at Marske-by-the-Sea.

Many old people have a lively remembrance of Peggy, with her tall hat and red cloak ; and the stories which are told to-day of the pranks she played and the wonders she worked, make us open our eyes with amazement, because we are not listening to the marvellous deeds of some person who lived in mediaeval times, but of one who lived amongst those now living. Do you wish to hear of her doings from one who knew her? then find your way to Boyes Wetherell's cottage, and have a chat with the old worthy, and you will have such an outpouring of ancient customs, rites, lore, smuggling stories, and the doings of days gone by, together with touches of his own eventful life, as will stock your mind with information such as it is only possible to obtain from an original source [1].

But of Peggy and her doings.

On one occasion Peggy is said to have cast a spell against one Tom Pearson (who lived on a farm near Marske), and every head of cattle he possessed died. Whether this ruined him or not, is not known, but he left the farm, and his cousin took it. As this cousin crossed the threshold for the first time, Peggy passed by. (This cousin, it seems, had once befriended Peggy.) She called out to him as she passed, 'Thoo 'ez mah good wishes,' and with that she turned three times round, threw her cloak on the ground, jumped over it, mumbled something, and walked away, and from that day everything prospered 'awlus wiv him.'

For three weeks in succession, Hannah Rothwell's butter didn't come rightly, churn as long as she might; and at the same time Mary Parker, her next-door neighbour, began to get very little milk from her cow. These two old worthies having talked the matter over, decided they would pay a visit to Jonathan Westcott of Upleatham, a wise man of that day [2]. Jonathan, on hearing what they had to say, declared it was all owing to Peggy's malice. So far as Mrs. Rothwell was concerned, she was told to return home, scald her churn out three times, first with boiling water, in which a handful of salt had been dissolved; secondly,

---

[1] Boyes Wetherell lost his wife on the birth of their first child, a boy. Boyes tended his bairn with a mother's love and care, and when the child was four years old, he tramped all the way to London with the lad on his back. Once they slept in a grave; but the journey is a story.

[2] A contemporary of the wise man of Stokesley, but having nothing like the same reputation.

with boiling water in which a handful of wicken-tree berries had been thrown; and, thirdly, with a large amount of plain boiling water. She had also to get two small wickenwood pegs and drive them into each end of the churn, and whilst turning the churn with the last filling of water, she had to repeat, as she pretended to look if the butter was coming,—

> This tahm it's thahn,
> T' next tahm it's mahn,
> An' mahn foor ivver mair.

This had to be repeated nine times, giving nine turns before repeating the lines, when the churn would be found to be all right. At least it would be quite clean, and that is needful for the making of good butter. The milk case was a much more difficult one to tackle. However, after Jonathan had consulted his almanack, and seen what direction and position the heavenly bodies were in—he was great on the planetary world—he advised the following: first, a good drench [1] must be given the cow, followed by gentle exercise; secondly, it was not to be milked to its full yield for nine days, but on the tenth, before seating herself to milk, Mary had to whisper in the cow's ear, 'Ah's milking tha foor Peggy Flaunders.' The cow would then yield its proper quantity. This pious fraud of deliberately whispering tarradiddles into the cow's ear had to be continued indefinitely. On the other hand, if after having so whispered Mary drew no more milk than usual, Jonathan declared Peggy had nothing to do with the case, that she would be free from all suspicion of milking the cow at home

[1] An aperient drink.

by magic art, and that it was nothing 'neea warse 'an
that t' au'd coo war a larl bit oot o' fettle, an' wad
mebbins cum roond iv a bit; if nut, sha mud git shut
on't sumhoo.'

On one occasion some sportsmen, coursing in the
old close field at the top end of Marske, put up
a hare, which was recognized as one the dogs had
often tried unsuccessfully to capture. Peggy's son
was one of the company. The lad, it seems, had
heard his mother say no hare could escape their
black bitch, but he was to be very careful not to
mention the fact, and never to slip it at one without
her consent. In the excitement the lad disregarded
his mother's commands, and repeated what she had
said. The black bitch was slipped, and, after an
exciting chase, seized the hare by the haunch just
as it was trying to enter Peggy's worral hole[1]. On
Peggy being examined, teeth-marks were found on
a corresponding part of her body.

The Guisborough witch, Jane Grear, was perhaps
more widely known than Peggy. She, like Peggy, was
bitten by a dog, and bore the marks until the day
of her death. She received her injuries when trying
to jump through her own key-hole: it must have been
either a very small hare she had turned herself into,
or she must have owned an abnormally large key-hole;
but this is a matter of detail. Whatever Jane may
have been like in the decline of her life, in her youthful
days she must have been quite a good-looking girl.

---

[1] A worral hole is a drain-pipe let in the wall immediately at the
back of the fire; this is to afford sufficient draught to burn the sea
coal which is daily gathered from the beach.

There are two old rhymes still remembered, one of which tells of her various charms, perhaps a little too freely. So much into detail does it go, that only a few lines can possibly be given. The second recounts a mighty hunt which once took place.

. . . .

Plump ez a suker[1] war Jinny whęn young,
Wi' t' waast an' t' bust[2] ov a queen;
T' gallants an' t' bucks did all on 'em sweear
Sha beeat owt 'at ivver tha'd seen.
Her hair it war black ez an au'd raven wing,
An' breet war t' glint ov her een;
Neea kerchief hauf hid sike an *ivory breast*[2],
Whahl her throat wad 'a'e deean foor a queen;
An' larl war her feet, an' trim war her waast,
An' reead ez a roaze war her lips,
Whahl her cheeks egg'd yan on for ti steeal a sly kiss,
An' shaply an' roond war her hips.

. . . .

An' when, tripping ti music, sha pulled up her goon,
Tweea feet war nivver mair nim (nimble);
Her ankles an' buckles fair 'wildered yan's seet,
An' seea, mun, did t' shap ov each limb.
Bud noo 'at Ah's au'd, Ah finnd 'at sha's t' seeam.
Her charms 'ev all swithered awaay;
Sha's ugly ez muck, wi' black blood iv her heart.
Au'd Scrat's[3] bowt her sowl, seea tha saay.

. . . .

It would seem that Jane, like Peggy, occasionally afforded sportsmen a good run; at least, so the following would lead us to believe. But here, again, much has had to be suppressed, being unfit for publication. The lines, however, which are given are valuable, show-

---

[1] A sucking-pig.
[2] A cant phrase of the time is used in the original.
[3] The devil.

ing as they do that several old customs were quite common at the time—about 1820, I should imagine.

Fra t' Applegarth, ti Slapewath slack,
Wi'oot a rist i' seet all t' waay,
Sha (the hare) teeak uz roond byv t' alum warks
Ti Aisdale gaate, an' gat awaay.

Wa knocked at Tom's, bud he warn't up;
Bud then, it's t' seeam wiv all. Besahd,
Yan may loup up ti cauv a coo,
Bud finnd t' bed pull ti leeave a brahd.

Wa drank ther healths at Jack's belaw,
Wa wished em weel, an' soup'd wer beer,
All hoaping when tha did git up
Tha wad tigither loup on t' fleear[1].

Jack leeaked bit dazed, an' hauf asleep;
Bud then, he's a fair Tyke wi' t' lasses.
He cuddles, kisses, drinks wiv all;
Neea hot pot ivver by him passes.

T' race he'd won, an' t' brahd he'd kissed,
On t' thresho'd knelt, her garter gitten,
Fra snowy breasts ther kerchiefs stown,
Then wi' ther budding charms war smitten.

Again they put up the hare, and the old dog gave chase.

Fra Scaling dyke ti Wapley end,
Thruff Tommy[2] geese an' Mary[2] stee,
Alang t' au'd to'npike, here then theer
That witched hare alang did flee.

[1] Hand in hand, both touch the floor together. This has already been referred to.
[2] Observe the lack of the possessive case.

Neea cleeaser did wa ivver git,
Neea gerter leead it ivver teeak;
Ten yards i' front o' Billy bitch—
Fra t' fost it seeam'd a narrer squeeak.
At last 'mang heather, brackken, whin,
Lang stanghow bru', wi' hosses blawn,
An' Billy bitch wi' tongue loll'd oot,
Fair beeaten it war fain ti awn.
Just when, wi' yah gert loup, t' bitch thowt
Ti grab t' hare haunch, t' poor spent au'd bitch
Fan nowt ti snap at; t' hare 'ed geean.
An' then wa kenn'd wa'd hunted t' witch[1].

I know a very similar set of verses exist, telling
of a wonderful run after a hare in connexion with
Bilsdale and that district. But the language, in fact
the whole tone of the rhyme, is much too loose for
the publication of any part of it.

A word here explaining what is meant by witches
milking cows may not be out of place. It has been
mentioned that Peggy Flaunders was thought to have
drawn the milk from one Mary Parker's cow. How
or by what means, deponent sayeth not, but one
Ann Allan, of Ugthorpe, who kept pigs, was almost
caught in the act. This was about 1780, and as Ann's
procedure was run on much the same lines as the
most respectable witches used some hundreds of years
before her time, we may take hers as a typical
example.

Not one, but three or four Ugthorpe cows ceased
to give their usual quantity of milk. Of course the
villagers talked, and at last the priest was visited;

---

[1] The ground covered would be about twenty miles—not bad.

but a hundred years ago many of the clergy, both of Rome and the Church of England, so far as learning was concerned, would have been knocked into a cocked hat by a Primitive Methodist local brother of these days. So it will be readily conceived the visit to the priest resulted in very little good. He declared the devil had got hold of the defaulting cows by the tail, and this made them hold their milk back; he further assured them the only way to get the devil to let go was to say three pater nosters and Ave Marias over their milk-pails, and to subscribe a certain sum, which had to be paid to him, to celebrate a mass to Saint somebody, who would send a holy angel to frighten the devil away. Now, I know nothing about doctoring cows, but I am inclined to the belief that old Jonathan Westcott, of Upleatham, was much nearer effecting a cure, when he ordered an aperient draught, to be followed by gentle exercise, than prayers muttered inside any number of milk-cans.

I believe the good people of that day would have fallen in with the prayers, but they drew a hard and fast line when the collection box obtruded itself. They returned home dissatisfied. They were losing their milk—that they could not help; but they could prevent their pockets being dipped into, and they did. Another meeting was held, and a watch was set on Ann, but nothing came of it. At last a neighbour's cow dried up altogether. At this the good man was so exasperated, that he went to Ann's and boldly accused her of milking the cows. Words ran high, till in the end he seized a three-legged stool, intending to hurl

it at Ann's head, when, lo ! a curious thing happened—
as he gripped the leg of the stool, a stream of milk
ran from it. The neighbours, who by this time had
flocked round the door, cried out with one voice :
' Thoo's gitten 't ; that's what sha milks wer coos wi'.'
And sure enough such was found to be the case. On
the name of any neighbour's cow being mentioned, and
a leg of the stool handled as in milking, a fine stream
of milk came from it, and the bag of that individual's
cow was found on examination to have shrunk. No
wonder she had fat pigs, when she could give them
new milk in any quantity and from any one's cow she
liked to name. Such a stool was not a fit piece of
furniture for any one to possess, so it was publicly
burnt on the moor just beyond the high end of the
village, near to where the windmill stands. Ann was
ordered to walk three times from one end of the
village to the other, clothed in nothing but her sark [1],
i.e. chemise. The Godivan rule, which compelled
every one to keep within doors during the time of
penance, seems (so far as Ugthorpe was concerned)
to have been absolutely reversed—they were all there,
even down to the babies in arms. From all accounts,
Ugthorpe has never had quite such a lively time
since. Before judging the people and the ways of
that time as altogether too idiotic, indecent, and
unjust, it is as well to bear in mind that every age
has its curious idiosyncrasies. In 1898 affiliation cases
are heard in open court ; a man may nearly kick the
life out of his wife with a pair of clogs at a small

[1] A woman was adjudged the same punishment at Bedale (for a
different offence) in the year 1779, also at Thirsk and Northallerton.

outlay of about seven-and-six ; but stealing a turnip necessitates a low form of diet, and enforced seclusion for three months. These masterpieces of our time will bring a smile to faces yet unborn.

Nan Hardwicke's fame at one time was great, and her name and deeds still live in many of the Cleveland dales. I remember once being driven to Westerdale by an old chap, who gave me the following story. I think the circumstance occurred to his father, and not himself—on this point my notes are silent, anyway. Either his mother or his wife was expecting the advent of a new baby, and the expectant mother's sister had to be sent for, to some place about five miles distant. That afternoon Nan Hardwicke called as she was passing (she must have been some miles from home), and asked for 'a shive o' breead an' a pot o' beer,' which were given her. Nan let them know she was aware of all that was about to transpire. Finishing her food, she opened the door of the room where the wife was lying, and poking her head inside, said, ' Ah wish ya weell ; ya'll 'ev a lad afoor morning, an' ya'll call him Tommy, weean't ya ? ' ' Whya, wa 'a'e made up wer mahnds ti call him John,' replied the wife. ' Aye, mebbe, bud ya'd best call him Tommy ; an' thanking ya, Ah'll be saying good-daay ti ya.' And with that she closed the door and departed. The husband, on being made acquainted with the witch's request, declared that nothing of the sort should happen—John they had decided to call the bairn, and John it should be—he dare not run the risk of changing its name then. About six o'clock that evening the husband put his horse in the gig, or whatever he had, and drove away to bring back the sister-in-law. About three miles on the journey, he had to cross a small bridge, but when within twenty or thirty yards of it, the horse stopped, and could not be persuaded to move a step further. The good man at last decided to get out and lead the mare over, but in this he was wrong. Much to his amazement, he discovered he could not leave his seat—he was 'ez fast ez owt.' Vainly did he strive, but it was of no use. At last he came to the conclusion that a spell was on them both, so he called out, 'Noo, Nan, what's ti eftther? this is thi wark.' Immediately he heard Nan commence to laugh, and then she shouted, but he did not know where the voice came from, 'Thoo'll call t' bairn Tommy, weean't ta?' The husband was desperately bold for those days, for he shouted, 'Neea, Ah weean't, nowther foor thoo na all t' Nan divils i' t' country.' 'Then thoo'll bahd wheer thoo is, whahl t' bairn's born an' t' muther dees,' croaked Nan. This, in its way, was a bit of a clincher, to sit stuck fast in a gig, neither able to proceed nor get out, at a time too when all speed was necessary; add to this a sinister threat of immediate death of the one he most loved, unless he consented to christen an unborn child Tommy, when he had decided to name it Johnny, and with a feeling at the bottom of his heart that there was a margin for uncertainty, and that after all it might happen to be a girl. Taking all these things into consideration, was it to be wondered that he gave way, and swore the child, if a boy, should be christened Tom? Having made this promise, he was allowed to proceed on his way.

But Nan did not always have her own way. She had a habit of hiding herself amongst the whins and brackens, which grew in abundance near her humble roof. The young men used to collect all the hounds together and put them on the scent of Au'd Nan. According to legend, they had many a good run, ' bud tha nivver catch'd her.' One other unrecorded story of Nan [1].

Nan had a relation living at Lowna Bridge, to whom she occasionally paid a visit. This relation, I believe, only looked forward with pleasure to Nan's departure. On this point, however, Nan seems to have been pretty thick-skinned. It is a mystery how this journey was accomplished. Some thought she turned herself into a hare and ran the distance of twenty miles easily in that form; anyway, the fact remains that now and again Au'd Nan turned up at Lowna Bridge. It may, *en passant*, be mentioned that human nature was very much the same in the early part of this century as it is to-day. I mean, poor relations are never welcome; their presence, or anything which calls them to mind, makes one feel we ought to do something which we had very much rather not do— their presence digs the spur into one's conscience, you know! But to return to Nan and her Lowna relations. I believe the following occurred on her last visit: she arrived just after the bridal procession of the daughter of the house had returned from church. By-and-by the question arose—where could Au'd Nan sleep? On this particular occasion every bed had more

[1] For other interesting matter concerning Nan Hardwicke, *vide* Henderson's *Folklore*.

than one claimant already. The matter was solved by a kindly bridesmaid offering to take Nan home and share her bed with her, and then bring her back when the guests had departed. Unfortunately, the bride, not knowing that Nan was near, said to her friend, ' Relation though the old thing is, I would not sleep with her for anything.' At this Nan turned round and, before the whole company, exclaimed, ' Neea, bud thoo wad sleep wi' him,' pointing to the bridegroom ; and then she added, shaking her stick,—

> Ah've let tha be wedded,
> Bud Ah'll stop tha being bedded ;

and so saying, turned about and left the house. Good cheer and bonny bridesmaids soon banished any gloom the old lady's words for the moment had cast over the party.

Late that evening, after the bride had retired to rest, one of the bridesmaids, sister of the bridegroom, whispered to him, that it would be useless trying to join his bride by way of the stairs, as there was a plot on foot to keep him with the revellers the night long—not an uncommon thing in those days—it often needing all the scheming of bride and bridesmaids, to outwit the well-laid plots of the bucks of those gay old times. The plan which the bridesmaids had arranged for the bridegroom's escape, was that a game of blindman's-buff should be played, and on a given signal a maiden was to call out, ' Kiss the girl you love in the dark'; on this being said, every candle was to be blown out, and the bridegroom had to seize the opportunity to escape.

A ladder had been placed underneath the bride's window, and although it was a little short, the bridesmaids had tied a long towel to the window-sash, by which he could pull himself through the window. Everything worked splendidly until he was just going to pull himself up by the towel, when some half-intoxicated idiot discovered he was escaping, and pulled the ladder from underneath him, bringing him to the ground with an awful bang. The poor fellow, on being carried into the house, was found to have broken his leg. The old lady was right after all. It seems they did have their little excitements in the good old days of yore—in these days it is a shower of rice [1] and an old shoe.

Wrightson, the wise man of Stokesley, although he died about seventy years ago, has left such a record behind as few men in his position ever build up to their credit [2]. He was known as the wise man of Stokesley. He was the seventh son of a seventh daughter; and whether such a concatenation of circumstances lift a man out of the ordinary rut, I am not in a position to say. But judging Wrightson from the lips of those who knew him—they are all about gone now—or from those who have heard of him from their parents, one cannot but come to the conclusion, that he was undoubtedly a man endowed with marvellous psychic power, and with the smallest amount of charlatanry possible. In fact, all agree in testifying to the fact that he claimed nothing beyond

[1] Observe rice is now being ousted by confetti, which is much better—rice is so dangerous.

[2] This statement has nothing to do with his private life, only as that of a wise man. 'De mortuis nil nisi bonum.'

the power which belonged to all such as are born under similar circumstances; and that sort of thing was fully believed in then, and, I might add, is yet, for the matter of that.

In dealing with such a celebrity—for such he was, his fame extending far beyond the boundary of the North Riding—one cannot be too particular as to the source from whence information is obtained. Fortunately, years ago, I knew an old Yorkshireman, already alluded to—William Scorer, a native of Basedale, but who for some years kept an inn at Fearby above Masham. During the time I knew him, he was the landlord of the Fleece, Bedale. He personally knew Wrightson.

Take the following as examples of the man's marvellous power. A friend of Scorer[1] had bought several head of cattle at Northallerton fair. These had to be driven to Stokesley; to this end they were given in charge of an old drover who was driving a lot to the same place for another buyer. The drover, arriving late at night, put the two droves into a field about a quarter of a mile on the other side of Stokesley, but in the morning two of Scorer's beasts were missing; the drover declared they were all there when he gated them the night before. A suspicion somehow arose that the old chap had sold them on the way, and pocketed the money. At that time they were altogether without any proof that he had done anything of the kind.

The only way to discover if their surmises were

[1] This would be the father of the Mr. Scorer I knew, who for many years lived at Basedale Abbey.

correct, was to visit Wrightson. But to put the wise man's power to the test, they decided to say it was a horse they had lost; arguing, if he really knew anything that could help them, he would find out the trick which was being played upon him. On entering his cottage, and before they could speak, Wrightson shouted from the scullery, where he was washing himself, 'Noo then, if you chaps is sharp eneaaf, an' ez that mich off' (i. e. know that much) ''at ya can manish ti to'n tweea coos intiv a hoss, it's neea ewse cumin' ti me, foor Ah can't to'n a hoss back inti tweea coos, an' seea ya'd better mak yersens scarce. Ah've nowt ti saay ti ya.' And for some time the wise man was past all persuasion. In the end he shouted, without leaving the scullery, 'Tha're baith i' t' beck, an' tha've been theer sen yester neet.' And sure enough both their bodies were found a good mile below the bridge; evidently they had missed the bridge when being driven over late the night before, and had both been drowned in the Leven, which was much swollen by recent rain. Here, as in many other stories told of the marvellous man, was an evidence of foreknowledge; and many of them rest upon what must be admitted to be very reliable testimony, and vouched for by most respectable people of that time[1]. Now for the other story, which occurred some years afterwards.

One Nathan Agar, for security, hid a stocking-foot (in which he had wrapped five golden guineas) under a portion of the thatch. One day, intending to add another golden one to his store, he found the stocking-

---

[1] I know that Mr. G. Markham Tweddle holds quite contrary views. His idea is that Wrightson was little better than a huge swindler.

foot, guineas and all, had vanished. Nathan said nothing to any one, but just went straight to Wrightson.
'Thoo'll knaw what Ah've cum'd aboot,' said Nathan.
Wrightson at once twitted the old man, touching
some previous conversation they had held as to the
advisability of Nathan, who was about sixty years
of age, marrying a girl not quite nineteen. But the
combined wisdom and unhappy future which had
been foretold by Wrightson, had not been sufficient
to overcome the old fool's idiotic passion for the buxom
lass. In the end he was told to go home, and when
no one was in the house, he had to lift up the flag in
front of the doorstep, and place a certain leaf of the
Bible underneath, and carefully watch who stumbled
over the threshold as they entered. This, Nathan
most carefully carried out. The first who entered
was their young lodger, and he stumbled ; after awhile
in came the wife, and she stumbled. I don't know if
the flag tilted, or whether the next person would have
stumbled also, because Nathan didn't wait to test
the result of a third entry, but hurried off to Wrightson,
to whom he made known the result. Wrightson told
him that his property was hidden in a certain part of
a pig-sty, together with an old watch, which up to
that time Nathan had not missed. Other and more
serious charges were made, which for ever destroyed
Nathan's hope of future happiness. Wrightson's advice
was that he should return home, secure his watch,
give them the five guineas, and send them about
their business. This was promptly carried out, and
I believe is the quickest and cheapest divorce proceeding on record. One other story has just come into

my mind, which, if true, proves to what a wonderful
degree he must have possessed a clairvoyant power.

A lady residing in some part of South Durham
was likely to die from a lump in her throat—possibly
a quinsy. Nothing that was done gave her ease;
at last some one suggested the wise man of Stokesley.
A man on horseback was dispatched—I believe the
son of the lady. On approaching Wrightson's house,
even before he got to the door, the wise man looked
out, saying, as the young man came up, 'Bait thi
hoss, git summat ti eat, an' git thisen back agaan;
t' bleb's brussen; sha's all reet now;' i.e. 'Bait your
horse, get some refreshment, and return home again;
the lump has burst; she is all right now.'

I have just had the following story given me by
Old Willie Bradley of Great Ayton. His father, who
was a quarryman, had some tools stolen, and, like
every one else in those days, he went to Wrightson.
'Noo, then,' said that worthy, on Willie's father
entering, 'thoo's cum'd aboot thi teeals, bud Ah can
deea nowt fur tha, ez they've been hugg'd accross
watter; bud Ah can let tha see wheear tha're liggin.'
Wrightson then put him in front of a seeing-glass
(looking-glass) in a darkened room, and told him to
keep looking at the glass, telling him if he took his
eyes off something awful would happen, but my informant cannot remember what. Anyway, his father
never was so terrified in all his life, and wished he had
never bothered about the lost tools. In a little while,
however, he saw them quite plainly, lying amongst
some bracken in a wood—the place he recognized
quite easily. On telling Wrightson what he had seen,

he was cautioned not to touch them. Wrightson said he must bring him a live magpie. This he tried to obtain, but failed; he could not catch one, neither, for some reason, would any boy who had one part with his pet; so, after a week, he had to tell the wise man that the task was impossible. 'Then,' said Wrightson, 'Ah caan't wark him onny harm, an' thoo'll 'a'e ti loss the teeals [1].'

Other stories of this man's foreknowledge could be given almost ad lib. Many of his methods suggested and adopted were of the heart-frizzling, pin-sticking, wickenwood, and bottery-tree order. His rites and ceremonies, too, occasionally savoured of the time in which he lived; and, after all, there is not much to wonder at.

We are most of us very much influenced by the environments of our own day; and after seeing a few of my own sex in Town, I can forgive Wrightson much. Like many another clever man, he played to suit his audience, and sang the songs of the day. There was, if all is true, no need that he should have done so, and possibly he knew it—who knows?

Nanny Pearson was held in great fear by the good people of Goathland, and that, too, a good way into the present century. As a witch of the old school, Nanny's fame was not confined to that locality. Many stories are still told of her and her doings, two of which I will give, as they afford a bit of new information, i.e. the power which holy water had over witches. I believe in her younger days she was

---

[1] For other authentic stories of Wrightson, *vide* Henderson's *Folk-lore.*

a communicant of the Roman Catholic faith; be that as it may, she was neither better nor worse than her sister witches of any other faith, or no faith at all. It seems that a Mrs. Webster had a goose, which, as was the custom of the time, was sitting on a cletch of eggs near the fireside. Now, Nanny came daily to Mrs. Webster's for milk, bringing an empty jug, which she left, taking a full one away with her. The goose was set one morning, and remained dutifully on her nest until evening; but as Nanny approached the house, off flew the goose in a great state of agitation, breaking two eggs, and could not be pacified until Nanny was well off the premises. The same thing occurred each time Nanny came for her milk, until some one, who was going to Scarborough, called upon the wise man and asked his advice. He told them to get a little holy water, put it in the jug with Nanny's milk, and her power would be broken—I suppose that meant her power over the goose, for she worked a vast deal of ill after that. This was done; the jug with the holy water and milk in due course was handed to Nanny, and just as she took hold of it, the goose plucked up courage and flew at her, knocking it out of her hand. It was broken in the fall, the contents splashing over her feet and gown; with a shriek she fled, and from that day the goose was never disturbed again.

Years ago, the Squire of Goathland had a very beautiful daughter. Some old chap with any amount of money, and quite ugly, wished to wed her, and for some unknown reason the Squire favoured his suit; but, as is often the case, the damsel had given her heart to a young farmer in the neighbourhood. The elder lover got it into his head the couple would elope, so he sought the aid of Nanny; and the old hag helped him with a vengeance, inasmuch as she so sorely afflicted the damsel that she could not rise from her bed, and her legs began to die—I don't quite know what that means; anyway, her limbs became useless. Her father told her that one of the female saints was greatly displeased with her obduracy, and would not restore power to her limbs until she consented to marry the man of his choice. This she flatly refused to do, choosing rather to die outright. The younger lover was distracted; he could not gain any reliable information, and a personal interview was impossible. So he did as every one else did in those days—he paid a visit to the wise man of Scarborough. The wise man, after a considerable performance of his own, placed a seeing-glass in front of the young fellow, desiring him to gaze steadily thereon, and to tell him if he saw the likeness of any one appear. Presently the young chap swore he had seen the face of Nanny Pearson. The wise man, on hearing this, declared that she was the origin of all the evil, and told him to return home, procure by some means a drop of Nanny's blood, and steal a few drops of holy water; these had to be mixed in a cup of milk drawn from a red cow, and rubbed by him on the soles and calves of his lady-love, when all would be well. This was a strongish order, and well-nigh staggered the young chap. Firstly, how was he to procure a drop of Nanny's blood? Stealing the holy water was a simple affair, as also was the red cow's milk; but how to gain admission to his lady-love's chamber, and apply the remedies when obtained, was not only a task of difficulty, but of danger. Bear in mind this was in the days of dogs and horsewhips, which were often freely used; but then, as now, love laughs at difficulties. Once let him become possessed of a drop of Nanny's blood, and he would overcome all the other obstacles. On making his trouble known to an old dame in the village, one Janet Haswell, she told him something he already knew in part, i.e. that in a certain field a hare nightly sat, which neither dog could catch nor man shoot; this hare, declared the old lady, was none other than Nanny herself. She further assured him that if he melted some silver and made shot of it, he would be able to hit the hare, and perhaps he might find some blades of grass stained with blood. Most carefully the young fellow carried out the old dame's advice. He was successful; he hit the hare, and found several blades of grass spotted with blood, which he carefully gathered. Next day Nanny was confined to bed, and for some weeks after. At the time, he alone knew the cause. Having procured a ladder, he invaded his love's room, and applied the remedy, when she recovered instantly; he then retired. The damsel, rising and dressing herself, descended the ladder, and was conveyed to a place of safety, where she remained until they were wedded. This, by-the-way, I believe is the first recorded case of massage.

A curious belief still clings to Gribdale Gate. Any one who dares to stand near the said gate on

New Year's Eve, will see an old man open it, pass through, and then vanish. This takes place just as the new year is born. There is one man still living in Great Ayton who has seen the old chap thus herald in the new year. Again, old people of Great Ayton still aver that on a certain night a once noted witch, Nanny Howe, may be seen riding astride on a broomstick over Howe Wood just at midnight. This witch, so mounted, is said once to have chased the devil for miles—on this occasion the two must have fallen out; perhaps at that time honest folk got their due. Howe Wood is near Kildale.

Ailer Wood, her real name being Alice, was a witch of considerable note throughout the Bilsdale district fifty years ago. In the form of a cat or hare, she seems to have cared little either what kind or colour the hounds were which chased her. She never was caught, but then she had a little way of making herself invisible when too hard pressed; but in this she was not alone, a case in point having already being mentioned. Innumerable times was she fired at, ' bud nivver nobody could hit her.' On one occasion a damsel named Annie Wilson felt sure the old thing had bewitched her sweetheart. The reason for such a supposition lay in the fact that the young fellow had transferred his affections to some other fair charmer. My idea is that the other girl had bewitched him; that, however, was not Annie's notion. She, like many another maiden of her time, went with the sorrow of her aching heart to the wise man of those parts, one Henry Wilson, who, after carefully listening to Annie's woeful story, told her how she could discover if it was the witch who had cast a spell on her lover. She was to return home, turn the cricket[1] wrong side uppermost, pushing pretty close together and very securely into the wood nine pins, saying, as she pushed in the last one, 'There's nine for him and her and the witch'; in another place she had to push in another nine, repeating at the ninth, 'There's nine for the witch and her and him'; and lastly, in another place, another nine, concluding at the ninth by saying, 'And there is nine more for all three of them, wi' her in t' middle.' By this arrangement, the vile creature who had stolen her lover, was always mentioned so that she occupied a place nearest the witch. All this having been accomplished, the stool had to be set on its feet, and, under some pretext or other, Ailer was to be induced to seat herself thereon. On doing so, she would be unable to get up again until she truly answered any questions Annie asked her. Everything was carried out as ordered by Wilson: Ailer was called in, and offered a cup of tea, the stool having been pushed toward her; she was invited to seat herself, and have her bite and sup comfortably. Now, was ever a maiden nearer finding out just why her lover had deserted her? The stool was even put in front of the fire, and Ailer again invited to seat herself; but no, the witch quietly replied, it would not be possible for her to enjoy the good things they had given her, seated on the back of a 'pricky-back otch'n[2].' Ailer by some means had found out what had been done, and so escaped the charm which had been prepared for her.

[1] A small four-legged stool.   [2] A hedgehog.

No doubt exists in the minds of many people now, that hedgehogs milk the cows[1]. It seems they creep up to them whilst they are resting, and draw their milk from them. My old friend told me they always killed a hedgehog whenever they saw one, for that reason.

One Nancy Newgill, a Broughton witch, used to set hedgehogs to milk the cows of those she had a spite against, and it was commonly believed that at times she used to turn herself into one, and then ' neeabody's coos had onny chance'; anyway, there was one hedgehog which could run as fast as a hare, and never was catched, ' ner killed ner nowt.' This Nancy Newgill cast a spell on a certain Martha Brittain, from which she could obtain no ease, no matter what she took ; so off to the wise man[2] Martha went. She was told to go to Stokesley, and buy a new fire-shovel, upon which she had to chalk Nancy's name[3]; then to make a cake—the ingredients need not be given—and, after closing her doors and window, the cake was to be baked upon the shovel resting on the fire. This was done at four o'clock in the afternoon[4]. Now, at the time this cake was being baked, Nancy Newgill was ' luking' weeds in a field a mile away, and standing quite close to her was my informant, Mrs. Peary. Suddenly Nancy clapped her hand on her stomach, crying out, ' Ah mun gan yam ! Ah mun gan yam !'

[1] I met a man in the train the other day who said he had often seen them sucking.
[2] Henry Wilson, of Broughton, was a wise man of some repute after Wrightson's time.
[3] Something like Sadler and Clarke's method.
[4] The usual time was midnight; this case, so far as I know, is unique.

She left the field, and was ill for days after; but Martha Brittain began to mend straight away, and was as right as ever she could be.

This, however, is a small affair, compared with the case of a man who lived at Broughton, and had a spell cast on him, by whom he did not know; at least, he was divided in his doubts. He suspected first Nancy, and also a man with an evil eye at Nunthorpe, but he could not really say which of them had cast the spell; so he went to the wise man, but in this he got little comfort. The wise man told him, before he could do anything he must be quite certain who had cast the spell, because if he worked a counter-charm on any one, and they were innocent, what he did would fall upon the complainant, in addition to what he was already suffering. He advised him to 'plump[1]' both Nancy and the Nunthorpe man with it. On accusing Nancy, she was so indignant, and looked him so straight in the face, and swore such a fearful oath, that he felt certain she for once was innocent; in such contrast was the behaviour of the evil-eyed one of Nunthorpe, that he was equally satisfied that he was the man. So sure was he, that he told the wise man he would chance it; so they set to work. A fire of wickenwood having been lighted close on midnight, a ball of clay was beaten flat with the back of an old Bible; on this a rude figure was scooped out in the shape of a man. Into this rough mould was poured a mixture of pitch, beeswax, hog's lard, bullock's blood, and a small portion of the fat from a bullock's heart. The whole having

[1] Accuse openly.

been melted and well stirred on the wickenwood fire, what remained of the mixture after filling the mould was divided; one-half was thrown into water, worked into a ball, and thrown away; the remaining portion was poured on to the fire, causing a most tremendous blaze; when this died out, the ashes were buried in the churchyard. The figure having been removed from its mould, and two small holes made to represent the eyes, a pin was thrust into one of these eyes, an incantation pronounced, and the spell was concluded. The pain left the man as he was returning home, and that very night the evil-eyed Nunthorpian was seized with a fearful pain, and before morning was blind of an eye—the eye corresponding to the one through which the pin had been thrust in the wax figure. I had the above from one who well knew the trio. My informant is still living.

Matthew Appleton, of Busby, for many years ruled the planets—it seems he ruled them so well that he found a pot of gold. This was ruling the planets to some purpose, and it is a great pity astronomers don't work this seemingly dead science up a bit.

In connexion with the witch-lore of the riding, it strikes one as singular, that whilst many of the stories told of local witches closely resemble those of other countries, yet other stories, equally common, both abroad and a little further north, so far as I have investigated, are with us conspicuous by their absence. Of witches turning their victims into horses by throwing a bridle over their heads and riding them the night through, or of a witch having been outwitted and treated in like manner, even in some instances casting a shoe, and of being reshod during the night, the shoe remaining nailed to the hand on regaining their natural form—of such stories, I repeat, not a vestige remains amongst us. Thorpe's *Mythology* and the Wilkie MS. give many instances; and though some of the stories are dated almost in recent times, doubtless their radicals are to be found in the myth of times remote.

Again, whilst we retain the belief in the efficacy of the dead hand in the curing of certain diseases, one never hears mention of the 'hand of glory[1].' There are old people to-day who tell you of its marvellous power, but their knowledge is that gained from hearsay. I have never met a single person who knew of an instance of its having been used in the North Riding; and if ever such was the case, it must have been long ago, for many of the old folk know absolutely nothing about it.

Silver shot was a deadly charge, because, in some way not explained, it was charmed. Jane Wood, who was accounted a witch about seventy years ago in the Basedale district, gave little heed either to dogs or guns; when she assumed the form of a hare, she escaped from the former quite easily, and the latter never could hit her. At last one sportsman, acting

---

[1] To prepare a 'hand of glory,' the hand of a man who had been hanged had to be left for some days in a special kind of pickle; afterwards it was dried in the sun, and then parched in the smoke of certain herbs. A special kind of candle had to be made from certain fats; with this candle lighted and stuck in the dead man's hand, a hypnotic sleep could be cast upon a whole household. Henderson's *Folklore*.

on the advice of a wise man, melted some silver coins in an iron ladle smeared with the blood of a hare. This was done at the blacksmith's forge, the same being plentifully supplied with wickenwood. The melted silver was poured into a basin of water, which divided it into fine particles; suitable pieces were collected, the gun charged, and next evening the venturesome hare was fired at. Though it escaped, it was evidently badly hit. Suspicion had for some time rested on Jane. Her cottage was visited; she declared she was too ill to rise and open the door, having, as she said, accidentally turned a beehive over and got severely stung. This statement did not satisfy those outside. The door was burst open, and Jane pulled out of bed; over one part of her body she was found to be covered with small sores, which there was no doubt had been caused by the silver shot. Anyway, that venturesome hare was never seen again, so no further proof was required.

There is one point which requires a few words of explanation, at least so far as it can be explained. We have heard of witches who allowed themselves to be chased as hares, some of which, if not caught, were bitten just as they were entering their own homes; on examination, teeth-marks were found on a corresponding part of their body. The same may be said of the injuries inflicted by the silver shot. The telling of these stories leaves no doubt in one's mind that the witches in the cases mentioned are supposed to have turned themselves into hares. This, however, was not always the case, as the following story will show. There was a woman on whom grave suspicion rested; for some reason or other she was never openly charged with being a witch, but old heads were ominously shaken when her name was mentioned. In the district in which she lived, there was a notorious hare, which simply jeered at dogs and guns alike. At length some one suggested silver shot; this was duly made, and the hare shot dead. Afterwards, on comparing the times, it was found that Mrs. —— had thrown up her arms the very moment when the hare was shot, ejaculating, 'They have killed my familiar spirit'; uttering these words, she fell dead on her kitchen floor. Now Mrs. —— had not been out that day—there were plenty of witnesses to testify that—so it would seem it was not always a case of transformation, but a familiar spirit which was chased, whilst the individual herself was at home attending to her household duties. Of course all such were subject to the ills which might befall their familiars.

There seems to be a very close connexion between a hare being shot and corresponding wounds being found on the person of those who had so transformed themselves, and the stories told of the witch mares being shod and the shoes remaining fixed to their hands when their original form was resumed.

Hobmen.

At one time the family of Oughtred, who lived on a farm near Hob Hill, Upleatham, were greatly assisted in their various occupations by the hobman, who lived in the Hob Hill. These hobmen are heard of now and again in the North Riding. The hobman[1] with us seems to hold the same place as the brownies of the north, and the pixies of Devonshire. Anyway, the hobman still did his work as recently as 1820; for the Oughtreds had their hay turned, their cattle brought home and driven back again, their corn and other grain winnowed, their turnips topped and tailed, and I do not know what all. What they did to offend the hobman, is not known. But it is thought that a man hung his coat on the winnowing machine, and forgot to remove it when his day's work was done. The hobman possibly thought, when he entered late at night, that it had been left for him; and no offence, it seems, could be greater than to offer a hobman clothes of any kind, so he went away, and has never been heard of since. It seems at the very time they unfortunately displeased their friend the hobman, they also incurred the ill-will of Peggy Flaunders; for about this time, late one evening, a fearful knocking came at the back door. The maid, on opening it, saw a fearful thing like a blazing pig standing on the step; with one wild shriek she fled, crying out to her master and mistress that the devil had come, and was standing on the back doorstep. They at once asked, had she closed the back door? On being told that she was too frightened to do anything else but flee from such a monster, they both sank back in dismay, well knowing the evil spirit had been given a chance to enter, which they rightly feared it would not fail to avail itself of. They rushed to the back door, but nothing was there;

[1] There was a marvellous hobman once lived near Ripon, but his deeds some one writing of the West Riding must chronicle.

still they had their misgivings—they were terribly
apprehensive. And sure enough it turned out not
without cause—crockery was smashed, machinery was
broken, cattle died; in fact things got into such a parlous state, that they decided to leave. On the day
when they were preparing to flit, a friend looked in,
and asked Oughtred if he really meant shifting. As
he asked the question, a queer little head popped out
over the top of the press, and a voice squeaked out,
'Aye, we're gahin ti flit ti morn'; on hearing which,
Oughtred said, 'Whya, if thoo's gahin wiv uz, it's teea
neea ewse gahin; wa mud ez weel stop[1].' The wise
man was eventually consulted. Legend sayeth not
where he lived; but under his directions a live black
cock bird was pierced with pins, and roasted alive
at dead of night, with every door, window, and cranny
and crevice stuffed up. By these means Peggy's power
and the imp were overcome.

Years ago, when the old church at Marske-by-the-
Sea was condemned, and a new one about to be built,
it was decided to pull down the old structure and use
the stone for building the new. This bit of vandalism
was duly commenced; part of the old building was
razed, and the stone carted to the new site[2]—so
far, so good. The old people murmured, for they
objected greatly to the demolition of the edifice in
which they and their fore-elders had worshipped;
but they were powerless—they could only stand by
and watch with aching hearts stone after stone

[1] With slight variation the same story is known in other parts of
the riding, also in Lancashire, and is as old as the hills throughout
Scandinavia.

[2] A similar story is told of Sir Francis Drake.

being carted away. And so the first day's work came to an end, which to them was work of desecration, and they returned home sad at heart. But if they were powerless, they had a champion, and one whom they had never dreamt of taking up their cause. Next morning, when the men returned to their work, what was their surprise, and the amazement of every one else, to find the old church whole again, without a stone displaced or a mark of the previous day's work to be found anywhere. Every stone had been brought back again and replaced *in situ,* and the mortar which had been used to reset the displaced stones was as hard and set as that of hundreds of years before.

This marvellous occurrence was duly reported at head-quarters. What the officials thought or imagined, is not recorded; they ordered the work to proceed, and even set on more men to pull the old place down, so that on the second day a considerable portion was carted away and stacked on the new site; but next morning the old church was found to have been fully repaired during the night, every stone having once again been brought back and placed in its original position. Things were now looking a bit serious. On the third day, however, work was resumed, a portion again pulled down and carted away, but this time men were set to watch the stones and find out who came for them. Now, whether these watchers fell asleep—they declared they did not—or whether in the darkness the stones were all stolen away so quietly that they never heard or saw anything of what was transpiring, cannot be stated; one thing is only known —when daylight appeared, every stone had vanished, and again the old church was found to have been restored, so perfectly that no one could tell that ever a stone had been removed. Those in authority were bound to admit that it was useless to contend further against such a powerful and invisible opponent. For long it was not generally known by what means the work of replacement had been wrought; but there were those who knew, and in time every one did. It was the hobman, assisted by others of his friends. In those days it was simply the essence of folly for architects and bricklayers to pit themselves against a hobman, just the same as it would be to-day, if the hobmen took it into their heads to undertake a job—but they don't now.

There was a hobman once had his home in a hill near to Hob Garth, and no doubt in his day performed many acts which are now forgotten; however, I had one related to me years ago by an old chap who at that time was working on the Mulgrave estate. His grandfather, Thomas Stonehouse, lived at Hob Garth for many years. I think he had a small holding; any-way, he kept sheep. It seems that some misunderstand-ing arose between him and one Matthew Bland, of Great Fryup. Bland was of a vindictive nature—at least, if the supposition was true that he broke Tommy's hedge down late one night, drove the sheep out, and left them to wander whither they liked. And wander they did to some purpose, for at the close of the day following, Stonehouse had only managed to find five out of forty. Next morning, what was his sur-prise not only to find his sheep back in the field, but the hedge repaired with new posts and rails. The neighbours knew that he could not have done the repairing, for he had caught a severe cold, having been wet to the skin searching for the lost sheep the day previous. Next night, however, every head of cattle belonging to Bland was turned loose. 'And great deed there was lating on 'em; it war ower a fo'tnit afoor they war all gitten tigither again.' That Stonehouse was quite innocent of this bit of retaliation was clear even to Bland, as it was well known he was too ill to stir out of doors. But when Bland had recovered all his lost cattle, Stonehouse's were set loose again, and the damage done was even greater this time; and as the poor fellow was still too ill to turn out to find them, the neighbours did what they could. This time, however, even fewer were found, but again on the following morning all but four were safely back in the field, and all damage repaired; subsequently the four were found dead, having fallen into a disused quarry. People talked, as naturally they would, and the bringing back of the lost sheep and repairing of the rails was put down to the hobman. When this conclusion was come to, heads were shaken in an ominous manner, for evidently if Tommy was be-friended by the hobman, Matthew would have to mind what he did. As soon as Tommy could, he set off to see his sheep. It happened to be rather late when he paid the first visit after his illness, owing to the fact that a neighbour was driving past where the sheep were, and as he was returning presently, he offered to put Stonehouse down and pick him up again as he returned. Tommy counted his sheep, and after cutting some hay for them—it was winter time—he sat by the gate waiting for the return of his neighbour. Presently an old man accosted him, and begged him not to fret about the lost sheep, as they would be more than compensated for when lambing time came. The old chap told him that Bland had on both occasions been guilty, but that he had not to mind. Just then his friend drove up. Tommy bade his new acquaintance good-night, thanked him, and got into the cart. No sooner was he seated, than the good neighbour asked him what he meant by saying good-night and thanking nobody at all. It transpired that the owner of the cart had not noticed any one speaking to Tommy. In the end he thought the old chap 'war a bit waak an' rafflin.' Anyway, when lambing time came, though the weather was very severe, and every one else, and more particularly Bland, lost many lambs, Stonehouse never lost one. Ewes, during Tommy's absence, were found safely delivered of their lambs, and mostly had two, and never a black one amongst them. 'An' noo that war a larl bit sing'-lar, warn't it? Bud then, ya knaw, i' them daays when t' hobman did tak ti yan, ya war yal reet i' t' lang-run; an' ivvery wo'd 'at Ah've tell'd ya's trew, 'coz Ah've heeard mah gran'father tell t' taal ower an' up agaan; bud it's a gay bit sen noo,' wound up my informant. The hobman was described as a little old fellow, with very long hair, large feet, eyes, mouth, and hands, stooping much as he walked, and carrying a long holly stick. The date of the story would be about 1760.

P

CHAPTER XI

SOME CHARACTERISTIC YORKSHIRE SAYINGS

Kindly contributed by the Rev. M. C. F. MORRIS, B.C.L., M.A.,
Author of *Yorkshire Folk-Talk.*

THERE is a saying current among us in the East
Riding that 'it takes a Yorkshireman to talk Yorkshire'; the very form of the expression smacks of
the county; and if this be true, as true it is, of the
mere pronunciation of the dialect, it is no less true
with regard to those other linguistic features—the
idioms, phraseology, and way of putting things, which
in this, as in every other folk-speech, go to a great
extent to make up the vernacular. We might even
advance a step beyond the statement just quoted,
for by no means the majority even of those who
have lived in the county all their lives can tongue
the speech aright, and many not at all. It is far
from uncommon to hear an accurate pronunciation
of the dialect from the lips of those who are supposed
to speak it well, and to find at the same time
that the speaker wholly lacks an appreciation of
those modes of thought, those turns and peculiarities
of expression in which the Yorkshire dialect is
peculiarly rich, and without which it sounds by
comparison only tame and feeble. As between dog-

Latin and the well-turned and polished, though often long-winded, sentences of Cicero, so is it in some sort between the two styles of dialectical Yorkshire to which I refer. The one grates upon the ear, while the other rings true. Over and above idiomatic usages strictly so called, there are many sayings more or less familiar which, though they cannot be brought under any rules of speech, like those of grammar, yet seem to possess a certain raciness all their own, and at the same time bring before us something of the Yorkshireman's force and character. To some of these I will here direct attention, though it must be understood that what are here cited are but a few disconnected specimens of many more which might be given.

We are most of us, no doubt, aware that in all his dealings and matters of business the Yorkshireman is pre-eminently of a strongly practical turn of mind. We 'reckon nowt' of a man who is not that.

It would be untrue to say that sentiment is a state of mind absolutely unknown to his nature; but its presence is so rare, and its hold upon him so feeble, that it need hardly be taken into account in considering his character. There may, no doubt, be times when such feelings are brought into play, but the strange thing is that when we might most reasonably look for them, we look in vain.

Those attractive personal charms of the gentler sex which with ordinary mortals are generally supposed to have their effect at times when a young man is seeking a partner for life, weigh but little for the most part with the matter-of-fact Yorkshire-

man who regards his intended from a severely
practical point of view. What, we may ask, would
the sentimentalist of the highly strung poetical
temperament think of this piece of advice which
was once given to a youth at an interesting period
of his life? 'Leeak at a lass's han's when thoo's
laatin' a weyfe; deean't be daffled wiv 'er feeace!'
It was said in the olden days that the lass who
churned 'wi' buckles on her shoon' was to be lightly
esteemed, but for sheer practicality the manual test
could hardly be surpassed. I well remember, many
years ago, the case of a man who was twice married.
His first wife proved herself an excellent one in every
way, and the couple lived happily together. When
she died, and he proceeded to look out for a successor,
his choice fell on one who also turned out a no less
industrious and tidy woman, though her personal
attractiveness was not of a specially pronounced
character. On being asked by a neighbour what
led him to make his selection in the way he did, he
made answer to the effect that his sole reason for
doing so was because his second wife's 'carcase'
reminded him so strongly of that of his first; she
was a lithe, active woman, and he thought, no doubt,
that she looked like work.

Despite these purely utilitarian considerations in
matters matrimonial, the saying we have heard that
the 'sweetness of a posy mainly hings on fra wheear
yan gits it,' indicates that some at least of our country-
folk, under certain favouring conditions, can say pretty
things, though it must be confessed such elegancies
are few and far between. The ordinary village gossip

who neglects her household duties for the sake of 'having a crack' with her neighbours, has from 'pre-historic times,' no doubt, come in for much plain-speaking, of which this may be given as an example: 'T' weyfe 'at can ho'd her au'd man up wi' t' news oot o' t' toon, meeastlins bakes bo'nt breead.' Such wives as these are not the ones to pay much heed to principles of domestic economy. Nevertheless, considerations of this kind are as a rule carefully thought out by our country-folk, if not scientifically, at least in a way that makes a shilling go as far as possible. It may be said, indeed, speaking generally, that domestic affairs receive, on the part of the York-shire wife, an amount of attention that is highly commendable, and adds not a little to the happiness of the family, and in no part of England do the people understand the meaning of the word 'comfort' better than they do in Yorkshire.

Cleanliness is a virtue for which our people have long been conspicuous, though even here extremes will sometimes meet, and excessive scrupulousness in this respect will at times be something of a burden to the household rather than a joy.

It was once said of a 'gudewife' whose washings, scrubbings, polishings, and brushings were performed with more than ordinary frequency and vigour, ' Sha scrats an' tews fra morn whahl neet; sha werrits an' natters an' grummels t' daay lang. . . . ' There's neea comfort i' t' hoos; an' ther nivver is wheear t' kettle's breet all ower.'

In days gone by it used to be said that a 'calling' wife and a dusty spinning-wheel were commonly associated together, and the saying, 'A mucky moos-trap shoots' (shouts) 'for t' cat,' was one of those standing rebukes to a slatternly *mater familias* which is tellingly put, while the following doggerel might well find a place on the walls of every kitchen :—

> A cobweb i' t' kitchen
> An' feeat-marks on t' step
> Finnd neea wood i' t' yewn
> An' neea cooals i' t' skep.

No theme is more frequently harped upon by our old folks, when contrasting present manners and customs with those of a generation or two ago, than the change that has come over the community in the matter of dress, and there is a moral which they commonly draw therefrom. 'There's sadly owermich prahd noo,' say they ; while the money that many of the young people spend upon their dress passes the understanding of their elders, who in their younger days were content with fustian jackets and print gowns. It was said, for instance, by one who held that a hood was a suitable head-covering for a woman, that 'she is a feeal 'at hugs a geease' (i.e. the price of a goose) 'on t' top of her heead.' In consequence of extravagancies of this nature, it is doubtful if, in spite of increased wages and cheapness of living, our farm lads and lasses save as much money as they did in the olden days. With corn at the high price it was, say, fifty years ago, the people were early inured to thrifty ways, and the absolute necessity for carefulness in all things was frequently insisted upon. Thus, for instance, a child would be told that 'a beean thrawn away at t' fore-end is a dinner lost at t' back-end.' Few of those living now would credit with what hard fare their grandfathers had often to be content, and yet the physique of the men which those times produced was probably not inferior, in point of endurance and capacity for work, to that at the present time.

Most of us, I dare say, remember the schoolgirl's reply when asked to define scandal, namely, 'When no one does nothing to nobody, and some one else goes and tells'; and although we cannot perhaps surpass even in Yorkshire that happy explanation of the term, yet we do own to certain sayings with reference to the unruly member, some of which may not be unworthy of being placed on record. There is one, for instance, which savours somewhat of the schoolgirl's definition just mentioned, and there are probably many similar ones; it runs thus: 'Them 'at says they deean't leyke saayin' nowt aboot nowt ti neeabody, meeastlins pass tahm by saayin' summat aboot summat ti somebody.'

Again, the following rhyme aptly hits off what, it is to be feared, is a not altogether uncommon failing in Yorkshire as elsewhere :—

> Them 'at says they weean't, an' diz it still,
> Dizn't deea it when they saay they will.

We all know what to expect from a 'slaap un'; he or she can never be depended on for anything. It was said of a female whose tongue could not be trusted, or, as we say in the East Riding, whom we could not 'talk after': 'Ah reckon nowt o' what sha says. . . . Praise frev a slaap tongue is nae better wo'th 'an rain i' haay tahm.'

That the idler is ever ready to make excuses for his idleness, and that half the 'loafers' who infest the country-side are as capable of doing a day's work as any one else in the community, we are well aware. We know, too, how any slight ailment is by many used as a plea for having an 'off-day'; it is to such 'ne'er-do-weels' as these that the saying applies: 'Yan's nivver ower waak to wark when yan's yabble ti bunch an au'd hat ower t' green.'

It is remarkable how few of the well-known English proverbs are in common use among our country folk in the form in which they have been handed down to us. They are for the most part either sup-planted by corresponding ones of more or less local growth or by extemporized expressions which do duty for the same and are of scarcely less force. Thus, for example, it was said of one who had been addicted to intemperate habits, and had at length given them up, but, alas! only to fall immediately into the wily snares of horse-racing and betting: 'Ah deean't think 'at he's mended hissen mich: they saay 'at he's signed t' pledge, bud started ti hoss-race; t' rabbit dizn't fare na betther 'at 'scapes fra t' fox an' meets wi' t' rezzil.'

The well-worn saying that 'prevention is better than cure,' is one which none of us will care to gainsay, and we are for the most part minded so to word the truism; the ancient statement is, how-ever, apt to take a different turn when uttered by Yorkshire lips. On one occasion a Yorkshireman

remarked to another countryman, with reference to
a certain fire in a house in the neighbourhood,
'He sleck'd t' fire oot afoor mich damage wer deean';
whereto the reply came, ''T may be clivver ti stop
a bull, bud it's wiser ti loup t' yat.'

An instance is recorded, and we fear it is by no
means a solitary one, of a certain would-be fine lady
in one of our Yorkshire villages who dressed herself
up in a manner singularly unbecoming for one in
her station in life, and withal gave herself highly
ridiculous airs. This kind of parade, as may be
supposed, gave no little offence in certain quarters,
while others of her sex, though not able or willing
to adorn their persons to the same absurd degree
of finery, were in no wise inferior in real worth to
this flaunty and gaily bedecked female. As 'my
lady' sailed down the 'town street' on one occasion,
a critical observer of her ways was heard to remark,
'Sha gans wiv her heead up as thoff yan wer nowt
bud muck; bud Ah'll tell ya what, Ah's as good
as sha is, if Ah's nut sa weel putten on—black fleeace
or white fleeace, t' mutton's t' seeam.' It would
be difficult to say whether such a one were the
more deserving of all the severe things that were
heaped upon her or another of whom we have heard—
Bessie by name. Her 'pleeanin'' ways were thus
described: 'It's awlus ower fine or ower wet for
oor Bessie, bud sum folks is that grum'ly, that they
awlus 'ev a steean i' ther shoon.'

The ordinary infirmities of the flesh are no doubt
the inheritance of the Yorkshireman equally with the
rest of mankind; we can claim for him no immunity

from these. He is 'hurt with the same weapons, subject to the same diseases, healed by the same means,' even as others. Fools are perhaps rather less frequently met with in this than in some other counties, and if there is one bump more clearly developed upon the Yorkshireman's cranium than another, it is that of caution. Those who happen to be deficient in that particular quality come in for no unfrequent reproofs and warnings from their more ' gaumish' fellows. Thus to one who was always being taken in by people of whom he knew nothing, this piece of advice was given: ' Afoor yan claps a stthrange dog uppo t' heead, yan s'u'd awlus leeak 'at it teeal;' while of another, whose propensity to spend money was in excess of that usually found among those who dwell between the Humber and the Tees, it was said, ' Aw deear, what a feeal he's been! bud Ah've telled him mair 'an yance 'at money ta'en oot o' t' pocket's mair 'an hauf spent.' Again, we have a Yorkshireman's equivalent of the brief injunction, ' look before you leap,' expressed as follows: ' Nivver loup a stell widoot ya knaw what sooart of a footho'd you'll leet on.'

To the same effect as the foregoing is a small bit of admonition that comes down to us from the days of the old tinder-box ; and for lack of its due observance, many a small trouble has been experienced. The word of warning shapes itself thus: ' Afoor yan flints tundther, knaw wheear t' rush-leet is.' A few old formulas of this kind may even still occasionally be heard. It was not long ago that I was told of one from the borders of Durham and Yorkshire which struck me as having an antiquated flavour, but yet, withal, one of a picturesque kind. The reason for its use was to reprove a child for displaying a certain greediness at table. It would sound strangely in modern ears to hear it said to a child in such a case: ' Thoo's 'greed wi' sham an' gi'en mense a grot' (you have made an agreement with shame, and given decent behaviour a groat).

There is no little truth as well as force in the old expression which says, ' Them 'at crack o' thersens awlus to'n' (turn) ' oot blawn eggs '; and those who have risen in the world, especially if it be by questionable means, may well take a lesson from the saying, 'Him 'at's gitten ti t' top o' t' stee, dhrops farest when he falls.'

In Yorkshire, as elsewhere, those who thus 'crack o' thersens,' besides being unpopular with their fellows, are, generally speaking, more easily daunted than those who are not given to blow their own trumpets.

That was a truly good specimen of our dialectical usages which had reference to one who was in the habit of sounding his own praises in no measured terms. ' Whya,' said a countryman, who took a fairly accurate measure of this vain boaster's ways, ' Ah deean't knaw; he'll mebbe nut deea sa mich when all cums ti all; Ah've heeard folk saay 'at a bragger taks a lang stthrahd when t' teeap' (the ram) 'grunds it heeaf' (stamps the ground with its hoof).

The most trifling and homely incidents frequently give occasion to a Yorkshireman for bringing out some of his flashes of wit and raciness of expression. I remember not long ago hearing of a native of the

North Riding who, one day in the fore-part of 'sheep-clipping time,' accompanied an old shepherd in order to have some sheep washed. . They had to wait near the appointed place until another flock had gone through the well-known process of cleansing, and as they were whiling away the time, the vicar's mother and sister drove by. Seeing what was going on, they pulled up and entered into conversation with the old shepherd, who, like every Yorkshireman, was a bit of a character. 'We do so like the smell of sheep,' they said; to which the old man replied, 'Yis, mum, an' seea deea Ah; bud Ah leykes t' teeast on 'em betther!'

In the few examples I have here given, it will perhaps be seen how that the Yorkshireman has a way of expressing himself which seems to be peculiarly his own, and how his utterances generally strike a stranger by their originality and quaintness. Refreshing is it to hear these when spoken with all the naturalness and force with which some of the older folk tongue them. They come upon us like whiffs of sea air laden with ozone, which put new life into us and make us walk with a lighter step.

I will bring my short chapter to a close by a characteristic little story which forcibly illustrates how strong the Yorkshireman's ruling passion— I mean, of course, his love of horseflesh—is in death.

I was told quite recently of a farmer who, at the time of the transaction to be related, was laid up with a dangerous illness; indeed, it proved to be his last. At this time he was possessed of a thoroughbred mare, which he was anxious to sell. A dealer in the neighbourhood had had his eye on the mare, and wanted at once to buy it. Accordingly he called on the farmer, and was shown into his bedroom. The bargain was not struck during the visit, though the difference between the two was only a matter of a sovereign or so.

A few days, however, after this interview, the dealer again presented himself at the house, not knowing that in the meantime the farmer had died. On entering the yard, the horse-dealer inquired of the man in the stables, how the master was. 'Oh! he's deead,' said the man ; 'he deed last Tho'sda, bud afoor he deed he said 'at thoo was ti 'ev t' meer !'

CHAPTER XII

IDIOMS AND THE PECULIAR USE OF CERTAIN WORDS

THE folk-speech of our county abounds in idioms, and possesses many forms of curious phraseology.

It is these and other peculiarities which add much to its forcefulness, and form one of its main features.

It will be the object of this short chapter to explain some of these usages and idioms.

In writing such a chapter there is one difficulty presents itself—where to commence. There is too much material. As a starting-point, let us take the following remark, which was made to me the other day by an old dame :—

'Them lads weean't deea ez tha're tell'd; Ah may shoot at 'em ez oft ez Ah leyke, tha deean't *mend ther waays*. Ah wadn't mahnd if tha war *onny bit leyke*;' i. e. 'Those boys will not do as they are told; I may shout at '*em* as often as I may, they do not mend their ways. I would not mind if they were any way reasonable.'

One word with reference to ''em.' Writers on

Yorkshire mark 'them,' so written, with an elision point ('em).

Is this correct? I offer an opinion for what it is worth. The vocabulary of our people dates back to a very remote period; the same may be said of many of the rules which govern their speech. May not this ''em' be a case in point; and instead of being a contraction of 'them,' only the plural form 'hem,' which they have retained along with many other old-time words?

Wicliff, in the parable of the Prodigal Son, translates as follows :—'And the younger of hem;' and a few lines below, we find, 'and he departed' (divided) 'to hem.' Although our people have not retained in their vocabulary the word 'departed,' they have held on to another equally archaic, i. e. parting, 'partinge,' to divide. I leave this for others better able than I to decide.

In the old dame's statement it was said that the lads would not mend their ways. 'To mend our ways' is equivalent to saying, 'improve,' 'to grow better'; and to be 'onny bit leyke '= being reasonable.

In the sentence 'Yon's nowt ti mahn,' the word 'yon' signifies 'that or those over there.' 'Yon chap' is 'that man over there'; or 'yon coos,' 'those cows over there.' 'That chap' points out a man near at hand; 'yon chap,' one who is a greater or less distance removed from the speakers. Hence, 'Yon is nothing to mine' tells that the thing spoken of was some distance away. 'To,' in the statement 'to mine,' is equivalent to 'compared with,' i. e. 'That (one) is nothing when compared with mine.'

'To' also='for,' e.g. 'good ti nowt,' 'good for nothing.' Again, 'to'='this.' And although to some it sounds odd to hear a farmer say, 'Wa s'all 'ev a good crop ti year,' 'we shall have a good crop to' (this) 'year,' it only sounds peculiar because it is unfamiliar. The same individual who would smile at such usage, would perhaps a moment afterwards ask, 'what have we *to* dinner *to*-day?' i.e. 'What have we for dinner this day?' The usage of the negative in the double, treble, or quadruple form is not infrequent. 'Ah nivver at neea tahm sed nowt aboot nowt ti neeabody neeaways; Ah'd nivver neea call teea,' literally, reads thus: 'I never at no time said nothing about nothing to nobody no way; I had never no reason to;' or, 'I never said a word to any one; I had no reason to.' 'Ah'd nivver neea call teea.' 'Call'='reason.' 'Ah'll gi'e him a good calling when he cums in; bud he wants his jacket lacing weel t' maist ov owt.' 'To call' here='to scold.'

'Sha called ma leyke all that; aye! ivverything 'at sha c'u'd lig her tung teea.' In this instance, 'called' means more than a scolding; it means, 'to defame,' 'to have said of the person shameful things,' 'to illify[1],' 'to speak evil of.' 'To lace any one's jacket,' is 'to administer a sound thrashing'; and to say 'ivverything 'at one can lay the tongue to,' is to heap upon a person all the opprobrious epithets we can remember or invent. We should not say to a child, 'What is your name?' Possibly did we do so, we should be met with a blank stare of amaze-

---

[1] See Glossary.

ment. The correct form would be, 'What do they call you?' and you would have an answer at once.

We should not say 'Shout to John,' but 'Call of John'; or 'Thoo'll 'a'e ti shoot on him looder na that, if thoo aims ti mak him hear,' i. e. 'you will have to shout to him louder than that, if you intend to make him hear.' This word 'call' caused considerable bewilderment to one who had to make a complaint to a mother of her son. Being a stranger, the mother replied to him in her best English, but although she managed to divest her speech of much of its usual vocabulary, idiom and the peculiar use of certain words were not so easily laid on one side. She began, 'It's ti little ewse, bud Ah'll call on him, an' Ah'll call him well when he cums; bud it's ti no good my calling him when he does cum, foor Ah've called him many a tahm afoor.'

Now, why the good lady should promise to call for him when he had come, and to assure the gentleman it was of no use calling him when he arrived, because she had done so many a time before, didn't leave things as clear as they might have been. What she really meant to say was, 'I will shout for him, and give him a scolding when he comes; but really scolding is of little use, as I have done so many a time before.'

A little way back the word 'aim' was used—'if thoo aims ti mak him hear.'

'Aim'='to intend,' 'to hope,' 'to think,' 'to go.'

'Ah aim ti git deean ti-day'=I intend to get done to-day; or, I hope to get done to-day.

'Ah aim 'at sha'll git better'=I think that she will get better.

Q

'Ah aim 'at he's a better talker 'an t' parson '=I think that he is a better speaker than the parson.

'He's aiming t' wrang road '=He's going in the wrong direction.

'Ah aim 'at it's *good* eneeaf ti deea '=I think that it is easy enough to do.

The word 'good'='easy,' also 'considerable.'

'Ther war a good lot o' sheep an' a goodish few pigs,' i.e. There were a considerable number of sheep, and equally so of pigs.

'Good' also='well.'

'Thoo mud ez good cum ti morn ez t' daay eftther '=You may as well come in the morning as the day after.

'To lap up a thing' is 'to conclude,' 'finish,' 'overcome.'

'Ah s'all lap it up iv a minit '=I shall be done in a minute.

'Ah'll seean lap yon job up '=I will soon end that affair.

'If Ah caan't lap yon chap up, Ah'll gi'e ower '=If I cannot overcome (thrash) yon man, I will give over; literally, I will admit my incapacity to do anything.

'To gi'e ower'='to cease.'

'Noo, bairns! gi'e ower potching steeans at t' ducks; ya'll be laamin' sum on 'em, an' then sum on ya'll be gitting ta'en afoor yer betters '=Now, children, cease throwing stones at the ducks; you will be hurting some of them, and then some of you will be getting taken before your betters.

'To be taken' or 'having to appear before one's betters'='appearing before the justices.'

'Bunch' and 'punch' are two words over which mistakes are often made. 'Bunch' is to kick with the foot or knee, 'punch' is to hit with the hand.

'He bunched, an' Ah punched, an' wa baith toupled inti t' beck tigither.'

'Mrs. Ridge, will ya mak your Sally gi'e ower? sha's bunching ma.'

'Nobbut when thoo lugs (my hair), Ah deean't bunch nobbut when thoo lugs, an' ivvery tahm 'at thoo lugs, Ah'll bunch. If it's gahin to be lug foor bunch, it s'all be bunch foor lug,' shouted Sally.

The very common occurrence of changing the past participle passive into the infinitive active, with 'be,' is somewhat curious.   Instead of saying, 'it will have to be seen to,' we should say, 'it'll be ti leeak teea'; or, 'the dog is dead, it will have to be buried,' would become, 't' dog's deead, it'll be ti sahd by.'   'To sahd by' is 'to bury,' and 'to put out of the road' is 'to kill.'   'Wa've 'ed ti put t' au'd meer oot o' t' road.'

As the following bit of information introduces many of our idioms, I will give it as uttered.

'Thoo maunt *let on* aboot it, bud oor Tom's *keeping company* wi' Hannah, Mary's lass; *an' Ah'll tell tha what*, she diz *git hersen up* when they gan oot. *Ah nivver thowt foor* oor Tom ti keep company wi' her; sha's *far an' awaay* t' best leeaking ov onny on 'em.   Aye! *byv a lang waay*; bud he's gitten weel in wi' *t' au'd woman*, an' he can gan an' *hing his hat up* onny tahm he 'ez a mahnd teea.   Ah've gi'en him *an inklin'* 'at he mun allus *mak hissen mensful*, an' ti *think on* nivver ti *let wit* owt aboot Nancy.   They 'ed a *few wo'ds* t'other daay aboot her; it war *all alang of* summat 'at Jack let slip; an', mah wo'd, bud Tom did *ramp an' rahve* when he gat ti knaw.   Sha sed 'at sha wadn't be played *fast an' loose* wi'; bud Ah

Q 2

tell't him ti *feeace it oot*, an' nut git oot o' heart, an' *fall oot* t' ane wi' t' ither ower a *larl matter* leyke that. Bud he sed 'at sha war *grieved an' vexed an' putten aboot*; an' *moreover 'an that,* Ah tell'd him nut ti *tak t' hig*, bud ti tak neea *'count on* what fau'k sed, bud ti deea his best ti *hit it off,* an' *gi'e ower* acting leyke ez if he'd gitten *a slaate off,* an' nut ti *fetch things up,* or else sha'd be gi'ing him t' *cau'd shou'der,* an' mebbe *gi'ing him t' sack* if he *gat her back up*; onny road, tha've *gitten things straighten'd up* a bit noo, seea lang ez it lasts.'

' To let on '=to tell, to divulge.
' Keeping company '=to be engaged.
' An' Ah'll tell tha what '=I assure you.
' To get oneself up ' is to pay great attention to one's appearance.
' Ah nivver thowt foor '=expected.
' Far an' awaay '=much.
' Byv a lang waay '=much.
' T' au'd woman '=either wife or mother.
' To hing one's hat up '=to be on very friendly terms.
' An inklin' '=a hint.
' To mak oneself mensful '=to put on one's best.
' To think on '=to bear in mind.
' To let wit '=to divulge.
' Few wo'ds '=a slight disagreement.
' All alang of '=owing to.
' Ramp an' rahve '=a violent passion.
' Fast an' loose '=first one way and then another.
' Feeace it out '=to meet an accusation boldly.
' To fall out with '=to quarrel with.
' Larl matter '=of small moment.
' Grieved an' vexed an' putten aboot '=to be annoyed.
' Moreover 'an that '=besides.
' Tak t' hig '=to take offence.

' 'Count on '=notice.

' To hit it off '=to agree.

' Gi'e ower '=cease.

' A slaate off : ' to have a slate off=to be an idiot.

' Fetch things up '=to mention bygones.

' To get the cau'd shou'der '=to be treated coolly.

' To give or get the sack '=to dismiss, to lose a situation.

' To get one's back up '=to be provoked to anger.

' To get things straightened up '=to arrange things in proper order, to settle matters in dispute.

To the above list may be added a few others which are equally common :—

'Ah'll mak sewer o' that, hooivver.' ' To make sure ' is to put a thing in a safe place.

'Ah'll mak an end on 't.' ' To make an end of' is to destroy, or conclude a matter once for all.

' Recollect ' is generally used instead of 'remember,' but ' beear i' mahnd ' is most commonly used.

' Ah nobbut want nobbut yan.' ' Nobbut yan ' is ' only one.' I only want one.

' Hard eneeaf '=without doubt. ' He'll deea 't hard eneeaf.'

' Ah put it all waays.' To put things all ways=explaining a thing in every conceivable manner.

' Ah feel *nobbut midlin* '=only moderately well.

' Ah's *neycely* noo.' ' Nicely ' is equal to almost quite well.

' Ah's *better* ' does not imply that the patient has recovered, but is recovering.

' It's nowt bud a *misfit*, onny road ya tak 't '=it is nothing but a bad fit (answers badly), or altogether out of place.

' Ah s'u'd be all reet if 'twarn't for this *naggin' pain* '= toothache.

' Nighest ov onny '=nearest of any. ' Ah gat nighest tiv him ov onny on 'em.'

' Not suited '=not pleased. ' Ah war neean seea suited at what sha sed.'

' *Naay, what!* wa s'all be *forced* ti gan.' ' Forced ' is to be obliged. 'Naay, what!' implies either surprise or disappointment.

'Whya, yan sees him *noos an' thens.*' 'Noos and thens'= occasionally.

'It won't be *lang fo'st*'=it won't be long before.

'Whya, Ah'll tell tha what; if thoo nobbut *taks* it this road. tho'll mebbe change thi mahnd.' To take=to consider.

'Ah *thowt for ti cum,* bud Tommy wadn't.' 'Thowt for ti cum'=almost decided to, intended.

'Ah caan't say hoo, bud *wa've gitten oot wiv* 'em.' To get out with, or fall out with=to be at variance.

'*Wa're kind* agaan noo; Ah've '*ed it ower wiv* him.' To be kind is to be friendly; and to have it over with is to have given and received a full explanation.

'It war that *pick dark* 'at Ah couldn't see t' hoss's heead.' 'Pick dark '=absolutely dark.

'He's sthrangely *setten up* wi' t' thing.' 'Setten up '=very pleased.

'Ah mun be gahin'; Ah 'ev ti ride on *shank's gallowaay ti neet,*' i. e. to walk.

'He'll 'a'e ti mahnd an' *treead his teeas streight,* or he'll be gitting t' sack.' To tread one's toes straight is to be careful to do right in all things.

'Ah caan't gan up Roseberry leyke Ah yance c'u'd, Ah git seea *oot o' puff* noo.' 'Oot o' puff,' and 'sho't o' puff,' is to be out of breath, and short of breath.

'Whya, Ah thowt 'at ther war nobbut varra *slack deed,*' i. e. dull, nothing doing.

'Ah nivver war oot i' sike a *steeping rain* afoor,' i.e. pouring down.

'Ah *laid it oot* tiv him *all roads,*' i.e. explained. I explained it to him every way.

'Thoo can saay what thoo leykes, bud Ah *reckon nowt on* him,' i. e. have a very poor opinion of him.

'Ah warn't *satisfied* aboot it, efter Ah'd seed it,' i.e. certain.

'Ah *start* ti morn; Bob dizn't want t' meer whahl t' daay efter, he's nut gahin' ti *start* whahl then,' i. e. begin.

'Ah's nut *thruff wi'* 't yet '=finished.

'Ah's be *agate* ti morn. 'Agate' is 'to commence.'

'He nivver did a *hand to'n* all t' tahm 'at he war here,' i. e. a single thing, or stroke of work.

'Ah maad fahve on 'em *hand running*,' i. e. without interruption, or without ceasing to work.

''Ez 't *kessen up* yet?'=has it been found?

'Tho'll 'a'e ti *knuckle down*,' i. e. humble oneself.

'Sha's a bad un, sha's allus *setting* things aboot.' 'To set about' is to spread reports.

'It gans weel wi' them 'at weel gans wi''=it goes well with those that well goes with, i. e. nothing succeeds like success.

'Tha're gahin' ti 'ev *grand deed*; sha's ti be *sahded by* o' Tho'sday.' 'Grand deed,' something out of the ordinary; 'sahded by,' buried.

'Ah've *wrought hard* all t' day, bud Ah've *brokken its heart* noo.' 'Wrought hard,' is to work hard; and 'to break the heart of an undertaking,' is to get the upper hand of it.

'Neea, Ah's a bit ta'en in; it *show'd* ti be a good un, bud it's warse 'an *a nahn wi' t' taal cut off.*' 'To show'=to appear, and a nine with its tail cut off stands a cypher.

'It didn't *fetch* what Ah *reckon'd* it wad.' 'Fetch '=realize, 'reckoned '=thought.

'Ah war *hard an' fast asleep* when 'Liza cam,' i. e. sound asleep.

'Martha sez 'at sha's *cumin' roond* neycely,' i. e. improving.

'Ah'll a'e neea mair o' that; Ah'll seean *steck t' yat* o' that gam.' 'To steck the gate '=to put a stop to, i. e. to close.

'Ah caan't forgit what he did ti ma; it's *stuck i' mah gizzard* ivver sen,' i. e. taken a thing very much to heart, something which can neither be forgotten nor forgiven.

'He'll be *dropping in* for 't yet; bud Ah've tell'd him *ower an' up agaan*, bud it's *teea neea good.*' 'To drop in ' has several meanings: (1) To look in—'Ah'll drop in an' see tha ti-neet;' (2) punishment—'Tho'll drop in for 't when ta gans yam,' i. e. you will either be thrashed, scolded, or punished in some form when you go home. 'Ower an' up agaan ' is a redundancy for 'many a time'; 'to neea good,' of no use, useless. 'It's teea neea good gahin', 'coz he's nut at yam'= it is useless going, because he is not at home.

'If it *fairs up* thoo maay *pop ower* ti Jane, bud thoo'll 'a'e ti *mahnd thisen* an' see 'at t' cau'd dizn't *sattle o' thi chist*; thoo's a *larl piece better* 'an what thoo 'ez been, an' *ther's nowt aboot that*; but thoo'll 'a'e ti *hap thisen up*, thoo seeams a bit *closed up* ez it is; an' Ah seear thoo diz *leeak a bad leeak*, bud thoo'll *cum on* neycely if thoo nobbut taks care.'

'To fair up'=to cease raining, to become fine.
'To pop ower'=to run, to go quickly to.
'To mahnd thisen'=to take care of oneself.
'To sattle o' thi chist' i. e. for the cold to attack the lungs.
'A larl piece better'=a little better.
'Ther's nowt aboot that'=no doubt of that.
'To hap up'=to wrap up.
'To be closed up'=difficulty in breathing.
'To leeak a bad leeak'=to leeak ill.
'To cum on'=to improve.

'Sha's cuming on neycely noo, sha's gitten a to'n foor t' better, bud Ah thowt it war gahin ti be all *owered wiv* her *yance ower*.'

'To be owered with'=to cease, to be the last end of.
'Yance ower'=once over,' once.
'Ah's gahin' ower[1] ti Bessy's; t' rest on ya mun stop wheer ya are, ther's ower[2] monny on ya ti cum wi' ma.'

'Ah war *hard set* ti git it deean byv t' tahm.'

'To be hard set'=to be much bothered, to find a thing difficult to do.

---

[1] 'Ower,' *prep.* over.
[2] 'Ower,' *adv.* too; 'ower' nearly always takes the place of 'too.' 'Ower mich,' 'ower monny apples,' 'ower big a load,' 'ower larl,' 'ower au'd,' &c.

'He *sidled aboot* t' Squire whahl he gat his rent sattled.'

'He's awlus *skewing aboot* t' doctor's; Ah aim 'at he's efter yan o' t' lasses.'

'To sidle about a person'=being obsequious.

'To gan *skewing about* a place'=to look or go about slily. 'To skew about'=to walk like a fool.

'If thoo's gahin ti *be agate*, Ah'll *get agate*, an' *set agate* Matther.'

'Be agate'=to be astir.

'Get agate'=to commence work; and 'to set agate,' to set another to work, or to start oneself. 'If you are going to be astir, I will commence (the job), and set Matthew to work (also).'

'*To hang in the bell ropes*' is either the time occurring between the first publishing of the banns, or that during which a wedding may be postponed.

'*To let oneself down*'=to perform some action which lowers us in the estimation of others.

'He's gitten neea *heart i' t' job*, nivver neeabody 'ez when tha're *rahding t' deead hoss*.'

'To ride the dead horse' is to do work for which payment has been made beforehand; hence, a man shews no energy in such work.

'It's a fine daay, ther's nowt aboot that; bud Ah's 'fraid it's nowt bud a *weather breeder*.'

This is often said specially of fine weather when inappropriate to the season.

'To *look hard* at anything' is to do so earnestly.

'*Noo leeak hard at it*, that's "C," nut "O"; noo leeak hard, an' bear it i' mahnd,' said an old country schoolmaster.

'*Ho'd on a bit*, thoo's nut gahin' *ti rahd rough-shod*
ower me.' 'Ho'd on a bit,' spoken in an ordinary
tone, means simply 'wait,' 'stay a moment.' But in
case of an argument, its utterance conveys the information that the tongue of one of the disputants
is wagging a little too freely, or it may imply, 'cease
speaking altogether.' E.g. I heard a man say the
other day to a fellow workman: 'Thoo ho'd on
a bit, wa've 'ed eneaf o' thi blather,' i.e. 'you cease
speaking (hold your noise), we have had enough of
your silly talk.' The tone of the 'thoo' gave such an
emphasis, that there could be no mistaking the command which it implied. On the other hand, 'Here,
Ah saay, ho'd on a bit,' carries no greater weight
than 'That will do for the present.'

'To ride rough-shod over any one '=utterly ignoring
or treating with contempt their desires and wishes.

'Wa've been tul him, an' wa've tell't him ez plaan ez
wa c'u'd what wa wanted an' what wa meant ti 'ev,
an' wa didn't *minsh matters* nowther; an' when wa'd
deean, he just to'n'd roond, an' tell'd uz 'at wa mud
jump up all t' lot on uz for owt 'at he cared; he s'u'd
gan his awn gate, neea matter what wa sed or did.
Ah tell ya what, chaps—it seeams ti me ez if he
meant ti rahd rough-shod ower t' lot on uz.'

'Minsh matters'=not speaking in a straightforward way;
another form of the same expression is, 'nut ti be ower
neyce,' not over-nice, careless as to expressions or the
method employed.

To tell a person he may 'jump up,' means he may just
do as he likes.

'To gan one's awn gate'=going our own way, i.e. acting as
we think best.

'Ah deean't *reckon* mich on him—he diz ivverything by *fits an' starts*, an' ya caan't *lay onny store byv* owt he sez he's at t' *beck an' call* ov ivverybody; an' he's *fo'st this road an' then that*, whahl yan caan't pleeace neea dependence on owt 'at he owther sez or diz.'

'Reckon '=think.
'Fits an' starts'=erratically and at odd times.
'To lay store by'=to value, to believe in, trust.
'Beck an' call'=to be the servant of any one who beckons or calls.
'Fo'st this road an' then that'=first one way and then another, unstable.

The following are also commonly heard :—

'To give oneself airs,' i. e. to ape manners, &c., above one's station in life.
'To be despert thrang,' i. e. being very busy.
'Almost any day'=at any time.
'Might as well be hung for a sheep as a lamb,' i.e. might as well be punished for committing a big fault as a little one.
'As good luck would have it'=as good fortune happened.
'Away'=continue. 'He may knock away, I shan't go to the door,' i. e. he may continue knocking.
'To fancy oneself' is to be conceited.
'As matters stand'=as things are.
'At all events'=in any case.
'From the bottom of the heart,' i. e. wholly, absolutely. Ex. 'I believe what you say from the bottom of my heart.'
'Cut an' come again'=help yourself; when you have eaten that, have more.
'Dragged by wild horses,' torture in any form. 'I wadn't 'a'e tell'd owt; neea, Ah'd 'a'e been dragged aboot wi' wild hosses fost;' i. e. I would have been put to torture first.
'To follow like a shadow ' is to keep close to.
'For my own part'=to my way of thinking.

' As far as in one lies '=to the best of one's ability.

' Not to allow the grass to grow under one's feet' is to be very energetic, diligent in business.

'To be hand and glove with any one,' is to be very intimately associated with them.

' For once in a way '=this time, just once.

' To scrape one's tongue '=to talk affectedly.

' To be over head and ears in anything '=to be completely so—over head and ears in debt, in love, &c.

' To hang heavy on one's hands'=to be difficult to dispose of.

' Not to know whether one is on his head or his heels ' is to be absolutely bewildered.

' On that score '=on that account.

' Over and above (ower an' aboon) '=more than. Ex. ' An' ower an' aboon that he sed——,' and more than that he said——.

'To pour into one's ears '=giving information with great unction.

' To quake in one's shoes (ti quake in yan's shoon) '=to be in great fear.

'Spoil the ship for a happorth of tar '=penny wise and pound foolish.

' To stir up strife '=making mischief.

' Stir your stumps,' or ' cut your sticks '=off you go.

' To the top of one's bent '=to fully carry out our inclination.

' That's telling,' often said after a question has been asked, and implies, ' You would like to know, but I shall not tell you.'

' Up to Dick '=just as it should be, perfection.

'To be wrang i' t' heead '=being out of one's mind.

' Not to be worth one's salt '=useless.

'To sleep like a top '=to sleep soundly.

To conclude. It was said of one, who was somewhat inclined to be a fop,

' He puts on airs, scrapes his tongue, skews aboot, an' fancies hissel' that mich, whahl he's mair leyke yan 'at's nicked i' t' heead, an' clean daft, 'an owt else ; he maay aim 'at he's up ti Dick, bud Ah aim 'at he's nut wo'th his sau't, an' Ah's reet.'

I am certain of one thing—a Yorkshireman, no matter what his position may be, never quite leaves his Yorkshire behind him. I was standing one day waiting for the steamer which was to bring me once again to old England, when a gentleman quite close to me said to his lady companion, 'It's a beautiful sight, is the sea[1].' I turned to him, and raising my hat, remarked, ' Ah's a York-shireman an' all.' That was enough, we were friends the whole of the voyage. No, we Yorkshire people cannot, if we would, leave our county behind us. And thank the gods for that.

. . . .

When cultured speech in tones refined
Lead us to dream all others blind,
'Tis well that we should bear in mind,
Though we may leave all else behind,
Our idiom goes with us.

[1] This peculiarity, even amongst many educated Yorkshire people, of repeating the verb is further illustrated in the concluding remarks at the end of the Glossary.

CHAPTER XIII

SIMILES, PROVERBS, AND SAYINGS

THE North Riding is very prolific in similes and quaint sayings. I have by me a collection of some hundreds, varying in degree of point and humour, but all worthy of being preserved. Many of them take us back to the time of our grandfathers, speaking of things and pointing to customs of other days. Still, they hang on the lips of the older people now; but to those who know nothing of their past, their sayings seem pointless and out of place. Nevertheless, 'Ez useless ez damp tunder' (tinder) would be as forceful in their day as our saying, 'As useless as a damp match.' In the days when many a pulpit was supplied with an hourglass—like a huge egg-boiler—to let the preacher know when to wind up his 'thirdly,' the old saying applied to those who were somewhat importunate, 'They hint ez plaan ez t' hoorglass,' and 'Sha's leyke t' hoorglass—sha uses t' same thing ower an' up agaan,' or 'Sha's ez careful ez a sand-glass,' which never wastes a grain, were in their day as pointed as any in use at the present time. A few remarks to elucidate the meaning of those in the following list which may be somewhat obscure to any lacking knowledge on certain points, will be found on page 243.

Those marked thus (†) are in daily use throughout the riding.
Thus (*), explanatory remarks will be found at the end.

1. Ez wise ez t' ullot.
† 2. Ez hung'ry ez a dog.
† 3. Ez patient ez a cat.
† 4. Ez whisht ez a cat.
† 5. Ez still ez a moose.
* 6. Ez friendly ez a bram'l bush.
*† 7. Ez walsh ez pump-watter.
8. Ez poor ez pauper soup.
*† 9. Ez thick ez inkle-weavers.
† 10. Ez reglar ez clockwark.
† 11. Ez sartin ez t' cess getherer.
12. Ez scarce ez guineas.
13. Ez noisy ez a tinker.
* 14. Ez common ez a deear-snek. Any one handles it.
† 15. Ez strang ez a steeple.
† 16. Ez hoarse ez a raven.
† 17. Ez soft ez pap, i.e. child's food.
† 18. Ez stiff ez buckram.
† 19. Ez deead ez a mauky ratten.
20. Ez sour ez a sloe.
† 21. Ez deead ez a hammer.
† 22. Ez deeaf ez a post.
† 23. Ez fit ez a fiddle.
24. Ez graspin' ez a toll-bar.
25. Ez tall ez a mill chim'ly.
† 26. Ez brant ez a hoos end.

† 27. Ez red ez a cherry.
† 28. Ez tough ez leather.
29. Ez seeaf ez a pig ring.
* 30. Ez soft-hearted ez a rezzil.
* 31. Ez slape ez a greeasy powl.
† 32. Ez rotten ez touch-wood.
33. Ez cruel ez a spider.
† 34. Ez red ez rud.
† 35. Ez lish ez a squirrel. Lish=active.
† 36. Ez friendly ez yan's shadder.
† 37. Ez hardy ez ling.
† 38. Ez impudent ez a cock sparrer.
† 39. Ez boddensome ez debt.
† 40. Ez bliew ez a whet-stone.
† 41. Ez saut ez sea watter.
† 42. Ez strang ez an onion.
† 43. Ez common ez weeds.
† 44. Ez sweet ez t' floors i' May.
† 45. Ez sweet ez a posey.
† 46. Ez sour ez a crab-apple.
*† 47. Ez femmur ez a mus-web.
† 48. Ez cracked ez a brokken pot.

*† 49. Ez polite ez t' divil.

† 50. Ez pricky ez a pricky-back otch'n.

51. Ez soft ez a geease-down pillow.

† 52. Ez common ez brack-k'ns.

53. Ez cheap ez promises.

† 54. Ez cau'd ez Kessamas.

† 55. Ez thrang ez bees iv a sugar cask.

† 56. Ez busy ez bees on t' moor.

† 57. Ez straight ez a bul-rush. Also 'as tall as,' &c.

† 58. Ez cheeap ez muck.

† 59. Ez soft ez muck. Also 'Ez soft ez a wesh-leather.'

† 60. Ez common ez muck.

† 61. Ez laam ez a three-legg'd dog.

† 62. Ez fast ez a rivet.

+ 63. Ez lazy ez a stee. A ladder generally leans against a wall.

† 64. Ez whisht ez yan's shadder. As quiet as one's shadow.

† 65. Ez true ez a die.

† 66. Ez mild ez a May morn.

†* 67. Ez tight ez a damp cleeas-line.

68. Ez slow ez a stutterer. Also 'Ez slow ez a snahl.'

† 69. Ez wick ez a lop—flea.

†* 70. Ez fond ez a yat.

† 71. Ez kittle ez a moose-trap.

† 72. Ez wet ez a dishclout.

† 73. Ez tired ez a dog.

† 74. Ez savage ez a wasp.

† 75. Ez black ez midneet.

† 76. Ez black ez sin.

† 77. Ez hard ez a steean.

† 78. Ez soond ez a bell.

† 79. Ez creeak'd ez a dog's hind leg.

† 80. Ez wet ez sump.

† 81. Ez wet ez thack.

† 82. Ez mucky ez a pig-sty.

† 83. Ez waak ez a kitten.

† 84. Ez oppen ez a skep.

† 85. Ez bold ez brass.

† 86. Ez lively ez a cricket.

† 87. Ez green ez grass.

† 88. Ez soft ez putty.

† 89. Ez deead ez a teead skin.

†* 90. Ez plaan ez a pike-staff.

†* 91. Ez plaan ez a yat-stoup.

† 92. Ez full ez an egg.

† 93. Ez dusty ez a flour pooak.

† 94. Ez white ez flour.

† 95. Ez mucky ez a duck pond.

† 96. Ez larl ez a flea-bite.

† 97. Ez still ez a finger-post.

† 98. Ez lonely ez a mile-steean.

†99. Ez slape ez an eel.

†* 100. Ez good-natur'd ez a pump.

† 101. Ez pure ez spring-watter.

† 102. Ez reight ez a trivet.

† 103. Ez thin ez a bubble skin.

† 104. Ez sticky ez glue.

†* 105. Ez meean ez bo'd-lahm (birdlime).

. † 106. Ez hard ez a nail.

† 107. Ez cau'd ez ice.

†* 108. Ez deep ez a well.

† 109. Ez strang ez a hoss.

† 110. Ez wet ez a mill-wheel.

† 111. Ez fond ez a goose nick't i' t' heead.

† 112. Ez lang ez a parson's coat.

* 113. Ez sartin ez t' thorn-bush.

* 114. Ez waffly ez a mill-sail.

† 115. Ez soft ez butter.

116. Ez empty ez a blawn egg.

† 117. Ez rank ez nettles.

† 118. Ez blinnd ez a bat i' daayleet.

† 119. Ez damp ez a cellar, or ' t' graav.'

† 120. Ez breet ez a new-made pin, or 'ez sun-leet.'

† 121. Ez fond ez a brush.

† 122. Ez greedy ez a rake.

† 123. Ez dhry ez a sarmon.

124. Ez tho'sty[1] ez a sponge.

† 125. Ez solemn ez a coo.

† 126. Ez breet ez a bald heead.

† 127. Ez bare ez a bald heead.

† 128. Ez roond ez a bullet.

† 129. Ez straight ez trewth (truth).

† 130. Ez mad ez a bull at a yat.

† 131. Ez phrood ez a banty cock.

† 132. Ez flat ez an iron.

† 133. Ez poor ez moor-land.

† 134. Ez hard ez t' to'npike.

† 135. Ez nak't ez a graav-steean.

†* 136. Ez strang ez a teeagle chaan.

†* 137. Ez tough ez a swipple.

† 138. Ez strang ez an oak.

†* 139. Ez warm ez a sheep-net.

†* 140. Ez catching ez t' scab.

†* 141. Ez bonny ez a sheep-cade.   In ridicule.

† 142. Ez drunk ez a fiddler.

* 143. Ez thrang ez a cob-bler's Monday.

144. Ez meean ez a cuckoo. The cuckoo lays its

[1] Thirsty.

R

eggs in other birds' nests.

† 145. Ez welcome ez t' floors i' May.

146. Ez larl wanted ez rain i' hay-tahm.

＋ 147. Ez hungry ez a dog.

148. Ez glib ez a leear's tongue.

† 149. Ez wo'thless ez an au'd shoe.

150. Ez larl value ez an au'd hat.

† 151. Ez tough ez pin-wire.

* 152. Ez neyce ez an otter [1].

†* 153. Ez greedy ez an otter [1].

154. Ez fat ez a tailor's goose. (The 'goose' is a tailor's iron.)

†* 155. Ez sweet ez a kern.

†* 156. Ez greedy ez a fox iv a hen-roost.

†* 157. Ez meean ez a cat wiv a moose.

† 158. Ez leyke ez tweea peas.

† 159. Ez bitter ez gall.

† 160. Ez big ez bull beef.

† 161. Ez leet ez a midge.

† 162. Ez limp ez a dishclout.

†* 163. Ez scraped ez a bath-brick.

* 164. Ez badly used ez a peggy-tub boddum.

†* 165. Ez gam ez a cock-roach.

† 166. Ez wet ez new pent (paint).

† 167. Ez sick ez a dog.

† 168. Ez flat ez a pancake.

* 169. Ez deead ez a red lobster.

† 170. Ez au'd ez my grand-father hat.

† 171. Ez merry ez a May-pole dance.

† 172. Ez white ez a sheet.

† 173. Ez catching ez t' mezzles (measles).

† 174. Ez bad tempered ez a nettle.

† 175. Awlus t' saam way leyke a bottle-jack (ironical, as a bottle-jack turns both ways).

† 176. Ez smooth ez a cat's back.

† 177. Ez rosy ez an apple.

† 178. Ez rotten ez (a bad) to'nip (turnip).

† 179. Ez bent ez a sickle.

† 180. Ez red ez raw beef, or 'ez a brick.'

† 181. Ez thrang ez a. wo-man's tongue.

† 182. Ez brazend ez a sun-flower.

† 183. Ez fresh ez new pent.

† 184. Ez breet ez a seeing-glass.

† 185. Ez wick ez an eel.

† 186. Ez slim ez a barber's powl.

[1] Really the same simile, common where otters fish.

No. 6. *As friendly as a bramble bush.* The way in which the bramble catches hold and clings to one is well known to all those who have had to force a passage where they grow.

7. *As walsh as pump-water,* or containing as little sustenance.

9. *As thick as inkle-weavers.* In the weaving of inkle, a kind of tape, the weavers had to sit quite close together.

14. *As common as a door-sneck.* This implies that a sneck is liable to be pressed or used by any one; the simile is one of an opprobrious nature.

30. *As soft-hearted as a weasel,* implies absolute cruelty, the weasel lacking the smallest spark of generosity in its nature.

31. *As slape as a greasy pole.* It is common at village feasts to erect a pole daubed thickly with grease, upon the top of which a ham, a leg of mutton, or a kettle is fixed; he who can climb to the top, which is a most difficult task, claims the prize.

47. *As femmur as a musweb.* 'Femmur' is slight, light, slender. 'Musweb,' a spider's web.

49. *As polite as the devil.* His Satanic majesty is said to be willing to shake hands with any one.

67. *As tight as a damp clothes-line.* A clothes-line, when left out in wet weather, becomes very tightly stretched between its two hooks.

70. *As fond as a gate.* The folly of a gate is admitted on all hands; does it not without any reason bang itself against the gate-post?

90. *As plain as a pike-staff*; and 91, *As plain as a gate-post,* denote both plainness of appearance, and a thing not difficult to understand. A pike-staff was just a bare pole, and a gate-post is usually lacking of all ornamentation; and both are fairly conspicuous objects.

100. *As good-natured as a pump.* A pump never grumbles, no matter how often or by whom it is handled.

105. *As mean as bird-lime.* It deceives those who rest upon it.

108. *As deep as a well.* 'Deep' is used in the sense of 'to hide from,' 'to be difficult to get at the bottom of.' In a modified sense, 'cunning.'

R 2

113. *Ez sartin ez t' thorn-bush.* It was the custom for the parson to collect the tithe by placing a branch of thorn in every tenth stook, he choosing the stooks, and sending his cart along for them.

114. *As waffly as a mill-sail.* 'Waffly' here implies 'unstable'; the mill-sail is turned about by every wind which blows.

136. *As strong as a teagle chain.* These chains are used to drag very heavy timber.

137. *As tough as a swipple.* The swipple is the short bar of the flail, used to thresh corn with—by hand—and was always made of the toughest wood.

139. *As warm as a sheep-net.* Used derisively; there is no shelter or warmth in a sheep-net.

140. *As catching as the scab.* The scab is a very infectious disease which sheep are liable to.

141. *As bonny as a sheep-cade.* The cade is a disgusting looking sheep-louse; hence the simile is used ironically.

143. *As busy as a cobbler's Monday.* It is generally supposed that a cobbler has to rest over Monday to work off his week's-end debauch; hence the simile is one of ridicule.

152. *As nice as an otter.* 'Nice,' in this case, means dainty, particular, eating as it does only the very best part of the fish it kills, leaving the rest untouched on the bank.

153. See 152.

155. *As sweet as a churn.* A churn, of all things, must be sweet and clean; hence anything which may be truly said to be as sweet as a churn, must excel in cleanliness.

156. *As greedy as a fox in a hen-roost.* The fox, having gained an entrance, not only kills the bird he intends to carry away for food, but any he can lay hold of; then, picking out the best, leaves the rest.

157. *Ez meean ez a cat wiv a moose.* 'Mean' is used in the sense of cruel. The way a cat plays with its victim before killing it, is the very essence of cruelty.

163. A bath-brick must be scraped each time it is used. Hence a person who has slipped down an incline, and so become bruised, will use the simile.

164. *As badly used as a peggy-tub bottom.* Surely whilst in use nothing receives more thumps than the bottom of the peggy-tub.

165. *As game as a cockroach.* No insect perhaps is so pugnacious as the common roach or black clock. The encounters which take place on our hearths after we have retired to rest are many and deadly.

169. *As dead as a red lobster.* As the lobster must be boiled for some time before assuming the red colour, we may with some certainty conclude the crustacean has ceased to exist ere it dons its red jacket.

If many of the sayings which fall from the lips of our country folk were only dressed in classic language, they would rank amongst the wisest saws ever uttered.

Take a few illustrations picked from a considerable number which I have jotted down as they have been uttered—I may say the circumstances which called each forth were as varied as they well could be. Some, I have little doubt, were impromptu, but in the main they belong to another age. It will perhaps add interest if the illustrations are given as uttered, followed by a literal translation, adding explanatory remarks when needful.

A raffle tung an' a race-hoss gan t' faster t' leeter wight tha hug. A foolish tongue and a race-horse go the faster the lighter weight they carry ; there will be more foolish talk, the lighter the weight of brains carried.

Them 'at grumm'ls sae mich aboot what tha 'evn't gitten, are maistly oot o' love wi' t' things 'at tha 'ev. Those who grumble so much about what they do not possess, are mostly out of love with the things they have.

Them 'at nivver diz nowt thersens, awlus 'magines 'at ther's nowt i' t' wo'lld 'at's hard ti deea. Those who never do nothing (anything) themselves, always imagine that there is nothing in the world which is hard to do.

Him 'at's gitten his heead screwed on t' reet road i' larl matters, weean't be leykly ti shut yah e'e when he's owt gert on hand. He who has his head screwed on the right way in little matters, will not be likely to close one eye when he has anything great on the way.

Impatience is t' hoss fau'k saddle and gallop on ti meet their troubles. Impatience is the horse people saddle and gallop on to meet their troubles.

It's easier wark feighting sin 'an nursin' 't. It is easier work fighting sin than nursing it.

Religion is offens mair laamed byv those whau attend tul 't, 'an them 'at feight shy on 't. Religion is often more injured by those who profess, than by those who are careless. There is another: ' No sinners are so intolerant as those just turned saints.'

Yan awlus 'es ti paay a seet mair foor repentance 'an yan c'u'd 'a'e bowt a vast o' common sense wi'. One always has to pay a great deal more for repentance than one could have bought a great amount of common sense with.

> *If wa wad lig i' peace an' rest,*
> *Wa mun see an' hear an' saay what's t' best.*
> If we would lie in peace and rest,
> We must see and hear and say what's the best.
>
> *'T'll save ya neea larl trouble,*
> *If when talking ya tak care*
> *Ov whaum ya speeak, ti whaum ya speeak,*
> *An' hoo, an' when, an' wheer.*
> It will save you no small trouble,
> If when talking you take care
> Of whom you speak, to whom you speak,
> And how, and when, and where.

Closed lips an' oppen een save yan fra monny a fratch. Closed lips and open eyes save one from many a quarrel (trouble).

Advising yan 'at's iv a passion's dafter 'an scrattin' a tup head. Advising one that is in a passion is sillier than scratching a tup's head, i. e. giving advice to one who is

in a passion, is equal in folly to that of scratching a tup
on the head, as there is no surer way of inducing it to
attack you than by following such a course.

*Him 'at's meead up his mahnd 'at he caan't deea a thing,
maistly maks up his mahnd afoorhand 'at he weean't try.* He
that has made up his mind that he cannot accomplish an
undertaking, mostly makes up his mind beforehand that he
will not try.

*Maist fau'k can see t' wrang they've deean, bud nut t' wrang
they're deeaing.* Most people can see the wrong they have
done, but not the wrong they are doing.

*Varra off'ns when a chap sez 'at he's deeaing nowt, he's
deeaing summat he s'u'dn't; an' when he aims ti mak ya think
'at he's deeaing summat 'at he s'u'd, he's off'ns deeaing nowt.*
Very often when a person says that he is doing nothing,
he is doing something that he should not; and when he
tries to make you believe he is doing something that
he should, he is often idling his time away.

Daftness nivver builds owght wo'th leaving up. Daftness
never builds anything worth leaving up. 'Leaving up'
means 'allowing it to stand.' The saying might be put this
way: folly never accomplishes anything worthy of being
handed on to posterity.

*Fame is a lump ov nowt putten insahd ov a bubble, which
bo'sts, an' it's all owered wiv it.* Fame is a lump of nothing
put inside a bubble, which bursts, and then it is all over
with it. To 'be overed with a thing,' is for it to be absolutely
annihilated.

*Good luck gi'es ti sum mair 'an what tha owt ti 'ev, bud nivver
mair 'an what tha want.* Good luck gives to some more than
what they ought to have, but never more than what they want.

*Cussing an' low-lived talk ther's nivver neea call for; ther's
nowt can hap it up, an' ther's nowt gitten byv it.* Cursing and
low-lived talk there is never no need for; there is nothing
can cover it up, and there is nothing got by it.

*Him 'at dis es he owt ti deea when young, 'll be yabble ti deea
es he wants ti deea when his warking days is owered.* He who
does as he ought to do when young, will be able to do as he

wants to do when his working days are over, i.e. he who diligently works when young, will be enabled to take his ease when old age overtakes him.

Them 'at weds wheer they deean't love, maistly love wheer they deean't wed.

It's a poor hedge 'at hezn't a bit of shelter.

Be friendly wi' all, bud familiar wi' few.

It saves neea end o' loss if ya sleck t' fire wi' yah bucket o' watter. Luke t' weeds afoor tha seed; an' let t' tap-reeat o' folly gan ez deep ez it leykes. It saves no end of harm if you put out the fire with one bucket of water. Pull up the weeds before they seed; and allow the tap-root of folly to go as deep as it may. A fire cannot have done much damage if it can be quenched with one bucket of water. ' Luke ' is ' to pull up.' Many methods are adopted to prevent the tap-root from growing deep into the ground; should such precautions not be taken, the root descends to where the ground is cold, and no fruit is borne. Hence the reason for desiring the 'tap-root of folly' to be allowed to grow deep into the ground.

Good behav'o'r nivver needs a drain-pipe; also, *good be-hav'o'r nivver needs pruning.*

He's nobbut hauf rocked 'at believes ivverything, bud he's cleean oot ov his heead 'at believes nowt. He is only a silly fellow who gives credence to everything he hears, but he is a hopeless idiot who believes in nothing.

Laziness ruins mair lasses 'an love, fancying thersens mair an' laziness; an' swallering ivverything 'at a chap sez tiv 'em, mair 'an baith putten tigither. Laziness ruins more girls than love, vanity more than laziness; and believing all that men flatteringly say, more than both put together.

Him 'at 'ez larl an' could mannish wi' less, is better off 'an him 'at 'ez mich an' caan't mak it fet. He that has little and could manage with less, is better off—richer—than he who has much and cannot make it serve.

Nivver judge a blade byv t' heft. Never judge a blade or knife by the handle; or, never judge a person's character by his clothes.

Ya'll 'a'e ti crack t' shells afoor ya can coont t' kon'ls. You will have to crack the shells before you can count the kernels; or, you must do your work before you can count your wages.

Sho't ez yan's tahm is, it's lang eneeaf foor sum ti ruin ther characters, ther constitutions, an' gan thruff all 'at tha 'ed at startin'. Short as one's life is, it is long enough for some to ruin their characters, their constitutions, and 'gan thruff,' i. e. spend, all they had to commence with.

T' furrows o' repentance are ploughed i' youth, and sow'd wi' t' seeds o' pleasure, bud t' harvest 'ez ti be reaped wiv a blunt sickle when yan's back is bent an' yan's gitten past wark. The furrows of repentance are ploughed during youth, and sowed with the seeds of pleasure, but the harvest has to be cut with a blunt sickle and gathered in when old age has made it impossible to repair the errors of youth.

Fooak 'at feight ower t' reet road ti heaven, off'ns finnd oot 'at t' far end 'at they've deean t' maist o' ther jo'ney i' t' hedge boddums. People who quarrel over creeds and forms discover, when life is drawing to a close, that often they have foolishly left the narrow but sure path, to stumble and struggle amongst the thorns and briars which overhang the ditch by the wayside.

T' loodist shooters i' t' fair off'ns 'ez bud larl o' ther stalls. The loudest criers in the fair often have the least on their stalls; i.e. those who make the most noise in the world generally display the least common sense.

Muschief is a fruit 'at nobbut needs a sho't summer ti repen 't, i. e. Mischief speedily comes to a head.

Ti stop lennin', start borrerin', i. e. To prevent borrowers coming to you, try to borrow from them.

It's better 'at fau'k s'u'd laugh at ya foor knowing larl aboot owt, 'an ya s'u'd loss yer brass byv pretending ti knaw owermich. It is better that people should laugh at your knowing little about anything, than you should lose your money by pretending to know too much.

When hooap dees, fear's born. When hope dies, fear is born.

Yan's nivver afeeard o' stepping oot o' t' waay ti deea a good to'n, if yan's on t' reet waay foor deeaing on't. One is never afraid of stepping out of the way to do a kindness, if one is in the right way for doing it; i.e. we are never unwilling to step out of our way to do a kindness, if we are sufficiently Christian to do what is right.

Since quite a boy I have jotted down any apt saying which I have heard. Many such, however, are so common, that they daily pass the lips of our country folk. These characteristic Yorkshire sayings, as already shown, are worthy of greater consideration than they have hitherto obtained. Why, I once heard an old Basedale man give a temperance lecture in a few words; he put the whole thing into a nut-shell. What he said was terse, brief, full of sound common sense, and decidedly smart. *We took it all away with us.* And just because it was what it was, we never forgot it—we never wished to forget it—whilst often we have no desire to remember the one-sided, long-winded, intemperate drivel we have to listen to nowadays. Said he, 'Drink, if nobbut weel followed up, awlus diz yan o' tweea things. If ya 'a'e gitten plenty o' brass, it'll kill ya; if nut, it'll beggar ya'; i.e. drink, if only well followed up, always does one of two things. If you have plenty of money, it will kill you; if not, it will beggar you.

'Some fau'k knaw better 'an ti swing on ther awn yat,' was said of one, who was an inveterate borrower of certain articles, which it was supposed he well could afford to buy for himself.

'Sha nivver will larn 'at yan s'u'dn't hug tweea eggs i' yah han',' was said of one who generally spoilt what she was doing by having too many irons in the fire at one time.

'Neeabody tries if a trap's kittle wi' ther finger.' The application is obvious.

To one who was in the habit of returning at a late hour from the weekly market, and sometimes not quite sober, it was remarked, 'Late yam fra t' market off'n spoils a good bargain,' implying that that which had been gained by the day's bargaining had been foolishly spent in the public-house.

'He's yan o' them 'at nivver hauf diz owt, bud then Ah've notished 'at them 'at leeavs t' hoos deear oppen, maistly foorgit ti steck t' yat.'

> 'Mair kindness, less lip,
> Mair corn, less whip,'

might well be hung up in every stable to-day, for certainly if our poor dumb servants were treated a little more kindly, they would need less shouting and bawling at, and when properly fed, the whip becomes but an ornament.

'Onny shufflin' taal diz ti shak off a needy relation, bud it dizn't mak 't reet foor 'em ti squander brass ti greease thersens wi',' said an old body who had asked assistance from a well-to-do sister, but who had been sent empty away with a most frivolous excuse. It seems her sister had shortly afterwards given a handsome donation at the laying of a foundation-stone upon which her name had been carved. 'Shufflin' taal' is equal to 'half a lie,' or, to put it in a milder form, 'a poor excuse.' 'To shak off' is 'to refuse'; and 'to grease yersen' is 'to please oneself,' 'to satisfy one's vanity.' The saying might be put this way: 'By the rich, any poor excuse is considered good enough to refuse help to a needy relation, but it is never just, whilst such are in want, to spend money in tickling their own vanity.'

'T' week 'ez tweea Mundaays foor t' hoss 'at ligs ower Sundaay,' implies that a Sunday's rest gives greater energy.

'Nivver tackle what ya caan't deea, bud allus deea what ya tackle,' is certainly an aphorism we should all do well to mark; the caution and advice which it contains, if acted upon, spells success in golden characters. 'Do not undertake anything beyond either your capabilities or resources, but whatever you once set your hand to, carry it through.'

At a funeral feast where one individual was rather too ready in handing the cake and wine round, one old body was overheard to say, 'He mebbe wadn't 'a'e been seea riddy wi' t' plate an' bottle 'ed he been iv his awn hoos, bud it maistly happens 'at them 'at's seea free wiv uther fau'k's hay, are varra skinny wi' ther awn corn.' That many people are exceedingly generous in dispensing the charity of others, and very careful in parting with anything of their own, is a fact too patent to dispute.

'T' chap 'at fishes for his breccus off'ns 'ez ti wait foor his dinner,' and 'A blinnd chap owt nivver ti lake wiv a crab whahl it's boil'd,' point their own moral.

At Great Ayton two neighbours were discussing one who had not long been a resident. 'Sha's gitten a pianer noo, an' it's nobbut t' other daay 'at sha bowt hersen new shades' (blinds) 'foor ivvery windther i' t' hoos. Wheer sha gits t' brass ti pay foor all t' new-fengl'd things 'at cum up, Ah deean't knaw, bud sha queerly cam, an' sha'll queerly gan; an' Ah'll tell tha what, a hoos gitten tigither by habs an' nabs, an' yan's sticks paid foor afoor they're fetched in, is comfortabler 'an yan filled wi' flee-by-neet stuff;' i.e. furniture, &c., got together at odd times and in odd ways, and paid for at the time, affords more comfort than possessing a houseful of things which possibly will have to be removed during the night to escape the landlord.

'T' yard's weel swept wiv a lent bizzum;' or, one does not fail to get the most out of any article which another has lent us. The following doggerel gives a phase of human nature common to all mankind :—

> Yan nivver thinks 'at t' egg 's new laid
> Yan's nahbor kindly lent yan,
> An' t' cream fra borr'ed milk is thin—
> Deean't len', if you'd content yan.

'Sha allus drives ivverything whahl t' last bat. Ya caan't insense it intiv her 'at them 'at git ther traps tigither iv a hugger-mugger, allus foorgits t' main thing 'at tha'll want.' This is a truism the world over. If we leave our packing to the last moment, we shall probably discover the very thing we mostly need has been left behind. Equally apt was the saying of one discussing a doubtful proceeding of some comrade: 'He'll deea 't whahl they catch him. It's a mistak at onny tahm ti sneeaf t' cann'l ti cleease ti t' wick.' It is a mistake to snuff the candle too close to the wick, for in so doing you may extinguish the light; i.e. it is unwise to tempt Providence.

'They've baith pulled yah road ; he's raxed an'
wrought, an' sha's scratted an' tew'd ; what yan thowt
t' other did, whahl i' t' end tha want foor nowt.
Bud a breet shool an' a well-worn thimm'l allus
mak a menseful hoos.' 'Raxed' and 'wrought' are
synonymous of working hard, and to 'scrat and tew'
is to be careful and ever toiling. 'What one thought
the other did' only strengthens the opening statement
that 'they both pulled one way.' To 'want for nothing'
is to possess all one needs ; and 'a bright shovel and
a well-worn thimble' clearly show that neither are
allowed a lengthy rest.

'It taks mair ti keep a pack o' hounds 'an t' damage
t' fox diz,' can be, and is, applied so variously that
explanation is needless.

> Deean't be ti pawky.
> Think on, thoo mun knaw
> If thoo starts wiv a chirp
> Thoo mud end wiv a craw,
> Bud if thoo 's seea feealish
> Ez ti be pawky an' pert,
> Maist leyke thoo'll start wiv a craw
> An' end up wiv a chirp.

The Yorkshireman is not one who believes in luck.
Hard work, toil from early morn till night, is the
daily lot of thousands. 'Luck!' said one ; 'ther is
neea sike thing ez luck ; what cums ti yan, 'ez ti be
fetched. Good luck's t' best gitten at wiv a wet
sark,' i.e. with a shirt wet with perspiration through
working hard. But hard work, if not applied in
a proper and sensible manner, will result in failure :
brute force is not everything. 'T' thickness gans for

nowt if t' roape isn't lang eneeaf;' i.e. the strength
of a rope goes for nothing if it is too short.

Can better advice be given than is couched in the
old saying of 'Deean't saay nowt on t' deearstan at'll
rax ya ti preeave ower t' thresho'd'? It is only one
stride from the doorstep over the threshold, therefore
it will be wise at all times to say nothing which will
cause you infinite trouble to prove immediately
afterwards.

The old saying, 'Buckles borrow, brussen tag-holes
beg,' clearly points that our fore-elders had a pretty
correct notion of human nature in their day. The short
saying embodies much. If the status of those who
needed assistance was such that they could afford to
wear nice buckles on their shoes, such obtained help
under the head of borrowing; but of those whose lace-
holes were burst, and buckles altogether wanting, it
was said they begged. Appearance goes a long way
towards giving a name to our actions.

Again, 'Pull t' bobbin wi' joy, bud knock wi'
sorrow,' and 'Ill news is shooted ti t' reeaks, bud
good news is whispered ti snahls [1],' both tell the same
story. In olden days a bobbin, attached by a string
to the sneck within, hung outside every door. The
saying urges us to haste with all speed to pull the
bobbin and enter if we have good news, but with
sorrow we are to be careful as to how we make it
known. Again, an evil report, it would seem, has
ever been urged on its hurtful career. The rook is a bird
which is not only noisy, but flies far afield, whilst, as

[1] Snails.

every one knows, the snail is silent and slow; but the truth of the old saying that ' Evil news is shouted to the rooks, whilst good tidings is only whispered to the snails,' is, we fear, as true to-day as when first uttered ages ago.

I will close this chapter with a few truisms, which fail to be hidden in the doggerel :—

IF.

'Twar a varra neyce wo'lld 'at wa live in,
An' bonny it still mud be maad,
If prahd an' au'd Harry wad give in,
An' pafty fooak putten i' t' shaad.
If t' pawky war nobbut all maastthered,
An' swaimish fooak nut ower green,
Sum neeams wadn't then be seea plaastered,
An' things wad be mair what tha seeam.
If scann'l war shun'd leyke a hag-wo'm,
An' fooak awlus thowt, 'foor tha spak,
Wa s'u'd aim ti deea all a good to'n,
Whahl ill-will wad tak off iv a crack.
If ti illify, spite an' sike uthers
C'u'd be deng'd cleean off t' feeace o' t' yeth,
Wa sud live mair leyke sisters an' bruthers,
An' 'ev mair ov innocent mirth.

CHAPTER XIV

CHILDREN'S LORE

THE North Riding is peculiarly rich in children's
lore. I remember when a lad it was considered
unlucky to hold a third place whilst crossing a stream.
To overcome the difficulty, two would walk abreast,
rather than cross last as third boy. A boy was
not considered a true grammarian[1] until he had
been subjected to the orthodox rule of bumping; and
any boy appearing in a new garment had to submit
to 'nips for new,' each one giving him a nip to
'handsel' the new garment. I remember, too, it was
considered unlucky to write one's name in a new
book with a borrowed pen. And whilst any one had
hold of wood, and cried 'Queenie,' or wet his finger,
calling out 'I'm wet,' such for the time being was
secure from receiving the last tig (bat or touch) on
parting for the night—a most desirable point of vantage
to gain in those days. But, be it remembered, this
last tig had to be given on the skin, not on the jacket,

---

[1] The name by which the Grammar School boys were known.

S

or the boy would call out, 'I wasn't born with my clothes on.'

To possess a white ally-taw was considered most lucky, a considerable number of marbles always being offered in exchange, though it was only dire poverty which would render such a transaction possible. One hears the same words and terms used now which thirty years ago came so glibly from our own lips, and how long before that, goodness knows; but old men tell us that they played the same games with the same terms and laws which govern them now. I remember seeing the look of astonishment which came into a South-country man's face as some boys rushed out of school to their usual ground, shouting at the top of their voices, 'Bags Ah fuggy, bags Ah seggy, thoddy thoddy'; and from another, 'Fowrt! fowrt! fowrt!' whilst a small scrap of a mortal yelled at the top of his voice, 'An' Ah bags laggy, Ah bags laggy.' Then it was demanded, 'What's t' steeak?' 'Tweea a go,' was the response, after which the game commenced, only to be followed by such expressions as—'Backs neea flies;' 'Ah bags brush;' 'Ah sed neea brush;' 'Noo, then, neea fullocking;' 'Here, thoo'll 'a'e ti gan ower agaan, thoo ramm'd.' And then up crept a bully of a boy, who screamed 'Brulley,' snatching every taw out of the ring and running off with them. And really, after all, one need not be very much surprised if a southern visitor does fail to understand what the boys are talking about. But then our lads would be equally at sea, and find it just as difficult to understand such a sentence as the following:—'Oi'll ketch yer one on yer blooming bouko, if yer deoun't 'old yer bally reow.' One is north, the other south, that is all—at least, nearly all.

For what untold ages our children's methods of counting-out have existed, it would be difficult to say. Some owe their birth to the times of the Reformation, when with a truly Christian spirit all things Romish were consistently or otherwise jeered at [1]; others to still earlier days, and a few to times remote. Take as an example the following :—'Ena, tena, tethra, pethra, pimps; sarfra, larfra, ofra, dofra, dix; ena dix, tena dix, tethra dix, pethra dix, bumpit; ena bumpit, tena bumpit, tethra bumpit, pethra bumpit, sigit—you're out.' Again it is repeated till another is out, and so on until only two remain, and then the last one is counted out.

The above is not very common, but still it lives; it is perhaps one of the oldest methods which has survived. Doubtless, during the centuries through which it has lived, as might be expected, many of the words have lost their original sound. It would seem to date from those days when a mixed race had for some time lived peaceably together, if ever such a thing did happen. The children know it, and that is all. Let us take the first ten words; I will leave my readers to form their own conclusions.

[1] I have heard children innocently repeating, as they counted each other out :—

> Prest an, pop an,
> Cock on t' spire,
> Holy Alice,
> Dah mell fire.

Did their parents or teachers but know what the youngsters were really saying, they would be no little shocked.

FROM ONE TO TEN IN VARIOUS LANGUAGES.

SIMILARITIES ONLY GIVEN.

The Children's Form.	Welsh.	Anglo-Saxon.	Old High German.	Modern German.	Gothic.
1. Ena	...	...	Ein	...	...
2. Tena[1]	...	Tu	...	...	...
3. Tethra	Tair	...	...	...	...
4. Pethra	Pedwar	...	...	...	...
5. Pimps	Pump	...	Finfe	Funf	...
6. Sarfra	...	...	...	...	Saihs
7. Larfra	...	...	...	...	...
8. Ofra	...	...	Ohto	...	...
9. Dofra	...	...	...	...	...
10. Dix	Deg	...	...	...	...

The comparative study of children's lore proves, perhaps more conclusively than that of anything else, how local circumstances in all things compel both alteration and modification. Our American cousins have retained with commendable accuracy most of the lore belonging to the old country; but as in some cases the nasal twang has altered the sound of words, so local and national peculiarities have influenced and modified them in others; it must, however, be admitted not to any vital extent. As an example of what I mean, take the following.

There is a very common girls' game not only in the North Riding, but in most parts of England, called 'Jennie o' Jones.' It is a singing game. One verse runs :—

> Red is for the soldiers,
> For soldiers, for soldiers;
> Red is for the soldiers,
> And that will never do.

[1] Probably this is the old form of two ones, for twice, hence *tuena* or *tena*.

Now, the American soldiers are not dressed in red coats, but some years ago their firemen were; this fact enabled the American girls (God bless 'em!) to shape the song so as to meet their case. So, without any other alteration worth noticing, they sing and act the song through just the same as our English bairns, until they come to this verse, and then, from one end of America to the other, where the Anglo-Saxon race predominates, they sing—

Red is for the firemen,
For firemen, for firemen;
Red is for the firemen,
And that will never do.

But to return to our counting-out games, some of which, by-the-way, originally were curses and anathemas, but as now sung by our children the original is lost in a meaningless jargon, often being devoid of rhyme, but always possessing rhythm. Many such are undoubtedly little else than so much gibberish, but in a few cases the rhythm is hoary with age, and possibly in the long past was listened to with awe and trembling. A very old and widely spread counting-out rhyme runs as follows :—

Eary, ory, hickory, on,
Philson, Valson, Dickson, John,
Squeaby, Squaby, Irishman,
Stiggerum, staggerum, buck [1].

The above is the North Riding version.

---

[1] Staggerum buck, or Staggerer Staggera bobtail, is the name of a boys' game, very commonly played. 'Philson,' 'Valson,' and ' Dickson ' are examples of the elision of the possessive case, i.e. Phil's son, Val's son, and Dick's son.

The American children sing :—

> One-ery, two-ery, ickery, Ann,
> Fillisey, fallisey, Nicholas, Jan ;
> Quiver, quaver, English Knave-a[1],
> Stringleum, strangleum, Jericho Buck.

One other :—

> Ena, mena, mina, mo,
> Catch a beggar by the toe ;
> If he squeals, let him go,
> Ena, mena, mina, mo.

Again notice the difference local circumstances give. The American children sing :—

> Ana, mana, mina, mo,
> Catch a nigger by the toe ;
> When he hollers, let him go,
> Ana, mana, mina, mo.

Of children's games no further notice can be taken, interesting though they be. To nursery stories, however, a short space must be devoted.

It is difficult now to discover in many of them any trace of religion, stories of the gods, or witchcraft, but the roots from which many of them spring were in existence thousands of years ago, and flourished in far-off lands. The similarity these stories bear to the myths of other countries greatly help in tracing that connecting link which shows the relationship of one race to another, when nearly all other landmarks and finger-posts have vanished[2].

Admitting the difficulty of assigning to every story its myth-root, it is easy enough in most cases to see the moral.

---

[1] 'Knave-a' became general during the War of Independence—we were a bit out of favour then.   [2] *Vide* Grimm's *Household Tales.*

THE LITTLE CROOKED OLD WOMAN AND THE PIG.

A little crooked woman had a little crooked broom,
She found a crooked sixpence when sweeping her little
    crooked room.
She set her off to market, which was a crooked mile,
Along a crooked pathway with a little crooked style;
With her little crooked sixpence a little pig she bought,
And with a band tied to its crooked leg, her homeward
    way she sought [1].

All went well until she came to the bridge quite
near to her own little cottage, but this the pig refused
to cross. At that moment a stick came by, and
the little old woman called out, 'Stick, stick, beat
the pig; for the pig won't go over the bridge, and
I shall never get home to get my old man his supper
ready.' The stick declined to help her, leaning itself
against the bridge end. Then came by a dog. To it
she cried, ' Dog, dog, bite the stick; for the stick won't
beat the pig, the pig won't go over the bridge, and
I shall never get home to get my old man his supper
ready.' But the dog refused to do any such thing, sitting down near by the stick. Just then a bull came
along. ' Bull, bull,' she shouted, 'toss the dog; for
the dog won't bite the stick, and the stick won't beat
the pig, and the pig won't go over the bridge, and
I shall never get home to get my old man his supper
ready.' But the bull refused to give her any help,
placing himself near to the dog. From a butcher's boy
passing at the moment, she begged assistance, urging
him to kill the bull, telling him how the bull, dog,
and stick had all refused to help her to induce
the pig to cross the bridge, winding up with the

[1] As the children tell the story, they pronounce *crooked*, ' crook-ed.'

sad assurance, that 'she would never get home to get her old man his supper ready'; but the lad only laughed at her, he taking his stand by the side of the bull, waiting to see how she would manage. Next came along a horse, which she besought to kick the boy, as the boy would not kill the bull, and the bull would not toss the dog, &c.; but still she fared no better, the horse standing by the side of the boy. Next a fire sprang up in the hedge bottom; this she implored to burn the horse, as the horse would not kick the boy, and the boy would not kill the bull, &c. The fire, like the rest, refused all help, quietly burning where it was. Then she begged of the stream to sleck the fire, as the fire would not burn the horse, &c.; but the water ran peacefully on, heeding not her prayers. Then she heard in the distance the sound of a mighty wind; to this she prayed, 'O wind, dry up the brook; the brook won't sleck the fire, the fire won't burn the horse, the horse won't kick the boy, the boy won't kill the bull, the bull won't toss the dog, the dog won't bite the stick, the stick won't beat the pig, the pig won't go over the bridge, and I shall never get home to get my old man his supper ready.' Then came a voice amongst the trembling leaves as the coming wind sighed through them, 'I will dry up the brook.' Then said the brook, 'Before I'll be dried up I'll quench the fire.' The fire at once cried out, 'Before I'll be quenched I'll burn the horse.' The horse neighed, 'I'll kick the boy before I'll be burnt.' The boy declared, 'Before I'll be kicked I'll kill the bull.' The bull said, 'Before I'll be killed I'll toss the dog.' The dog declared, before it would be tossed it would bite the stick. The stick at once offered to beat the pig, at which resolution on the stick's part the pig said, 'Before I'll be beaten I'll go over the bridge'; and so it did, and the old woman got home and made her old man his supper.

It was not until the old lady besought the aid of Woden, that her petition was granted. Little doubt can exist that, as told in the north, the approaching storm-wind represents that god [1].

The next story, under various garbs, is told to the little folks in nearly every corner of the earth. The connexions between the various forms and alterations (which different local peculiarities have demanded) are not difficult to trace, as the connecting links are all there. Possibly its root originated in the far East. Though our version comes from the Scandinavian race, they learnt it from some other nation, probably Germany.

NORTH RIDING VERSION OF THE BOY AND HIS WAGES.

A boy once had a very cruel stepmother; so cruel was she, that the lad determined to run away. In the end he did so, and hired himself to a farmer. Now when a year had passed, the kind farmer gave the lad for his wages an ass which dropped gold. Off home went the boy, driving his ass in front of him. On coming to a wayside inn, the landlord asked him why he did not ride such a fine-looking ass. The lad in reply foolishly told Boniface that his ass was much too valuable a one to ride; adding, 'Would you ride an ass that dropped gold?' To this the man asked him to make it drop gold where it stood. The boy wisely

[1] The story in its original form was a prophetic hymn sung by the Jews at the Passover, the animals and elements representing their enemies and deliverers.

explained that it was only when nature's call had to be obeyed that it did so, and quite beyond his power to command it. Whilst the boy was having refreshment, the ass was put in the stable, the landlord keeping his eye on it; before the lad had eaten and rested, evidence was given that he had spoken nothing but the truth. It happened the landlord had a very fine ass of his own; this he fetched from the field, and whilst the lad slept he groomed it, trimmed its ears and tail, and blacked its hoofs, till in the end it exactly resembled the gold-dropping one. This he took away and hid, putting his own ass in its place. The boy never noticed it was a changeling which he was driving home. On his arrival he told his step-mother what a treasure he had brought her. Hearing such good news, she received him kindly, giving him a supper of fried eggs and bacon. For three days he was, as she told him, treated like a prince; but the third morning, instead of his breakfast, she gave him a worse thrashing than ever, and turned him to the door, calling him all the names she could lay her tongue to. He returned to his master, who kindly received him, and on the completion of his second year's labour, gave him for his wages a hamper, which every day, on the command being given to fill itself, would be found packed with choicest food, sufficient to feed a large household. Again he stopped at the inn on his way home; calling for a glass of beer, he ordered the hamper to fill. On beholding such a wonderful hamper, the landlord determined to steal that also, so whilst the lad slept, he took it away, replacing it with one of his own exactly similar. To the lad's discomfiture, the fraud was discovered the moment he returned home. Once again he was severely beaten and turned adrift. Again his kind master took him in, and at the end of his third year gave him a bag containing a thick stick, which on the command being given, 'Come out, stick, and bend yourself,' would immediately leap out and unmercifully thrash the individual who at the time was holding the bag. On his way home, the landlord spied him approaching, and with smiles and kind words asked him in. 'And, pray, what does your bag contain?' asked he, as soon as the lad was seated. 'The most wonderful thing you ever saw,' said he; 'but let me have a good dinner, and then I will show you.' The landlord, thinking to have another good haul, served him with the best of everything, going even so far as to give him a glass of wine. All impatience, he waited until the repast was finished. 'Now,' said the youth, smacking his lips, as he swallowed the last bite, 'stand in the middle of the room and hold the bag in your hand, and I'll promise you the biggest surprise you ever had in your life. That bag is just wonderful.' Before the lad had finished speaking, the landlord had taken his place in the middle of the floor, holding the bag in his hand. 'Now open it,' said the boy—which Boniface did. 'Why,' said he, in a tone of great disappointment, 'it is only a stick.' 'Yes,' replied the boy, 'but it is a wonderful stick. Now just watch what it can do;' and then he shouted, 'Come out, stick, and bend yourself.' Immediately the stick jumped out of the bag, and bent itself about the back of the landlord until he howled with pain. Do what he would, go where he might, the stick leapt after and beat him, till at last, almost dead, he cried out, 'Put it in the bag again ; I will return thee thy ass and hamper,' which he did. On nearing home, the lad saw his cruel step-mother waiting for him with a thick stick in her hand. 'Wait a while,' he called, 'until you see what I have brought you in my bag.' Thinking it would be wiser to wait, she laid down her stick, and let him enter. 'Now, before I show to you what I have in my bag, give me a good tea; you can thrash me afterwards quite as well as now,' said he. After his tea, he asked the cruel old dame to take hold of the bag and open it. This she readily did, little dreaming of what was to follow. Again he shouted, 'Come out, stick, and bend yourself' ; and for once the old hag knew what a stick laid across the back meant. She begged, she implored, she promised she would be good and kind to him, if he would only call off the stick. At last, when he considered she had been sufficiently punished, he ordered the stick back into the bag. And from that day she behaved herself in a decent manner.

As has been said, there are many forms of this story. This one differs slightly from that told in the West Riding, and considerably from that of other countries, but one and all contain the same mythological essentials.

The kind master is the all-ruling God. The ass is typical of spring, yielding that which gives all good things. And the hamper undoubtedly represents the earth, which is full of all things necessary for our happiness and existence. But there comes a time when the gods, displeased with our ungratefulness or other sins, permit evil spirits to either steal or withhold the good blessings from us; then follows a chastising of the evil spirits, who are driven away, and the earth becomes once again plentiful.

The gold-dropping ass, and in some collateral form the hamper, bag, and stick, are old friends in Eastern tales, which were told when the world was very young. Possibly their radicals, if ever discovered, will be found in some early religious creed.

Perhaps some student will work out the meaning and application of the following; it is beyond me. An old servant of ours was taught it by her grandmother :—

> There was a man who lived in Leeds,
> He set his garden full of seeds,
> And when the seeds began to grow,
> It was like a garden full of snow;
> But when the snow began to melt,
> It was like a ship without a belt;
> And when the ship began to sail,
> It was like a bird without a tail;

And when the bird began to fly,
It was like an eagle in the sky;
And when the sky began to roar,
It was like a lion at my door;
And when my door began to crack,
It was like a penknife at my back;
And when my back began to bleed,
I was dead, dead, dead in*deed*.

I remember, when this doggerel was repeated, we all sat round the kitchen fire, the maid sitting by the table with her hand near the lighted candle; towards the last few lines her voice would drop, until, on repeating the last line, it almost became a whisper. With ears strained, and eyes nearly out of our heads, we awaited the dramatic *dénouement*, which most of us well knew; but in those days the excitement never waned, always the same intensity of feeling was duly worked up, as she repeated in a hoarse whisper, ' dead, dead, dead in*deed*,' extinguishing the light, as she uttered the last syllable with a fearful shriek, whilst we all yelled in one mighty chorus. Houses in those days were built, not held together by the tacks in the carpets and the paper on the wall; such a yell as we gave would have shaken the ornaments from off every bracket nailed to the walls of a whole row of modern blown-together domiciles.

The Story of the Poor Old Cobbler and the Wicked Knight.

There was once a poor old cobbler had twelve children, all girls. He was quite broken down with the hard work of finding food and clothes for them. One night, when he was working very late, he suddenly heard a laugh, and on looking up, saw the queerest little man his eyes had ever beheld sitting by the stove door. 'And who may you be?' inquired the cobbler, resting from his work. But the queer little man did nothing but laugh and shake his head. After a while, however, he said, 'I have a bit of news for you.' 'Good, I hope,' said the cobbler, waxing a thread. 'You won't think so; there is another daughter going to be added to your little family,' chuckled the old chap. On hearing this, the poor old cobbler fainted; the shock was too much for him. He had hoped it would be a boy, who would in time grow up and help him; but a girl! it was too much. However, when he came to himself, the baby was born, and sure enough the queer little old man had been right. It was a sweet babe, and when three years old the wee thing showed promise of growing up to be a most beautiful maiden. One day, whilst the little lass was playing about the shop door, a knight rode by; seeing the child, he was struck with her marvellous beauty. Never before had he seen such beauty and shapeliness of limb in one so young. As he rode along, he consulted his book of fate, for he was a wicked wizard knight, and discovered the child was fated to be the bride of his own son. This he determined should not be. Turning his horse about, he returned to the cobbler's shop, and after some conversation offered him a sum of money, and promised to take the child along with him, adopt her, and leave her all his wealth. To this the poor old man agreed, and away rode the knight with the lovely child in his arms. Now, he dare not kill the child himself, because the book of fate told him if any one did so before she had been kissed by the man she would wed, the same should die that day. So he determined her death should be an accident. Riding to the banks of the Ouse, he jumped his horse off the bank, leaving hold of the little lass as he did so. As they sank beneath the flood, she was washed away, and the wicked wizard left her to her fate. Her clothes, however, buoyed her up, and as she floated along, she heard a voice call her by name, and a queer little old man, who was fishing, threw his line over her, and dragged her to shore. Taking her to a cottage near by, he gave her in charge of the good wife and her husband, begging them to take great care of her until he came that way again ; placing a large sum of money on the table to pay for her keep, he departed on his way. So she lived with these kind people, until she was eighteen. At this time her many charms of form and face had become the talk amongst the courtiers at York. To such an extent was her wondrous beauty famed abroad, that she was even toasted in the castle. A certain wizard knight, hearing her so extolled, rode out one day to where she lived. Seeing her standing by the door, he passed on, and again consulted his book of fate, and discovered she was the very maiden he had looked upon as drowned years ago. Turning back, he offered the good woman a large sum of money if she would permit the maiden to carry a note to his brother who lived at Scarborough Castle. The dame said it was too far for the maiden to walk ; however, just then a queer little old man drove by with an ass yoked to a cart, and offered to give the maiden a lift most of the way, so she was permitted to go. When the queer little old man and the maiden rested for the night, he stole into her bedroom, and removed the note, which she had pinned within her chemise for security ; so gently was this accomplished, that she never awoke. He broke the seal and read, 'Let the bearer see my son, command him to kiss her, and then cast her into a dungeon, and let her starve to death.' 'I knew,' muttered the old man. Returning to the sleeping maiden, he gently pinned within her chemise another note, with just the same seal on, and written in exactly the same writing. But written in this note was a command that the brother should at once marry his nephew to the bearer. In the morning, when the girl arose, she found the ass, cart, and little old man had left very early ; however, she was quite near to Scarborough, for never had an ass trotted like the queer little old man's had done. On arriving at the castle, she was speedily married to the wizard knight's son, and they were as happy as they could be. Two months afterwards, the father-in-law came to stay at the castle. No sooner did he behold the bride, than he saw that he had been baulked again, but he held his peace. Early next day he met his daughter-in-law in a wood: she had been seeing her husband off on a hawking expedition. The wicked knight asked her to walk with him along the shore, and when they came to a lonely place, he told her she must prepare to die. Plunging his sword into the sand, he scratched a mark on the beach, telling her that when its shadow reached that mark, he would draw it from the sand and run it through her heart. So eloquently did she plead, and her beauty was so great, that he relented so far as to offer her her freedom if she would swear to go away and never see his son again, until she wore upon her finger the ring which he held in his hand. She swore she would do as he wished if he would only spare her life. He then by magic art threw the ring into the very middle of the sea, where it sank.

Broken-hearted, she left her cruel father-in-law, and wandered far away, feeling that she would never see her husband again. For more than a year she travelled from place to place. At last the poor young wife was engaged as cook by a great baron's lady. Some time afterwards her father-in-law and her husband came to stay at the castle. The very day they arrived, the queer little old man and his cart drew up at the servants' door, offering fish for sale. The cook purchased a large turbot, and on opening it, she found inside it the very ring which her wicked father-in-law had thrown into the middle of the sea. She cooked the dinner so well, that the guests begged to see the cook; to this end she dressed herself in her best gown, put the ring on her finger, and appeared before them. The wicked knight recognized her at once, and rushed forward to slay her with his uplifted sword. But the delighted husband folded her in his arms, so that his father must have slain both had he dared to strike. Freeing herself from her husband's loving embrace, she held up her hand. The knight saw the ring. He then knew she was guarded beyond the reach of any machinations of his; so he gave them his blessing, and they all lived happily ever afterwards.

Although in another form the same story is told by Grimm, and is known to-day in every country in Europe, originally it was two separate stories, which have grown into each other. The first part is closely related to a Swedish and Norwegian story, whilst the second is from a different root, which is common to many others. One having a strong resemblance is that of 'Mageloné,' and of mythological signification. Regarding the story itself, I dare not venture an opinion. But the guardian spirit, in the form of the little old man, comes out much more strongly in the North Riding version than in that of any other. Again, the act of throwing the ring into the sea, which was followed by total darkness being cast over two lives, may be typical of the sun[1] sinking into the middle of the universe. And the fish bringing it to light may be symbolical of its rising again; anyway, the act brought light, life, and hope for the future. I leave it with you—I have only suggested, not laid my ideas before you as the opinion of one able to give an *opinion* on a question of this kind.

The story of the 'Golden Ball' and others are common with us; but they must be passed by, as space only remains for one other.

THE CRUEL STEP-MOTHER AND HER LITTLE DAUGHTER.

Once upon a time, years and years ago, when animals possessed the power of speech, a cruel woman lived with a son of her own, and a little step-daughter of her husband's

[1] Henderson's *Folklore.*

T

whom she hated—but then she was a wicked step-mother. This poor little girl never knew what it was to have a kind word spoken to her, though she tried in all things to win her step-mother's love, but it was a hopeless task. One day she was sent to the neighbouring village for some candles, her step-mother giving her a silver piece, telling her to be sure and bring the change back. On returning home, she had a stile to climb, and it was such an awkward stile. There was no other way but to push the candles under the lowest bar, and then climb over; this she attempted to do, but when on the topmost rail, a black dog snatched up the candles and ran off. In great trouble she returned to the grocer's, and with some of the remaining money bought another pound of candles; but this time, when she came to the stile, a white dog ran away with them. Again she went to the grocer's, and found she had just sufficient money left to purchase a third pound. This time she was wiser, and balanced the candles on the topmost rail; but just as she did so, a great black bird swooped down and flew away with them. On her return home she told her cruel step-mother all that had happened. Instead of scolding and beating her, she told the child to come and rest her head on her knee whilst she combed her hair; and the cruel woman's heart was filled with envy and hatred when she saw the wealth of golden hair which fell about the child, hiding her from view. 'Your head tires my knee,' said she; 'fetch in the stick-block, and rest your head upon it whilst I comb out the cotters[1].' There really wasn't a cotter in her hair, it was only a wicked excuse. Whilst the child was gone for the wooden block, she took a sharp axe from its nail and hid it under her apron. 'Put your head on the block, my dear,' said she—oh, so kindly—and the little child, never dreaming what her cruel step-mother contemplated, laid her head upon the block. Then the cruel woman brought out the bright sharp axe, and with one blow severed the head from the body. This wicked step-mother then tore the child's heart from her

[1] Knotted hair.

little breast, put it in a pan, and set it upon the fire to boil, whilst she buried the body. On the father's return home, she said that his daughter was chopping sticks. She then offered the father some of the broth she had made from his own dear child's heart. He tasted it, but said he did not like the flavour, and would not drink any more; her own son refused even to taste it. Next evening, when the father asked for his little daughter, the woman lied again. She made the excuse that she had sent her with the carrier to stay with her grandmother, a great way off, declaring that she would not return for a whole year.

In a short time, on the very spot where she had buried the child, there sprang up a most wonderful rose-tree, which bore one large bud; this presently bloomed into a lovely white rose, when lo! from its petals, there flew forth a little bird as white as the purest snow. The bird did not stay in the garden, but flew into the town, and alighting on the window-sill of a toy-maker, at once commenced to sing more sweetly than he had ever heard a bird sing before. So charmed was he that he begged of it to sing again. 'I will,' said the bird, 'if you will give me the best toy sword you have,' which he gladly promised to do. So the bird sang again, and flew away with the sword to the door of a watchmaker. Here again it sang: this time it received a gold watch and chain. With this and the sword it flew to where some stone-masons were working; to them it promised to repeat its song if they would tie to its neck a large round stone which they had just finished making. This they readily did, and away it flew, alighting on the chimney of its former home. After resting awhile, it rattled the stone against the chimney side, which sounded in the house like thunder. 'It thunders down the chimney,' said the mother; so the little boy thrust his head under the chimney, to hear better. No sooner had he done so, than the bird let the sword drop, the leather belt falling round his neck. 'See,' cried the lad, 'what the thunder has sent me,' jumping about with joy. Again the bird rattled the stone against the brickwork. 'It thunders again,' said the father, thrusting his head into the chimney, when round his neck fell a gold chain with a beautiful watch attached. 'And see what the thunder has sent me,' said the father, removing the chain from his neck, and admiring his present. A third time the stone was shaken against the chimney side. Pushing the other two aside, the cruel step-mother cried, 'It is my turn this time.' So saying, she thrust her head up the chimney, when the bird let the stone ball drop, which falling on her head crushed her skull, and she fell back dead on to the kitchen floor. Such was the sad end of the cruel step-mother.

The variety of forms which this story has taken, and its wide distribution over perhaps the greatest area of any of our early-life stories, gives it a prominence and distinction second to none. In many of the stories of other places, the stone ball is described as a millstone. Possibly this is nearest to the original, as in many early fables the millstone figures as thunder. But to the eminently practical mind of the Yorkshire folk, it has been discarded, owing possibly to the unlikelihood of finding a chimney big enough to admit of its being dropped down. If its mythological root is somewhat obscure, its close relationship to other stories hoary with age is as clear as the noonday sun.

Passing on to other branches of childhood's lore, we call to mind the many charms of our youthful days. Were we stung with a nettle, we at once searched for a dock-leaf, and rubbing the part stung, repeated with all due solemnity :—

Docken in drahve t' nettle oot,
Just leyke an au'd dishcloot;

or,

> In docken, oot nettle,
> Deean't let t' warm blood sattle.

The snail-charm is as follows:—

> Sneeal[1], sneeal, shut oot yer horn,
> Or Ah'll kill yer feyther an' muther ti morn;

or,

> Snahl[1], snahl, cum oot o' yer shell,
> Or Ah'll bray yer flat wiv a wooden mell.

The crow-charm, as sung by the bairns, is:—

> Craw, craw, flee oot o' seet,
> Or else Ah'll eat yer liver an' leet.

The rain charm is:—

> Raan, raan, go away,
> Cum agaan anuther daay;

or,

> Raan, raan faster,
> T' bull's in t' pastur.

It is curious how spitting has come to play such a prominent part as it has. In certain games of catching, a boy may be quite securely caught, so far as actual grip is concerned; but until he has been hit three times on the back, and the operation of spitting over his head duly carried out, the capture is not fully concluded. Again, when two boys quarrel, one will be asked if he dare give the other 'his buff.' This is a slight blow, struck on any part of the opponent's person. Virtually, it is a challenge. Up to this point, however, the actual fight may or may not come off. The opponents, if left to themselves, are still open to arrange matters amicably. But if some boy hold his finger under the chin of one of them,

---

[1] Both pronunciations are equally common.

and ask him 'if he dare spit over,' and some lad make the same demand of the other, and both spit over, then utter disgrace and obloquy would for ever cling to the boy who, after the performance of such a sacred rite, dare refuse to do battle.

What boy does not yet fully believe that a horse-hair, either pushed up the cane or held in the hand, will split it, so as to render it useless as a means of correction? And which of us in our younger days did not accept in full faith the belief that horse-hairs steeped in water turned to eels. Why, I can well remember the time that every man jack of us, when we passed Sharrow Cross, always touched the old stone and wished, and many a pin have I dropped into St. Helen's Well and done the same.

> Rob a Robin,
> Go a-sobbing,

so we used to say, and for that reason we never stole their eggs—that is, we did not actually take them out of the nest with our fingers. No, to save ourselves from sobbing, we poked one out with a stick, and then picked it up—under such conditions, we found it lying outside. Don't smile, please. Grown-up people now-adays round the corners of their consciences in quite as barefaced a manner, and with fewer qualms.

Other children's lore must with reluctance be omitted. May what has been written be acceptable to them.

CHAPTER XV

ODD SCRAPS OF OLD YORKSHIRE, ETC.

SONG.

[*Published at Bedale*, 1800-1815.]

WHEN Ah war a wee lahtle tottering bairn,
An' 'ed nobbut just gitten sho't frocks,
When ti gan[1] Ah at fo'st war beginnin' ti larn,
O' mah bru[2] Ah gat monny hard knocks;
Foor sae waak an' sae silly an' helpless war Ah,
Ah war awlus a tumm'ling doon then,
Whahl mah muther wad twattle ma gently, an' cry,
'Honey, Jenny, tak care o' thisen.'

Bud when Ah grew bigger an' gat ti be strang,
'At Ah cannily toddled aboot
Byv mysen wheer Ah leyked, then Ah awlus mud gan
Wivoot being tell'd aboot owt.
When hooivver Ah cam ti be sixteen year au'd,
An' rattl'd an' ramp'd amang t' men,
Mah mother wad call o' ma in, an' wad scaud,
An' cry—'Huzzy! tak care o' thisen.'

Ah've a sweetheart cums noo upo' Seterdaay neets,
An' he sweears 'at he'll mak ma his weyfe;
Mah mam graws seea stingy, sha scauds an' sha fleets,
An' twitters ma oot o' mah leyfe.
Bud sha may leeak soor, an' consate hersen wise,

---

[1] Walk.   [2] Brow.

An' preeach ageean leyking young men—
Sen Ah's a woman, her clack Ah'll dispise,
An' Ah s' marry! tak care o' mysen!

A DIALOGUE BETWEEN TWO YORKSHIRE FARMERS, ON THE INDECENCY OF DRESS ADOPTED BY FASHIONABLE LADIES.

[Date about 1800-15. Published at Bedale.]

Simon.

Good morrow, Johnny, hoo d'ye deea?
If ya're ganning mah road, Ah'll gan wi' ya.
Hoo cau'd this mornin' t' wind diz blaw—
Ah think wa seean s'all 'a'e sum snaw.

Johnny.

Aye, Simon, seea wa s'all ere lang.
Ah's Bedale wards; Ah wish ya'd gan,
Foor Ah've a dowter leeatly deead—
Ah's boon ti git her coffin meead.

Simon.

Heigh! Johnny! deead? Wha, seear, thoo's wrang,
Foor sha war wiv uz e'er seea lang.
An' oft wiv her i' yonder booer
Ah've joked and laugh'd full monny an hoor.
Bud fo'st, good Johnny, tell ma this,
What maad her dee? what's been amiss?

Johnny.

Ti tell tha, Simon, noo Ah's boon.
Thoo sees, Ah sent her ti yon toon
Ti skeeal, an' next ti larn a traad
Byv which sha war ti arn her breead.
Bud when sha fo'st cam yam ti me,
Sha 'ed neea petticoats, ya see.
Ah fan sha'd larl on bud her smock,

An' ower that a tawdry frock.
Sike wark ez that, it raised my passion,
An' then sha telt ma it war t' feshion.

. . . .

Her hat sa fine to'n'd up afoor, .
It made her leeak just leyke—Oh lor !

Simon.

Wha, Johnny, stop, thoo's oot o' breeath.
Bud hoo cam sha ti git her death ?

Johnny.

Whya, ho'd a bit, an' thoo s'all heear.
I' t' next pleeace, mun, her breasts war bare ;
Her naaked airms, teea, sha mun show,
E'en when t' cau'd bitter wind did blaw.
Her clock'd hose, ez ower t' street
Sha tripp'd, sha show'd, a sham'ful seet.
An' when Ah spak aboot it, then
(Ya see, Ah's awlus by mysen)
Her muther maistly leean'd her waay—
It matter'd nowt what Ah'd ti seeay.
Ah tell'd mah deeam hoo it wad be,
An' seea sha caan't lig t' blaam o' me :
Sez Ah, ' Afoor sha's twice ten au'd,
Sha's seear ti git her deeath o' cau'd.'

. . . .

Ah's seear it's all t' gert fau'ks' pursuit
Ti 'ev, like Eve, a birthday suit.

Simon.

Thoo's reet good, Johnny ; reet, Ah saay.
That Ah've obsarved afoor ti-daay ;
Foor t' maist o' wimmin nooadaays
Nobbut put on ther goon an' staays.
An' noo i' t' toon, ez each yan passes,
Ya caan't ken deeams fra sarvint lasses.

. . . .

Johnny.

Aye, Simon, thoo sez reet, Ah sweear;
Bud noo, ez Bedale's drawing near,
Deean't let on wiv owt Ah've sed
Aboot mah dowter ligging deead.

. . . .

Simon.

Neea, that Ah weean't; but whahl Ah've breeath,
Ah'll nobbut saay 'sha starved ti deeath.'

NOTE. Much of the above has had to be suppressed.

SONG.

T' Lass fra Lunnon.

Yan nivver 'ed seean sike a yan
Foor dhriss an' feathers spik an' span;
Sha war maistly t' match foor onny man,
    War t' lass fra Lunnon.
Sha c'u'd raffle on, an' tell a taal
'At put i' t' shaad Jonah an' t' whaal;
Bud sha wadn't hug a hauf-filled paal,
    That lass fra Lunnon.

Sha c'u'd slather oot a bit o' Frinch,
An' sit an' swing her legs on t' binch;
Sha warn't partic'ler tiv a pinch,
    Warn't t' lass fra Lunnon.
Sha c'u'd sing yan comic songs byv t' year—
Sike songs yan dizn't offens hear—
Bud sha wadn't scrub a kitchen fleear,
    That lass fra Lunnon.

A bisittle sha'd larnt ti rahd;
When dancing, wha, sha seeamed ti glahd;
A chap sha wad 'ev byv her sahd,
    Wad t' lass fra Lunnon.

Her waist war nobbut bud a span ;
Sha c'u'd ommaist cum roond onny man,
Bud sha wadn't cleean a pot or pan,
      That lass fra Lunnon.

Sha c'u'd plaay t' pianner, sing an' all ;
Sha'd read all t' luv taals gert an' small ;
Sha war sharp eneeaf foor yan an' all,
      War t' lass fra Lunnon.
A leet daay's wark sha wadn't start,
Ti muck hersen sha 'edn't heart,
An' sha c'u'dn't bake a leeaf or tart,
      That lass fra Lunnon.

Sha'd lig back iv a basket cheear,
An' fairly cap yan wiv her hair—
Ah've seen mah missus stan' an' stare
      At t' lass fra Lunnon.
Sha wad laak at crickets leyke a lad,
An' carry on leyke yan 'at's mad,
Bud sha wadn't mend a thing sha 'ed,
      That lass fra Lunnon.

Ah've seean her smeeak a larl cigar,
An' sha didn't seeam a bit the war,
Bud then sha war a mo'tal star,
      War t' lass fra Lunnon.
Her shoon war oppen doon ti t' teeas,
Her hat stuck on all macks o' waays,
Bud sha wadn't wesh her mucky cleeas,
      That lass fra Lunnon.

Sha'd row on t' pond just leyke a chap,
An' iv a net sha'd tak a nap—
Sha didn't seeam ti mahnd a rap,
      That lass fra Lunnon.

Foor fun an' gam sha seeam'd fair rife,
Bud wark sha wadn't thruff her leyfe—
Sha'd nivver mak a poor man's weyfe,
    Wad t' lass fra Lunnon.
                    B——.

THA'RE KITTLISH THINGS TI DEEA.

Deean't aim ti stop a bull by t' e'e,
Deean't gan far up a rotten stee,
Deean't ho'd i' t' han' a bumm'l bee—
    Tha're kittlish things ti deea.

Deean't tak a straange dog byv its taal,
Deean't mak yer naabor's pigs ti squeeal,
Deean't call yer maaster's lad a feeal—
    Tha're kittlish things ti deea.

Deean't aim ti alter wimmin's waays,
Deean't conterdict what t' maaster saays,
Deean't hark him back tiv uther daays—
    Tha're kittlish things ti deea.

Deean't saay ti t' muther t' babby 's plaan,
Deean't tell a chap his lass is t' saam,
An' nivver saay 'at t' weyfe 's ti blaam—
    Tha're kittlish things ti deea.

Deean't drahve a lent hoss ower fast,
An' when ya've wo'ds, deean't try foor t' last
Wi t' weyfe, or else sha'll ommaist brast—
    Tha're kittlish things ti deea.

Deean't gicken when yer betters slip,
Deean't be ti pawky wi' yer lip,
An' frev anuther's glass deean't sip—
    Tha're kittlish things ti deea.
                    B——.

SONG.

A Blighted Young Man.

Noo stan's afoor ya a blighted young man
Wheeas leyfe is fast slithering awaay;
Ah's dowly an' dwining, an', deea what Ah mud,
Ah caan't lig mah troubles awaay.

Chorus.

Yance Ah war happy, leetsome, an' gaay;
Bud Ah gat wed, an', varra sad ti saay,
Ah seean fan t' mistak oot, an' noo ivvery daay
Ah wish Ah war a sing'l young man.

Ah offens calls ti mahnd noo when Ah war a lad
T' fussack Ah rade on ti skeeal;
Ah nivver thowt i' them daays 'at woman sae coy
C'u'd ivver mak a man sike a feeal.

Chorus.

Aa, bud Ah's dowly an' stalled o' mah leyfe,
Ther's nowt noo bud waiting for t' end,
Ah 'livvers up my wages Ah arns ivvery week,
An' fow'pence sha gi'es me ti spend.

Chorus.

Ah weshes all t' taters, Ah maks all wer beds,
Ah fetches all t' coals in, an' t' hearth Ah cleans up;
Ah peeals ivvery onion, an' monny a tear Ah sheds
Ez Ah sups fra leyfe's bitter cup.

Chorus.

Ah diz all t' possing, Ah hings oot all t' cleeas,
Ah hugs in all t' watter, an', ez ya maay suppose,
Ah meng'ls, Ah irons, Ah diz all 'at Ah can,
Bud Ah's nowt na mair ner a poor wedded man.

Chorus.

When Ah went a-courting, sha seeam'd ti be
Ez meek an' ez mild ez meek an' mild can be;
Bud ther's tweea sahds tiv a woman—deea what ya can,
T' Missus will be t' maastther of a poor married man.

B ——.

NOWT BUD LUV COULD BE.

T' meean war leeaking doon on t' yeth
Leyke a silver ball yah neet,
An' stars war twinkling ivver seea,
Whahl t' sky war all aleet
Wi' t' gems ov Heaven up aboon.
Seea gran' tha leeak'd ti t' e'e,
Yan felt fair capp'd ti think doon here
'At owt bud luv c'u'd be;
Foor t' beetles hum'd ez roond tha swirl'd,
An' t' crake call'd foor its maate,
An' t' bleeat o' monny lambs yan heeard,
An' t' moths cam oot ti late
Ther suppers fra some neetly bloom,
An' t' wo'lld war fair ti see,
Whahl sumhoo yan felt bet ti knaw
Hoo owt bud luv c'u'd be.
A twittering noos an' thens yan heeard
Fra t' larl bo'ds i' ther nist,
Ez croodled under t' muther wing
Tha teeak ther neetly rist.
T' noisy creeaks 'ed geean ti reeast,
Ther war nowt yan c'u'd see
Ti mak it hard upon this yeth
Foor owt bud luv ti be.
Bud whahl yan tried ti mak it oot,
A flittermoose fligg'd by,
An' t' ullot's shadow darken'd t' grund,
An' t' neet-jar gav its cry,
An' t' fox yapp'd wiv its neease ti t' grund,
Whahl t' rezzel slank alang,

An' t' rabbit's squeeal tell'd plaan eneeaf
O' parlous deed amang
T' weeak critters, whahl yan's forced ti awn
It's seeam amang wersels—
I' t' heart, wheer nowt bud luv s'u'd be,
Unkindness offen dwells.

B——.

. . . .

Yan better wed when t' glamour's on
Ez wait whahl t' heart graws cau'd;
It's better deean i' t' spring o' leyfe
Ez when yan's grawing au'd.
Yan better wed foor luv ez brass,
Just when oor een is breet;
Yan better wed when toilsome wark
Upon yan's rig ligs leet.
Yan better fetch wer baans all up,
Whahl ivvery gam tha plaay;
Baith them an' uz can laak ti t' end—
It's better mich that waay.
Yan owt ti be just gahin' doon t' hill
Ez tha tak frev uz t' pleeaf,
An' if thruff leyfe yan's deean yan's best,
Yan's awlus deean eneeaf.

B——.

. . . .

Nivver belder at yer bairns,
Whisht wo'ds is awlus t' best;
An' nivver let a tear-drop damp
Ther een when gahin ti rist.
Deean't let 'em doot yer larlest wo'd,
Bud let 'em ho'd ti be
Nowt else bud t' trewth iv all ya saay,
An' let 'em awlus see
'At ivverything ya daily deea
Thersels mud pattern tak—
I' deeaing this, ya're deeaing mich
Bonny bairns ti mak.

B——.

THE BALLOON.

From the Author's series of Yorkshire Sketches.

' What is 't, mun ? '

' It's t' b'loon.'

' Is 't t' thing 'at tha gan up inti t' sky wiv ? '

' Aye.'

' Hoo deea tha mannish 't ? '

' Naay, that licks ma ; bud it gans up leyke all that.'

' What's ho'ding 't up noo ? '

' Ah deean't reetlings knaw. Ah ax'd t' chap 'at awns 't, an' he tell'd ma 'at it war thrussen up wi' gas.'

' Aye, an' what did thoo saay ti that ? '

' Whya, Ah tell'd him 'at Ah'd cutten my back teeth.'

' An' what did he saay then ? '

' Nowt ; he nobbut ax'd ma if Ah'd leyke ti gan up wiv him, an' Ah tell'd him 'at he wadn't catch me sailing thruff t' cloods sitting on t' top ov a gert blether, an' he did nowt bud laugh at ma.'

' Ah didn't knaw 'at tha sat on t' top ; Ah awlus thowt 'at tha gat insahd t' b'loon. Bud Ah deean't see hoo tha'd git inteea 't. Ah's t' maist capped ti knaw what ho'ds 't up.'

' Aye, bud what diz ta mak on 't gahin up byv itsen, when tha let it off ? '

' Ah deean't knaw, that's a capper. An' thoo sez 'at it gans up leyke all that ? '

' Seea fau'k saay. Think on, Ah've nivver seen yan git awaay wiv itsen.'

' Ah saay, efter tha've gitten 't up, hoo deea tha mannish ti fetch 't doon agaan ? '

' Ah nivver thowt o' that. Ah wunner hoo tha deea deea 't. Bud Ah s'u'd think 'at tha mebbe fling a roap oot an' swarm doon 't.'

' Mebbe, bud Ah's leathered ti knaw what ho'ds 't up.'

' Whya, Ah s'u'd think 'at ther's mebbe a chap insahd ho'ding it up wiv a powl ' (pole).

' Aye, mebbe seea; Ah nivver thowt o' that. What's that thing; is 't a bee-skep?'

' It leeaks despert leyke yan.'

' It's a varra gert un. Mah wo'd, what a swarm it wad ho'd.'

' Sitha, mun ! if tha ar'n't tying t' bee-skep ti t' b'loon; an' ther's a lass gitting insahd.'

' Ther is, hooivver. Ah nivver seed sike a thing i' mah leyfe; it waggles aboot sairly.'

' Leeaks, ta ! Ther's a chap gitting in noo; depend on 't, tha're foor off.'

' Tha're larl better 'an tweea feeals. Ah wadn't leeave t' grund tied tiv a thing leyke that; neea, nut foor a ransom.'

' Whativver are tha efter noo ?'

' Ah caan't mak oot.'

' Bless mah leyfe, tha're lowsing t' thing.'

' Tha are, hooivver. Tha're gahin' ti let it off.'

' Ther's na doot aboot it.'

' Well, ov all t' crack-brained undertakkings 'at ivver Ah've clap'd mah een on, this carrying on licks au'd Mother Shipton.'

' T' Queen owtn't ti 'low this.'

' Sitha, tha're gahin' up.'

' Sha owtn't. It's nut reet, a-gahin' on leyke this; neeabody 'ez onny reet ti start foor heaven, owther insahd or ootsahd a b'loon, wivoot tha've deed fo'st. It's warse 'an t' tooer o' Babel.'

' It seeams ti gan stiddy, Ah will saay that.'

' That's nowt ; tha're nut i' t' reet on 't.'

' Tha'll 'ev a gran view, onny road.'

' Thoo dizn't meean ti saay, John, 'at thoo'd leyke ti gan, diz ta?'

' Whya, mebbe Ah wad ! sha's a neycish leeaking lass.'

' Whya, then, Ah'll tell tha what, if ivver Ah catch thee gahin' inti t' cloods, dengling belaw a b'loon iv a bee-skep wiv a straange lass, thoo'd better stop up wiv her altigither, foor thoo'll 'a'e larl peace if thoo ivver darr's ti cum doon agaan. Beear i' mahnd, noo, when thoo leeaves ma for t' cloods, it'll 'a'e ti be ez an angel, or thoo'll rue 't.'

U

Mrs. Waddleton travels by train for the first time to see her daughter, residing at Whitby, to whom she gives a full description of her journey.

Whya, noo, Ah'll tell tha all aboot it reet away fra t' starting. Thoo knaws Ah went ti what they call t' station, an' Ah seed a young chap stannin' at t' back ov a thing leyke a ratten trap, an' Ah sez tiv him, 'Noo, then, what's thoo been efter ti git thisen stuckken theer foor?' An' he séz, 'Naay, nowt; Ah's nobbut here ti sell t' tickets, that's all.' 'Oh, whya,' sez Ah, 'if that's all, let's be 'evving ho'd o' yan.' An' he sez ti me, 'All reet, wheear are ya gahin'?' 'Stop a bit,' sez Ah; 'that's neea business o' thahn.' 'Whya,' sez he, 'Ah caan't gi'e ya a ticket if ya deean't tell uz wheear ya gahin' tul.' 'Well,' sez Ah, 'Ah s'all deea nowt o' t' sort; an' if Ah've onny mair o' thi impidence, Ah'll tak tha byv t' hair o' thi heead an' Ah'll pull tha thruff t' larl hoal—that's what Ah'll deea.' An' then a young lady cam up, an' sha sez, 'If Ah war yow, Ah'd tell t' young chap wheear ya're gahin' tul, an' it'll mense things up a bit, an' ya'll git yer ticket an' git awaay neycely.' 'All reet,' sez Ah. 'Noo, then, cu' thi waays back, impidence; Ah's gahin' ti Whidby ti see my dowter. Sha lives on t' cliff, an' sha's gitten a pianner, an' bowt a pig, an'——' 'Naay, what!' sez he; 'Ah deean't want ti knaw all t' family history, hooivver.' 'Well,' sez Ah, 'thoo seeam'd that 'quisi-tive aboot it, 'at Ah thowt Ah'd best tell tha t' lot whahl Ah war at it.' 'Whya, noo then,' sez he, 'theear's yer ticket, an' it's yan an' fow'pence.' 'Whya,' sez Ah, 'thoo needn't be seea chuff aboot it; theer's thi yan an' fow'pence.' 'That's reet,' sez he; 'an' ya mun tak care on 't.' 'Thoo gert dunder-nowle!' sez Ah; 'Ah's nut gahin' ti fling 't awaay when Ah git ootsahd. Ah s'all tak care on 't ti t' end o' mah daays.' 'Naay,' sez he, 'bud ya weean't.' 'What foor?' sez Ah. ''Coz theer's a chap at t' tother end 'll want it.' 'Oh, is theer?' sez Ah; 'whya, then, he weean't git it.' 'He'll tak it fra ya,' sez he. 'Nut if he's leyke what thoo is,' sez Ah, 'or hauf a dozen on 'em.' An' then Ah went ootsahd, on ti what tha

call t' platform. ' Noo, then,' sez Ah, ' is this t' traan thing?'
An' a porter chap sez, 'Aye, that's it.' 'Oh! an' wheer's t' hoss?'
sez Ah. ' What hoss?' sez he. 'Whya, t' hoss 'at's gahin'
ti drag t' thing ti Whidby?' ' Bud,' sez he, ' it dizn't gan wiv
a hoss.' ' Then what diz it gan wiv?' sez Ah. 'Whya, that
thing 'at's at t' front end on 't.' ' Hoo can a thing leyke yon
knaw t' road ti Whidby? Ger away wi' tha.' ' Oh,' sez he,
' ya're gahin' ti Whidby, are ya?' ' Ah is,' sez Ah; an' wi'
that he gat at t' back o' mah, an' afore Ah knew wheer Ah
war, Ah war hauf lifted an' hauf thrussen inti ti carridge.
An' ther war nowt bud a young chap sitting up i' t' far
corner; an' Ah sez tiv him, 'Ah, saay, 'ev yow ivver been
iv a train afoor?' ' Aye, monny a tahm,' sez he. 'Is this all
reet?' sez Ah. 'Aye, it's reet eneeaf,' sez he. An' seea Ah
sat ma doon. Ah thowt it 'ud be seea neyce ti leeak oot
o' t' winder an' see Tom Robison's coddy fooals an' John
Williams's pigs, bud it's ez trew ez Ah's sitting byv thi fire-
sahd, t' fo'st thing 'at Ah seed war a chetch run reet across
a field, an' t' next minit ther war tweea coos, three pigs, a man,
an' a haystack flew past that quick, whahl ya c'u'dn't keep
yer e'es on 'em at all, an' then ivverything went ez pick
dark ez neet. ' Noo, then,' Ah shooted, ' what's up noo?'
' Naay, nowt,' sez he; ' wa've nobbut gane insahd ov a funnel,
that's all.' ' Insahd ov a funnel!' sez Ah; ' then s'all wa be
dragged oot o' t' narrer end on 't?' ' Noo, it's all reet,' sez
he. 'Ah deean't knaw sae mich aboot its being all reet,' sez
Ah. 'Ah've neea reet ti be locked up i' t' dark wiv a young
chap 'at Ah've nivver seen afoor.' 'Whya, noo, sit ya still,'
sez he; ' Ah isn't gahin' ti mell on ya.' ' Thoo'd better nut,'
sez Ah, ' or else tho'll git thi hair combed foor nowt.' .An'
then wa flew inti dayleet, afoor Ah knew wheer Ah war.
Efter a bit wa began ti slack up a piece. ' Noo, then,' sez
Ah, ' what's up noo?' ' Nowt,' sez he; ' wa've nobbut gitten ti
Whidby, that's all.' ' Oh! well,' sez Ah, ' if that's all, that's
wheear Ah want ti be.' An' Ah oppen'd t' deear an' stepped
oot, an' afoor Ah knew wheer Ah war, Ah war laid flat o' mah
back on t' platform. When Ah'd gitten mysen upended agaan,
Ah seed a chap at t' far end o' t' station clicking ther tickets

U 2

frev 'em leyke all that, an' Ah thowt ti mysen, 'Thoo'll finnd
thisen wrang when Ah cum up.' Hooivver, he nobbut tried ti
git hauf o' mahn, an' seea it didn't matter; bud Ah've ta'en
'em in, foor all that. Ah wadn't 'a'e deean 't if they'd nobbut
behaved thersens, bud tha didn't, chucking yan in an' potching yan oot. What diz ta saay, thoo wants ti knaw hoo Ah've
mannished ti tak 'em in? Whya, noo, Ah'll tell tha—Ah've
bowt a return ticket, an' Ah isn't gahin' back. Tha caan't
git t' best o' me.

WENSLEYDALE NICKNAMES.

Ov all the straange plaaces 'at ivver wur knawn,
Wensleydale bangs 'em all, ez noo s'all be shown,
Fur naams 'a'e been gi'en ti women an' men—
Yow'd wunner hooivver tha gat 'em, an' when.

'Drummer Tom' is t' naame 'at's sattled o' yan,
An' 'Sheggy' is t' naame o' 'Mary Toms'' son;
Ther's 'Bell Taylor Johnny' 'at lives up at Gayle,
An' 'Brissy' 's a man bred an' born iv oor dale.

'Cobbler Jack' drahves a bus fra Leyburn ti Hawes,
An' 'Wingy' uz sartinly been i' the wars;
Ah caan't tell hoo 'Hiapath' cam byv his naame,
An' ti call a man 'Shinnock' is sewerly a shaame.

'Ball Joan' is a chap ya'd awn ti be tall;
His weyfe, 'Lile Bella,' is sartinly small;
Her brother-i'-law is called 'Peggy Tom,'
An' 'Pop' 's a chap Ah knaw nut wheer from.

'Tom Kiss' is a tailor, a scheealmaister 'Paul,'
Whahl 'Jeff Boat,' a cobbler, wurks hard wiv his awl;
'Jim Nip' is a good un wi' pickaxe or speead,
An' 'Shetty' maks brass i' t' grossery traade.

'Spinner Niddy' an' 'Chapir' wurk up at t' au'd mill,
'Arry Ann' uz a doctor is faam'd fur her skill,
'Sailor Jack' Ah wad sweear nivver hann'l'd an oar,
Bud 'Planks,' the young joiner, 'll mak ya a doour.

'Dicky Flesk' is a grosser, an' 'One Boy' maks shoes,
An' 'Snegram' 's a naame 'at Ah wadn't choose;
'Sophy John' keeps a lodging-hoos noo at t' Toon foot,
An' tweea uther chaps are called 'Puin' an' ' Put.'
My frien's 'at are left Ah'll clap iv a lump,
Fur wa've 'Gaggon' an' 'Crackon' an' 'Bridney' an'
    ' Stump.'

The above would be written about twenty-five years ago. The verses were given to me by my old school-fellow, T. Fairbank King, Esq., West Witton. The two following verses are the sole remains of a much older rhyme, probably about 1800, and may have suggested the idea to the author of the above, whose name is unknown.

Ther's 'Jack's lass wi' cauves' an' 'Sally wi' Shanks';
Ther's 'Miss Nancy Prim,' an' young 'Tommy Pranks,'
An' 'Mucky stee Tom,' an' 'Hopplin' Bill';
Ther's 'Mary wi' t' scar' an' 'Au'd Muther Dill';

Ther's 'Tommy wi' t' warts,' an' 'Sticker Bull Coo,'
An' 'Sniftering Tom lass,' an' 'Ugger-a-boo';
Ther's 'Snouty' an' 'Corker,' an' 'Annie fra Gayle,'
Wheeas legs caan't be matched iv all Wensleydale.

The symmetry of Annie's legs must have been quite phenomenal, as my informant gravely told me that 'A chap cam all t' waay fra Lunnon ti tak t' pattern on 'em fer a statta' (i.e. statue) 'he war makking fur sumbody.'

Nicknames are quite common in Yorkshire. Take the following (some I do not know the surnames of, though well knowing the persons):—Jamma, Muca-

duck, Midge, Boxer, T' au'd bo'd, Blash, Tarra, Au'd
Willie, Bunks Canary, Black Jack, Coy Duck, Calcraft,
Fishy, Tankard, Trucky, Radden, Shut, Moudy,
Tramp, Slackbags, Jump a Bush, Dog Tom, &c.

A COMPARISON OF TWO LANGUAGES AS SPOKEN AT THE PRESENT DAY.

Ther war a chap fra Lunnon cam—
Fau'k said he war a swell.
He mebbe war ; yah thing Ah knaw,
He did his varra best ti draw
        T' soft oot o' yan.

He cam ti me yah daay an' sez,
'Oi sai, old chep, look h'yar,
Oi've lorst my bally self, yew kneow,
End jest which wai I orter gou
        To me aint cleah.

'Deoun't cher kneow, 'pon my word!
A fellah feels a fool;
Oi sai, look h'yar, I want to kneow,
Old cheppy, the best wai to gou
        To—er—the hall?

'Oi kneow yew Johnnies kneow a lot,
Beout land end worms end grubs;
Yew're beastly clevvah, deoun't cher kneow?
But deoun't yew find it bally sleow,
        This sort of life?'

'Noo, then,' Ah sez, 'ho'd on a bit,
Deean't ramm'l on seea fast;
Thoo sez thoo's lost, an' wants ti knaw
T' gainest road foor thoo ti goa
        Ti git ti t' hall.

'Noo, if thoo aims that road ti gan,
Just to'n thisen aboot,
Thruff t' staggarth tak an' to'n ti t' reet,
Mak foor t' larl yat thoo'll finnd i' seet,
       Nigh hand t' faud-yard.

'Thoo maun't gan thruff 't, bud to'n agaan,
Keep t' muckheap weel ti t' reet,
Tak t' pastur path, deean't laak wi' t' steg,
Foor he's neean ower neyce wheea's awe t' leg—
       He'd neb thi breeaks.

'Ah mak na doot aboot this tahm
Thoo'll sairly daffled be,
Bud theer's a lad theer flaying creeaks;
Thoo'd best ass him, an' when thoo speeaks,
       Talk plaan.'

'Thenks, awf'ly, but deoun't cher kneow,
Deah cheppie, 'pon my word,
Oi deoun't quite ketch what yew do sai,
The fect is, Oi hev lorst my wai—
       Yew understend?'

'Ah understand tha hard eneeaf,
Bud leeaks ta, mun, Ah s'u'dn't,
Bud a frien' o' mahn fra Lunnon cums,
An' just leyke thee, he 'aws an' 'ums,
       Whahl Ah caan't bahd.

'Noo, if thoo aims Ah's gahin' ti try
Ti scrape mah tongue, thoo's wrang;
Thoo cums an' slaps yan on yan's back,
An' eggs yan on ti talk, ti mak
       Nowt else bud gam.

'Ah've tell'd tha t' road ez plaan ez nowt,
An' Ah'll tell tha summat else—
Deean't aim at t' reeaks an' shut a craw,
Deean't slavver fau'k thoo dizn't know;
       Noo off thoo gans.'   B——.

THE SELL IN THE CELLAR.

Being fond o' sweets ov ivvery kahnd,
Nut lang sen, mun, Ah 'ed a mahnd
Ti help mysen tiv a lahtle teeaste
O' summat neyce i' puffy peeaste.
Thieves, thoff, awlus 'ev a fear,
Seea Ah lissen'd, an' Ah fan t' road clear;
Seea being a sharpish soart o' feller,
Ah teeak mysen reet doon i' t' celler,
An' theear on shelves afoor my een
War pies an' tarts fit foor a queen.
Ho'd on a bit! what's this Ah see?
A pankin full o' rich jelly.
Ah war fairly capp'd at fo'st ti see
Seea gert a bowl full ov jelly;
But theear it war, ez plaan ez daay,
An' tempting teea. Ah've heeard fau'k saay
When t' divil maks ya try yer luck,
He awlus leeaves ya stuck i' t' muck.
He 'ez a waay, he 'ez, by gock!
O' makking plother leeak leyke rock.
Whether 't be wenches, drink, or money,
T' divil daubs 'em all wi' honey,
Or summat else 'at catches t' e'e.
Noo Ah war 'ticed wi' that jelly,
Seea wi' mah whittle a shive o' keeak
'At 'ed been cutten, Ah did teeak.
Theer's a saying, mun, which rhymes wi' rhahm,
It's 'yah good thing tak at a tahm';
Bud t' lump o' keeak Ah felt wad be
Nowt mich bidoot Ah 'ed t' jelly.
Seea Ah laid a lump on t' top o' t' keeak,
An' sed, by gum! hoo neyce ya leeak!
Mah mooth war wattering foor a teeast,
An' Ah just war gahin' ti start mah feeast,
When Ah thowt Ah heeard sumbody cumin'—
Mah fo'st thowt war ov up an' runnin'.

Inti mah gob Ah cramm'd all t' lot,
Then nut a minit did Ah stop;
Up t' cellar steps Ah quickly flang,
Thruff t' kitchen deear went wiv a bang,
Whahl t' garden roond Ah madly rushed,
An' plants an' shrubs Ah sairly crushed
Wi' baith mah stamping feet;
Foor t' stuff 'at Ah'd thowt foor ti eat,
Oha! war nut it a sell!
Tak mah wo'd for 't, Ah scarce da'st tell.
Ti think o' t' trouble 'at Ah teeak
Ti git that jelly an' that keeak,
An' efter all mah langing hoap,
Ti finnd Ah'd gitten nowt bud soap.
Ya tumm'l teea 't; Ah needn't saay,
Sum stuff they'd made foor t' weshing daay.

B——.

A SPECIMEN OF YORKSHIRE FOLK-SPEECH, AS SPOKEN IN THE NORTH RIDING.

A Sketch. One of the 'Waddleton' series, by the Author.

Mrs. Waddleton goes to Stockton Races, and her friend Mrs. Bubbles is told all about it.

Sit tha doon, Mary, an' Ah'll tell tha all aboot it reet awaay fra t' starting. It war leyke this, thoo knaws. Ah sed tiv oor John yah daay when he cam in; Ah sez tiv him, 'Noo, then!' an' he sez ti ma, 'Noo, then!' An' Ah sed, 'Whya, noo, Ah'll tell tha what; what diz ta think if wa gan ti Stockton Races?' An' he sez, 'Wha, Ah's'u'd think 'at wa war daft—that's what Ah s'u'd think.' Ah seed 'at he war t' wrang sahd oot, an' seea Ah sed nowt neea mair just then. Bud bliss yer leyfe, Ah 'evn't been wed tiv a man fahve an' twenty year nut ti knaw t' reet end o' yan, ez a body might saay; seea Ah let things bahd whahl he cam intiv his supper, an' Ah' gat him a neyce bit o' liver an' bacon riddy. Ah seed him

soffen t' minit 'at he clapp'd his een on 't. Bud, what! ya
can ommaist awlus tattle onny man thruff his stomach. Ah
waited a larl bit, whahl he'd gitten a mouth or tweea full,
an' then Ah sat ma doon on t' cheer-airm, an' started ti
git ower him wi' mah au'd cunnin' waays, leyke what Ah used
ti deea i' daays geean by. Ah put mah airm roond his neck,
an' sed, 'Noo, that's a bit o' neyce, isn't it?' An' he sez, 'Aye,
lass.' An' Ah sed, 'Aye, it is; ther's neeabody else wad 'a'e
bothered to 'a'e gitten tha sike a neyce bit o' supper riddy.'
An' then Ah ran mah fingers thruff his hair. 'Neea,' sez he,
'ther's nut.' An' then efter a bit, he sez, 'Ah'll tell tha what,
lass; if thoo wants ti gan ti t' races, whya, what, Ah s'all 'a'e ti
tak tha.' 'Nut if ya doan't want ti go, mah luv,' sez Ah. Bud
Ah maad up mah mahnd 'at he s'u'dn't back oot on 't then. 'Bud
Ah'll tell tha what,' sez Ah, 'if thoo wants ti gan, Ah'll gan
wi' tha.' Thoo knaws it's best foor t' men ti deea ez t' weyfe
wants 'em at t' fo'st, acoz thoo knaws wa awlus deea git wer
awn way owther thruff t' yat or ower t' hedge. Bud ez he'd
sattled ti gan, theer war nowt neea mair ti saay aboot it. An'
seea when t' morning cam, wa gat up a bit seeaner, an' set
off foor Guisborough Station—ma, Sairy Jane, an' Jimmey,
an' oor John, wi' t' ten pund 'at mah aunt Martha 'ed left
uz ti buy a bit o' betterly furniter wi'.

Weel, thoo knaws, when wa gat ti t' station, oho—oo! Ah
think 'at Ah nivver war i' sike a hubbleshoe i' all mah leyfe.
Ah sed ti Sairy Jane, 'Noo, thoo mun tak ho'd, an' keep ho'd
o' thi feyther's coat-taal; an' thoo, Jimmey, lig ho'd o' mah sket,
an' see 'at nowther on ya leeaves go whahl wa're all safely
inti t' carridge.' Wa 'ed nobbut been studden that waay hauf
a minit, when oor Sairy Jane let oot t' gertest skrike 'at Ah've
ivver heeard; an' when Ah leeaked roond, if sha warn't i' the
cruel clutch ov a bobby. 'Noo, then,' sez Ah, 'what's up wi'
t' lass?'

'Ah've catched her i' t' act,' sez he.

'I' t' act o' what?' sez Ah.

'O' picking this chap's pocket,' sez he.

'Thoo gert dunderknowle!' sez Ah. 'Thoo's deean nowt
o' t' sooart; that's her feyther, an' sha's nobbut ho'ding on

tiv his coaat-taals, seea ez sha dizn't git hersen lost amang all this thrang. Leeave lowse, an' let her gan, an' mak a shift ti leet o' sumbody 'at's up ti neea good ; or else thoo'll finnd thysen i' t' wrang box, Ah can tell tha.' An' wi' that, Ah marched all t' three on 'em inti t' traan, which 'ed just puff'd itsen inti t' station. Sitting reet i' t' front o' ma, war a young chap wiv a rug ower his knees, potching three cards aboot maist miracklous leyke.

'What are ya trying foor ti deea?' sez Ah.

'Whya, it's a trick,' sez he.

'Whya,' sez Ah, 'Ah deean't see mich ov a trick i' owt 'at ya've deean up ti noo; onny bit baan could hann'l three cards i' that road. What is 't ya're efter?'

'Whya,' sez he, 'it's a trick 'at Ah seed a chap deeaing yesterdaa, bud Ah's nut weel up in 't yet. Ah's trying ti thraw 'em doon seea ez ya weean't ken wheer t' pictur-card tumm'ls.'

'Oha, that's it, is 't?' sez Ah. An' then Ah sez, 'Ah'll tell tha what, thoo'll 'a'e ti lig 'em doon vastly different ti what thoo 'ez deean up ti noo, afoor thoo'll mannish ti deea 't, foor Ah've seen wheer it's tumm'l'd ivvery tahm.'

'Maist leykely,' sez he; 'bud ya knaw it's ez Ah sed—Ah's nut t' maaster on 't yet.'

'Neea,' sez Ah, 'Ah seear thoo isn't.'

'Whya, noo,' sez he, chucking 'em doon agaan, 'which on 'em's t' pictur-card this tahm?'

'T' far ended!' sez Ah. An' Ah lifted it up, an' o' course it war, 'coz Ah'd seen it tumm'l theer.

'Aye, ya've mannished it this tahm,' sez he.

'Aye, an' ivvery uther tahm!' sez Ah, 'if ta caan't deea 't neea better 'an that!'

'Whya, noo then,' sez he, chucking 'em doon agaan. 'Deean't touch 'em, bud tell uz which on 'em is 't this tahm?'

'T' middle yan!' sez Ah, ez bou'd ez brass.

'Whya!' sez he, 'mebbe it is. Ah deean't knaw neea mair 'an what ya deea, but Ah's yan o' them 'at backs mah fancy, an' Ah'll bet yer a suverin 'at it's nut it.'

'Young man!' sez Ah, solembly, 'diz yowr muther knaw 'at

ya cum'd awaay wiv a suverin, foor ya're gahin' on iv a straange leykely way foor lossing on 't.'

'Nivver ya mahnd,' sez he ; 'Ah'll bet a suverin 'at it's nut it. Ah've gitten mah idea, an' ya've gitten yowrs—will ya bet?'

'Well!' sez Ah, 'Ah deean't ho'd wi' betting, an' Ah nivver at neea tahm did; bud if so be ez hoo an au'd boddy leyke mysen can larn ya hoo easy a suverin can be slithered awaay by backing up sike consate ez 'ez gitten ho'd o' ya, whya, here gans.' An' Ah pulled mah pess[1] oot, teeak t' on'y suverin 'at Ah 'ed, and handed it tiv a chap ez war sitting byv his sahd; t' young chap handed him yan an' all, an' then Ah lifted t' card up, an'—oho——o! Ah nivver war seea capped iv all mah leyfe—it warn't it. Ah trimm'l'd an' dithered fra t' top ti t' boddum o' ma; Ah felt just ez if mah back war stuffed wiv aspen leeaves.

'John!' Ah gasped, 'it's a swinn'l, it's a swinn'l; keep thi han' i' thi pocket, or thoo'll be lossing t' ten pund 'at mah aunt Martha left uz ti buy a bit o' betterly furniter wi'. An' deean't let on 'at thoo 'ez ten pund aboot tha,' sez Ah, foorgitting 'at Ah war letting ivvery yan on 'em i' t' carridge knaw 'at he'd gitten seea mich on him. Hooivver, Ah hedn't neea tahm ti saay owt else, foor just then wa gat ti Stockton, an' Ah think ther war a warse hubbleshoe on i' Stockton Station 'an what ther war i' Guisborough. 'Noo, then!' sez Ah tiv a gert fat woman 'at cam thrussin' up agaan ma, 'deean't ya cum shuvvin' ma aboot i' that road.' 'Noo, then, Victoria!' sez sha, 'what's t' matter wi' thoo?' 'Ah's nut Victoria!' sez Ah; an' leeak ya, Ah deean't think sha thowt 'at Ah war. Just ez Ah sed that, ther war anuther woman stood hersen reet on t' top o' mah pet bunion. 'Oh deeary ma, missus!' Ah skriked oot, 'Ah cannut bahd this, hooivver, ya're laaming ma sadly; deea tak yer foot off.' 'Noo, then,' sez she, 't' station isn't yowrs!' 'Neea,' sez Ah, 'bud t' bunion is.' An' wi' that Ah tell'd John an' t' childer ti follow cleease at t' back o' ma, an' Ah boudly pushed mah waay oot o' t' station. Neea seeaner 'ed wa gitten ootsahd, 'an Ah seed clagg'd on a wall a gert big bill, wi'

[1] Purse.

theease wo'ds printed on 't, 'BEWARE O' PICKPOCKETS.' An'
what d'ye think? Ah felt i' mah pocket, an' mah pess, eight-
an'-six, an' mah railway ticket 'ed all geean, geean ez cleean
ez a whistle. Ah didn't tell John ; Ah just sed, 'Thoo mun
keep thi han' i' thi pocket, or else sumbody 'll be takking t'
ten pund fra tha, if thoo dizn't mahnd.' He sez ti ma, 'Tha
weean't git nowt oot o' mah pockets, if tha deea shuv ther
han's in.' Ah sez, 'Thoo dizn't meean ti saay 'at tha've
gitten 't fra tha alriddy, diz ta?' 'Neea,' sez he, 'Ah 'evn't
gitten t' brass i' mah pocket—Ah've putten 't i' mah hat.' An'
then Ah notished 'at he 'ed his hancutcher tied ower his
hat an' unner his chin, leeaking foor all t' wo'lld leyke yan
'at war iv an extremity wi' t' teeth wark ; bud Ah thowt it
war t' capitalist idea 'at onnyboddy could 'a'e thowt on. Ah
didn't saay seea tiv him, acoz if yer praise t' men tha seean
git past thersens—bud ya knaw that bidoot ma telling ya.
Hooivver, Ah did wish 'at Ah'd putten mah pess i' mah
bonnet, an' then Ah s'u'dn't 'a'e lost it an' all 'at war iv it.
'It'll be t' best,' Ah sez, 'foor uz ti finnd wa waays ti t' course,
git summat ti eat, see a race, buy t' furniter, an' gan yam
ageean.' Noo, hoo can Ah picter ti tha a race-course? If
yer can 'magine all t' rackapelts an' raggamuffins gedered
tigither i' yah crood, shooting men an' screeaming women,
wi' rows o' carridges filled wi' lords an' ladies stuffing
thersens wi' pies an' pop, ya can 'ev summat ov a idea what
a race-course is leyke. Whahl wa war stannin' fair capped
wi' t' carryings on, whau s'u'd cum up bud t' varra seeam
young chap 'at Ah'd lost t' pund teea i' t' carridge. 'Ah's
glad 'at Ah've tumm'l'd across ya ageean,' sez he. 'Mebbe
ya may be,' sez Ah. 'Ya see, ya wan t' pund an' Ah lost it,
an' that maks all t' difference i' being glad ti see onnybody.'
'Aye, bud that's nut it; Ah've gitten a gert frien' o' yer
muther's wi' ma,' sez he. 'Oh, indeed,' sez Ah. 'An' whau
may that be?' 'This is the gentleman,' sez he; 'let ma mak
him knawn ti ya. This is Lord Swin'lton, whau knew yer
muther varra weel.' 'Ah didn't knaw 'at mah muther ivver
war acquainted wiv a lord,' sez Ah, leeaking t' chap ower;
bud ther war neea doot aboot his being a lord—Ah seed

that t' minit Ah clapped mah een on him. Oh yes, he war all there—ulster, eye-glass, di'mon' pin, an' ivverything. Ther's no mistakking a lord when ya see yan, tha're good eneeaf ti challenge. 'This is yer husband?' sez his lordship, leeaking at John. 'Got t' feeace-ache?' sez he. 'Noa, mah lord,' sez Ah, 'it's nut t' feeace-ache 'at he's suffering fra. It's leyke this, doan't yer see, mah lord : mah aunt Martha left us ten pund ti buy a bit o' betterly furniter wi', an' seea ez neeabody 'll finnd oot wheer it is, he's tied it up iv his hat, foor safety leyke, ez a body might saay, ez ya may term it so ti speeak.'

'An' a varra good plan an' all,' sez he.

Just at that minit t' young chap whau Ah'd lost t' pund teea teeak a fit, an' fell wiv his han's roond oor John's neck, an' doon tha baith went tigither, an' ez tha tumm'l'd on ti t' grund, Lord Swin'lton swiped oor John's hat off wiv his stick, an' next minit Sairey Jane beald oot, 'Oha, muther ! Lord Swin'lton's off wi' mah feyther's hat, an' it's gitten t' ten pund in 't.' Ah didn't stop ti think, thoo knaws, bud just off efter him ez hard ez ivver Ah could gan. Ah heard a man saay 'at he'd nivver seen a woman leg it leyke what Ah did. Ah s'u'd 'a'e catch'd him an' all, bud just when Ah war gahin' ti click ho'd ov his coat taals, Ah catched mah foot iv a tentroap, an' afoor Ah knew wheer Ah war, Ah war laid wi' mah heead iv a box o' cokernuts. 'Noo, then,' shooted t' man 'at awn'd 'em, 'cum oot o' that. Deean't ya cum cracking mah cokernuts, an' sucking t' milk oot; ther's neea free sucks here.' Ah gat up, an' Ah let that man 'ev t' length o' mah tunge— Lord Swin'lton 'ed ta'en hissel off by that tahm. Ther war nowt else for 't bud ti git wersens heeam ez best wa could. An' when Ah'd putten Sairey Jane an' Jimmy ti bed, Ah sed tiv oor John, Ah sez, 'Noo, John, Ah deean't want ti upbraad tha—it's been a sad daay foor uz—bud efter all's sed an' deean, thoo owt ti be asham'd o' thisel foor ivver letting a woman 'tice tha inti takking her ti sikan a blackguardy pleeace ez Stockton Races.

NOTE.—Wensleydale and Swaledale readers will

find it both interesting and instructive to compare
the above sketch, which is given in the Clevelandic
speech, with the folk-speech as spoken in their own
dale, which to a slight degree in pronunciation
tends toward that of Lancashire in one direction and
to that of Cumberland and Westmoreland in the
other. The two latter, however, on all counts,
bear a closer relationship to our North Riding
speech than either that of the West Riding or
South Lancashire.

It must always be borne in mind that the dialect
along the north-east coast of Yorkshire approaches
nearer to its original source than that of any other,
and especially so may this be said of Cleveland.

A HUNDERD YEARS HENCE.

[Date about 1800.]

A hunderd years hence
What a chaange 'll be maade
I' politics, morals, religion an' traade.
I' statesmen whau wrang'l
Or rahd upo' t' fence
Maist things 'll be diff'rent
A hunderd years hence.

T' heeads ov oor lasses
Sike changes 'll show;
It's nut ov ther mahnds
'At wa aim ti speeak noo,
Bud ov three-bishel bonnets,
Ther gypsies an' flats,
Ther scoops, navarinoes,
Ti snug lahtle hats

Wi' furs an' wi' ribbons,
Wi' feathers an' flooers,
Sum feshioned byv artists
An' sum plucked fra t' booers.
Bud heeads 'll be chaang'd teea,
Far larnt an' i' sense,
Afoor wa' 'ev coonted
A hunderd years hence.

Oor laws 'll be then
Nivver maade, mun, by feeals,
An' prisons Ah aim
'Ll be to'n'd inti skeeals;
Foor t' pleasurs o' vice
Are a feealish pretence,
Bud Ah doot if tha'll awn it
A hunderd years hence.

Noo vice 'll be kenn'd,
When at last fau'k awakken,
Ti be t' warst kind o' daftness,
Or else Ah 's mistakken.
T' lawyers an' t' doctors
And t' parsons wi' sense
Will 'ev altered ther waays
A hunderd years hence.

An' you an' me, reader,
Wheer s'all wa be fund?—
It 's wer souls 'at Ah meean,
Nut wer bodies i' t' grund.
S'all wa be wheer it 's joy,
Or i' sorrow intense?
Wa s'all all on uz knaw
A hunderd years hence.

                                   Anon.

THE SWEEPER AN' THIEVES.

By D. Lewis.

[Date about 1800–15. Published at Bedale.]

A sweeper's lad war late o' t' neet,
His slaape-shod shoon 'ed leeam'd his feet;
He call'd ti see a good au'd deeam
'At monny a tahm 'ed trigg'd his wame[1]
(Foor he war then fahve mile fra yam).
He ax'd i' t' lair[2] ti let him sleep,
An' he'd t' next daay the'r chim'lies sweep.
Tha supper'd him weel wi' country fare,
Then show'd him tul his hoal i' t' lair.
He crept intul his streahy[3] bed,
His pooak o' seeat[4] beneath his heead;
He war content, ner cared a pin,
An' his good frien' then lock'd him in.
T' lair fra t' hoos a larl piece stood,
Atween 'em grew a lahtle wood.
Aboot midneet, ur nigher morn,
Tweea rogues brak in ti steeal ther corn.
'Eving a leet i' lantern dark,
Tha seean ti winder fell ti wark;
An' wishing tha'd a lad ti fill,
Young brush (wheea yet 'ed ligg'd quite still),
Thinkin' 'at t' men belang'd ti t' hoos,
An' that he noo mud be ov ewse,
Jump'd doon directly on ti t' fleear,
An' t' thieves then baith ran oot o' t' deear,
An' stopp'd at nowther thin na thick—
Fully tha aim'd it war Au'd Nick.
T' sweeper lad then ran reet seean
Ti t' hoos, an' tell'd 'em what war deean.

---

[1] 'Trigg'd his wame,' filled his stomach.   [2] 'Lair,' a barn.
[3] 'Streahy,' strawy.   [4] 'Seeat,' soot.

X

Maister an' men then quickly raase,
An' ran ti t' lair wi' hauf ther clais[1];
Tweea hosses, secks, an' leet tha fand,
Which 'ed been left by t' thievish band.
Theease all roond t' countrysahd tha cry'd,
Bud nut an awner e'er apply'd,
Foor neean dast t' hosses awn na t' secks,
Tha war seea freeten'd o' ther necks.
Yah hoss an' seck war judged ez t' sweeper's share,
Acoz he'd kept baith t' farmer's corn an' lair.

The following note is appended to the original :—
'This tale is founded on fact, and happened at
Leeming Lane a few years ago.'

The student will find the above and four following
pieces interesting, as showing the alteration in the
pronunciation of certain words which has locally
taken place during the last eighty years in the
Bedale district.

DARBY AN' JOAN AN' THEIR DAUGHTER NELL.

A DIALOGUE BY W. HIRD.

[Date 1800-15.   Published at Bedale.]

Darby.

Joan! Ah noo 'ev thowt seea mich about it,
Ah seearly nivver mair s'all doot it;
At moorn an' neet, an' neet an' moorn,
Ah sumtahms wish Ah'd ne'er been born.

Joan.

Whya, Darby, prethee, let ma see,
Ah whoap it's nowt 'at's bad o' me.

[1] ' Clais,' clothes.

Darby.

Thee, Joan! neea, marry, neea sike thing.
Think bad o' thee! 'twad be a sin.
Ah think, indeed, Ah war a feeal
Ti send oor Nell ti t' Boordin'-skeeal.
Sike mauky feeals ez them, Ah think,
'Ev filled her heead wi' prahd an' stink,
Foor, sin' sha went, sha's grown seea fine,
Sha caan't deea nowt wi'oot her wine,
When t' dinner's owered, an' sha's seea neyce,
Sha weean't eat puddin' meead o' rice,
Thoff when at skeeal an' put ti t' pinch,
Fra sike good stuff sha'd nivver flinch.
An' all her notions are seea raased,
It's fit ti to'n her feyther crazed,
Fer leyke a toon wench, Ah declare,
Sha walks abroad wi' breasts all bare—
To show her shoon, an' hosen clocked,
Sha lifts her sket whahl Ah's fair shocked;
Nut 'at Ah care aboot t' fond lass,
Neea mair 'an this—it taks mah brass,
An' wiv her fine lang labbering tail,
Sha'll git her faththter inti jail.

Joan.

Whya, Darby, bud thoo knaws ther's t' Squire,
An' he, mayhap, will Nell admire,
An' efter all ther noise an' strife,
Thoo knaws t' young Squire he wants a weyfe.
Then let's be seear ti mak her smairt,
An' teeach her hoo ti plaay her pairt;
Sha seean 'll mak him towards her leean,
An' then thoo knaws 'at t' wark is deean.
Ez fer her breasts an' bare at t' airms,
It's feshion noo ti show yan's chairms.
Men leyke ti knaw, Ah've heeard it sed,
What's real an' fause afoor they wed;

X 2

Hoose'er, Ah'll try an' deea mah best,
An' leeave ti thee ti mannish t' rest.

Darby.

Bud, then, suppooase oor plot s'u'd fail,
An' me foor debt be sent ti jail,
Poor Nell wad nivver be a weyfe,
An' 'ev ti laabur all her leyfe;
Foor efter sha's seea browten up,
Hoo can sha ivver bahd ti stoop
Ti gan ti sarvice, ur ti spin,
Or ivver ti deea onnything?

Joan.

Whya, Darby, leeave it all ti me,
Ah'll mannish 't weel, an' that thoo'll see;
Ah'll be her pilot all mah leyfe,
An' mak her sum rich farmer's weyfe.
Then ez tha gan ti chetch, doon t' toon,
Ah's seear thoo'll saay, 'Weel deean, oor Joan.

T' DEEATH OV AWD DEEASY.

An Eclogue.

GEOORGY AND ROBIN.

[Date about 1800.]

Geoorgy.

Weel met, good Robin. Seed ya my au'd meer?
Ah've laated her an hoor i' t' looaning here,
Bud hoosumivver, spite ov all mah care,
Ah caan't spy her, nowther heead na hair.

Robin.

Whah, Geoorgy, Ah've ti tell ya dowly news,
Sike ez varra leyke 'll mak ya muse.
Ah just this minit left yer poor au'd tike,
Deead ez a steean, i' Johnny Dobson's dyke.

Geoorgy.

Wheer! What's that, Robin? Tell uz ower agaan.
Thoo's jokin'—ur ya've mebbe been mistaan.

Robin.

Neea, marry, Geoorgy; Ah's seear Ah caan't be wrang.
Ya knaw Ah've kenn'd au'd Deeasy noo seea lang.
Her breead-ratch'd feeace, an' tweea white hinder legs
Preeav'd it war her, as seear ez eggs is eggs.

Geoorgy.

Poor thing! What, deead then? 'ed sha ligg'd theer lang?
Wheeraboot is sha? Robin, will ta gan?

Robin.

Ah care nut, Geoorgy; Ah 'a'en't mich ti deea—
A good hoor's laabor, or mayhappen tweea;
Bud ez Ah nivver leyke ti hing behinnd
When Ah[1] can deea a kahndness tiv a frinnd,
An Ah[1] can help ya wi' mah hand or teeam
Ah'll help ti skin her, ur t' fetch her heeam.

Geoorgy.

Thank ya, good Robin. Ah caan't think, belike,
Hoo t' poor au'd creature tumm'l'd inti t' dyke.

Robin.

Ya mahnd, sha'd fun hersel just boon ti dee,
An' seea laid doon byv t' sahd (ez 't seeams ti me),
An' when sha felt, mun, t' paans o' deeath wi'in,
Sha stakker'd, tumm'l'd, fick'd, then toupled in.

Geoorgy.

Maist leykly—bud—what, war sha deead ootreet
When fo'st thoo fand her, when ta gat t' fo'st seet?

---

[1] E is used in the original.

Robin.

Ya s' hear, ez Ah war gahin doon t' looan, Ah spy'd
A scoore or mair o' creeaks byv t' gutter sahd,
All seea thrang, hoppin' in an' hoppin' oot,
Ah wunder'd what i' t' wo'lld tha war aboot.
Ah leeaks, an' then Ah sees t' au'd yode[1] leead,
Gaspin' an' pantin' sair, an' ommaist deead.
An' ez tha pick'd it een, an' pick'd ageean,
It just could lift it leg, an' give a greean;
Bud when Ah fand au'd Deeasy war ther prey,
Ah wav'd mah hat, an' shoo'd 'em all awaay.
Poor Deeas'! Ya mahnd, sha's noo worn fairly oot,
Sha's lang been quite hard-set ti traail aboot—
Bud yonder, Geoorgy, leeak ya, wheer sha's leead,
An' tweea 'r three nanpies chatt'rin' ower her heead.

Geoorgy.

Hey, marry! This Ah nivver wished ti see;
Sha's been seea good—seea trew a frinnd ti me.
An' 'ez ta cum'd ti this, mah poor au'd meer?
Thoo's been a trusty sarvant monny a yeear;
An' better treeatment thoo's desarv'd fra me,
'An thus neglected iv a dyke ti dee.
Monny a good day's wark wa've wrowt tigither,
An' bodden monny a blast o' wind an' weather;
Monny a lang dree mahle, ower moss an' moor,
An' monny a hill an' deeal wa've toddled ower.
Bud noo, wae'st[2] me! thoo'll nivver trot neea mair,
Ti nowther kirk, na market, spoort, na fair;
An' noo foor t' futur', thoff Ah's au'd an' leeam,
Ah s'all be forced ti walk, ur stay at heeam.
Neea mair thoo'll bring ma cooals fra Blakey-Broo,
Ur sticks fra t' wood—Ah s' 'a'e ti drag 'em noo.
Ma poor au'd Deeas'! afoor Ah dig thi greeave,
Thi weel-worn shoon Ah will foor keepseeaks seeave;
Thi hide, poor lass! Ah'll 'ev it tann'd wi care,

---

[1] Horse.   [2] Should be 'wae's t' me,' lit. 'woe is to me.'

'T'll mak a cover ti mah au'd airm-cheer,
An' pairt an appron foor mah weyfe ti weear
When cardin' woul ur weshin' t' parlour fleear.
Deep i' t' cau'd yeth Ah will thi carcase pleeace,
'At thi poor beeans maay lig an' rist i' peeace;
Deep i' t' cau'd yeth, 'at t' dogs mayn't scrat tha oot,
An' rahve thi flesh an' trail thi beeans aboot.
Thoo 's been seea faithful foor seea lang ti me,
Thoo s'annot at thi deeath neglected be.
Seldom a Christian 'at yan noo can finnd,
Wad be mair trusty ur mair trew a frinnd.

Anon.

THE INVASION.

An Eclogue.

[Date 1810.]

A wanton wether had disclaimed its bonds
'At kept him cleease wivin Au'd Willie's grunds,
Brakt thruff t' hedge an' wander'd far astraay,
He kenn'd nut whither, alang t' au'd to'npik waay.
Ez Willie wrowt wi' neea larl care
T' fence wi' stake an' thorns t' gap ti repair,
His neighbour Roger, heeam fra t' fair reto'n'd,
Then cam i' seet, i' rahding graith[1] weel don'd[2],
Wheea seean ez Willy, fast drawing nigh he spies,
Thus tiv his frinnd fra t' back o' t' hedge he cries.

Willy.

'Noo, then; what, Roger! 'a'e ya been ti t' fair?
Hoo gans things? Maad ya onny bargaans theer?

Roger.

Ah knaw nut, Willy, things deean't leeak ower weel;
Coorn sattles fast, thoff beeas 'll fetch a deeal.

---

[1] Riding apparel.   [2] Well dressed.

Ti sell t' au'd intak barley, Ah desaund[1],
Bud c'u'dn't git a bid ti suit mah mahnd[2].
What wi' rack rents, an' sike a want o' traad,
Ah knawn't hoo yan's ti git yan's landloord paad;
Mairower an' that, tha saay i' t' spring o' t' year
T' Franch is intarmin'd[3] ti 'tack uz here.

Willy.

Yea, mun! What are tha cummin' hither foor?
Depend on 't, they'd far better nivver stor.

Roger.

True, Willy—nobbut Inglishmen 'll stand
By yan anuther; o' ther awn good land
Tha'll nivver suffer, Ah s' be bun ti saay,
T' Franchmen ti tak a sing'l sheep awaay;
Feightin' foor heeam upo' ther awn fair field,
All t' poo'r o' France c'u'd nivver mak 'em yield.

Willy.

Whya, seear yan cannot think, when put ti t' pinch,
'At onny Inglishmen 'll ivver flinch.
If t' Franch deea cum, wha, Roger, Ah'll be hang'd,
An tha deean't git thersens reet soondly bang'd,
Ah can't bud think—thoff Ah may be misteean—
Nut monny on 'em 'll git back ageean.

Roger.

Ah think nut, Willy; bud sum fau'k 'll say
Oor Inglish fleet let t' Franch ships git awaay
When tha war laid—thoo knaws—i' Bantry Bay,
'At tha c'u'd nivver all 'a'e gi'en 'em t' slip,
Bud t' Inglish wanted nut ti tak a ship.

Willy.

Eah! that's all lees!

---

[1] Designed.   [2] Mind.   [3] Determined.

Roger.

Ah dunnot saay it 's trew,
It 's all unknawn ti sike ez me an' yow.
Hoo deea wa knaw when t' fleets deea reet ur wrang?
Ah whooap it 's all on 't fause [1]— bud seea talks gan.
Hoosivver, this Ah knaw, 'at when tha pleease,
Oor sailors allus beeat 'em upo' t' seeas,
An' if tha nobbut sharply leeak aboot,
Tha needn't let a sing'l ship cum oot;
At leeast, tha'll drub 'em weel, I dunnot fear,
An' keep 'em fairly off fra landing here.

Willy.

Ah whooap seea, Roger; bud an' if tha deea
Cum ower, Ah then s'all sharpen mah au'd leea [2].
What thoff Ah can bud ov a lahtle boast,
Ya knaw yan wadn't 'a'e that lahtle lost.
Ah s' send oor Molly an' all t' bairns awaay,
An' Ah mysen 'll byv t' au'd yamsteead staay.
Ah'll feight, if need; an' if Ah fall, wha, then
Ah s' suffer all t' warst mishap mysen.
War Ah bud seear my weyfe an' bairns war seeaf,
Ah then s'u'd be ti dee content eneeaf.

Roger.

Reet, Willy, mun! What an tha put uz teea 't,
Ah will mysen put forrad mah best feeat;
What thoff Ah 's au'd, Ah 's nut seea easily scar'd—
On his awn middin, an au'd cock feights hard.
Tha saay a Franchman 's to'n'd a different man,
A braver, better sojer ten ti yan;
Bud let t' Franch be to'n'd ti what he will,
Tha'll finnd 'at Inglishmen are Inglish still—
O' ther awn grund tha'll nowther flinch na flee,
Tha'll owther conger, or tha'll bravely dee.

Anon.

[1] False.   [2] Scythe.

COMIC SONG.

A Beautiful Boy.

[*Date about 1750.*]

'Twar yance on a tahm, aboot six i' t' morn,
When fo'st Ah saw leet—Ah meean, Ah war born.
Ther war t' doctor an' t' nuss, an' a gert monny mair,
Bud neean on 'em 'ed seen sike a babby afoor.
Ah'd t' neease o' mah dad, an' t' een o' mah mam,
Seea wi' sleet alterations Ah varra seean cam
Wivoot onny doot or the sleetest o' sham
    Ti be a maist beautiful boy.

Ti mak ma a beauty, skriked oot Mrs. Sneer,
'He'll be t' taal end o' nowt, bidoot a sweet leer.'
Seea ti gi'e ma this leer, yan on 'em shoots oot,
'When he's tumm'l'd asleep, lig a weight on his snoot.'
Which maad ma ti wink an' ti blink O!
Whahl t' ladies kenn'd nut what ti think O!
Bud tha mannish'd ti gi'e ma a squint O!
    An' maad ma a beautiful boy.

Ti finish ma off, Ah needed yah thing.
My gob ower-straight war—Ah meean for ti sing—
Seea ti lug it an' tug it all t' lot on 'em tried,
Whahl they stritched mah poor gob ommaist hauf a
        yard wide,
Shooting, 'Pull awaay, noo, Mrs. Ryder,
It's stritching a lahtle bit wider,'
An' Dolly, wheea stood just ashad her,
    Sed, 'Oh! what a beautiful boy!'

When they'd finish'd ma off, tha sent ma ti skeeal.
T' lads an' t' lasses all gen'd ez Ah sat o' mah steeal,
An' when they went yam tha sed 'at tha'd seen
T' fresh lad at skeeal wi' sike beautiful een.

'He can leeak onny road, an' that's handy,
His gob's reetly shapp'd ti suck candy,
Whahl his legs are what tha call bandy—
    Gocks! bud he's a beautiful boy!'

T' uther daay Ah war ax'd i' t' city ti din e,
When t' lasses i' rapters all thowt ma divine;
An' t' lot, whahl admiring mah elegant grace,
Let ther dinners aleean ti gaze i' mah feeace,
Then sigh'd, 'Ah s'all swound wi' surprise O!
T' sunleet caan't match his dear eyes O!
He's sike a neyce mooth foor mince-pies O!
    Oh! kiss uz, you beautiful boy!'

Ah sed, 'Lasses, beware o' love's piercing darts,
Foor feearful Ah be Ah s'all steeal all yer hearts;
An' then, mah deear lasses, ya'll sob an' ya'll sigh,
When you think o' mah charms, whahl ya'll langwish
    an' dee.
Ah can kiss, bud Ah caan't wed ya all,
Bud Ah wad if Ah mud, gert an' small;
Ah lang for ti cuddle ya all,
    For, ya ken, Ah's a beautiful boy.'

Mr. Fossick, of Carthorpe, kindly gave me the above
(and several others). He tells me it was sung when
his grandfather was a boy. As Mr. Fossick was born
in the early years of this century, I am not in the
least antedating it. Though turned eighty, the last
time I saw Mr. Fossick, for two hours he recited
poetry without having to halt for a single word. It
is in a great measure owing to the wonderful memories
possessed by our old people that I have been able to
collect the matter for this work.

CHAPTER XVI

A FEW SIMPLE HINTS ON THE GRAMMAR OF THE FOLK-SPEECH

THE ARTICLE.

THERE is no variation in the usage of the indefinite article, save that it still retains its place before participles and the adjectives *few*, *many*, and *great many*.

Ex.—'He started a calling o' ma, an' Ah started a genning at him, an' then wa set ti wark a lethering yan anuther.'

Educated people do not nowadays say, 'I sat a sipping of my tea, and a smiling at the kettle a singing on the hob.' No, it sounds quaint. And to those who know as little of their Shakespeare as they do of their Bibles, such speech is put down to ignorance, or a lack of education, when in point of fact they are listening to an echo of that old-time speech which was in full swing long before their great grandmothers were born, and used by really quite respectable people; e.g.—

'As he was yet *a* coming' (Luke ix. 42).
'I go *a* fishing' (John xxi. 3).

'While the ark was *a* preparing' (1 Pet. iii. 20).
'His greatness is yet *a* ripening' (*Henry VIII*).
'There is some ill *a* brewing towards my rest' (*Merchant of Venice*, Act ii. Sc. 5).

In such cases, however, 'a' cannot be parsed as an article. Many opinions have been given, but perhaps Cobbett, who holds it to be an abbreviation for 'at,' meaning 'without doubt,' has gained the most supporters. In the *Spectator*, No. 86, we find, 'Socrates' disciples burst out *a* laughing,' and in No. 420, 'The spirits which set the springs *a* going.' Such are by no means archaic forms of speech in the North Riding, 'bud ez common ez pigs *a* grunting at yan anuther.'

The definite article, as mentioned elsewhere, is 't'.' To this rule there are very few exceptions. Before certain letters it is almost inaudible; nevertheless, it is always there. It may be said, and with truth, that a perfect mastery of the definite article, both in speaking and hearing it spoken, has advanced those desirous of knowing something of our folk-speech— rather more than half of their journey. I know many people who are fluent speakers of the dialect, but who read it, even when in printed form, with the greatest difficulty; others who can read fairly well, but so far as understanding the dialect when spoken, might as well listen to a batch of Chocktaw Indians, as two or three good old Yorkshire dames when fairly letting out.

A Frenchman once said to me, ' I could understand you English people, if you did not speak so quickly.' Aye, just so, and so would many another body from

other counties understand a great deal of what our
country folk say if each word was uttered separately,
but with us, as in standard English, very frequently
no pause is made between commas ; so the difficulty
increases tenfold, when a stranger strives to follow
a fairly classical dalesman or woman. Take, for
instance, a few words which the other day I heard
a woman shout across a village street to her daughter.
Firstly, as they sounded when uttered, then the same
as they would be written, and thirdly, the translation.

As spoken. Teggattenlaadsitwinner.

As written. T' egg 'at t' 'en laad's i' t' winner [1].

Standard English. The egg (that) the hen laid is
in the window.

NUMBER.

This, with only a few exceptions, follows the
ordinary rule of grammar.

CASE.

The possessive case is noted elsewhere.

GENDER.

The same as in standard English, with this slight
deviation : many things which are neuter are spoken
of as being of the feminine gender. Ex.—'Sha's
a fine stack;' 'Sha's a bit rough ti-daay,' speaking
of the sea; 'Sha's gitten a fine bole on her,' speaking
of an oak. There can be no rule given for guidance,
because in a compound sentence the same noun is

---

[1] 'Window' is commonly pronounced *winder, winner*, and *windther*.

sometimes both feminine and neuter. A man speaking of his watch said, ' It's yan ov t' best 'at Ah ivver 'ed ; sha's a good un,' i.e. ' It is one of the best that I ever had ; she is a good one.'

ADJECTIVES.

Adjectives which in standard English are compared by the addition of *more* and *most* to the positive, generally form their degrees of comparison by the addition of *er* or *r* for the comparative, and *ist* or *st* for the superlative ; e.g.—

POSITIVE.	COMPARATIVE.	SUPERLATIVE.
True	truer	truist.
Expensive	expensiver	expensivist.
Dangerous	dangerouser	dangerousist.
Okkad (awkward)	okkader	okkadist.
Forrad (forward)	forrader	fo'derist.

Though it is quite common to hear such expressions as ' mair okkader ' or ' t' maist okkadist,' and the like, with other adjectives, it is also not uncommon for the adjective to be used as an adverb, as ' It's easy deean.'

PERSONAL PRONOUNS.

FIRST PERSON.

SING.	I, thou, he, she, it. Ah, thoo, tha, *or* ta, he, sha, it, 't.		

		Nom.	Poss.	Obj.
SING.	I		mine	me.
	Ah		mahn	ma.

PLU.	We	you	they	us.
	Wa	ya	tha	uz.

PLU.	Thou	thine	thee.
	Thoo	thahn	thee.

There is no rule to guide the student in the use of *thoo, tha, ta.* In a general way *ta* follows an auxiliary verb, and *thoo,* used in the accusative case, is definite in its application. 'He's shooting o' thoo,' and 'he's shooting o' tha,' have a well-marked distinction of meaning. 'He's shooting o' thoo' implies that the person told of the fact is the actual person being shouted of; not only does it point him out from amongst many, but the fact that *thoo* was used further implies that the shouting had better be attended to at once. 'He's shooting o' tha,' is merely certain information given, making known to some other person that he was being called for without regard to others.

RELATIVE PRONOUNS.

Who	which	that.
Wheea *or* whau	which	that *or* 'at [1].

Who and *which* are declined as follows. *That* and *what* as in standard English.

SINGULAR AND PLURAL.

STAND. ENG.	NTH. RIDING.	STAND. ENG.	NTH. RIDING.
Nom. Who	whau, wheea.	Which	which.
Poss. Whose	whaus, wheeas.	Whose	wheeas, whaus.
Obj. Whom	whaum.	Which	which.

The compound relatives are formed by the addition of *ever* and *soever*; 'at forming the compound 'ativver, i.e. *whatever.*

[1] *At* is often used instead of *who, which,* and *that.*

POSSESSIVE PRONOUNS and the compound personal and possessives are formed as under :—

STAND. ENG.	My	mine	thy	thine	his	her
NTH. RIDING.	Mah	mahn	{ thah / thi }	thahn	his	her

STAND. ENG.	Its	our	your	their	own
NTH. RIDING.	Its	oor *or* wer	yer	ther	awn

STAND. ENG.	Myself	thyself	himself	herself
NTH. RIDING. {	Mahsel	thisel	hissel	hersel
	Mahsen	thisen	hissen	hersen

STAND. ENG.	Itself	ourselves	yourselves
NTH. RIDING. {	Itsel	oorsels *or* -sens	yersels
	Itsen	wersels *or* -sens	yersens

STAND. ENG.	Theirselves	ownselves.
NTH. RIDING. {	Thersels	awnsels
	Thersens	awnsens.

DEMONSTRATIVE PRONOUNS.

This and *that* are used as follows :—

This refers to an object near at hand, *that* is rarely used, *yon* being almost universal, e. g. ' Yon man ower theer 'll tell tha.' *Q.* ' Which is Mister Thompson?' *A.* ' Yon chap's him,' i. e. ' That man is Mr. Thompson.'

INDEFINITE PRONOUNS.

Any	both	some	other	another	one	none	such
Onny	beeath	sum	uther	anuther	yan	neean	sich, sike

Yan and *yah* are noticed elsewhere, also *vide* Glossary.

Y

ADVERBS.

Adverbial peculiarities are fully noticed in the Glossary.

The PREPOSITIONS and ADVERBS mostly in use are :—

About, *aboot.*

Above, *aboon.*

Across, *quarrelled.* 'Him an' me's gitten across.'

After, *efter* or *efther*[1].

Against, *ower agaanst*, near to.

Among, *amang.* Amongst, *amangst.*

Before, *afoor.* 'For afore the harvest, when the bud is perfect' (Isa. xviii. 5).

Behind, *ahint.*

Between, *atween.*

Betwixt, *atwixt.*

Beyond, *ayont, beyont.*

By, *byv* or *by*, pronounced *be.*

From, *fra* before a consonant, *frev* before a vowel.

In, *i'*.

Into, *intiv, inti, intil.*

Near, *nearhand.*

Nigh, *near, ommaist*, also *nigh.*

Of, *ov* and *foor.*

Over, *ower* and *aboon.*

Beyond, *past.* 'He did entreat me *past* my saying nay' (*Merchant of Venice*, Act iii. Sc. 2).

Too, *ower.*

With, *wi', wiv.*

Until is never used, *whahl* always taking its place : no exception to this rule.

It may be noted this peculiarity extends to the south of Northamptonshire.

THE VERB.

It will only be possible to note one or two of the more striking peculiarities.

TO BE.

Indicative Mood.

Has two forms of the present tense.

[1] The *th* and *dh* sound, found in so many East Riding words, is not nearly so marked in the speech of the North Riding.

SINGULAR.		PLURAL.	
Ah is, *or* Ah's. *I am*, &c.	Wă		Wa're, *we are.*
Thoo is, *or* Thoo's.	Yă	are, *or*	Ya're.
He, Sha, *or* it is.	Thă		Thă're.

Also the older form is quite common—

SINGULAR.		PLURAL.
Ah be. *I am*, &c.	Wă	
Thoo beest *or* byst.	Yă	be.
He be.	Thă	

Examples :—

'Ah be gahin' ti morn.'
'Thoo byst efter neea good.'
'We be twelve brethren' (Gen. xlii. 32).
'If thou beest he' (*Paradise Lost*, Bk. i. 84).
'If thou beest death' (*Henry. VI, Part II*, Act iii. Sc. 3).
'If thou beest rated by estimation' (*Merchant of Venice*, Act ii. Sc. 7).

IMPERFECT.

SINGULAR.		PLURAL.
Ah war, wur, *or* wuz. *I was*, &c.	Wa	
Thoo war, wur, *or* wast.	Ya	war, wur, *or* wuz.
He war, wur, *or* wuz.	Tha	

PERFECT.

'Ev *or* hev. The aspirate is rarely heard.

SINGULAR.		PLURAL.
Ah 'ev been. *I have been*, &c.	Wa	
Thoo 'est been.	Ya	'ev been.
He's *or* he 'ez been.	Tha	

PLUPERFECT.

Ah hed *or* 'ed been, &c.

FIRST FUTURE.

Ah s'all *or* will be, &c.

Y 2

Second Future.

Ah s'all *or* will 'ev been, *or* Ah s'all 'a'e been.

Imperative Mood.

SINGULAR.	PLURAL.
Let ma be.	Let uz be.
Be thoo.	Be ya.
Be he, let him, her, *or* it be.	{ Let 'em be. Be tha.

Subjunctive Mood.

SINGULAR.

Ah be, *or* Ah maay *or* can be.
Be thoo, *or* thoo mayest *or* canst be.
He be, *or* he may *or* can be.

PLURAL.

Wa
Ya } may *or* can be.
Tha

IMPERFECT.

SINGULAR.

Ah war, mud, c'u'd, wad, *or* s'u'd be
Thoo wert, mudst, c'u'dst, wadst, *or* s'u'dst be } loved.
He war, mud, c'u'd, wad, *or* s'u'd be

PLURAL.

Wa war,
Ya war, } wur, mud, c'u'd, wad, *or* s'u'd be loved.
Tha war,

PERFECT.

Ah maay *or* can 'ev
Tho maayst *or* canst 'ev } loved.
Tha may *or* can 'ev

PLUPERFECT.

SINGULAR.	PLURAL.
Ah mud, &c.	Wa mud, &c.

Infinitive Mood.

PRESENT.	PERFECT.
Ti be.	Ti 'a'e *or* 'ev been.

Participles.

PRESENT.	PERFECT.	COMPOUND PERFECT.
Being.	Been.	'Evin' been.

TO HAVE.

SINGULAR.	PLURAL.
Ah've, Ah 'a'e, *or* Ah 'ev. *I have*, &c.	Wa've, 'a'e, *or* 'ev. *We have.*
Thoo's *or* thoo 'ez.	Ya've, 'a'e, *or* 'ev.
He's *or* he 'ez.	Tha've, 'a'e, *or* 'ev.

PERFECT.

Ah'd, Ah 'ed. *I had.*	Wa'd, wa 'ed.
Thoo'd, thoo 'ed.	Ya'd, ya 'ed.
He'd, he 'ed.	Tha'd, tha 'ed.

Affirmative.

Ah've, *or* Ah 'ev tă'en. *I have taken.*	Wa've, *or* wa 'ev tă'en. *We have taken.*
Thoo's tă'en.	Ya've, *or* ya 'ev tă'en. *You have taken.*
He's tă'en.	Tha've, *or* tha 'ev tă'en. *They have taken.*

Negative.

Ah 'evn't, *or* Ah 'a'en't ta'en. *I have not taken.*	Wă 'evn't, *or* wă 'a'en't ta'en. *We have not taken.*
Thoo's nut, *or* thoo 'ezn't ta'en.	[1] Yă've nut, *or* yă 'a'en't ta'en. *You have not taken.*
He's nut, *or* he 'ezn't ta'en.	[1] Thă've nut, *or* thă 'a'en't ta'en. *They have not taken.*

[1] 'Ya 'evn't' and 'tha 'evn't' are not so emphatic as 'ya've nut' or 'tha've nut,' &c.

Interrogative.

SINGULAR.	PLURAL.
'Ev Ah ta'en? *Have I taken?*	'Ev wă, *or* 'a'e wă ta'en? *Have we taken?*
'Ez tă ta'en?	'Ev' yă, *or* 'a'e yă ta'en?
'Ez ă[1] ta'en?	'Ev thă, *or* 'a'e thă ta'en?

IMPERFECT TENSE.

Ah'd, *or* Ah 'ed. *I had.*	Wa'd, *or* wa 'ed. *We had.*
Thoo'd, *or* thoo 'ed. *Thou hadst.*	Ya'd, *or* ya 'ed. *You had.*
He'd, *or* he 'ed. *He had.*	Tha'd, *or* tha 'ed. *They had.*

Imperative Mood.

'A'e *or* 'ev (have).

Infinitive Mood.

Ti 'ev, *or* ti 'a'e. *To have.*

Participles.

PRESENT.	PAST.
'Evin', *having.*	'Ed *or* 'ad, *had.*

TO DO.

Indicative Mood.

PRESENT TENSE.

SINGULAR.		PLURAL.	
Ah deea, diz, *or* duz. *I do.*		Wă	
Thoo diz *or* duz.		Yă	deea *or* div.
He diz *or* duz.		Thă	

---

[1] Throughout, save in this example, 'He' has been so printed, but without exception its utterance approaches nearer to that of 'a' or 'eh,' e.g. "'Ez he ta'en 't fra tha?' would certainly appear as if the speaker had said "'Ez *a* (or *eh*) ta'en 't fra tha?' But to save the reader much needless confusion, *he* has been retained, though it is rarely heard save at the commencement of a sentence.

SINGULAR.	PLURAL.
Ah deean't. *I do not.*	Wa deean't *or* divn't [1].
Thoo dizn't *or* deean't.	Ya deean't *or* divn't.
He dizn't.	Tha deean't *or* divn't.

MAY.

Ah maay.	Wa ⎫
Thoo maayst.	Ya ⎬ maay.
He maay.	Tha ⎭

IMPERFECT TENSE—Might.

Ah mud *or* might.	Wa ⎫
Thoo mud.	Ya ⎬ mud *or* might.
He mud.	Tha ⎭

Must.

SINGULAR.	PLURAL.
Ah ⎫	Wa ⎫
Thoo ⎬ mun.	Ya ⎬ mun.
He ⎭	Tha ⎭

Must not.

SINGULAR.	PLURAL.
Ah ⎫ maun't	Wa ⎫ maun't
Thoo ⎬ *or*	Ya ⎬ *or*
He ⎭ munnot.	Tha ⎭ munnot.

TO GO.

ACTIVE VOICE.

Indicative Mood.

PRESENT TENSE.

SINGULAR.	PLURAL.
Ah gan, *or* goa.	Wa ⎫
Thoo's gahin' *or* gannin'.	Ya ⎬ gan *or* goa.
He gans.	Tha ⎭

INDEFINITE—I was going.

Ah war, wur, *or* wuz ⎫ gahin'	Wa war, wur, *or* wuz ⎫ gahin'
Thoo wast *or* wart ⎬ *or*	Ya war, wur, *or* wuz ⎬ *or*
He war *or* wuz ⎭ gannin'.	Tha war, wur, *or* wuz ⎭ gannin'.

[1] ' Divn't ' is quite a common form of ' do not.'

INDEFINITE PERFECT—I have gone.

Ah 'ev *or* Ah've
Thoo's *or* thoo 'ez } gane *or* geean.
He's *or* he 'ez

Wa 'ev *or* wa've
Ya 'ev *or* ya've } gane *or* geean.
Tha 'ev *or* tha've

Infinitive Mood.

PRESENT.	PROGRESSIVE.
Ti gan. *To go.*	Ti be gahin' *or* gannin'. *To be going.*

PERFECT.	PROGRESSIVE.
Ti 'ev gane *or* ti 'a'e geean. *To have gone.*	Ti 'ev been gahin'. *To have been going.*

PRESENT.
Gahin' *or* ganning. *Going.*

PERFECT.
Geean *or* gane. *Gone.*

COMPOUND.
Having geean *or* gane. *Having gone.*

Observe *is* and *be* generally take the place of *are* and *am*. In fact, the latter word is very rarely heard amongst the country people. 'Are you Tom?' in the folk-speech, would be, 'Is ta Tom?'—the answer would not be 'Ah am!' but 'Ah is!'

Q. 'Is ta gahin' wiv uz[1]?' i.e. 'Are you going with me?'

A. 'Neea, Ah's nut,' or 'Neea, Ah isn't,' i.e. 'No, I is not' (I am not).

Nobbut, as a sign of the conditional mood, is quite as general as *if*.

Q. 'Will ta cum?' Will you come?

---

[1] 'Uz,' 'us,' is often used for 'me.'

A. 'Nobbut it be owt leyke, an' nobbut I git deean;' i.e. 'If it be anything like' (as to weather), 'and if only I finish my work.'

It is not uncommon to hear the future tense used for the present, and in many instances the country people, as it were, confuse the perfect tense and perfect participle. 'Ah've chose t' whip 'at Ah want.' 'I have chosen the whip I want (*or* like).'

''Ez ta broke t' winder?' would be asked in a whisper,. but 'Aye, he's brokken 't,' would certainly be the form in which it would be shouted to the other boys. 'Ah've spoke tiv him mair 'an yance,' would be the form such a declaration would take from one confiding to another the hopelessness of making any further entreaties; but 'Ah've spokken tiv him ower an' up agaan,' would be the language used when temper was in the ascendent. Nevertheless, those who would consider vulgar such sentences as have been given, are apt to forget that the accepted rules which govern the speech of to-day are only correct because they are of to-day. The rules which were once accepted may have been laid aside in favour of others; but the country people move slowly—their speech is that of their grandparents, and it is what they have been used to all their lives. They know nothing of the new order of things. And again, they keep very good company.

Examples:—

'I have already *chose* my officer.'

Othello, Act i. Sc. 1.

'Methought this staff, mine office badge in court, was *broke* in twain.'—*Henry VI, Part II*, Act i. Sc. 2.

' By what yourself too late have *spoke* and done.'
King Lear, Act i. Sc. 4.

' Why was this *forbid*?'—*Paradise Lost*, Bk. ix. 703.

' Waiting desirous her return, had *wove*
' Of choicest flowers a garland.'
Paradise Lost, Bk. ix. 839.

Steele, in the *Spectator* (No. 344), has, ' I have *wrote* to you three or four times.' And he is generally acknowledged to have been a fairly good scholar, but then his writings go back a hundred years, and they spoke differently then. Our people speak very much like it now.

The formation of the perfect and of the participle vary considerably from that of ordinary grammar. As a rule the past participle is formed by the addition of *en*. There are other striking peculiarities in the vowel changes. A list of some of the leading ones is here given.

Present.	Perfect.	Participles.
Build	Belt	Belt
Beeat (beat)	Bet	Betten
Bid	Bad	Bidden, bodden
Binnd (bind)	Bun *or* bund	Bun, bund, *or* bunden
Bleead (bleed)	Bled, blaad	Bledden
Break, breek (break)	Brak	Brokken
Brust (burst)	Brast	Brussen, brossen
Cast	Kest	Kessen
Cheease (choose)	Choaze	Chozzen
Coss (curse)	Coss'd	Coss'd, cossen
Cost	Cost	Cossen
Creeap (creep)	Crep *or* crop	Croppen
Cum (come)	Cam, com	Cum'd
Cut (cut)	Cut	Cutten
Darr (dare)	Dast	Darrd

Present.	Perfect.	Participle.
Drahve (drive)	Drave	Drovven or druvven
Felt (hide)	Felt	Felted
Feyght (fight)	Fowt	Fowten
Finnd (find)	Fan	Fun
Flig (fly)	Fligg'd	Fligg'd
Fling (fling)	Flang	Flung
Flit (to change one's abode)	Flitted	Flitten
Freeze (freeze)	Fraze	Frozzen
Gi'e (give)	Gav or ga	Geen [1]
Git (get)	Gat	Gitten, getten, or gotten
Greeap or group (grope)	Grape	Groupen or groppen
Grund, grahnd (grind)	Grund	Grun or grunded
Ho'd (hold)	Ho'ded	Ho'dden
Ho't (hurt)	Ho't	Ho'tten
Kep (catch)	Kept	Kept, keppen
Lap (wrap)	Lapt, lapp'd	Lappen or lappen'd
Let (let)	Let	Letten
Lig (lay)	Lig'd, lihd	Lihn
Lig (lie)	Lig'd	Liggen or lig'd
Leet (light)	Let	Letten
Loose (loose)	Lowse	Lowsen
Loss (lose)	Lost	Lossen
Preeave (prove)	Preeav'd	Provven or pruvven
Put (put)	Put	Putten
Rahd (ride)	Rade	Ridden or rodden
Rahse (rise)	Roase	Risen or rosen
Rahve (tear)	Rave	Rovven
Set	Set	Setten
Shak (shake)	Shak't	Shak't or shakken
Shed (shed)	Shed	Shedden
Shoe (shoe)	Shod	Shodden

[1] Written *gi'en*.

Present.	Perfect.	Participle.
Shut (shut) *or* shoot	Shut	Shutten
Sit (sit)	Sat	Setten
Slet (slit)	Slet	Slitten
Smit (infect)	Smitted	Smittel'd
Snaw (snow)	Snew	Snawn *or* snaw'd
Speeak (speak)	Spak	Spokken
Splet (split)	Splet	Spletten
Spreead (spread)	Sprade	Sprodden
Stan (stand)	Steead	Stooden
Stick (stick)	Stack	Stucken
Straad (stride)	Stroade, straad, *or* strahd	Strodden
Strahve (strive)	Strahve *or* stroave	Struvven *or* strovven
Strike (strike)	Strake, strak	Strukken
Tak (take)	Teeak, teuk	Ta'en, takken, *or* tuckken
Tell	Tell'd, tell't	Tell'd, tell't
Thrahve (thrive)	Throv, thrahve	Throvven
Thrust (thrust)	Thrast, throst	Throssen *or* thrussen
Treead (tread)	Trade, tred	Trodden
Wet (wet)	Wet	Wetten
Win (win)	Wan	Won
·Worrk (work)	Wrowt, wark'd	Wrowt *or* wrowten
Wreyte (write)	Wrate	Written

Conjunctions.

Some of those generally in use will be found contained in the following request :—

'Tommy's cum'd, *an'* Jimmy *an' all.* Noo, *if so be as* hoo 'at wa caan't finnd hoos-room for baith *on*[1] 'em, could thoo, *wivoot* putting thisen aboot, mannish ti tak Jimmy in? *Bud, hooivver,* thoo knaws *if in case 'at* thoo caan't mannish ti deea

[1] 'On,' prep. 'of.'

't foor all t' tahm tha're here, can ta *whahl* t' daay efter ti morn? Tha've cum'd *for ti* see Mary. *Nowther* on 'em's clapt ees on her *sen* sha went ti pleeace, *an' seeaner 'an* tha s'u'dn't 'a'e seen her, Ah wad 'a'e geean ti my aunt Martha; bud Ah'd better stop at yam *es* gan theer, *if so be 'at* thoo can mannish 't onny road. *Besides, thoo knaws* thi larl Lizzie could cum *an'* lig wiv oor Freddy, *bidoot* thoo *ligs* her on t' sŏfy. Ah think *'at* that wad be t' better waay; noo, what diz ta saay?'

Key.

'Tommy has come, *and* Jimmy *as well.* Now, *if* we cannot find room for both on them, could you, *without* inconveniencing yourself, manage to take Jimmy in? *Still, if* you cannot manage to do so for all the time they are here, can you *until* the day after to-morrow. They have come to see Mary, *neither* of them having seen her *since* she went to place—i.e. situation. *And rather than* they should have missed seeing her, I would have gone to my aunt Martha; but I had better stay at home *than* go there, *if* you can manage it anyway. *Besides,* your little Lizzie could come *and* sleep with our Freddy, *unless* you *lay* her on the sofa. I think *that* would be the best; now, what do you say?'

In reading the key over, it will be found, in several instances, that a single word does duty for several. This tendency towards redundancy is very common, e.g. 'If so be as how 'at wa cannot,' simply means 'If we cannot'; and 'Besides, thoo knaws,' is 'besides.' Instead of the last word, 'besides,' the usage of 'An' moreover 'an that' is very common.

The rule that prepositions govern the objective case, expressed or understood, the conjunction never, holds good in the folk-speech.

The conjunctions in italics are very rarely used, those in brackets commonly taking their place.

'Ah s'all be theer (an' all),' *as well.*
'(Bud hooivver) thoo mun cum,' *still.*
'(Wivoot) Ah cum, deean't start,' *unless.*
'(Ez) stop wiv him, Ah'll cum,' *rather than.*
'Ah've cum (for ti) see Tom,' *in order to.*
'Deean't leeave t'hoss (bidoot) he gi'es tha t'brass,' *unless.*
'Thoo wait (whahl) Ah cum,' *until.*

There are many who consider the folk-speech of our country people little better than a mixture of about equal parts of bad grammar and mispronunciation. Such a notion, I feel sure, can only have arisen from either a lack of information or undue haste. From such I would humbly crave a reconsideration of the case.

I can well understand those who know little of the various sources through which the standard English of to-day has come down to us, considering such words as those contained in the following list as being vulgar — *backerly, balk, belly-wark, botch, cant, chaamer, clag, cleg, drukken, flacker, flit, fra, lake, lang, leck, lig, lop, lown, luke, mirk, neeaze, owerwelt, raun, roke, rud, scraffle, shive, snite, steg, stob, stower, sump, theeak, thrave, till,* &c. Though some words in the list may be new to the reader, they are in common usage amongst our people. And what is much more to their credit, every one of them were doing duty hundreds of years ago. And as in many cases the pronunciation is identical with that of their Danish relations, we have grounds for assuming that not only has the word itself been pre-served, but the actual sound in which it was formerly uttered, though the spelling often differs greatly in the two countries. Take, as a single example, the North Riding word 'stower'; the Danish word is spelt 'staver,' but the pronunciation is exactly the same in both countries. Therefore, as Angus says, if the sound rather than the spelling be taken, the similarity of the languages will be found to be much more striking. A few so-called vulgar words and their respectable relations are given in the following list.

NOTE.—Scandinavian in this list must be taken in its widest sense, as including Old Norse, Frisian, Swedish, and Danish.

North Riding.	Scandinavian.	Anglo-Saxon.	English.
Backerly	Bagerlig	...	Late
Backstan	Bage-sten	...	A stone for baking cakes on
Balk	Balk	Balca	Beam
Band	Baand (O. N.)	...	String
Belly-wark	Bælg-værk	Bælig-wærc	Stomach-ache
Bid	Byde	Beódan	To invite
Bor	Borre	...	Seed of the burdock
Blendcorn	Blandkorn	...	Mixed corn
Botch	Bota	Botian	To mend clumsily
Brave	Brav	...	Goodly
Brede	Bredde	Bræd	Breadth
Cant	Kante, Kanta	...	To tilt on end

North Riding.	Scandinavian.	Anglo-Saxon.	English.
Calf	Kalve, v. to calve	...	Calf
Chaamer	Kammer	...	Chamber
Clag	Klæg	Clæg	To stick
Clap	Klap	...	To pat
Cleg	Klæge	...	Horse-fly
Clovver	Klaver	Klaver (Dutch)	Clover
Clip	Klippe	...	To clip
Drukken	Drukken	...	Drunken
Eaves	Ovs	Efesse	The eaves
Fau'k, Folk, Fooak	Folk	...	People
Felt	Fela, fiæle	Feolan	To hide
Flacker	Flagre	...	To flutter
Flittermouse	Flaggermus	...	The bat
Flit	Flytte	...	To remove to another house
Fore-elders	Forældre	...	Forefathers
Fra	Fra	Fra	From
Gimmer	Gimmer	...	Ewe lamb
Glooar	Gloe	...	To stare
Gob	Gab	...	Mouth
Havermeal	Havre mel	...	Oatmeal
Handsel	Handsel	Handselen	First money received
Holm	Holm	...	Low-lying land
Hoos	Hus	...	House
Humble-bee	Humlebi	...	Humble-bee
Kist	Kiste	Cist	A chest
Laat, lait	Lait	...	To seek
Lake, laak	Leka	Lacan	To play
Lake, laak	Leg, lec	Lac	A game
Lang	Læng	...	Long
Leck	Lække	Leccan	To leak
Lig	Ligge	Liggan	To lie down
Lop	Loppe	...	A flea
Lown	Luun	...	Calm, still

North Riding.	Scandinavian.	Anglo-Saxon.	English.
Luke	Luge	...	To weed
Middin	Modding	Midding	A dunghill
Mirk	Mork	Mirc	Dark
Neeaze	Nyse	Niesan	To sneeze
Owerwelt	Awvælt	...	To lie on the back as a sheep
Raun	Rawn	...	Fish-spawn
Riggintree	Rygtræ	...	The topmost spar in the roof
Roke	Rok	...	A misty rain
Rud	Rod[1]	...	Red ochre
Scraffle	Scravle	...	To walk in a feeble way
Shive	Skive	...	A slice
Snite	Snyde	...	To blow the nose
Steg	Steggi	...	A gander
Stob	Stub	...	The stump of a tree
Stower	Staver	...	A stake, a rung
Sump	Sump	...	Boggy place
Theeak	Tække	...	Thatch
Thrave	Trave	...	A number of sheaves of corn
Till	Til	...	To
Yule keeak	Yule kage	...	Yule cake

This list might have been greatly extended, but the above suffices for the purpose of proving that many of the words considered vulgar are simply venerable through age. If we inquire a little further, we shall find not only the words, but the form of speech used

---

[1] Rod = red.

Z

by our people, which so often seems ungrammatical, is actually that of the best writers of bygone ages. The fact is, as has been already stated, our vocabulary and mode of speech is not of to-day, but belongs to the time of long ago.

From Spenser's *Faerie Queen* take as examples the following words and grammatical forms, which are quite common with us to-day :—

That seemed both shield and plate it would have *rived*.
For to avenge that foul, reproachful shame.
To lose long *gotten* honour with one evil hond.
Much greater grief and *shamefuller* regret.
In hope her to attain by *hook or crook*.
To *tossen* spear and shield.
Me leifer were with point of foeman's spear be dead.
. . . how stout Deborah *strake*.
Inglorious now lies in senseless *swownd*.
But *lapped* up her silken leaves most *chare*.
Fast *bounden* hand and foot with cords of wire.
But, glancing on the tempered metal, *brast*.
And ever and anon, when none was *ware*.
And from her head oft rent her *snarled* hair.

In *Piers Ploughman*, 1362, by R. Langton :—

Under a brood bank—By a *burn's* side.
.   .   .   .   .
Some *putten hem* to the plough.

The Parsone's Tale :—

And *axeth* of the old ways.
. . . ought to *plain*.

Wicliff, 1380 :—

And he eat *honeysoukis*.

The Prodigal Sone, 1380 :—

> Tweie sonnes. And the younger of *hem.*
> A ryng on his hond, and *schoon* on his feet.
> And when he *cam.*

Tyndale, 1534 :—

And not long after the younger sonne *gaddered* all that he had *togedder.*

And when he *cam.*

And *axed* what these things meant.

From the Epistle to the Romans.

Also— *Geven, goven, moun, quyt* (quit = to repay), *stakker trone* [1] (throne), and scores of others are quite common with us.

The following past tenses are given by Angus as obsolete, and as having been so for long :—*fand, flang, slang, stang, wan, wrang,* every one of which are in frequent use.

In Wicliff's edition of the Bible we have :—

'The keperis weren *afeered.*' 'And *brak.*' 'The wisdom of this world *fonned.*' 'Clensed with *besyms.*' 'Mayster Moses seide if *ony* man.' '*Twey* men.' '*Ridile* as whete.' 'Joseph *lappide* it ' (St. Matthew). '*Moun* comprehende with alle seyntis which is *breed*' (Eph.). 'He *concitide*' (St. Luke). 'And *telde* him' (Acts). 'It schal not *rewe* Him' (Hebrews).

Such words, when uttered by our country people, are not vulgar, though they may sound odd, but that is because they are old fashioned and unfamiliar; and if their utterance has no charm for you, then it is music you never heard in your youth, and which your ear can never rightly appreciate. So

---

[1] The old pronunciations of 'trashing' for 'thrashing,' 'trepence' for 'threepence,' 'trive' for 'thrive,' &c., are frequently heard in Cleveland.

that you may see at a glance to what extent the
language has altered, and how the folk-speech has
remained almost stationary during the last three
or four hundred years, let us compare a few of the
commonest North Riding words of to-day with the
standard English of the thirteenth, fourteenth, and
fifteenth centuries.

Words of the 13th, 14th, and 15th centuries, taken from the best authors.	Common North Riding words, 1898.	Standard English as pronounced in 1898, or giving the word which has supplanted the older one.
Afeered	Afeeard	Afraid
Axed	Axed	Asked
Besyms	Bizzums, buzzums	Broom
Bounden	Bounden	Bound
Brak	Brak	Broke
Brast	Brast	Burst
Breede	Breed	Breadth
Burn	Burn	Stream
Cam	Cam	Came
Chare	Chare	Carefully
Concitide	Consated	Imagined, opinionated
Fain	Fain	Gladly
Fand	Fand	Found
Flang	Flang	Flung
Flig	Flig	To fly
Fonned	Fond	Foolish
Gaddered	Gaddered	Gathered
Geven	Geven [1]	Given
Goven	Govven [1]	Given
Gotten	Gotten	Got

[1] 'Gi'en' is by far the most general. Still, amongst the older people, one often hears 'geven' and 'govven.'

13th, 14th, and 15th century.	Common North Riding words, 1898.	Standard English.
Lapped Lappide	Lapped ⎫ Lapp't ⎭	Wrapped
Laverock	Lairock or lave-rock	The lark
Leifer	Leif or leifer	Soon, willingly
Moniment	Moniment	Monument
Mown	Mun	Must
Ony	Onny	Any
Partinge	Parting	Division
Plain	Pleean	Complain
Putten	Putten	Put
Quyt	Quit	To repay
Rewe	Rewe	Repent
Ridile	Ruddle or riddle	To sift
Shamefuller	Shamefuller	Very disgraceful
Snarled	Snarled	Knotted
Stakker	Stakker	Stagger
Strake	Strake	Struck
Swownd	Swound or soond	To faint
Telde	Tell'd or tell't	Told
Threpe	Threeap	Argue, contend
Togedder	Togedder	Together
Tossen	Tossen	To throw
Twey	Tweea	Two
Ware	Ware	Beware
Wrack	Wrack	Destruction
By hook or crook ⎫⎭	By hook or crook	By any means

Need I add more to prove my case? I think not.

Those interested are requested to read the concluding remarks at the end of the Glossary.

GLOSSARY

OF ABOUT FOUR THOUSAND NORTH RIDING WORDS

Giving only those daily in use at the present time, 1898, together with more than 1000 sentences as examples of the dialect.

FOR RARE AND OBSOLETE WORDS, SEE OTHER GLOSSARIES.

N.B.—Some words as we pass from east to west of the North Riding differ slightly in pronunciation; such, when established over a sufficiently wide area, have been included in the Glossary. It is owing to this that the spelling of the same word varies throughout the work, as in all cases the dialect has been given in accordance with the pronunciation of the locality in which the incident or word uttered occurred. As a single example, take 'fau'k,' which is universal along the coast; further inland, in the Great Ayton and Stokesley district 'fau'k' and 'fooak' are equally common, whilst in Wensleydale and Swaledale 'fooak' is only heard.

ABBREVIATIONS.

abv. = abbreviated.	ex. = example.	part. = participle.
adj. = adjective.	intj. = interjection.	pp. = past participle.
adv. = adverb.	n. = noun.	prep. = preposition.
conj. = conjunction.	N. R. = North Riding.	pret. = preterit.
pron. = pronoun.	v. = verb.	num. = numeral.

A.

A or **Eh,** *p. pr.* He. *Vide* footnote, p. 326.

A, *num. adj.* One. *Vide* **Yah, Yan.**

A', *adj.* All.

Aa! *intj.* Exclamation of surprise, admiration.

Aa, but. Aa, but Ah saay! *intj. of comparison.*

    Ex.—*Aa, but Ah saay! Ah aim at yon pig's better 'an oors.*

Aback, *adv.* Behind.

Aback o' beyont, *adv.* Out of sight, out of the way.

    Ex.—*Them things is sadly i' t' road. Ah wish thoo'd git 'em aback o' beyont.*

Abeear, *v.* To endure.

    Ex.—*Ah caan't abeear t' seet o' yon lass.*

Aboon, *prep.* Above.

Aboon-heead, *adv.* Overhead.

    Ex.—*It leeaks a bit blackish aboon-heead.*

Abraid, *v.* To wake, to stir up.

Abrede, *adv.* Width.

Accorn, Yackron, *n.* The acorn.

Acoz, *conj.* Because; often abv. to ''coz.'

Actilly, *adv.* Actually.

Addle, *adj.* Barren.

Addle, *v.* To earn.

Addlin', *n.* A term of contempt.

    Ex.—*Thoo larl addlin', ger awaay wi' tha.*

Addlin's, *n.* Wages.

Admire, *v.* 1. To approve, to like. 2. To wonder.

    Ex.—1. *Ah deean't admire a job o' that soart. Ah admire t' maist o' what he did.* 2. *Ah caan't bud admire at t' waay he did it.*

Adreead, *adj.* In a state of fear.

'A'e, 'Ev, *v.* Have.

Aether, Owther, *conj.* Either.

Afeear'd, *adj.* and *part.* Afraid, seized with fear.

Afoor, Afur, *prep.* Before.

Afoor- or **Afur-lang,** *adv.* Before long, very shortly.

After- or **Efter-birth,** *n.* Placenta.

Afterwit, Efterwit, *n.* An idea which strikes one often when too late to remedy a mistake.

Agaan, Ageean, *prep.* Again.

Agaanst or **Ageeanst,** *prep.* Against.

Agaate, Ageeat, *adv.* 1. On the way. 2. Begun; also used as a *part.* 3. To disturb. 4. To set going.

    Ex.—1. *Wa s'all git agaate ti morn at morn.* 2. *Ak's agaate wi' 't noo.* 3. *Naay, what! Ak'd gitten all sattled peeacably, an' thoo gans an' sets 'em all agaate agaan.* 4. *Ak've putten a new pin in, an' sha's agaate agaan noo.*

Agee, *adv.* Askew.

Ah, *per. pron.* I.

Ah'll. I will.

Ah'll awaand. I will warrant.

Ah'll be bun. I will be bound, I am sure.

Ahint, *adv.* and *prep.* Behind.

Aiblings, *adv.* Maybe, perhaps.

Aim, Aam, Yam, *v.* 1. To intend. 2. To be under the impression. *Vide* chapter on 'Idioms.'

    Ex.—1. *Wa aim ti start ti flit ti morn fust thing,* i.e. 'We intend to remove our goods first thing to-morrow.' 2. *Ah yam'd 'at he war Tommy's bairn,* i.e. 'I thought that he was Tom's bairn.'

Airm, *n.* Arm.
Airt, *n.* Point of the compass.
　　Ex.—*What airt is t' wind in ? Whya, sha's nobbut iv
　　a bad airt; Ah doot 'at it's nut gahin' ti tak up.*
Al, Yal, *n.* Ale.
Alaane, Aleean, *adj.* Alone.
Aliments, *n.* Elements.
All of a heh, *adj.* Inclining to one side.
All out, *adv.* Altogether, absolutely.
All ti nowt. Gone to nothing, dwindled away.
Ally, Ally-taw, *n.* A boy's taw of white marble, distinct from
　either a stony or glassy.
Along of, *prep.* Owing to, in consequence of.
Amaist, Omaist, *adv.* Almost.
Amang, *prep.* Among.
Amang-hands. Implies the doing of certain work coincidently
　with other labour.
Amell, *prep.* In the midst, between.
Ance. *Vide* **Yance.**
An', *conj.* And.
'An, *conj.* Than.
An' all, *conj.* and *adv.* As well as, besides, truly.
Ane, *num. adj.* One, usually followed by 'ither,' i.e. other.
　　Ex.—*If Ah'll tak t' ane, will thoo tak t' ither ? Vide* **Yan.**
Anew, *adj.* Enough in number.
Angry, *adj.* Inflamed.
Anotherkins, *adj.* Different altogether.
　　Ex.—*Sha sartinly raffled on tiv a gert len'th, bud sha
　　nivver tell'd ma 'at Willie hed offered ti gi'e ma summat —
　　that's anotherkins, thoo knaws.*
Anters, *conj.* For fear, lest.
Any, Onny, *adv.* At all, in the least.
　　Ex.—*Ah doan't aim 'at he'll help onny*, i.e. 'I do not think
　　that he will help at all.' *He teeak ho'd, bud he didn't lift
　　onny*, i. e. 'He took hold, but he did not lift in the least.'
Apace, Apaace, *adv.* With great speed.
　　Ex.—*He's gitten tweea mair lads; he'll git on apaace noo.*
Appron, *n.* The fat covering the belly of ducks and geese.
Arf, Arfish, *adj.* 1. Timid, fearful. 2. Unwilling.
　　Ex.—1. *He wur a bit arfish when t' dog boonced oot.*
　　2. *Naay, Ah deean't think he'll cum, he seem'd a bit arfish
　　when Ah ax'd him.*
Argify, *v.* To argue.
Arn, *v.* To earn.
Arr, *n.* A scar.
　　Ex.—*Ah's afeear'd he'll be arr'd sairly on his feeace, he gat
　　sae badly bo'nt.*

Arran web, *n.* A cobweb.

Arridge, *n.* The rough edge left after either sawing or filing; the edge of a squared stone, of furniture, &c.

Arse-end, *n.* The end of a stook which rests upon the ground.

Arsey-varsey. Upside down, great confusion.

Ashads, *prep.* Beside.

Asher, *adj.* Ashen.

Ask, Esk, *n.* The newt.

Aslew, *adj.* Not perpendicular.

Ass, *v. Vide* **Ax.**

Asseer, *v.* To assure. *adv.* Instead, in the place of.

Assel-tree, *n.* Axle-tree.

Ass-hoal, *n.* A hole with a grate over it, usually under the kitchin fire, to hold the fine ash.

Assil-teeath or **-tewth**, *n.* A molar, a back tooth.

Ass-manner, *n.* Manure obtained from the ash-midden.

Ass-midden, *n.* The place in which ashes and other refuse is thrown.

Asteead, *adv.* Instead.

As tite, Ez tite, *adv.* As soon, rather, readily.

> Ex.—*Ak'd ez tite gan ez stop*, i.e. 'I would as soon go as stay.' *Ak'd ez tite kiss t' dowter ez t' muther*, i.e. 'I would rather kiss the daughter than the mother.'

'At, *rel. pron.* and *conj.* 1. Who. 2. That. 3. Which.

> Ex.—1. *Him 'at tell'd tha, tell'd tha wrang*, i.e. 'He who told you, told you wrongly.' 2. *Ah caan't saay 'at ivver Ah did*, i.e. 'I cannot say that ever I did.'

At, *prep.* 1. To. 2. Also used in a verbal sense of to worry. 3. To attack. 4. To bother.

> Ex.—1 and 3. *What's he deean at tha 'at thoo s'u'd at him leyke that?* i.e. 'What has he done to you that you should attack or illuse him like that.' 2 and 4. *Ah s'all 'ev ti let her 'ev t' pup, sha's awlus at ma aboot it.*

Atefter or **Atefther**, *adv.* Afterwards.

> Ex.—*Whya, noo, Ak'll see tha atefter aboot it. Aye, that's what he sed at fo'st, bud he tell'd a different taal atefter.*

Athout, *prep.* and *conj.* Without, unless.

Atop o', *prep.* On the top of.

Atter, *n.* Matter, mucus.

Atween, *prep.* Between.

Au'd-feshioned, *adj.* Precocious, antique.

Au'd-leyke, *adj.* Aged.

Aught, *n.* Anything.

Aund, Awned, *pp.* Possessed.

Aw, *adj.* All.

Aw, *intj.* Oh.

Awaay, *intj.* Go on, continue doing the same thing.

Ex.—*It maay scream awaay foor owt 'at Ah care,* i.e. 'Scream on.' 'Fight away, my lads.' 'Shout away, my boys.'

Awaay-gannin' crops, *n.* The crops an outgoing tenant sows and reaps on the farm he is leaving, in consideration of certain other land which he has fallowed and manured.

Awanting, *adj.* 1. Needed. 2. Lacking sense.

Ex.—1. *T' land's vastly awanting a sup o' rain.* 2. *That bairn's a bit awanting.*

Awe. *Vide* **Owe.**

Awhahl, *conj.* Awhile. *Vide* **Whahl.**

Awkward. *Vide* **Okkad.**

Awlus, Allus, *adv.* Always.

Awm, *n.* The elm.

Awn, *v.* 1. To own. 2. To admit.

Ex.—1. *Ah awn t' dog,* i.e. 'I own the dog.' 2. *Did ta awn tiv owt?* i.e. 'Did you admit anything?' *Neea, Ah awned ti nowt,* i.e. 'No, I admitted nothing.' *Ti awn ti,* is 'to confess.'

Ax, Ax'd, Ass, or **Ast,** *v.* To ask.

Ex.—*Ah ax'd him, bud he wadn't 'a'e neea truck. Ah's ast oot ti tea ti morn at neet. Ah wadn't ax him owt,* or *ass him.*

Ax'd at chetch or **chŭch** }
Ax'd oot } Publishing the banns.

Ex.—*Tha'll be ax'd at chetch o' Sunday; he's putten t' spurrings in.*

Aye, bairn. Assent.

Aye, foor seear. Aye, for sure.

Aye, marry, *adv.* Certainly, yes.

Ex.—*Diz ta believe what sha's sed aboot Hannah? Aye, marry, that Ah deea—Hannah war sadly flowtered t' other daay, when Ah plump'd her wi' 't.*

B.

Bab, Babby, *n.* A baby.

Babbles an' Saunters. 1. Wearying repetitions. 2. Unreliable information.

Ex.—1. *T' sarmon war larl better 'an babbles an' saunters.* 2. *Tak neea notish ov owt 'at sha sez, all 'at sha knaws is babbles an' saunters.*

Back, *v.* *Vide* **Backen.**

Back-bearaway, *n.* The common bat.

Back-burden, *n.* A load carried on the back.

Backen, *v.* 1. To retard. 2. To hold in check.

Ex.—1. *T' frost 'll backen things a gay bit.* 2. *Wa did*

all 'at ivver wa c'u'd, bud wa c'u'dn't backen t' inflamma-
tion; 't 'ed gitten past deeaing owt, afoor t' doctor cam.

Back-end, *n.* The time following harvest.

Backendish, *adj.* Winterly.

Ex.—*It's cau'd, an' begins ti feel a larl bit backendish.*

Backerly, *adj.* and *adv.* Late, backward.

Backly, *adv.* Late, backward.

Backreck'nin'. *n.* A misunderstanding.

Ex.—*Noo Ah've maad it plaan, 'evn't Ah? foor Ah*
deean't want neea backreck'nin' at efter.

Back-talk, *n.* Impudently answering again.

Back-side, *n.* 1. The back of the house. 2. That part which
is opposed to the front of anything.

Ex.—1. *Put t' barrer at t' back-side.* 2. *It's at t' back-side*
o' t' barn.

Backstan, *n.* A sheet of iron, sometimes a stone, having an
iron hoop to hang it over the fire by, used to bake cakes upon.

Back up, To get one's. To make angry.

Back-word, *adv.* To countermand, to decline.

Bad, *adj.* 1. Difficult. 2. Unwell.

Ex.—1. *Ah finnd it varra bad ti deea.* 2. *Ah feel ez bad*
ez ivver Ah can.

Bad, Bod, *pret.* of ' to bid.'

Ex.—*Ah bad, an' sha bod, an' Tommy gat it.*

Badger, *n.* A huckster.

Badger, *v.* To beat down in a bargain.

Ex.—*Thoo mun ass him a lump mair 'an what thoo wants,*
foor he's a despert yan at badgering.

Badly, *adv.* 1. Sickly, ill. 2. Very much.

Ex.—1. *Mah wo'd, bud Ah is badly.* 2. *Ah's badly i' want*
ov a self-binnder. It badly wants leeaking teea.

Badness, *n.* Wickedness.

Ex.—*He's full o' nowt bud badness.*

Bags Ah fuggy. ' I claim the first,' whether it be innings or first
place in a game, &c.

Bahd. *Vide* **Bide.**

Bainest, *adj.* The nearest.

Ex.—*It's t' bainest waay ti gan byv t' pastur.*

Bairn, Barn, Baan, *n.* A child.

Bairn-birth, *n.* Lying-in.

Bairnish, *adj.* Childish.

Bairn-lakings, *n.* Playthings.

Bakin', *n.* The whole of the bread baked at one time.

Bakus, Bakehoos, *n.* The bakehouse.

Balk, Bawk, *n.* A beam, also a worthless corner of a field.

Ball, *n.* The palm of the hand, or sole of the foot.

Bally-bleeazes, *n.* A bonfire.

Bam, *n.* and *v.* 1. A cheat, a joke, to cheat. 2. To play a joke.
> Ex.—1. *He bamm'd ivvery hand he played.* 2. *He went all*
> *t' waay ti Stowsla ti see her, an' sha nivver cam oot; it*
> *war nowt bud a bam o' Jack's.*

Band, *n.* String, twisted straw used by the harvesters to bind sheaves with.

Band-maker, *n.* A maker of bands in the harvest-field.

Bang, *v.* To thrash.

Bangs all, *v.* Surpasses everything.
> Ex.—*He bangs all, yon youth. That's a capper; it bangs*
> *all, it diz.*

Bank up, *v.* To collect in masses, as clouds.

Banky, *adj.* Hilly, applied to road or land.

Bar, *adj.* Bare.

Barfan, *n.* A horse-collar.

Bargh, Barugh, Barf, *n.* A hill forming part of a low ridge, as Lang Barugh, Great Ayton.

Bargollies, *n.* Young birds before they are feathered.

Barguest, *n.* An apparition, applied to ghosts in general.

Barken'd, *v.* Encrusted.

Barley-bairn, *n.* A child born shortly after marriage.

Barm, *n.* Yeast.

Barren, *n.* The external part of the sexual organ of a cow.

Barrow, *n.* The flannel in which a newly-born child is wrapped.

Bass, *n.* Any kind of matting made from reeds or grass.

Bat, *n.* 1. A blow. 2. A condition. 3. A small amount of work.
> Ex.—1. *Ah gav' him sike a bat ower t' lug.* 2. *He's awlus*
> *at that bat,* i.e. ' game.' 3. *Ah've nut deean a bat sen*
> *yesterdaay.*

Bate, *v.* To reduce in price.
> Ex.—*Thoo'll 'a'e ti bate summat afoor wa can barg'in.*

Bath, *v.* To wash a child; to foment with hot water.

Batten, *n.* Two sheaves of straw.

Batter, *n.* An inclination inwards, a narrowing towards the summit. A wall which is wider at the base than at the summit is said to ' batter.'
> Ex.—*Thoo'll be leyke ti gi'e it a bit mair batter, foor if*
> *t' bank at t' back gi'es waay, it'll nivver bahd it thrussin'*
> *agaan 't.*

Batter-fanged, *adj.* Beaten and scratched by a woman.
> Ex.—*He nobbut sed tweea wo'ds ti Ann, when sha batter-*
> *fang'd him sairly.*

Battin, *n.* A rafter of any length, 7 × 2½ in. thick.

Baufy, *adj.* Strong.

Bavin, *n.* A bundle of sticks.

Bawks, *n.* The yoke.

Bazzak, *v.* To strike with force.

Beck, *n.* A small stream.

Bedfast, *adj.* Confined to bed.

Bed-happings, *n.* Bedclothes.

Bed-heead, *n.* The pillow end.

Bedho'dden, *adj. Vide* **Bedfast.**

Bedoot, Beoot, *prep.* 1. Without. 2. Unless.
    Ex.—1. *He's gahin' ti gan bedoot tha.* 2. *Bedoot thoo cums an' all, Ah saan't gan, soa thoo knaws.*

Bedstock, *n.* The wooden frame of a bed.

Bed-twilt, *n.* Bed-quilt.

Beeaf, *n.* The bough of a tree. *Vide* also **Bugh.**

Beeak, *v.* To bake.

Beeal, *v.* 1. To roar as an animal. 2. To cry out in pain. 3. To shout loudly.
    Ex.—1. *He beeal'd leyke a bull when tha catch'd him.* 2. *Ah nivver heeard a lass beeal oot leyke what sha did when t' doctor cut her wicklow.* 3. *When he calls o' yan, he beeals ez if yan war deeaf; he ommaist deavens yan.*

Beean, *n.* A bone.

Beean't. Be not (am not).

Beearer, *n.* Martingale.

Beeas, Beeos, Beeast, *n.* An animal of the ox kind.

Beeaslings, *n.* The first milk drawn from a cow after calving.

Beeldin', *n.* A building.

Bee-skep, *n.* A straw hive.

Behappen, *v.* To happen to, perhaps.

Behauf, *n.* Behalf, sake.

Beho'dden, *pp.* To be indebted to.

Belang, *v.* To own, to belong to.

Belder, *v.* To bellow as a bull, to cry out loudly.

Beleyke, *adv.* Probably.

Belk, *v.* To belch.

Bellacing, *part.* A sound thrashing.

Belly-cheer, *n.* Good cheer.

Belly-glut, *n.* A greedy glutton.

Belly-timber, *n.* Food.

Belly-wark, *n.* A pain in the stomach.

Belt, *pp.* of ' Build.'

Bensil, *n.* A blow.

Bensiling, *n.* A sound chastisement.
    Ex.—*Ak'll gi'e tha sike a bensiling if ivver thoo cums that gam agaan.*

Benty, *adj.* Wiry, blue-looking, applied to pasture herbage.

Berry-tree, *n.* The gooseberry tree.

Bessy-babs, *n.* One who behaves like a child.

Bessy-bainworts, *n.* Daisies.

Bessy-ducker or -douker, *n.* The water-ousel.

Best leg first, To put one's = To hurry.

Ex.—*If ya aim ti catch t' traan ya'll 'a'e ti put yer best leg fo'st.*

Best and Bested. Used in a verbal sense—1. To get the better of. 2. To overcome.

Ex.—1. *Ah bested him,* i. e. 'I got the better of him.' 2. *Ah can seean best yon youth,* i. e. 'I can soon vanquish that fellow.'

Bethink, Bethowt, *v.* To recollect.

Ex.—*Ah caan't bethink ma ov hauf o' what sha sed. When Tom ga' ma a inklin' Ah bethowt ma ov ivverything 'at 'ed ta'en pleeace; aye, all 'at t' ane 'ed sed ti t' other, thoff afoor that all t' lot 'ed cleean slipped fra mah mahnd.*

Better, *adj.* and *v.* 1. More. 2. To gain by. 3. Improved in health.

Ex.—1. *It's better 'an a month sen.* 2. *Ah s' better mysel by changing pleeaces.* 3. *Ah's a lot better ti-daay.*

Bettering, *n.* An improvement.

Bettermy, *adj.* 1. Used to denote those in a higher position. 2. Polished.

Ex.—1. *T' bettermy fau'k 'ez their waays, an' wa' 'ev oors; bud when onny on 'em cums inti mah cottage, Ah awlus puts on mah bettermy manners, an' Ah can scrape mah tongue an' knack a bit wi t' best on 'em.*

Beyont, *prep.* Beyond.

Bickerin', *n.* A wordy conflict, quarrelling.

Ex.—*Tommy an' Mary's at it agaan; Ah nivver heeard sike bickerin' deed ez yon twea 'ev, tha're awlus at it.*

Bid, *v.* To invite to a funeral.

Bidder, *n.* The person deputed to bid guests to a funeral.

Bide, Bahd, *v.* 1. To endure. 2. To wait. 3. To dwell.

Ex.—1. *Ah caan't bahd yon chap.* 2. *Ah'll bahd here whahl ya cum.* 3. *Wheear did ta bahd afoor thoo cam ti live here?*

Big, *adj.* Strong—of the wind.

Ex.—*It war a fairly big wind last neet.*

Bigg, *n.* Barley having four rows of ears on one stalk.

Bike, *n.* The nest of the wild bee.

Bile, *n.* A boil.

Binch, *n.* A bench to work upon.

Bink, *n.* A long seat of either stone or wood.

Binnd, *v.* To bind.

Binnder, Binndther, *n.* The tier-up of sheaves.

Birk, *n.* The birch-tree.

Birr, *n.* Rapid motion accompanied with a sound like whirr-r-r.

Ex.—*T' bo'ds gat up an' went wi' sike a birr, 'at Ah aim he war ti freet'n'd ti shut at 'em.*

Bishel, *n.* A bushel.

Bishopped. *Vide* Set on.

Biv, Byv, *prep.* By.

Bissum, Bussum, *n.* A broom.

Bissum-heead, *n.* A person who is equally foolish and stupid.

Bissum- or **Bussum-heeaded,** *adj.* Stupid and foolish.

Black-clocks, *n.* Black beetles.

Blacking, *n.* A severe scolding.

Bladdry, Blathery[1], *adj.* Muddy, applied to soft splashy mud.

Blaeberry, *n.* The bilberry.

Blair, *v.* To roar loudly, to shout loudly.

Blake, *adj.* Of a light golden hue, pale.

Ex.—*Noo, thaťs a bit o' neyce blake butter. Thoo nobbut leeaks blakeish.*

Blake, *v.* Intoxicated.

Ex.—*Jim war fairly blake last neet.*

Blane, *n.* A small boil.

Blash, *v.* 1. To splash with water. 2. *adj.* Nonsense, idle talk.

Blashment, *n.* Melted snow or soft mud.

Blashy, *adj.* Applied to wet weather. The roads are said to be 'blashy' when the snow melts.

Blather, *adj.* and *n.* Nonsense.

Bleb, *n.* A blister, a small bubble.

Bleck, *n.* The dirt and oil worked together on a machine.

Bleea, *n.* The inner bark of a tree.

Blendcorn, *n.* A mixture of wheat and rye.

Blendings, *n.* A mixture of peas and beans.

Blether, *n.* Noisy foolish talk.

Bletherheead, *n.* One full of silly talk.

Blew milk, *n.* Skim milk.

Blind-worm, *n.* A non-venomous snake.

Blirt, *v.* To tell anything suddenly.

Ex.—*Yan caan't trust Sally wi' nowt, sha blirts oot all sha knaws.*

Blish-blash, *n.* Tittle-tattle.

Blo', *n.* Bloom.

Blob, *v.* To bubble, as air rising in water.

Ex.—*He tumm'ľd blob inti i' beck* is quite a common form of speech. The original meaning may have been that the falling in caused many bubbles.

Bloss, *v.* and *n.* 1. To make ugly, to disfigure. 2. A dowdy.

Ex.—1. *Her feeace war bloss'd wi' blebs an' blanes.* 2. *Sha is a bloss is yon lass.*

Blotch, *n.* A blot, a spot.

---

[1] Along the borders touching the West Riding 'Blathery' is in common use. 'Bladdry' it should be.

Blubber or **Bluther**, *v.* To cry.
Blur, *v.* To blot or smear.
Blurt, *v.* To suddenly weep.
Blustery, *adj.* Squally.
Blutherment, *n.* Puddle, slush of any kind.
Bobblekins, *n.* The water buttercup.
Bodden, *v.* 1. To impose too heavy a task. 2. To accuse, to charge with.
> Ex.—1. *He's bodd'n'd t' lad wi' mair an' a day's wark.*
> 2. *Well, an' thoo'd 'a'e slapt her a feeace an' all if sha'd bodd'n'd thee wi' t' seeam ez sha plump'd me wi'.*

Bodden, *pp.* of ' to bide.'
Boddum, *v.* To thoroughly investigate.
> Ex.—*Ah'll boddum 't if it cost ma fahve pund.*

Boddums, *n.* and *adj.* Lowest, lowest ground.
Boddy, *n.* A person.
> Ex.—*Sha's a deeacent body, is 'Liza.*

Boggart } *n.* A ghost.
Boggle }
Boggle, *v.* To jib, to frame badly; also a *n.* inaptitude.
> Ex.—*He'll mak nowt bud a boggle on 't.*

Boiling, *n.* The whole lot, whether of persons or things.
Bolden, *v.* To encourage, to incite.
> Ex.—*Yance ower Ah felt a larl bit fearsome, bud he bolden'd ma ti deea 't, seea Ah bunched him.*

Boll, *n.* The trunk of a tree.
Bonny, *adj.* 1. A large quantity or number. 2. Strange. 3. Good-looking.
> Ex.—*Aye, ther' wur a bonny lot on 'em, a vast mair 'an Ah'd aim'd ti see.* 2. *Ther'll be bonny deed i' Bedale a week cum Mundaay.* 3. *It's a bonny-leeaking meer.*

Bon't! *intj.* Bother it (literally, burn it).
Bo'nt, *pp.* Burnt.
> Ex.—*Sha's bo'nt her pinny wiv a cat'ren wheel.*

Booak, Bowk, *v.* To retch, to vomit.
Book, Bouk, *n.* Bulk.
Bool, *v.* To trundle a hoop.
Booler, *n.* A child's hoop.
Bor, *n.* The seed of the burdock.
Borril, *n.* The gadfly.
Bost, *v.* To burst or break in small pieces.
Botch, *v.* To repair in an unworkmanlike manner.
Botchet, *n.* Mead, made from honey.
Bottery, Bore-tree, Bur-tree, *n.* The alder-tree.
Bottom. *Vide* **Boddums.**
Boult or **Bou't upright.** Upright, erect.

Boun, Bun, *adj.* Going, on the point of.

 Ex.—*Ah's bun ti deea't t' next job. Ah doot t' au'd thing's boun ti dee. Ah war just boun ti pop ower, if thoo 'edn't dropt in.*

Bound, Bun, *adj.* Compelled.

 Ex.—*Ah s' 'a'e ti gan, in fact Ah's bound ti gan.*

Bounder-marks or **-steeans,** *n.* Stones erected to mark boundaries.

Bow-bridge or **-brigg,** *n.* A one-arched bridge, several of which still exist.

Bowdykite, *n.* An impudent child.

Boxin, *adj.* Buxom.

Brack, *pret.* of ' to breke,' ' breck,' or ' breeak.'

Bracken, *n.* The common fern (*Pteris aquilina*).

Brade, *v.* To spread abroad.

Brading aboot, *part.* Gossiping.

Brae, *n.* The overhanging portion of the bank of a river.

Braeful, *adj.* Bankful.

Brag, *v.* To boast.

Brahdal-bands. *Vide* **Bridal-bands.**

Brahd-wain, *n.* A wagon laden with furniture, &c., taken from the home of the bride.

Braid-band, *n.* A sheaf of corn laid out to dry.

Bramlings, *n.* The red worms used as bait for trout.

Bramm'l, *n.* The bramble.

Brander, *n.* An arrangement varying in design — often in the shape of a tripod—fixed over the fire to support pans, &c.

Brander, *v.* To cook over the fire.

Brandery, *n.* A wood frame used in making wells.

Bran-new, Brander spander new, *adj.* Quite new.

Brant, *adj.* Steep.

 Ex.—*Thoo'll 'a'e ti put t' skid on, it's varra brant.*

Brash, *n.* Useless refuse, a rising of acid into the mouth.

Brashy, *adj.* Worthless.

Brass, *n.* 1. Money. 2. Impudence.

 Ex.—1. *Brass nivver chinks sae sweetly ez when t' soond cums fra yan's awn pocket.* 2. *If he'd nobbut hauf ez mich brass iv his pocket ez he 'ez iv his feeace, he nivver need deea a hand stroak.*

Brassend, Brazzend, *adj.* Impudent. When applied to a female, immoral.

Brat, *n.* A child.

Brattice, *n.* A wooden partition dividing two rooms.

Bratty, *adj.* Applied to cream or milk when turning sour.

Brave, *adj.* Good in quality as well as in appearance.

Bravely, *adj.* and *adv.* Exceeding, exceedingly well.

Bray, *v.* 1. To thrash, flog. 2. To overcome.
    Ex.—1. *Ak'll bray tha when thoo cums in.* 2. *Ah can bray yon chap wi' yah han' i' mah pocket.*

Brazent, Brazened. Impudent. *Vide* **Brassend.**

Breaks, Brooks, *n.* Boils.

Breeath, To take away one's = To overcome.
    Ex.—*It teeak mah breeath away when tha tell'd ma 'at he'd deean foor hissen,* i.e. 'It filled me with surprise when they told me that he had *deean for hissen,*' i.e. committed suicide.

Brede, *n.* Breadth.

Bree, Breeoe, *n.* The gadfly.

Breer
Breear } *n.* The briar, the dog-rose.

Breeaous, Breokus, *n.* Breakfast.

Breead leeaf or **loaaf,** *n.* A bread loaf.

Breead meal, *n.* Flour from which brown bread is made.

Breead-ratched, *adj.* Broad-striped.

Breeak, Breek, Brek, *v.* To break.

Breeak one's day, To = To fail to keep an appointment; to spoil a day's employment by having to attend to some trivial duty.

Breeam, *n.* The broom (*Genista scoparia*).

Breed, *n.* A brood, a litter.

Breekin', *n.* That part of a tree where the stem breaks into branches.

Breekless, *adj.* Without breeches.

Breeks, *n.* Breeches.

Breke or **Breear,** *v.* To break.

Bridal-band, *n.* The name given to the bride's garter (*obsolete*).

Bride-ale, *n.* Another form of hotpot. *Vide* chapter on 'Customs.'

Bride-wain, *n.* *Vide* **Brahd-wain.**

Brief, *n.* A begging letter.

Brigg, *n.* A bridge; a natural bed of rocks standing considerably out of the water and projecting into the sea.

Briggsteean, *n.* Flags or stones covering a culvert in front of a gateway, or in other places, so as to serve the purpose of a bridge in miniature.

Brim, *v.* Applied to a sow when inclined to the boar.

Brissling, *adj.* A slight gale of wind.

Brook, *n.* The badger; the frog-hopper or cuckoo-spit (*Aphrophora spumaria*).

Brog, *v.* To feed on the young hedge-shoots.

Brokken-bodied, *adj.* Suffering from hernia.

Brole, Browl, Brul, *n.* An impudent, saucy girl.

Bru, *n.* The brow, forehead.

Bruff, Bluff, *adj.* Fresh-complexioned, rough in speech, brusque.

Brully, *n.* A squabble amongst neighbours, a broil, a storm at sea of short duration.

Brully ⎱ *n.* A stealer of marbles.
Brullier ⎰

Brully, *v.* To steal marbles (taws) from the ring whilst a game is in progress, by some bully having no part in the game.

Brumm'l-neeased, -nooased, -noased ⎱ *adj.* Rubicund.
Brumm'l-snouted ⎰

Brumm'ls. *Vide* **Bramm'l.**

Brunt. *Vide* **Brant.**

Brussel, Brissel, *v.* To hector, swagger, show off.

> Ex.—*He went bruss'ling aboot ez if t' field war hisen, bud when Jack's lad offered him oot ti feight, he 'edn't a wo'd ti saay foor hissel.*

Brussen, *pp.* of Burst.

Brussen-hearted, *adj.* Broken-hearted.

Brussen oot, *adj.* Covered with blotches or sores.

Brussen or **Brusten up,** *adj.* Burst, broken into small pieces.

Buckheeads, *n.* The living stump of a thorn hedge left to grow after slashing.

Budge, *v.* To move, to give way in a bargain.

> Ex.—*Ah weean't budge an inch foor neeabody. Ah weean't budge a farden.*

Buer, *n.* The gnat.

Buff, *n.* The blow given as a challenge to fight.

Bugh, Bew, *n.* A bough.

Bull, *v.* To serve a cow.

Bullace, *n.* Wild plum, of a green colour when ripe.

Bull-feeaces, Bull-fronts, *n.* The hair-grass (*Aira caespitosa*).

Bull-heead, *n.* A small flat-headed fish found under stones, the miller's thumb.

Bullock, *v.* To bully, to be overbearing.

> Ex.—*If thoo aims 'at thoo can cum a bullocking o' ma, thoo's wrang, sae thoo'd better off wi' thisel.*

Bulls, *n.* Bulrushes, also the cross-beams of a harrow which carry the tines.

Bulls and segs, *n.* The name often given to the stalk and seed-head of the bulrush, the leaves being called 'segs'; hence 'bulls and segs.'

Bull-seg. A bull castrated in its prime.

Bull-spink, *n.* The chaffinch.

Bull-stang, Bull-teng, *n.* Dragon-fly.

Bull-steean, *n.* A stone used for sharpening tools.

Bullyrag, *v.* To be exceedingly overbearing.

Bum-bailiff, *n.* A bailiff.

Bumm'l-barfan, *n.* A horse-collar made of reeds.

Bumm'l-bee, *n.* The humble-bee.

Bumm'l-kites, *n.* The fruit of the bramble.

Bumper } *Vide* { **Thumper.**
Bumping } *Vide* { **Thumping.**

Bumping, *n.* An initiating ceremony at some schools of bumping a new boy on a stoop or otherwise.

Bunch, *v.* To kick with the foot, or violently bump with the knee. N.B.—'To bunch' is 'to kick,' 'to punch' is 'to hit.'

Burden, Bod'n, *n.* Anything one has to bear, whether mentally or physically.

Burden-band, *n.* A hempen band used to bind hay, to be carried on the back.

Burdened, *adj.* Insane.

Burn, *n.* A brook.

Burr, *n.* Anything used to prop a wheel from running backwards downhill. A burr proper is a round cylinder of wood with a loose iron pin through it; this is so fixed that it runs on the ground behind the wheel, and automatically prevents the wheel running back.

Burr-thistle, *n.* The spear-headed thistle.

Busk, *n.* A small bush.

Bustard, *n.* A witch bereft of power to work ill (*obsolete*). *Vide* chapter on 'Witchcraft.'

Butch, *v.* To kill as a butcher.

Butt, *n.* The halibut.

Butter-fingered, *adj.* Applied to one who lets things drop.

Butter-mouthed, *adj.* Flattery.

Butter-scotch, *n.* A superior kind of toffee.

Buzzard, *n.* A large moth.

Buzznacking, *part.* Gossiping.

By mich, *adj.* By a good deal.

By noo, *adj.* By now, by this time.

Ex.—*Thoo owt ti 'a'e lap't t' job up by noo.*

Byre, *n.* A cow-house.

C.

Caan't, pronounced 'carnt,' *v.* Cannot, must not.

Ex.—*You caan't do that,* i. e. 'You must not do that.'

Cabbish, *n.* Cabbage.

Cade, *n.* A sheep-tick. *Vide* **Kead.**

Cadge, *v.* To beg.

Cadger, *n.* A carrier, a beggar.

Caff, *n.* Chaff.

Caffed, *adj.* Cowed, dispirited.

Caff-hearted, *adj.* Nervous, cowardly, unprincipled.

Caffy, *adj.* Worthless.

Caggy, *adj.* Touchy, disposed to quarrel.
Cagmag, *adj.* and *n.* Worthless.
Caingy, *adj.* Fretful, peevish.
Cake, *v.* To cackle.
Caling, *v.* To gossip.
Call, *n.* Occasion, necessity, reason.

> Ex.—*Ah's nut gahin', Ah've neea call ti gan,* i. e. 'I am not going, I have no occasion to go. *Ther wur neea call for tha ti deea that.*

Call, *v.* 1. To scold. 2. To quarrel. 3. To call to or for.

> Ex.—1. *Sha's nobbut calling o' ma ti call ma,* i. e. 'She is only shouting for me to (give) me a scolding.' 2. *Tha're calling yan anuther leyke all that,* i. e. 'They are quarrelling with one another like anything.' 3. *Ah'll call on him ti cum,* i. e. 'I will shout for him to come.'

Callet, *n.* A scold, a railing woman.
Callet, *v.* To scold.
Callety, *adj.* Scolding, nagging.
Call of, Call on, *v.* To cry to.
Calven-coo, *n.* A cow recently calved.
Cam, Camside, *n.* A raised earthen bank, the sloping bank from a hedge bottom.
Cambril, Caumbril, Caum'ril, *n.* The notched wooden bar which is thrust through the tendons of the hind legs of a slaughtered beast to suspend it by.
Can, *v.* May. 'Can' is commonly used for 'may.'

> Ex. Q. *Can I smoke here?* Ans. *No, you caan't,* i. e. 'No, you may not.'

Canker, *v.* To rust.
Cankery, *adj.* Cross, rotten.
Cannily, *adv.* Wisely, with subtilty, nicely.
Canny, *adj.* Pleasing, judicious, skilful, considerable as to number.

> Ex.—*Sha's a canny lass,* i. e. 'pleasing.' *Thoo fraam'd varra cannily wiv him,* i. e. 'You set to work very judiciously with him.' *He did it varra cannily,* i. e. 'He did it very skilfully.' *Whya, ther wur a cannyish few on 'em,* i. e. 'Why, there were a considerable number.'

Cant, *v.* To raise one end.
Canty, *adj.* Full of spirits, lively.
Cap, *v.* To fix a piece of leather over the toe of a boot; to surprise, bewilder, excel.

> Ex.—*Ah nivver war sae capped i' mah leyfe,* i. e. 'I never was so surprised in my life.' *Ah caan't tell hoo he mannish'd ti deea 't, he capped me,* i. e. 'I cannot say how he managed to do it, he bewildered me.' *Yon caps 'em all,* i. e. 'That one over there excels them all'

Capper, *n.* Something which surpasses all others.

Caps all=Exceeds in everything.

Capster, *n.* A piece of wood roughly shaped like the bridge of a bagatelle board, each arch being numbered, the boy winning by that number placed over the arch he shoots through; should he not succeed in passing through any arch, he loses his taw.

Card up, *v.* To sweep and tidy up the fireside.

Cark, *v.* To be careful, anxious.

Carlings, *n.* Peas cooked in butter, prepared for Carling Sunday.

Carneyed, *pp.* Flattered, coaxed.

Carp, *v.* To doubt without reason.

Carr, *n.* Low-lying boggy land.

Carryings on, *n.* Lively, disorderly proceedings.

Cassen. *Vide* **Kessen.**

Cast down, To be, *v.* To be downhearted, dispirited.

Cast, Kest, *adj.* Not straight, warped.

Cast, Kest, *v.* To cease wearing.
> Ex.—*Ah kest yan o' my petticoats, and Ah've catch'd my deeath o' cau'd.*

Cast, To be, *v.* To be bent, warped.

Cast up, *v.* 1. To twit a person with some past failing. 2. To happen unexpectedly. 3. To come to light.
> Ex.—1. *Ah think 'at Ah wadn't kest that up at him.* 2. *Well, it caps yan when a thing leyke that kests up.* 3. *Ah thowt 'at Ah'd lost it, but it kest up i' yan o' ma au'd coats.*

Catch it, *v.* To be reprimanded, punished.
> Ex.—*Thoo'll catch it when thi mudher sees tha.* I heard a woman say to her daughter, when giving the child a jug of milk to take to a neighbour's, *If thoo lets it drop, thoo'll catch it.*

Cat-collop, *n.* Cat's-meat.

Cat-gallows, *n.* Two upright forked sticks upon which a cross-bar rests as an obstacle for boys to jump over.

Cat-haws, *n.* The fruit of the hawthorn.

Cat-jugs. *Vide* **Dog-choops.**

Cats and eyes, *n.* Seeds of the ash-tree.

Cat-trail, *n.* The root of valerian.

Cau'd, *adj.* and *n.* Cold.

Cauf, Cauff, *n.* A calf.

Cauf-heead, *n.* A stupid fellow.

Cauf-lick, *n.* A tuft of hair on the forehead which cannot be parted or made to lie flat.

Cauf-riddling. *Vide* chapter on 'Superstition.'

Caul, *n.* *Vide* **Keld.**

Causer, Caus'ay, *n.* A causeway, a paved footpath.

Cess, *n.* A rate for parish relief; the amount paid to the poor by the overseer.

Cess, *n.* 1. Extra effort. 2. Punishment.

> Ex.—1. *Gi'e't cess, an' thoo'll seean'a'e't deean*, i. e. 'Give it an extra effort, and you will soon have it done. 2. *Ah'll gi'e tha cess when Ah git ho'd on tha.*

Cess getherer, *n.* Rate collector.

Chaff, *v.* To tease by using playful but provoking language.

Chaff, Chafts, *n.* The jaw, generally that of a pig.

Chaffer, *v.* 1. To banter or beat down in a bargain. 2. An interchange of provoking remarks.

> Ex.—1. *He chaffered that mich, whahl Ah ax'd him if he wanted t' meer foor nowt?* 2. *Dolly's chaffering wi' Sally agaan.*

Chaff-fallen, *adj.* Dejected.

Challenge, *v.* To recognize.

> Ex.—*Ah c'u'd challenge oor bitch amang all t' dogs i' t' show. Sha's good ti challenge onnywheer.*

Chamber, Chamer, *n.* A room above the ground-floor.

Champ, Champion, *adj.* Excellent, very well.

Chance bairn, *n.* An illegitimate child.

Chander, *n.* A chaldron.

Change, *v.* To turn sour.

Channely, *adv.* Grandly.

Chanter, *n.* A chorister.

Chare, *adv.* Careful, doubtful.

Chass, *n.* Haste. *v.* To follow quickly.

Chatt, *n.* A fir cone.

Chatter, *v.* To make an uneven surface; to shake, as machinery running unevenly.

Chaudy-bag, *n.* The stomach of an animal.

Chaudy-guts, *n.* A greedy, gluttonous fellow.

Chavel, *v.* To chew as one without teeth, to gnaw.

Cheean, *n.* A chain.

Cheeany. The common pronunciation of 'chinaware.'

Cheeat'll chow. *Lit.* 'Cheating will show itself.'

> Ex.—In a dispute boys will say, *Let him 'ev anuther goa, cheeat'll chow.*

Cheek by chowl or **jowl**=Close together.

> Ex.—*Theer tha gan, cheek by chowl; Ah doot tha're up ti neea good.*

Cheep, *n.* The cry of a young bird, generally a chicken, partridge, or grouse.

Cheeper, *n.* A young partridge or grouse.

Cheesfat, *n.* A press used for extracting the whey from the curds.

Chetch, Chuch, *n.* A church.

Chetch or **Chuch priest**, *n.* A Church of England clergyman.

Chevin, *n.* The chub.

Childer, *n.* Children.

Chimbler, **Chim'ly**, *n.* A chimney.

Chip, *v.* To chip anything; to crack an egg when boiled, or when hatching commences.

Chip up, *v.* To trip up by holding the foot out in front of any one running past.

Chisel, **Chissel**, *n.* Bran, husks of grain.

Chissel, *v.* To cheat, to impose upon.

Chist, *n.* The chest, a chest of drawers.

Chitterlings, *n.* The small entrails of a pig.

Chitty, *adj.* Childish.

Chock-full, *adv.* Full to overflowing.

　　Ex.—*Thoo caan't git neea mair in, it's chock-full noo.*

Cholter-headed, *adj.* Thick-headed.

Chop, *v.* To trade by exchanging.

Chops, *n.* The jaws. *Vide* **Chaff**.

Chow, *v.* To chew.

Chucky, *n.* A hen, a term of endearment applied to a child.

Chuff, *adj.* Healthy-looking, pert, determined.

Chunter, *v.* To mutter in a complaining tone.

Churlish, **Chollus**, *adj.* Bad-tempered.

Churr, *v.* The murmuring sound made by birds when roosting.

Clack, *n.* Lit. the tongue, scolding, advice.

Clack, *v.* To admonish, to talk much.

Clag, *v.* To stick to or on.

Claggum, *n.* Any sticky mass, applied generally to sweets.

Claggy, *adj.* Sticky.

Clam, *v.* 1. To climb. 2. To squeeze, to nip as a vice. 3. To adhere to, stick to, owing to mosture.

　　1. Ex.—*Ah clam up t' tree an' gat t' nist an' t' eggs an' all.*
　　2. *Ah gat mysen clamm'd atween t' wall an' t' wagon.*

Clam, **Clem**, *v.* To faint for want of food.

　　Ex.—*Ah's fair clamm'd foor a bit o' summat ti eat.*

Clam, *n.* Damp, sticky moisture.

Clame, *v.* To smear with anything sticky.

　　Ex.—*Tha saay what it's t' chaange o' watter what's deean 't. That maay be ; onny road sha's a perfect picter noo, covered wi' watter-blebs an' larl reead spots ivvery bit ower her ; an' t' doctor's clamed her all ower wi' sum soart o' clarty, bladdry, muckment stuff, whahl sha kittles that bad 'at sha dizn't knaw wheear ti put hersel.*

Clammy, *adj.* Parched with thirst, sticky, moist, adhesive.

Clamoursome, *adj.* Noisy.

Clamper, *v.* To make a loud noise with the feet when walking or running.

Clampers, *n.* Feet or claws of any metal object, also the fingers and claws of things animate.

Clap, *v.* 1. To pat a dog. 2. To sit down, or set anything down.
> Ex.—2. *Clap yersel i' that cheer. Clap it doon onny-wheear.*

Clap back, *v.* To encore.

Clapt een on, *v.* To see. Really *part.*, saw.

Clart, *v.* To smear, to flatter.
> Ex.—*Ah've gitten mysen clarted all ower wi' t' bladdry blashment. Noo, then, deean't cum clarting ma up leyke that; gan thi waays an' clart Mary ower. Whya, he clarted her up whahl he's fair to'n'd her heead.*

Clarty, *adj.* 1. Sticky. 2. Untrustworthy.
> Ex.—2. *Deean't len' him owt, he's nobbut a clarty customer.*

Clash, *v.* To hurry work, to close a door with force, to bring together suddenly.

Clat. *Vide* **Clack.**

Clatter, *n.* A blow, a noise.
> Ex.—*Ah'll gi'e tha a good clatter if thoo clatters on leyke that.*

Clavver, *n.* A rowdy rabble.

Clavver, *v.* To clamber like a child.

Clawt, *v.* To attack with the nails.

Clear up, *v.* To become fine after rain.

Cled, *adj.* Clothed.

Cleean, *v.* To tidy oneself.

Cleean, *adj.* and *adv.* 1. Right. 2. Quite. 3. Well, adroitly, completely.
> Ex.—1. *He flang t' steean cleean thruff t' winner*, i.e. 'He threw the stone right through the window.' 2. *Ah cleean foorgat all aboot it*, i.e. 'I quite forgot all about it.' 3. *Ah've nivver seed a chap sae cleean deean iv all my leyfe*, i.e. 'I never saw a fellow so completely taken in.'

Cleean up, *v.* To tidy the house.

Cleeas ⎰ *n.* Clothes.
Clais ⎱

Cleease, *adj.* Near, close, greedy.

Cleease-fisted, *adj.* Greedy.

Cleeat, *n.* A piece of iron or wood used to add strength.

Cleg, *n.* The horse-fly, a begging friend.

Clem. *Vide* **Clam.**

Cletch, *n.* A brood of young birds.

Cleugh, *n.* The race of a mill, terminating often at one end by cleugh-gates or gate, or door, which winds up and down by means of a wheel and ratchet, admitting more or less water according to the height it is lifted.

Clever, *adj.* Well done or made.

Clever-headed, *adj.* Wise beyond his fellows.

Click, *v.* To snatch, to snatch quickly.

Click-hooks, *n.* Three or four hooks joined together and attached to a rope, used to drag ponds or a river with in search of a body, &c.

Clim, *v.* To climb.

Clinch, *v.* To grasp tightly with the hand.

Clink, *n.* A stinging blow.

Clinker, *n.* A heavy blow.

Clinking, *adj.* Very good, first-class.

Clip, *v.* To shear sheep.

Clipping tahm, *n.* Shearing time.

Cloam, Clooam, Claum, *v.* To grasp with both hands at the same time, to pull about not only roughly but rudely.

Clock, *n.* Black clocks, black beetles.

Clock-seves, Bulrush. The names not only vary in different localities, but are given first to one and then another of the water-side flags, rushes, and seves or seaves. *Vide* **Bulls and segs.**

Clog, *n.* A log of wood.

Clogged, *adj.* Asthmatical (of people), stopped by bleck (q. v.) or other filth (of machinery).

Clooase. *Vide* **Cleease.**

Clooased, *part.* Closed up, as in a cold in the chest.

Clooase-neifed, *adj.* Niggardly, greedy.

Closing, *n.* A difficulty in breathing.

Clot, *n.* A clod of earth, a portion of blood when set.

Clot bur, *n.* The burdock.

Cloth, To draw the=To remove the white tablecloth on the meal being concluded.

Clotter, *v.* To make thick or lumpy.

Clout, *n.* An old piece of cloth, a patch.

Clout, *n.* A blow.

Clout, *v.* To strike at.

Clow-clags, *n.* Dried dung adhering to the hind parts of animals; in the case of sheep they are termed 'doddings.'

Clow-clash, *n.* Things all in confusion.

Cloy, *v.* To eat until sick at the sight of the same dish.

Clubster, *n.* The stoat.

Cludder, Cluther, *v.* To huddle together.

Clue, *n.* A ball of cotton or string.

Clum, *adj.* Sodden, heavy; generally applied to clayey land.

Clunter, *v.* To go heavily on the feet.

Cob, *n.* A small-sized horse, a small bread bun.

Cobble, Cobble-steean, *n.* A small paving-stone.

Cobble, *v.* To pelt with stones, to mend anything roughly to serve for the time being.

Cobble-tree, *n.* The wooden bar which connects the swingle-trees with the beam of the plough.

Cobby, *adj.* Lively, brisk, stout, decent.

Cŏble, *n.* A fishing-boat.

Cocker, *v.* To fondle, to indulge.

Ex.—*Thoo'll spoil t' bairn if thoo cockers it i' that road.*

Cocker, *n.* Conceit.

Cockerate, *v.* To boast.

Cockeration } *n.* Uncertainty.
Cockle-spell }

Cockertraps, *n.* Traps to catch cockroaches.

Cockle, *v.* To be unsteady, to curl when drying.

Cockle boat, *n.* A small pleasure boat.

Cock-leet, *n.* The dawn of day.

Cookly, *adj.* Unsteady, insecure, likely to fall over.

Cock o' t' middin, *n.* The one who claims supremacy.

Cock-shot, *n.* The boy who chances being caught in a certain game.

Cockshut, *n.* Twilight.

Cock-sure, *v.* To be quite certain.

Cooky, *adj.* Self-assertive, domineering.

Cod, *n.* The cod or pod of peas, beans, &c.

Cod, *v.* To impose upon, to stuff with nonsense.

Coddle, Couther, *v.* To indulge oneself, to use unnecessary wraps.

Collar, *n.* A horse-collar.

Collar, *v.* To lay hold of.

Collier, *n.* The swift.

Collop, *n.* A slice of bacon.

Collop Monday, *n.* Monday before Shrove Tuesday.

Colly, *adj.* Curly.

Come¹ again, *v.* To appear after death.

Come by, *v.* To stand aside.

Come by chance. *Vide* Chance bairn.

Come fra, *v.* To come from.

Come on, *v.* To improve, to grow.

Ex.—*Thi cabbishes is cummin' on champ.*

Come round, *v.* 1. To recover from fainting. 2. To reconsider. 3. To agree with.

Ex.—1. *Slap her han's, an' sha'll seean cum roond.* 2. *Tak neea notish o' what he sez, i' t' end he'll cum roond an' foorgi'e ya baith.* 3. *Whya, Ah've cum roond ti thi way o' thinking.*

Come to, Cum teea, *v.* To regain consciousness.

Ex.—*When Ah cam teea, Ah didn't ken wheear Ah war.*

¹ 'Come' is always pronounced 'cum.'

Come-to, *n.* Place of abode.

 Ex.—*Maist fooak 'ev a cum-teea o' sum soart.*

Commin's, *n.* Barley-sprouts formed during fermentation.

Comp'ny, *n.* Several people gathered together with one object.

 Ex.—*Ther war a fairish comp'ny geddered up ti lissen ti*
  t' new parson.

Con, *v.* To scan, to observe critically.

 Ex.—*Efter Ah'd conn'd it ower, Ah thowt varra larl aboot it.*

Conceit, Consate, *n.* Imagined.

 Ex.—*He consated hissen 'at he knaw'd a lot, bud it wur*
  all blather when he wur oppen'd oot.

Conger, *v.* Conquer.

Conny, *adj.* Neat, nice; when applied to things, ' little.'

Conquerors, *n.* Horse-chestnuts when dried, or even freshly
 gathered, are so called when used by boys to play the game of
 conquerors with. The game consists of threading a chestnut
 on a string and striking it against a similar one held by an
 opponent—the one breaking the other, conquers.

Consarn, *n.* Business, the object or matter seen or discussed.

 Ex.—*It's a gert consarn yon,* i. e. 'A big affair or undertaking.' *Ak've nowt ti deea wi' 't, it's neea consarn o'*
  mahn, 'No business of mine.'

Consumpted, *part.* Suffering from phthisis or consumption.

Continny, *v.* Continue.

Cook thi goose=To completely vanquish.

Cool. *Vide* **Coul.**

Coom, *n.* Dust. **Sawooom,** sawdust.

Coo-tie, *n.* A band, usually made of hair, used to secure the
 hind legs of a cow.

Cop, *v.* 1. To be caught. 2. To be punished.

 Ex.—1. *He'll cop us if wa deean't leeak sharp.* 2. *Thoo'll*
  cop it when thoo gans yam.

Corker, *adj.* Large of its kind. *n.* A lie.

 Ex.—*Ah saay, bud that's a corker.*

Corn-creeak, *n.* Field-crake.

Corr'n-berries, *n.* The red or white currant.

Cossen, *v.* 1. To cost. 2. To inconvenience.

 Ex.—2. *It wadn't 'a'e cossen him mich,* i. e. 'It would not
  have inconvenienced him much.'

Cot, *n.* One who manages his domestic affairs without any
 female help, an effeminate fellow.

Cott, *n.* A tangled mass of wool or hair.

Cotten, *v.* 1. To have a liking for. 2. To discover.

 Ex.—1. *Ah cotten'd tiv him fra t' fust.* 2. *He cottened ti*
  what sha wur efter afoor sha'd ommaist gitten started.

Cotter, *v.* To work hair or wool into knots. *Vide* **Felter.**

Cottered, *pp.* Entangled, knotted.

Coul, Cool, *n.* A weal or swelling caused by a blow.

Counting, *n.* Arithmetic.

Coup, *v.* To exchange in barter, to empty a cart by tilting.

Coup ower, *v.* To fall over.

Couther. *Vide* **Coddle.**

Cout, *n.* A colt.

Cow- or **Coo-byre,** *n.* A cow-house.

Cow- or **Coo-clags,** *n.* Dung adhering to the buttocks of cattle.

Cow- or **Coo-footed,** *adj.* Awkward in gait.

Cow- or **Coo-gate, Coo-yat, Cow pastur,** *n.* Cow pasture.

Cow- or **Coo-grip,** *n.* The channel to carry off the urine.

Cow- or **Coo-leech,** *n.* A cow-doctor.

Cowdy, *adj.* Lively, pert, active.

Cower, *v.* To crouch in fear.

Cowl, *v.* To scrape together towards one.

Cowler, *n.* A scraper.

Cowl-rake, *n.* A small scraper used to rake ashes together.

'Coz. *Vide* **Acoz.**

Crab, *v.* To vex.

Crabbed, *adj.* Peevish, in a bad temper.

Crack, *n.* A loud noise like thunder.

Crack, *v.* 1. To boast. 2. To praise.

    Ex.—1. *He crack'd a deeal aboot it.* 2. *Ah crack'd it up fur tha. He cracks a seet ti mich ov his awn deeds.*

Crack, *n.* and *v.* A chat, to chat. *Vide* **Rap.**

Crack, *n.* A short space of time, immediately.

    Ex.—*Ah s'all be deean iv a crack.*

Crack'd and Cracky, *adj.* Not quite *compos mentis.*

Crafty, *adj.* Skilful, original.

Crake, Creeak, Cruke, *n.* A carrion crow.

Crake. *Vide* **Corn-creeak.**

Crake, *v.* To speak hoarsely.

Cramm'l, *v.* To walk haltingly, tottery.

Cramm'ls, *n.* The gnarled and twisted boughs of trees.

Cramped, *part.* Perplexed.

Cramper, *n.* Any matter difficult of settlement or solution.

    Ex.—*Noo, that's a cramper fur tha.*

Cramp-ring, *n.* A charm-ring made from coffin tire, and worn as a preventive against cramp, &c.

Cramps, *n.* The term given to the playing of either the octave or the scales.

Cranch, *v.* To grind the teeth together when eating.

Cranky, *adj.* Idiotic, able to move with difficulty through stiffness, likely to overbalance, insecure.

Cranky, *n.* A checked material, usually of blue and white checks, used for aprons. Often called 'Kinky-cranky.'

Craps or **Crappin's,** *n.* The pieces left after rendering fat into lard.

Crashes, Creeases, *n.* Watercress.

Craw, *v.* To crow. *n.* A crow.

Crazed, *pp.* In a violent passion.

Creckits, *n.* The game of cricket.

Cree, *v.* To soak grain in water.

Creeak. *Vide* **Crook** and **Cruke.**

Creel, *n.* The wooden frame pigs are laid upon after slaughtering.

Creepin's, *n.* A shivering sensation usually foretelling a cold.

Cricket, *n.* A small four-legged stool.

Crook, Creeak, Crewk, *n.* The hinge upon which a gate swings, a bent piece of iron to hang anything upon.

Crook, Crewk, *n.* An abrupt corner in a field.

Crooked, *adj.* Bent.

Crowberries, *n.* The crowberry fruit (*Empetrum nigrum*).

Crowdy, *n.* Oatmeal porridge.

Crow-ling, *n.* The heath (*Erica cinerea*).

Crown, *n.* Top of the head.

Crowp, *v.* To croak like a toad.

Crowse, *adj.* Lively. *n.* A drinking bout.

Cruddle, *v.* To curdle.

Cruds, *n.* Curds.

Cruke, Crewk, Creeak, *n.* The rook. *Vide* **Reeak.**

Crunkle, Crinkle, *v.* To crease, rumple.

Crush, *n.* A great crowd.

Cuddle, *v.* To fondle by embracing.

Cuddy, *n.* A donkey, a hedge-sparrow.

Culler'd, *pp.* Blushed.

Cum, *n.* Sweepings of sawdust.

Cum, *v.* Come.

Cumber-ground, *n.* Any thing or person of no value.

Cumly. *Vide* **Comely.**

Cummer, *v.* To encumber.

Cummersome, *adj.* Burdensome.

Cungle, *v.* To influence by charms or prayers.

Cup-rose, *n.* The common poppy.

Cushat, *n.* Ring-dove.

Cush-pet, *n.* Pet name for a crow ; also **Cushy-Cushy.**

Cut, *v.* Be off.

Cut and run } *v.* To retire hurriedly.
Cut wer sticks }

Cutter, *v.* To whisper.

Cuvvins, *n.* Periwinkles.

Cuz, *n.* Cousin.

D.

'D. Would, had.

Daam, Deeam, *n.* A lady, the wife, an aged person.

Dab, *adj.* Dexterous, skilful. *n.* A blow.

Ex.—*He's a dab hand at t' job,* i.e. 'He is skilful at the business. *Catch him a dab on t' feeace.*

'Dacity, *n.* 1. Ability to accomplish. 2. Presumption, impudence.

Ex.—1. *He's gitten 'dacity fur owt, 'ez that lad.* 2. *Ah didn't aim 'at he 'ed t' 'dacity ti 'a'e spokken ti t' parson i' that waay, hooivver.*

Daddle, *v.* To walk unsteadily, to trifle.

Daff, *n.* A coward, a fool.

Daffle, *v.* To confuse, to bewilder with noise.

Daffly daffled, *pp.* Bewildered.

Daffy-down-dilly, *n.* The daffodil.

Daft, *adj.* Foolish, lacking common sense.

Daftish, *adj.* Foolish, like a fool.

Dagg, Deggle, *v.* To sprinkle with water.

Dainish, Densh, *adj.* Over particular.

Daized, *pp.* Stupefied, suffering from the effect of cold.

Dakky, *n.* A pig.

Dale, *n.* A valley varying in extent. 'Dale' is usually pronounced 'deeal.'

Dale-end, *n.* The end or widest part of a dale.

Dale-heead, *n.* The upper and narrowest portion of a dale.

Dander, *n.* Rage, temper.

Dander, *v.* To tremble, to vibrate.

Danger, *n.* Risk, probability, doubt.

Ex.—1. *He's lost hauf on 'em, an' ther's a danger 'at other hauf 'll dee an' all.*

Dangerous, *adj.* Doubtful, risky.

Ex.—*It's nobbut a dangerous consarn ti sink yan's brass in.*

Dangle efter, *v.* To follow as a lover.

Danglements, *n.* Superfluous trinkets, trimmings of beads, &c.

Dank, *adj.* Damp, moist.

Dapper, *adj.* Sharp, active, nimble.

Dappers, *n.* Birds ready to leave the nest.

Dark, *v.* To follow or move slily about, to listen unperceived.

Darkening, *n.* Twilight.

Darrn't, *v.* Dare not.

Darr, *v.* To dare.

Ex.—*Ah darr tackle yon job.* To tell any one they dare not do a certain thing, is to dare them to it, e.g. *He darrn't jump whahl Ah darr'd him ti 't, an' then he went that cauf-hearted at it, whahl he tumm'ld blob in.*

Dased, Deeased. *Vide* **Daized.**

Datherin'. *Vide* **Ditherin'.**

Daul'd, *pp.* Tired, weary.

Ex.—*Ah daul'd on 't,* i.e. 'I tired of it.'

Daul'd oot, *part.* Tired out.

Daupee, *n.* The grey-headed crow.

Daytal, *adj.* By the day.

Daytalman, *n.* A farm labourer hired by the day.

Deaf, Deeaf, *adj.* Lacking a kernel, barren.

Deaf or **Deeaf nettle,** *n.* The blind or hemp nettle.

Deary, *adj.* Puny, lovable.

    Ex.—*Sha's a deary larl honey.*

Deave, Deeave, *adj.* Deaf.

Deaven, *v.* To deafen.

Decoy-duck, *n.* A by-name given to one who leads others astray.

Dee, *v.* To die.

Deea, *v.* 1. Do. 2. To swindle.

    Ex.—2. *He'll deea him if he dizn't watch him,* i.e. 'He will swindle him if he does not take care.'

Deead, *adj.* Dead.

Deeafly, Deavely, *adj.* Alone, by oneself.

Deeak, *n.* Duke.

Deean, *pp.* of Do. Also swindled overmatched.

    Ex.—*Ah've deean him neycely,* i.e. 'I have taken him in nicely.'

Deean't, Doan't, *v.* Do not.

Deear, Doour, *n.* Door.

Deearstan, *n.* *Vide* **Doorstan.**

Deearsteead, *n.* The framework of the door; also **Doourstead,** &c.

Deeatchess, *n.* Duchess.

Deeath, *n.* Death.

Deeath-smear ⎫
Deeath-clam ⎬ *n.* The clammy sweat of death.
Deeath-sweeat ⎭

Deeazment, *n.* Chilled to the bone.

Deed, *n.* Doings, applied indiscriminately to events of a joyous or sorrowful nature.

    Ex.—*Ther war straange deed at Willie's wedding. Ah nivver seed sike deed ez ther war at Ann's funeral.*

Deedless, *adj.* Useless, helpless.

Deggle. *Vide* **Dagg.**

Deft, *adj.* Quick, clever, neat.

Delf-rack, *n.* An arrangement of wooden bars to hold plates and dishes.

Dempt, *pp.* Deemed, thought.

Deng, *v.* To knock off with violence, to throw down, to wrench off.

Densh. *Vide* **Dainish.**

Deny, *v.* To refuse.

    Ex.—*Ah'll see 'Tommy mysel, he'll nut deny me. Ah weean't deny tha fishing, hooivver.*

Despert, *adv.* Exceedingly, used as an augmentative.

Ex.—*Ther war despert grand deed at t' Squire's dinner.*

Dess, *n.* A mass built up by degrees; a block cut out, as a dess of hay.

Dessably, *adj.* Orderly.

Devil-screamer, *n.* The swift.

Dhriss. *Vide* **Dress.**

Dib, *v.* To dip.

Dibbing, *v.* To dip, as with a fly on the top of the water.

Dice, *n.* A small portion, as a dice of cheese; a square piece of anything.

Dicky, *adj.* Doubtful.

Ex.—*It nobbut leeaks a bit dicky.*

Dicky, *n.* A louse.

Dicky-ass, *n.* A donkey.

Didder. *Vide* **Dither.**

Differ, *v.* To quarrel.

Differing bout, *n.* A wordy quarrel.

Dike, *n.* A ditch.

Dike-back, *n.* The bank forming one side of a ditch.

Dike-cam, *n.* The bank-side of a ditch.

Dildering, Dilder, *v.* To shake, unstable, silly.

Dill, *v.* To lessen, to deaden.

Ex.—*Clap a plaaster on, it'll dill t' paain.*

Dilldam, Dilldum, or **Dilldrum,** *n.* A loud noise, boisterous merry-making.

Dindle, *v.* To have a tingling sensation after a fall or blow.

Ding. *Vide* **Deng.**

Dingle, *v.* To tingle after a blow.

Dint, *n.* Energy, force, power.

Ex.—*By dint an' sticking ti 't, he'll mannish 't.*

Dither, *v.* To shiver, to shake with fear.

Doan't, Deean't=Do not.

Docken, *n.* The dock plant. Also denotes of little value.

Ex.—*Ah wadn't 'a'e gi'en a docken for 't.*

Dodded, *adj.* Hornless.

Dodderums, *n.* Shaking violently, unnerved.

Doddery, Dothery, *adj.* *Vide* **Dither.**

Doddings, *n.* Matted wool on the hind quarters of sheep.

Doff, *v.* 1. To remove the garments. 2. To raise the hat.

Ex.—1. *Ah'll doff mah duds iv a crack.* 2. *Ah doff'd mah cap tiv her.*

Dog, *v.* To set a dog to drive sheep.

Dog, *n.* A piece of iron fitted within the fire-grate, thereby reducing its size, so as to save coal.

Dog-choops, *n.* Hips, the fruit of the dog-rose.

B b

Doggers, *n.* Nodules containing a fossil, and used in the making of Roman cement.

Dog-jumps. *Vide* Dog-choops.

Dog one's footsteps, To, *v.* To persistently follow any one.

Doit, *n.* A small portion.

Dole, *n.* The distribution of money left to some charity, or that given at a funeral.

Dole out, *v.* To give in small quantities.

Dollop, *n.* A clumsy person or badly-formed thing, a number or quantity of persons or things.

Dolly-stick, *n.* A handle to which is affixed an arrangement like a small four-legged stool, being used to give a half-circular motion to the clothes in the tub, which is termed dollying.

Dolly-tub, *n.* A round tub used to wash clothes in.

Don, *v.* and *adj.* 1. To put on one's better attire. 2. Clever.

　　Ex.—1. *Ah'll don mysel up a bit, ez Janey's cumin' ti tea.*
　　2. *He's a don hand at deeaing owt o' that sooart.*

Donk. *Vide* Dank.

Donnot, *n.* An immoral female.

Doody-cow, *n.* The ladybird beetle.

Door, Deear, Doour-cheek, *n.* Sidepost of a door.

　　　　,,　　　,,　　　,,　　**sill,** *n.* The threshold of the door.
　　　　,,　　　,,　　　,,　　**stan,** *n.* The flagstone in front of the doorway, often mistaken as meaning the doorstep.

Door, Doour, Deear, To get to the=Able to walk abroad.

Doory, *adv.* Very little, a trifle.

Dordum, *n.* A dreadful uproar.

Dorse, Duzz, *v.* To shake out from the ear by reason of over-ripeness.

Dossel, *n.* A bunch of wheat, the finest ears being selected to be used as an ornament; formerly such bunches were fixed on the top of corn-pikes.

Dossel-knob, *n.* The straw knob at the top of a stick which terminates the thatch.

Dothering-grass. *Vide* Trimm'ling-gess.

Dotteril, *n.* A dotard.

Douk, *v.* To duck under, to dive as a water-fowl.

Doup. *Vide* Daupee.

Dou't, Doot, *v.* Almost certain.

　　Ex.—*Ah doot he's laam'd fur leyfe. Ah doot wa saan't git it.*

Dow, *v.* To thrive.

Dowdy, *n.* An untidy woman.

Dowled, *adj.* Flat, said of long-drawn beer.

Dowly, *adj.* Sad, poorly, down-hearted.

Down, *v.* To knock or throw down.

　　Ex.—*Ah've doon'd tha yance, an' if Ah 'ev onny mair o' thi lip, Ah'll doon tha ageean.*

Down-come, *n.* A spout at the side of the house, a heavy downpour of rain.

Down-dinner=Afternoon allowance.

Dowse, *n.* A blow from the fist.

Ex.—*Ah'll catch tha a dowse on t' sahd o' t' heead.*

Dowse, *v.* To wet to the skin.

Ex.—*He dowsed t' lot on uz wi' t' hose. Ah gat sike a dowsing,* said one who fell into a stream.

Dozzen'd, *adj.* Withered, blighted.

Drab, *n.* A dirty slut.

Drabbletail. *Vide* **Flappy-sket.**

Draff, *n.* Refuse from a brewery for pigs, grains.

Draker-hen, *n.* Corn-crake.

Drape, Dreeap, *n.* A cow not giving milk.

Drate, *v.* To drag one's speech, to drawl.

Draught, *n.* A team of horses, not less than three.

Draw up, *v.* To gather together.

Ex.—*Thoo mun ring t' bell an' call oot, an' they'll seean draw up.*

Drazzle, *n.* A shower of fine rain and mist.

Dree, *adj.* Tiring, weary.

Ex.—*It's nobbut a dree job this.*

Dree, *adv.* Slowly.

Dree, *v.a.* To deliver tediously.

Dreeap. *Vide* **Drape.**

Dreep, *v.* Drop by drop.

Dress, Dhriss, *v.* 1. To tidy up. 2. To correct, to punish.

Ex.—1. *Ah s'all 'a'e ti dhriss things up a bit afoor sha cums.*
2. *Thoo impident young raggel, thi fatther owt ti dhriss thi jacket weel foor tha,* i. e. 'Your father ought to chastise you.'

Dressin', Dhrissin', *part.* and *n.* 1. Preparing. 2. Chastisement, severe scolding. The use of this word is peculiar.

Ex.—1. *Things 'll want dhrissing up a bit afoor Ah start ti wark,* signifies that a certain amount of work not actually connected with the 'thing' itself must be done or prepared beforehand, such as tidying up the bench, or rough planing before marking out. *He nivver gits neea fother 'an dhrissing things afoor he starts o' summat else.*
2. *He'll nut foorgit ma, Ah nivver gav onnybody sike a dhrissing afoor.*

Dribblet, *n.* A small quantity at a time.

Ex. *He'll pay ma back, Ah've neea doot, bud Ah s'all 'a'e ti tak 't noos an' agaains i' dribblets.*

Drinch, *n.* An aperient drink for a cow.

Drinching, *part.* To be drenched.

Drinkin' tahm, *n.* The usual extra allowance during hay or harvest time.

Drippling, *adj.* Weak, small.

    Ex.—*Sha's nobbut a drippling bairn.*

Drive, Dhrive, *v.* To procrastinate.

    Ex.—*Thoo dhrives ivverything whahl t' last bat, an' then thoo nivver gits nowt deean.*

Droll on, *v.* To half promise, to lead one to believe.

    Ex.—*Ah nobbut drolls him on a bit, Ah saan't tell him nowt 'at's owt.*

Drolly, *n.* *Vide* **Capster.**

Droothy, Drouthy, *adj.* Suffering from excessive thirst.

Drooty, *adj.* Very dry, a long continuance of fine dry weather.

Drop, *v.* 1. To lose. 2. To fell with a blow. 3. To kill a bird on the wing.

    Ex.—1. *He'd drop a canny bit ower that last bargain.* 2. *He up wi' his neeaf an' dropped him leyke an ox.* 3. *He fired in amang 'em an' dropped three.*

Drop-dry, *adj.* Water-tight, as of a roof.

Drop in, *v.* To pay a casual visit.

Drop it or that, *v.* To cease doing.

    Ex.—*Noo drop it,* i. e. 'Discontinue the act.' *Drop that racket,* i. e. 'Cease that noise.'

Drop on, *v.* 1. To surprise. 2. To discover.

    Ex.—1. *Ah nivver wur seea dropped on afoor,* i. e. 'Never so surprised,' or 'suddenly caught in the act.' 2. *Ah dropped on it all at yance,* i. e. 'I discovered it all at once.' It also implies a sense of shame, e. g. *Ah did feel dropped on when he catched ma.*

Droppy, *adj.* Applied to rain long continued.

    Ex.—*It's nobbut a droppy tahm.*

Drubbin', *n.* A thrashing.

Dub, *n.* A large pond.

Dubbin', *v.* and *n.* 1. To lower one's dignity. 2. A thrashing.

    Ex.—1. *He's ti clivver by hauf is yon youth, he wants dubbin' a bit.* 2. *Ah'll gi'e tha sike a dubbin' ez thoo 'ezn't 'ed ov a piece, if thoo dizn't mahnd thisel.* 'Dubbing' originally meant cutting the comb and wattle of a gamecock.

Duck, *v.* To drop the head so as to evade a missile.

Ducks and drakes, *v.* A stone thrown so as to skim with short leaps along the water.

Duds, *n.* Clothes, usually applied to old garments.

Dulbert, *n.* A stupid fellow. Also **Dullard.**

Dump. *Vide* **Dub.**

Dunderheead, Dunderknowle, *n.* A blockhead.

Dundy-cow or Dowdy-cow, *n.* The ladybird.

Dwine, *v.* To pine away, to fade.

Dwinn'l, *v.* To decrease.

Dwiny, *n.* and *adj.* Fading, small.
Dwiny-voiced, *adj.* Weak-voiced.
Dwizzend, *adj.* Thin, wrinkled, shrunk.

E.

Ě, *per. pron.* I. The short sound of 'Ah,' as *Mun ĕ cum?* i. e.
'Must I come?' Although rarely used by writers, it must be
admitted, when speaking the dialect, it is as commonly used
as 'Ah.'
Eak, *n.* The oak.
Earan, *n.* An errand.
Earnest, *n.* A sum of money paid to bind a bargain.
Earning. *Vide* **Yearning.**
Ease, *v.* To spatter with mud, to accede to the demands of
nature, to obtain ease from pain.
Easement, *n.* Alleviation from pain, the remedy applied.
Easings, *n.* The eaves.
Easter-shells, *n.* The periwinkle.
E'e, *n.* The eye, that part of a potato from which the sprout leads.
Een, *n.* The eyes.
Een, *n.* 1. The evening, as 'yester een.' 2. The eve of any fast-
day, as 'All Hallows' Een.'
Een-holes, *n.* The eye sockets.
Efter, Efther, *prep.* After. 'Efther' becomes general as we
approach the East Riding.
Efterneean, *n.* Afternoon.
Egg on, *v.* To incite, to urge.
   Ex.—*It wer yowr Tom 'at egg'd him on ti kiss ma. Ah
   nivver s'u'd 'a'e set mysel ti loup t' beck if he hedn't egg'd
   ma on and darr'd ma tiv it.*
Eldin, *n.* Firewood of any kind.
Eller, *n.* The alder-tree.
Elsin, Alsin, *n.* A shoemaker's awl.
'Em, *pro.* Them.
End-board, *n.* The tail-board of a cart.
Endeavouring, *adj.* Striving, industrious.
   Ex.—*Sha's a fendy endivering lahtle body. He's a varra
   endivering young chap, an' he'll mak a man ov hissel.*
End, Girt. *Vide* **Gret end.**
End na sahd. 1. Nothing. 2. Not understandable.
   Ex.—1. *Ther's nowther end na sahd tiv owt 'at he diz,*
   i. e. 'Neither beginning nor end,' nothing. 2. *Ah c'u'd
   nowder mak end na sahd ov owt 'at t' chap war raffling
   on aboot.*
End, Reet upon, *adv.* Upright.
   Ex.—*Let's git it reet upon end fust, an' then wa s'all mannish.*

Enoo, Enew, *n.* 1. Enough in number. 2. Sufficiently cooked.
　　Ex.—1. *Thoo wants neea mair, thoo's gitten mair 'an enew ez it is.* 2. *It owt ti be enew by this, it's been i' t' yewn ower an hoor.*

Enow. *Vide* **Inoo.**

Entry, *n.* The passage within the house, or small entrance hall.

Ept, *adj.* Handy.

Esh, *n.* The ash-tree.

Ewse, *n.* Use.

Expect, *v.* 1. To imagine, to suppose. 2. Not quite certain.
　　Ex.—1. *Ah expect it war him 'at did it.* 2. *Yan nivver can saay, bud Ah expect sha'll win t' prize. Sha's neea waays sure, sha nobbut expects seea.*

Extremity, To be in an=To be at the far end.
　　Ex.—*Ah war in an extremity o' paain. Nowt c'u'd 'a'e been warse, sha war in a complete extremity.*

Es, as. *'Es,* has.

F.

Fadge, *v.* Between a walk and a trot.
　　Ex.—*T' au'd meer an' me, wa've fadged alang monny a mahl tigither.*

Fadgy, *adj.* Fat, unwieldy.
　　Ex.—*Buxom at twenty, fadgy at fo'tty.*

Faff, *v.* To blow in puffs.

Faffle, *n.* A light intermittent wind.

Faffle, *v.* To flap gently, as a ship's sail.

Fahve o' clocks, *n.* Ripe seed-heads of the dandelion, which children blow at to ascertain the time.

Fail, *v.* To show signs of growing weakness day by day.

Fain, *adv.* Gladly.

Fair, *adv.* Altogether, absolutely.
　　Ex.—*Ah's fair bet wi' t' lad. Ah nivver war sae fairly takken in wiv a lass ez Ah 'a'e been wi' Tom's weyfe.*

Fairish, *adj.* Just moderate.

Fairlings, *adv.* Clearly, distinctly.
　　Ex.—*Naay! he fairlings gat t' best o' thah that tahm.*

Fair to see. Easy to see or understand.

Fair up. *Vide* **Clear up.**

Fairy butter, *n.* A yellow fungus found growing on dead wood.

Fairings, *n.* Presents bought at a fair.

Fall, *v.* 1. To happen. 2. To become finely divided, as lime when slaked.
　　Ex.—1. *Whya, it mebbe mud fall i' that road,* i. e. 'Why, it maybe might happen in that way.'

Fallen away, *v.* To have decreased in bulk, to grow thin.
　　Ex.—*Whya, it's fallen awaay ti nowt.*

Fall in, *v.* To meet accidentally.

> Ex.—*Oor Martie war pleased ti fall in wi' John an' Annie at Bedale.*

Fall out, *v.* To quarrel, to have a misunderstanding.

> Ex.—*Tha're nut kind noo, tha fell owt ower Tommy's pig. Ah nivver knew sike nibors ez them tweea, tha're awlus quarting an' fratching, an' falling oot t' ane wi' t' uther.*

Fall teea, *v.* To commence.

> Ex.—*Noo all t' lot on ya fall teea an' set ti wark.*

Fan, Fand, Fun, Fund, *part.* and *pp.* of 'to find.'

Fangle, *v.* To seize, to entrap.

Fangled, *pp.* Caught.

Fantickle, *n.* A freckle.

Far, *adj.* Further, more distant than.

> Ex.—*Ah ligg'd it doon i' t' far sahd o' yon field.*

Far an' awaay, *adv.* Much, decidedly.

> Ex.—*Sha's far an' awaay t' best-leeaking lass aboot here; often* **Far awaay.**

Farantly, *adj.* Decent, well behaved; neat, nice, orderly.

Fardel, *n.* A small bundle.

Farden, *n.* Farthing.

Fare, *v.* 1. To approach, to draw nigh to. 2. To seem. 3. To succeed. 4. To conduct oneself, to behave.

> Ex.—1. *Sha fares o' cauvin'.* 2. *Yon lass fares dafter na Sally Ridge.* 3. *Thoo's gahin' ti fare t' warst wi' t' cauves, Ah think; thoo mun git sum keeak intiv 'em.* 4. *He fares foor gitting t' sack.*

Far end. The close of anything, almost *in extremis.*

> Ex.—*Tell her Ah'll cum when Ah've deean; Ah saan't be lang, Ah've ommaist gitten ti t' far end. Ah've just left him; Ah deean't aim 'at he'll see t' neet throw, he's ommaist at t' far end noo.*

Far-fetched, *adj.* Unlikely, improbable.

Farness, *n.* Distance.

> Ex.—*T' farness on 't taks all t' profit awaay, gahin' an' cumin'.*

Farrish, Fairish on, *adj.* Considerably advanced.

> Ex.—*He mun be gitting fairish on i' years noo. He gat farrish on at t' dinner, did Tommy, afoor he gat to'n'd ti t' doour.*

Far-side, *n.* The further side, the right-hand or off side; the **Nar-side** being the left-hand.

Fash, *v.* 1. To worry. 2. To inconvenience oneself.

> Ex.—1. *Just thee tak thi awn gate, an' deean't fash thisen aboot nowt.* 2. *Ah wadn't fash mysel a larl bit fur owther him or her.*

Fast, *adj.* 1. At a standstill. 2. In a fix.
> Ex.—1. *Ah caan't deea nowt, Ah's fast foor a sup o' wet.*
> 2. *Ah think 'at Ah nivver war sae fast iv all my wick.*

Fasten or **Fass'n oot,** *v.* Said of sheep when turned from the grass on to the moor for the season.

Father, *v.* 1. To impute. 2. To bear witness of itself, as an illegitimate child.
> Ex.—1. *He's awlus tryin' ti father his misdeeds o' sumbody. Ah wadn't let him father his lees o' me.* 2. *Ther's neea call ti mak t' poor lass gan afoor her betters, t' bairn sha hugs fathers itsel.*

Fatrascal, *n.* A cake made with butter, flour, and currants; a rich kind of small tea-cake.

Faugh, Fauf, *n.* Fallow land.

Fause, *adj.* False.

Fayther, Fadder, *n.* Father.

Fear'd, To be, *v.* To be apprehensive of, to be afraid.
> Ex.—*It's to be fear'd t' warst 'll happen.*

Fearful, *adv.* Exceedingly, used as an augmentative.

Fearsome, *adj.* Awful, terrifying.

Feather-fallen, *adj.* Crestfallen.

Feather-fowl, *n.* Birds.

Featly, *adv.* Dexterously.
> Ex.—*Noo, he lapp'd that job up weel. Aye, it war varra featly deean.*

Feck, *n.* Ability, quantity, mass.

Feckless, *adj.* Lacking management, wanting ability to provide for oneself.
> Ex.—*Sha's a feckless miss, is yon; sha's up ti nowt, good ti nowt, an' warse 'an nowt.*

Feeal, *n.* A fool.

Fegs, *n.* Dead grass-stems, anything of small value.

Fele, Felt, *v.* To hide.

Fell, *v.* To knock down.

Fell, *n.* An undressed hide or skin, a moorland summit, a hill.

Fell, *adj.* Keen, striving.

Fell'd, *v.* To be prostrate, knocked down.

Felon bone, *n.* An abscess on the finger or some other part of the hand, from which, during suppuration, small pieces of rotted bone are ejected.

Felon o' t' yuer. A disease the cow's udder is liable to.

Fellow-fond, *adj.* Wild after the men. A girl is said to be 'fellow-fond' when her arts and guiles to gain a lover are too plainly manifest.

Felt. *Vide* **Fele.**

Felter, *n.* One who hides things.

Felter, *v.* To entangle, to twist, to clot. NOTE.—**Cotter** is much more commonly used now.

Feltrics, *n.* A disorder horses are liable to.

Femmer, *adj.* Slight, light, weak.

Fend, *v.* To provide, to be able to do.

Fendable, Fendy, *adj.* Capable of doing.

Fengle. *Vide* **Fangle.**

Fent, *n.* A vent or slit in a garment.

Fent, *v.* To bind the edge of anything.

Fer, Foor, Fur, *prep.* For.

Fest, *v.* To bind an apprentice.

Fet, *v.* To last out, serve round, to serve.

> Ex.—*If'll fet us ower Sunday. If'll fet t' lot on us if Tom carves.*

Fetch, *n.* A stitch or catch in the side, difficulty in breathing.

Fetch, *v.* To give, to bring.

> Ex.—*Ah'll fetch tha yan ower t' feeace. Ah'll fetch tha 't when Ah cum fra t' market. Fetch t' barrer ower here,* i. e. 'Bring the barrow over here.'

Fettle, *v.* 1. To repair. 2. To put in order. 3. To be in good order.

> Ex.—1. *Thoo mun fettle t' au'd cart up a larl piece,* i.e. 'You must repair the old cart a little.' 2. *Ah'll fettle things up a bit afoor ya cum back,* i. e. 'I will put things in order by the time you return.' 3. *T' machine's i' grand fettle.*

Few, *n.* Amount, generally used with some qualifying adjective, as 'a good few,' 'a larl few,' 'a gay few.'

Fick, *v.* To struggle under restraint.

Fik, *v.* 1. To strive. 2. To obtain.

> Ex.—1. *He fick'd on whahl he gat it.* 2. *He fick'd it i' t' end.*

Find heart, To, *v.* To make up one's mind.

> Ex.—*Sha's blinnd, bud Ah can't finnd heart ti put t' poor au'd critter oot o' t' road.*

Finnick, *v.* To be over-particular in doing things.

Fire-flaught, *n. and adj.* A lighted coal which leaps from the fire, a meteor; passionate.

Fire-smatch. *Vide* **Stithe.**

Fire-steead, *n.* Fireplace.

First-foot. *Vide* **Lucky bird.**

Fisk, *v.* To dance about.

Fit, *adj.* 1. Equal to. 2. Ready. 3. Inclined.

> Ex.—1. *Ah's fit foor that job, hooivver.* 2. *T' meer's fit onny tahm.* 3. *Ah's ommaist fit ti gan.*

Fizzle, *v.* To fidget.

Flabbergasher, *n.* A poser. *Vide* **Cramper.**

Flacker, *v.* 1. To flutter. 2. To flicker. 3. To waver.

> Ex.—1. *T' au'd bo'd flackered ower t' hedge.* 2. *T' cann'l*

flackered whahl Ah thowt it 'ud gan oot. 3. *Ther's neea dependence on him, he flackers aboot sae.*

Flag, *n.* A snow-flake.

Flags, *n.* The yellow iris.

Flam, *v.* To flatter, to make believe.

Flappers, *n.* Young birds nearly ready to fly.

Flappy, *adj.* Unstable.

Flappy-sket, *n. and adj.* An immoral woman; untidy.

Flappy-tongue, *n.* One whose word cannot be relied upon.

Flatch, *n.* A flatterer, also used as a *verb.*

Flather. *Vide* **Blether.**

Flaum, *v.* 1. To blaze, to burst out in flame. 2. To demonstrate great affection so as to gain some advantage.

　　Ex.—1. *It flaum'd up leyke all that, bud then it war ez dry ez a kex.* 2. *Sha flaum'd aboot ma that mich, whahl i' t' end Ah 'ed ti gi'e waay an' let 'em git wed.*

Flaumy, *adj.* Common, tawdry. *n.* Fulsome caresses.

Flaun, *n.* A custard tart.

Flaup, Flauping, *n.* **Flaupy, Flaupish,** *adj.* Senseless talk.

Flawter, Flowter, *v.* To unnerve, to flurry.

　　Ex.—*Ah war sairly flowtered when Ah heeard o' Jimmy's deeath.*

Flay, *v.* To frighten. Also **Fley.**

Flay-boggle, *n.* A ghost.

Flay-craw, -creeak, or **-cruke,** *n.* A scarecrow.

Flaysome, *adj.* Causing fear.

Flee, *n.* A fly.

　　Ex.—*Ah deean't meean fleas 'at's fleas, bud flees 'at flee,* i. e. 'I do not mean fleas that are fleas, but flies that fly.'

Fleead, *n.* A flood.

Fleead, *v.* To flood.

　　Ex.—*Ah's gahin' ti let t' dam off an' fleead t' boddums.*

Fleear, *n.* A floor.

Fleece, *n.* Obesity.

　　Ex.—*Wait whahl he gans throw all 'at Ah've gane throw, an' he weean't hug sike a fleece.*

Fleece, *v.* To take all that a man has.

　　Ex.—*Oh, sha's a rank bad un; tha saay 'at sha's fleeced him ov ivvery haupenny he 'ed.*

Fleeing-aither or **-ask,** *n.* The dragon-fly.

Fleer, *v.* To laugh at, to ridicule.

Flesh-fly, *n.* The common bluebottle.

Flesh-meat, *n.* Butcher's meat, not pork.

Flick, *n.* A flitch of bacon.

Flick, *v.* To remove any light dust or thing with a rapid motion, as with a duster or whip-lash.

Flicker, *v.* and *n.* To exist for an instant, as a smile; the action of a dying flame.

Flig, *v.* To fly.

Fligged, *part.* Having left the nest.

Fliggers. *Vide* **Flappers.**

Flipe, *n.* The brim of a hat.

Flipe, *v.* To remove dust by any quick, light motion, as with a handkerchief. *Vide* **Flick.**

Flisk, *n.* A light tap.

Ex.—*Sha nobbut flisk'd him wi' her larl finger.*

Flit, *v.* To remove to another house.

Flite, Fleeght, *v.* 1. To scold with many words. 2. To quarrel.

Ex.—1. *Sha nivver lets ma be, sha's awlus fliting at ma.*
2. *Tha're fliting t' ane agaain t' ither that mich whahl Ah've cum'd awaay.*

Flither, *n.* The common limpet.

Flittermouse, *n.* The common bat.

Flitting, *v.* The act of removing.

Flity, *adj.* Unstable.

Ex.—*Ah wadn't trust her, nowder yah waay ner anuther, sha's sike a flity body.*

Flobbed up, *part.* Swollen.

Flop, *v.* To sit down with a sudden drop, to set things down of a sudden and carelessly.

Floss-docken, Fox-docken, *n.* The foxglove (*Digitalis purpurea*).

Floss-seave, *n.* Cotton-grass.

Flowtered, *part.* Upset, nervous.

Flowterment, *n.* Excitement in speech and behaviour.

Flowtersome, *adj.* Excitable, tomboyish.

Fluff'd, Fluff'd up, *adj.* Conceited.

Fluffy, *adj.* Covered with down, light, feathery.

Fluke, Fleeak, Fleuks, *n.* A small maggot found in the liver of sheep.

Fluky, Fleeaky, Fleuky, *adj.* Maggot-eaten, fly-blown.

Flushy-feeaced, *adj.* Red complexioned.

Fluster, Flusterment, *n.* A state of being heated by excitement, agitation.

Ex.—*What a flusterment that bairn' ez putten uz all inteea ! wa thowt 'at he'd gitten hissel lost.*

Fly, To let, *v.* To strike with force.

Foal's-foot, *n.* Coltsfoot (*Tussilago farfara*).

Fod, *n.* A small bundle of straw.

Fodder-hoos, *n.* A barn for storing fodder.

Fog, *n.* The grass which grows after the hay has been removed.

Fog-field, *n.* A field left for the second growth of grass to spring up after haytime.

Foisty, *adj.* Musty, damp, mouldy.

Fold- or **Fod-garth, Fod-yard,** *n.* The farmyard where the beasts are fed.

Folk, Fau'k, Fooak, *n.* The people, often used with and generally qualified by a prefix, as *T' au'd folk, T' young fooak, Chetch-fau'k, Chapel-fau'k.*

Fond, *adj.* Silly.

Fond-head, *n.* A silly fellow.

Fondness, *n.* Nonsense.

Fondy, *n.* A simpleton.

Foor, Fur, Fer, *prep.* For.

Foorced, *part.* Compelled.

> Ex.—*Ther's neea waay o' gittin oot on 't, Ah s' be foorced ti gan. He'll foorce tha ti deea 't.*

Foot, The length of my=A kick.

> Ex.—*If thoo isn't off iv a quickstick, Ah'll gi'e tha t' len'th o' mah foot.*

Foot, To get or take the length of one's=1. To judge a person accurately. 2. To have completely won another's confidence.

> Ex.—1. *He'll nut best ma, weean't yon; Ah teeak t' len'th o' his foot lang sin.* 2. *Sha lets him deea just what he leykes wiv her brass; he's gitten t' len'th ov her foot, an' ther's nowt aboot that.*

Footing, *n.* Money claimed from a new apprentice on commencing his apprenticeship, commonly called paying his footing; the sum paid is always spent in drink.

Footings, *n.* The lowest foundations.

For, Fur=In what direction.

> Ex.—*Noo, then, wheear's thoo for? Ah's for Ayton, is thoo for Stowsla?*

Fore, *prep.* Before. **Afoor** is much more general.

Fore-elders, *n.* Forefathers.

Fore-end, Forr-end, *n.* 1. The beginning of a season or time. 2. The springtime.

> Ex.—1. *At t' forr-end he war ez reet ez a trivet, bud he maad a varra poor finish on 't.* 2. *If t' back-end be owt leyke t' forr-end wa s'all mannish grandly.*

Forking-robin, *n.* The earwig.

Forks, A pair o', *n.* The centre timber of a roof.

For-wandered, *adj.* Bewildered.

Fo'st, Fust, *adj.* First.

Fo'ther, *adv.* Further.

Foul-fingered, *adj.* Given to stealing.

Foul-lipped } *adj.* Given to swearing or lewd talk.
Foul-mouthed

Foulmart, Fumart, *n.* The polecat.

Foupe, *v.* To drive sheep, &c., too quickly.
 Ex.—*Thoo'll 'a'e sum o' them sheep deead beeat if thoo foupes 'em i' that road.*
Fou't, *n.* A fault.
Fou'ty, *adj.* Badly made, ill fitting.
Fowt, *part.* Fought.
Fowt, Fout, *n.* An idiot, a spoiled child.
Foxy, *adj.* Cunning.
Fra, Frav, Frev, *prep.* From. 'Fra' is used before a consonant, 'frav' and 'frev' before a vowel.
Fraby, Frebby, *prep.* 1. Beyond. 2. Compared with. Still common in parts of Cleveland.
 Ex.—1. *'T'll be fraby ten mahl ti Yarm.* 2. *Thahn frebby mahn's t' best o' t' tweea on 'em.*
Framation, *n.* Dexterity, ability, skill shown at the commencement of any work.
 Ex.—*Noo, yon chap hez a bit o' framation aboot him.*
Frame, *v.* To show good management, contrive well.
 Ex.—*T' lass frames weel ti milk.*
Fratch, *v.* To quarrel.
Fraunge, *v.* To play a joke.
Fresh, *adj.* Intoxicated.
Fresh-wood, *n.* The threshold of a doorway.
Fridge, *v.* To rub against so as to cause a sore.
Frightened, Freetened, *adj.* and *part.* 1. Doubtful as to. 2. Apprehensive of. 3. Bashful.
 Ex.—1. *Ah's freetened he weean't mannish ti cum.* 2. *Sha war despert freetened 'at he war gahin' ti splet aboot what tha'd deean.* 3. *Gi'e t' lass a kiss, deean't be freetened.*
Frog-fry, *n.* Frog- or toad-spawn.
Fromward, *prep.* Away from.
Frough, *adj.* Soft, spongy.
Frow, *n.* An untidy person, generally a female.
Frowsy, *adj.* Applied to a forbidding countenance, untidy, musty.
Frutas, *n.* A kind of tea-cake made of batter and fruits fried in butter on Ash Wednesday.
Fuggy, *adj.* First. *Vide* **Laggy.**
Full, *adv.* An intensive, as 'Full seean,' i. e. 'full soon.'
 Ex.—*Ah'll be on full seean efter dinner*, i. e. 'very soon.'
Full-fligged, *adj.* Full-feathered.
Fullock, *v.* To shoot a marble with force, and by unfairly overreaching the line; to do anything with considerable force.
 Ex.—*He went at it wi' sike a fullock.*
Full-up, *adv.* Quite full.
Fun, *pp.* of Find.
Fur. For.

Furmety, Frummety, *n.* Creed-wheat boiled in milk, thickened with lithing, sweetened, and flavoured with cloves, nutmeg, &c., only eaten at Christmas time.

Furrh, *n.* A furrow.

Fustilugs, *n.* A low fellow.

Fuzzack, *n.* A donkey.

Fuzz-ball, *n.* The common field-fungus which, when ripe, on being nipped emits a cloud of brown dust-spores.

Fuzzle, *v.* To intoxicate.

G.

Ga', *v.* Gave.

Gaa, *v.* To go.

Gab, *n.* Senseless chatter.
> Ex.—*Ho'd thi gab,* i. e. 'Cease your foolish talk,' or 'hold your tongue.'

Gabber, *v.* To talk foolishly.

Gabriel-ratchet or **T' Gabby-ratch.** A sound heard overhead in the still hours of the night, somewhat resembling the yelping of dogs ; generally thought to be due to a flock of geese. When heard by the country folk it is looked upon as an omen of death.

Gad, *n.* A pointed rod, a whip-stock fitted with a thong. To guard against the power of witches the whip-stock was often made of rowan-tree wood.

Gad, Gadder, Gadabout, *n.* A gossip.

Gadding, *part.* Gossiping.

Gaddish, *adj.* Inclined to gossip.

Gadling, *adj.* Applied to a gossiping person.

Gae. *Vide* **Gaa.**

Gaed, *pret.* of **Gae.**

Gaffer, *n.* The master.
> Ex.—*Leeak oot, here's t' gaffer cumin'.*

Gag-bit, *n.* A powerful bit used when breaking horses.

Gah, *v.* To go.

Gahins on. Doings, festivities, proceedings.
> Ex.—*Ther's been straange gahins on at Bessy's sen Martha cam yam. Noo, wa 'ed grand gahins on at t' Jubilee.*

Gahlfat. *Vide* **Gilevat.**

Gain, Gainest, *adj.* Shortest, quickest, easiest.
> Ex.—*It's t' gainest waay ti gan byu t' wood,* i. e. 'It is the shortest way,' &c. *Ther's a gainer way ti deea 't 'an that,* i. e. 'There is a quicker or easier plan to do it than that.'

Gainable, *adj.* Obtainable.

Gain-hand, *adj.* Easily reached.

Gainly, *adv.* Easily gained, of access.

Gains, *n.* An advantage.

Gainstrive, Gainstand, *v.* To oppose.

Ex.—*Yan caan't gainstrive owt o' that soart. Neea-body can gainstand thersens agaain t' railway cump'ny.*

Gain-way, *n.* A shorter path.

Gairn, Garn, *n.* Worsted, yarn.

Gaitings, *n.* Bundles of clover tied at the top and left to dry.

Gallac-handed, *adj.* Left-handed.

Ex.—*Fau'k 'at's gallac-handed's awlus a larl bit tricky, Ah think.*

Gallivant, *v.* To flirt, to be continually in the society of ladies.

Galloway, *n.* One of a small breed of horses.

Gallowses, Gallasses, *n.* Trouser braces.

Gally-bauk, *n.* An iron bar attached to the rann'l bauk, from which pans are hung either on or off the fire.

Galore, *n.* A superabundance.

Gam, *n.* 1. A game. 2. Fun. 3. Ridicule.

Ex.—1. *Wa'd a rare gam at creckets last neet.* 2. *He's a grand hand at makking gam.* 3. *Ah thowt sha was deeaing nowt bud mak gam o' ma.*

Gamashes, *n.* Gaiters, leggings, now applied to all kind of leg-coverings.

Gammer, *v.* To waste time, to be slow.

Gammer-stag or **-stang,** *n.* An immodest female.

Gammish, *adj.* Lively, full of frolic, plucky.

Gan, Gang, *v.* To go, to go on foot. 'Gang' is often added to the direction pointed out.

Ex.—*Thoo'd best tak by t' mill gang,* i. e. 'Go by the mill way,' or 'go by the mill,' or 'by t' stell gang,' 'up gang,' &c.

Gane, *v.* Gone.

Ganger, *n.* A goer, usually applied to a horse.

Ex.—*Sha's nut mich ov a ganger. That's a good ganger,* i. e. 'A good goer.'

Gangeril, Gangril, *n.* A worthless fellow, a vagrant, a toad.

Gannings on. *Vide* **Gahins on.**

Gans, *v.* Goes.

Gant, *adj.* Thin, puny, half-fed.

Gantree, *n.* A low wooden stand for barrels to rest on.

Gap, *n.* An opening in a hedge through which sheep may stray, a rift in the hills.

Gape, Gaape, Geeap, *v.* To bawl loudly, to stand open-mouthed.

Garb, *v.* To dress vulgarly, or in tawdry finery.

Garfits, *n.* Entrails. In some parts goose giblets are known as 'garfits.'

Garland, *v.* A white glove decorated with ribbons and carried at funerals. *Vide* Chap. VIII, on 'Customs.'

Garsel, *n.* Rotten sticks, last year's undergrowth.

Garth, *n.* A small enclosure of land.

Gate, Geeat, *n.* A way, road, street ; there is also a secondary meaning of 'manner.' Adverbially as 'all gates,' 'onny gates.'
Ex.—*What gate mun Ah tak ti Easby ?* i.e. 'Which road must I take to Easby ?' *If he gans on i' yon gate, he'll seean lap t' job up,* i. e. ' If he goes on in that manner, he will soon end the business.' *Leeak at what he's deean onny gate an' all gates, an' yan's boun ti awn he's been a feeal all roads,* i.e. 'Look at what he has done any way and all ways, and one is compelled to admit he has been a fool every way.' *Thoo diz things all gates an' onny gates, an' it's neea gates i' t' end.*

Gate, *n.* An acquired right or privilege of pasturage for cattle.

Gate, *v.* To arrange clover in small bundles to dry.

Gauk, Gawk, *n.* A stupid fellow, the cuckoo.

Gauky, *adj.* Clumsy, idiotic.

Gaum, *v.* To pay attention intelligently.

Gaumish, *adj.* Intelligent.

Gaumless, *adj.* Lacking intelligence.

Gaup, *v.* To stare and gape with astonishment.

Gauve, *v.* To stare vacantly.

Gauvison, *n.* Silly of either sex. Usually applied to a female.

Gauvy, *n.* A silly fellow.

Gavelock, *n.* A crowbar.

Gay, Gayish, *adj.* 1. Considerable in number. 2. Nice, pleasing. 3. Fairly good, both as to size, quality, and number.
Ex.—1. *Ther war a gay few fau'k gethered up ; Ah gav a gayish bit mair 'an that for 't.* 2. *It's a gay bit o' stuff.* 3. *It's a gayish field o' to'nips.*

Gayly, *adv.* 1. First-class. 2. Exceedingly well as to health.
Ex. 1.—*Ah's gittin' on gayly,* i.e. 'first-class.' 2. *Sha war nobbut dowly a piece sen, but sha's gayly noo.*

Gear, Gearing, *n.* That part of a machine which alters the speed of running, harness.

Gear, *n.* Worldly possessions, raiment.

Geb. *Vide* **Gib.**

Geck, *n.* A stupid oaf. *Vide* also **Goffen.**

Geean, *part.* Gone.

Geeaping, *pp.* Gaping, staring.

Gecken, *v. Vide* **Goffen.**

Gee, *v.* The wagoner's command for the horse to take the right-hand side of the road.

Geen, Gi'en, Gi'n, *v.* Given.

Geld, *adj.* and *n.* Barren; single unmated birds, as of partridges.

Gell, *n.* Girl.

Gen, Girn, *v.* To grin.

Genning, *adj.,* also *part.* of **Gen.** 1. To grin. 2. To find fault.
Ex.—1. *Thoo genning munkey, Ah'll gi'e tha summat ti*

gen at if thoo disn't shift thisel. 2. *Sha's awlus genning an' fliting at yan.*

Gep, *v.* To eavesdrop.

Ger, *v.* To get, go.

Ex.—*Ger ho'd on 't.*

Gert, Gret, Greeat, *adj.* Great.

Gesling, *n.* Gosling.

Gess, Gerse, *n.* Grass.

Gessing-land, Gersing-land, *n.* Grass-land.

Get, *v.* Beside being used in the ordinary sense there are several curious usages. 1. To get to. 2. Is called. 3. To come.

Ex.—1. *Ah aim ti gan ti Brotton when Ah git to Boosbeck.* 2. *T' chap 'at 'ed it afoor called it Jack, bud it awlus gits Flip wiv uz.* 3. *Wa thowt ya warn't gahin' ti mannish ti get.*

Get, Able to. *Vide* **Yabble.**

Get agate, *v.* To commence.

Get away with, To, *v.* To push forward work.

Ex.—*Noo 'at t' wood's cum'd wa s'all be yabble ti git awaay wi' t' job at yance.*

Get on, *v.* To succeed.

Ex.—*He's sartin ti git on, is yon chap.*

Get the length of, *v.* To get as far as, either of place, distance, or work.

Getherer or Gedderer, *n.* A collector of taxes, one who gathers the corn into bundles.

Gether or Gedder up, To, *v.* To collect together.

Getten, Gitten, Gotten, *part.* To get.

Gew-gaws, *n.* Jewellery, &c.

Gew-gow, *n.* A Jew's harp.

Gib, *n.* The hooked handle of a stick.

Gib- or Geb-stick, *n.* A hooked stick.

Gicken. *Vide* **Goffen.**

Gi'en. *Vide* **Geen.**

Giglet, *n.* A giggling girl.

Gilder, *n.* A horsehair snare.

Gilevat, *n.* The vat or tub in which ale is stood to ferment.

Gill, *n.* A half-pint.

Gill, *n.* A narrow rock valley, a ravine.

Gillifer, *n.* An immodest woman; one who pretends to good looks, or dresses younger than her years.

Gilt, *n.* A young sow.

Gimmal, *n.* A narrow passage between two houses.

Gimmer, *n.* A young female lamb.

Ginger-heead, *adj.* and *n.* One having red hair.

Gingerly, *adv.* Cautiously, ticklish to do.

C c

Ginnel. *Vide* **Runnel.**
Ginner, *adv.* Rather, quite as soon as.
    Ex.—*Ah'd ez ginner gan ez stop.*
Girt, *adj.* Great. *Vide* **Gert.**
Girt shakes, Neea. Nothing to boast of.
Gissy-gissy, *n.* The call for the young pigs to be fed.
Git. *Vide* **Get.**
Give, *v.* To stretch, to give way, to yield to force, to thaw.
Give agaan, *v.* To thaw, to return something when bargaining for luck.
Give back, *v.* To recede, to yield through lack of courage.
Give in, *v.* To tender an estimate, to give notice to a land-lord of intention to quit his farm or house, to admit being vanquished.
Give out, *v.* To fail in supply.
Give ower, *v.* Leave off, desist, cease.
    Ex.—*Gi'e ower at yance,* i. e. ' Cease at once.'
Gizzen, *n.* The gizzard.
Glazzen, *v.* 1. To glaze a window. 2. Become glassy.
    Ex.—2. *It'll seean be deead, its een 's glazzen'd noo.*
Glease, Gleeaze, *v.* To run swiftly.
Gleasing, *n.* A race after, the cost of a suit at law.
Gleen, *v.* To shine.
Gleg, *v.* To peep slyly, to cast one's eyes about furtively.
Glent, *v.* To glance off at an angle.
Gliff, Glift, *n.* A passing glance, a glimpse.
Gloaming, *n.* Twilight.
Gloor, Gloar, *v.* To stare intently.
Glorr, *n.* Soft, fat.
Glow. *Vide* **Low.**
Glump, *v.* To sulk.
Glumpy, *adj.* Sulky.
    Ex.—*If he's glumpy, let him glump.*
Glut, *n.* A wooden wedge used to split timber with.
Gnag, *v.* To weary one with reproaches, to continually assail one with remarks of an irritating nature.
Gnaggy, *adj.* Bad tempered, continually scolding.
Gnarl, *v.* To gnaw, as rabbits do trees during a hard winter.
Gnarr. *Vide* **Knar.**
Gnarr, *v.* To growl.
Gnatter, *v.* To find fault of a petty nature continuously.
Gnattering, Nattering, *adj.* Fault-finding on all occasions.
    Ex.—*Oh, sha's a gnattering au'd thing, sha's nivver off his beeans.*
Gnipe. *Vide* **Knep.**

Go or Goa, *n.* 1. Attempt, try. 2. Event, circumstance.

Ex.—1. *Cum by, an' let me 'ev a go at it. He fetched yan doon fust go. All t' three on us 'ed a go, bud neean on us hit it.* 2. *Well, this is a go; it beeats ivvery go, diz this.*

Gob, *n.* The mouth.

Gobble, *v.* To reply in a sulky, indistinct manner.

Ex.—*Noo, git thisel oot o' t' glumps, an' deean't gobble i' that road when Ah ass tha owt.*

Gob-string, *n.* A bridle.

God's penny, *n.* A sum of money paid by the master when hiring a servant to bind the transaction.

Goffen, Gecken, Gicken, Geck, *v.* To laugh like an idiot.

Goings on. *Vide* **Gahins on.**

Goke, Gowk, Gooak, *n.* The core of an apple, the hard part of a boil or ulcer; also used to denote the centre of many things, as 't' gowk o' t' stack.'

Goldens, *n.* The charred stems of burnt ling.

Goldie, *n.* The yellow-hammer.

Golly, *n.* A newly-hatched bird.

Gomerill, *n.* A born idiot.

Gone away. *Vide* **Fallen away.**

Good, *adj.* 1. Considerable. 2. Easy. 3. Well. 4. Almost. 5. Kind, obliging.

Ex.—1. *Whya, noo, ther war a good few on 'em.* 2. *That's good eneeaf ti deea.* 3. *Yan mud ez good talk tiv a yat-post ez yon lad.* 4. *Ah've ez good ez deean noo.* 5. *Ya'll mebbe be seea good ez ti fetch ma a bit o' bacca back wi' ya?*

Good, *adv.* Altogether, entirely.

Ex.—*Wa'd gi'en ya up foor good, wa thowt ya warn't gahin' ti mannish to get.*

Goodies, *n.* Sweetmeats.

Good-like, *adj.* Of pleasing appearance.

Goodman, *n.* The husband.

Good riddance. Lit. Very pleased you have gone away.

Good-stuff, *n.* Sweets.

Good-woman, *n.* The wife.

Goose- or Geeasegogs, *n.* Gooseberry.

Gorpie, *n.* *Vide* **Golly.**

Gossamer, *n.* Fine cobwebs found during dry weather, either on the herbage or floating in the air. *Vide* **Musweb.**

Gote, *n.* A narrow passage often running between two rows of houses, a rent in rocks sufficiently wide to admit the passage of one man at a time, a natural narrow ravine. A mill-race is often called a 'mill-gote.'

Goupen, *n.* A handful.

Goupenful, *n.* A double handful.

Gowden, *adj.* Golden. The 'ow' is pronounced as in 'show.'

Gowk, *n.* A fool, a clumsy fellow.

Gowky, *adj.* Clumsy.

    Ex.—*A gret gowky good ti nowt.*

Gowland, *n.* The corn marigold.

Grace, *n.* Advantage, benefit.

    Ex.—*Ther weean't be mich grace i' deeaing a thing leyke that.*

Graft or **Graff,** *n.* A spade depth.

Grain, *v.* To grumble.

Graining, *n.* The fork, the division into branches.

Grains, *n.* Branches.

Graithing, *n.* Clothes.

Grapplement, *n.* A grasping in a struggle.

Grass widdy, *n.* An immoral woman.

Grave, *v.* To dig.

Grawn up, *adj.* Grown up, adult.

Greean, Girn, Gairn, *v.* To groan, as when lifting a heavy weight.

    Ex.—*Thee lift, an' Ah'll deea t' gerning.*

Gree, *v.* To agree, to assent.

Greease-horn, *n.* A toady, a sycophant.

Greease in, *v.* To win over by flattery.

Greed, *n.* Avarice.

Greet, *v.* To weep silently.

Grenky, *adj.* Complaining, unwell, irritable.

Gret. *Vide* **Gert.**

Gret end, *adv.* Almost.

    Ex.—*Ther'll be t' gret end o' fowr scoore. Whya, Ah gav' t' gret end o' twenty pun for 't.*

Gret likelihood. Almost a certainty.

    Ex.—*Tha've been keeping cump'ny foor sum tahm, ther's gret likelihood 'at tha'll be gittin' wed afoor lang.*

Griff, *n.* A small ravine.

Grime, Grahm, *n.* Soot.

Grime, Grahm, *v.* To black with soot.

Grime ower, *v.* To spread a light covering of dust or other light matter.

Griming, *n.* A light covering of snow.

Grip, *n.* A narrow trench.

Gripe, *n.* A pronged fork for digging.

Grip ho'd, *n.* A handle. *v.* To take hold of firmly.

Grissy, *adj.* Damp and warm, of the weather.

Grob, *n.* An undersized, badly-built man.

Grob, *v.* To search with the hand under conditions where the eyes cannot assist.

Grobble, *v.* To grope, to search for with a stick or hand, as under a stone for fish.

Ex.—*Ah's grobbling unner t' steean foor a treeat,* i. e. trout.

Gross, Grossy, *adj.* Rapid growth, plants too close together, fat.

Growt-heead, *n.* A blockhead.

Grozy, *adj.* Well-to-do.

Grue, *adj.* Sullen, lowering, dismal, also applied to discontent freely expressed.

Gruff, *adj.* Brusque.

Gruff, *v.* To express dissatisfaction, to grunt, to snort in temper, to snore.

Grump, *v.* To sulk.

Grumps, *n.* *Vide* **Brully.**

Grumpy, *adj.* Bad tempered, sulky.

Grund, *n.* Ground.

Grundage, *n.* Ground rent.

Grun'lstan, Grunstan, *n.* Grindstone.

Gruntle, *v.* To give low grunting sounds of discontent.

Grutch, *v.* To envy, to grudge.

Ex.—*Ther's nowt 'at he dizn't grutch yan. He mud 'ev 'ed t' tweea pigs, bud Ah did grutch him t' coo.*

Gulch, *v.* To swallow like a dog.

Ex.—*Thoo gulches thi puddin' doon warse 'an a dog.*

Gumption, *n.* Tact, general capability.

Ex.—*He'll nowther fick na fend, foor he wants baith mense an' gumption.*

Gush, *n.* A rush of air, a gust.

Gutter, *v.* To waste, as a candle in a draught.

Ex.—*Put t' deear teea, t' cann'l 's sweealing an' guttering awaay leyke all that.*

Gutter eaves, *n.* The gutter which carries the water from off the roof.

H.

Hack, *n.* A small pickaxe.

Hackle, *n.* The natural covering of an animal, or the clothes of man.

Hackle, *v.* 1. To dress, to put on one's best attire, to make smart. 2. To turn the soil lightly.

Ex.—1. *Sha's hackled hersel wiv all t' gew-gaws 'at sha's gitten.* 2. *Thoo mun just hackle aboot t' reeats.*

Had away. A corruption of the Scotch 'haud awa.' It is quite common, and used in the sense of 'come or go quickly.'

Haffle, *v.* 1. To hesitate when speaking, to stammer, to appear desirous of keeping something back. 2. To exhibit indecision of character. 3. To quibble.

> Ex. 1.—*Deean't haffle leyke that, bud speeak plain.* 2. *Naay, what! he's lost t' job, he haffled seea; just he wad an' then he wadn't, whahl t' gaffer gav it ti sumbody else.* 3. *He awlus haffles on that mich, whahl neeabody ho'ds ti owt he sez.*

Hag, *n.* A thick white fog which, when followed by a frost, forms frost-hag; a coppice, such as often grows on a rough bank or broken ground; a broken rugged bank.

Hag-berry, *n.* The fruit of the bird-cherry (*Prunus padus*). NOTE.—In many parts of the North Riding Bug-berry is the common name, *bägg* being the Swedish for the same.

Hag-clog, *n.* A wooden block, varying in size, used as a chopping block.

Haggle, *v.* To chop or cut anything unevenly, to tease, to beat down in a bargain, to argue in a contentious spirit.

Haggy, *adj.* Rough, boggy, always applied to land.

Hag snars, *n.* The stubs left standing after the chopping down of young trees.

Hag-worm, *n.* The viper or adder (*Pelias berus*). The name is never applied to the blind-worm.

Hair-breed, *n.* 1. By little and little. 2. Slow degrees. 3. The narrowest margin.

> Ex.—1. *Wa're bodduming what tha did byv hair-breeds,* i. e. 'We are finding out what they did little by little.' 2. *Willie mends, bud it's nobbut byv hair-breeds.* 3. *He 'scaped wiv his leyfe, bud it war nobbut byv a hair-breed,* lit. 'A hair's breadth.'

Hairy-worm, *n.* Any caterpillar of a hairy kind.

Hake, *n.* An importunate beggar, not necessarily a pauper; a greedy, grasping person.

Hake, *v.* To be pertinacious, to weary with importunities.

Hale, *v.* To empty a vessel by inclining it to one side.

Hales, *n.* The handles of a plough.

Half-marrow, *n.* One considered as but a youth at his calling, half-grown.

Half nowt. Beneath consideration, either as to money or character.

> Ex.—*Ah gat it foor hauf nowt. It's nobbut a hauf-nowt when it's deean. T' father's i' prison an' t' lad's a hauf-nowt.*

Half-rocked or -**baked,** *adj.* Half-witted, foolish.

> Ex.—*He knaws nowt, he's nobbut hauf-rocked. It's nobbut a hauf-rocked thing foor onnybody ti deea.*

Hallock, *v.* To wander aimlessly about.

> Ex.—*If he isn't risting up agaain a wall, he'll be hallocking*

sumwheear. If thoo aims 'at hallocking aboot 'll finnd tha a job, thoo's grandly mista'en.

Hames, Heeams, *n.* That part of a horse's collar to which the traces are fixed.

Hammer, *v.* To stammer.

Hampered, *adj.* 1. Hindered by difficulties. 2. Overrun by vermin or insects.

Ex.—1. *Ah've been hampered wi' all maks an' manders o' things.* 2. *T' farm's fairly hampered wi' rabbits an' rats.* 3. *Them to'nips leeak a bit hampered wi' t' fly.*

Ham-sam, *v.* To pack or hurriedly put away things anyhow so as to get them out of sight, to throw together anyhow.

Ham-shackle, *v.* To tie the head to one of the fore feet to prevent driven cattle from running away.

Hanch at, *v.* An attempt to bite from behind.

Hand, To bear at. *v.* 1. To blame. 2. To blame with a feeling of resentment.

Ex.—1. *Ah beear him at hand foor all sha knaws aboot what wa did at Sally's.* 2. *It war nowt bud a dirty trick, an' Ah s'all awlus beear him at hand for 't.*

Hand-clowt, Han'-cloot, *n.* A towel.

Hand-ho'd, *n.* That which admits of being firmly gripped, the act of gripping.

Ex.—*It 'ez a good hand-ho'd ti 't. Ah gat a good hand-ho'd, an' Ah nivver let go.*

Handle, Hann'l, *v.* 1. To treat. 2. To manage.

Ex.—1. *Tha hann'ld t' lad varry badly.* 2. *Sha's varra kittlish an' bad ti hann'l.*

Hand-running, *adv.* In regular succession.

Ex.—*He's ta'en fowr prizes han'-running.*

Handsel, Han'sel, *n.* and *v.* 1. The money received on or before the commencement of any work so as to make the agreement binding. 2. To give something on using a thing for the first time. 3. The act of using a thing for the first time.

Ex.—1. *Ah'll pay tha summat noo ti han'sel t' job.* 2. *Whya, thoo'll be leyke ti han'sel t' new hoss, wa s' want a glass apiece.* 3. *Ah've han'sel'd t' new reaper ti-daay.*

Hand-staff, *n.* The handle of a flail.

Hand-turn, *n.* A small amount of work.

Ex.—*Sha's that lazy 'at sha weean't deea a hand-to'n foor hersen, let aleean foor onnybody else.*

Handy, *adj.* 1. Skilful, apt, clever with one's hands. 2. Useful, just the very thing needed.

Ex.—1. *He's a varra handy chap.* 2. *It's yan o' t' maist handy things 'at Ah've ivver clap't my een on.*

Hang-dog, *adj.* Sullen.

> Ex.—*Deean't gan aboot wiv a hang-dog leeak o' thi feeace leyke that.*

Hang-dog, *n.* A worthless fellow.

Hangedly, *adv.* Without heart, despondent.

Hank, *n.* A latchet or loop of band or rope used to secure a gate; a skein of wool or string, &c.

Hank, *v.* To hang the bridle to a hook, gate, &c.; to fasten, as a gate.

Hank, To get things in a=To get one's circumstances involved.

Hankle, Henkle, *v.* 1. To become entangled. 2. To greatly desire, used in a very wide sense.

> Ex.—1. *Ak've gitten t' kite band sadly hankled,* i.e. entangled. *He's gitten hankled on wi' yon chap, an' he'll deea him neea good. Ah weean't be hankled on wi' neea sike leyke carryings on,* i.e. mixed up with. 2. *Ah awlus hed a hankling foor Tom's meer. Neea, wa didn't bargain, bud Ak've a gert hankling foor 't.*

Hant, *v.* To frequent.

> Ex.—*He fairly hants t' hoos sen Polly cam.*

Hanted, *v.* 1. Frequented by a ghost. 2. To be always at one's heels.

> Ex.—1. *Ah wadn't gan neear t' pleeace at neet, tha saay it's hanted.* 2. *He's awlus sumwheear nigh at hand, Ah's fairly hanted wi' t' lad sen Ah gat t' larl pony.*

Hap, *v.* 1. To cover over. 2. To wrap up. 3. To bury. 4. To discontinue. 5. To happen, chance, befall.

> Ex.—1. *Thoo mun hap t' strawberries up wi' a bit o' streah.* 2. *Noo ya mun hap up well, it's a cau'd neet.* 3. *Ak've just happ'd Willie's grave up.* 4. *Let's hap t' job up noo an' saay neea mair aboot it.* 5. *If nowt s'u'd hap ti stop ma, Ah s' cum.* NOTE.—Lap is often used instead of ' hap ' in 2 and 4.

Happen, *v.* 1. Possibly. 2. To meet with. 3. Perhaps.

> Ex.—1. *Will ta cum? Happen Ah maay.* 2. *He's happen'd a bad accident.* 3. *Ass him, an' happen he'll gi'e tha 't.*

Happing, *n.* Covering of any kind, usually bed-clothes.

Haps, *n.* Any covering which may be used over the ordinary clothes.

> Ex.—*'A'e ya browt plenty o' haps wi' ya?* meaning topcoats, jackets, rugs, &c.

Harbour, *n.* Shelter, lodging.

> Ex.—*Wa mun finnd a harbour sumwhere whahl t' shooer's ower'd. Seea lang ez it's cleean Ah deean't mahnd, bud Ah mun 'ev a harbour foor t' neet.*

Harbour, *v.* To shelter, to hide, generally used in a derogatory sense.

> Ex.—*Sha's neeawaays neyce whaw sha harbours*, i. e. 'She is not particular what kind of people she takes in, shelters, or lets her rooms to.' *Tha'd harbour t' devil if tha thowt tha c'u'd mak owt byv it.*

Hard, *adj.* Sour, said of beer; difficult to do or manage, close, much.

> Ex.—*He's a hard un ti bargain wi'. It ficked that hard, whahl Ah c'u'dn't ho'd it,* i. e. much. *He awlus drahves a hard bargain,* i. e. close. *It's ommaist neea ewse assing him; he said he wadn't, an' he's hard ti to'n.*

Hard eneeaf, *adv.* Without doubt, certainly, of a truth.

> Ex.—*Ah'll deea 't, hard eneeaf. He'll tell tha what he thinks, hard eneeaf.*

Hard, To look. *v.* To pay great attention, to observe closely.

> Ex.—*Thoo mun leeak hard at it, an' then thoo'll seean git thi task off. Ah hed ti leeak hard at him afoor Ah kenn'd whaw it war.*

Harden, *v.* 1. To bring oneself to do a thing. 2. To clear up after rain.

> Ex.—1. *Ah deean't leyke t' job, bud Ah s'all 'a'e ti harden mysel ti 't.* 2. *It's neea ewse to'ning t' hay, whahl it hardens up a bit.*

Harden-feeaced, *adj.* Threatening, lowering—of the sky or weather.

Harding, *n.* A coarse kind of material for making aprons or wrappers of.

Hardlings, *adv.* Not quite, scarcely.

Hard o' hearing, *adj.* More or less deaf.

Hardset, *adj.* With difficulty able.

> Ex.—*Sha's hardset ti mak ends meet. Ah wur hardset ti git t' job deean i' tahm.*

Hark back, To. *Vide* **Harp.**

Hark ya, *intj.* Hear you! listen!

Harled, *adj.* Mottled.

Harn, *n.* *Vide* **Harding.**

Harp, *v.* To continually refer to some annoying circumstance, some mistake, or disgrace.

> Ex.—*Sha nivver lets t' thing dee, sha's awlus harping on aboot it.*

Harr, *n.* A thick fog inclining to rain.

Harrish, *n.* Worry, annoyance, trouble.

> Ex.—*It's a bit of a harrish, bud then wa s' git ower 't sumhoo.*

Harrish, *v.* To be worried owing to some misadventure,

distressed through not knowing how some undertaking may turn out.

Harrow, To trail a light=To have a small family, to have few worries or difficulties.

Hartree, *n.* The tail-piece of a gate.

Harv, *v.* The word for a horse to turn to the left hand.

Hasky, Hask, *adj.* Dry, rough, coarse.

Hat up, To hang one's=To be quite at home, welcome.
> Ex.—*Ah can hang mah hat up yonder when Ah've a mahnd teea.*

Hatter, *v.* To mix or confuse things, to knot, to throw in disorder. *See also* **Hotter.**

Hause, *n.* The throat or neck.

Hauve, *v.* To stare stupidly.

Hauvey-gauvey, *n.* A stupid fellow, a lout.

Hauvish, *adj.* Lacking common sense, stupid.

Havver, *n.* Oats; hence **Havver-cake.**

Havver-meal, *n.* Oatmeal.

Hay-bauks, *n.* Poles or sticks so arranged to hold hay for cattle to feed from.

Hay-bay, *n.* A wild uproar.

Hay-chat, *n.* The whitethroat.

Hazel. *Vide* **Hezzle.**

Hazled, *adj.* An intermixture of red and white hairs. When the red preponderate, the beast is dark hazled; when white, vice versa. Often designated roan or roaned.

Head, *n.* The upper part of a dale.

Head-gear, *n.* 1. The blinders and bit, &c. 2. Head-dress. 3. Good sense, brain power.
> Ex.—1. *He's putten t' heead-gear on afoor t' barfan.* 2. *Did ti notish her heead-gear? It wur grand.* 3. *Ez far ez a bit o' heead-geear gans, he's ez sharp ez onny on 'em.*

Head-rigg, *n.* That part of a field on which the horses and plough are turned about.

Head screwed on the right way. Knowing what is best to be done, sensible, having good judgement.

Head-stall, *n.* A halter, usually made of hemp.

Head-tire, *n.* Head-dress.

Heap, *n.* In measure a quarter of a peck.

Heart-brussen or **Brussen-hearted,** *adj.* Heart-broken.

Heart-bun, Heart-grown, *adj.* Strongly attached to a place; also having a great desire to accomplish something in the future.

Heart-eased, *adj.* Freed from pain or distress.

Hearten, *v.* To encourage, to give hope.

Heart-sick, *adj.* Without hope, despondent.

Heart, Soft at
Heart, Warm at } *adj.* Easily appeased, kindly disposed.

Heart-whole, *adj.* 1. True-hearted. 2. Fancy-free.

Ex.—*Tak him all ends up he's a heart-w'oll, canny chap. Ah's heart-w'oll yet; ther's nowt aboot here 'at's ta'en mah fancy,* i. e. not in love.

·**Heave,** *v.* To scatter corn, to winnow it.

Heave and throw. To retch and vomit.

Heave up, *v.* To retch.

Heck, *n.* The upper part, containing the latch, of a door made in two parts. A rack for fodder; hence **Stand-heck.**

Heckling, *n.* Being much questioned whilst being scolded.

Heckling, *v.* To pester with many pertinent and impertinent questions.

Hedge-dike, *n.* A bank with a hedge on it, forming a fence.

Hedge-dike-side, *n.* The part of the hedge-bank on the water-channel side.

Heead-wark, *n.* Headache.

Heeaf, *n.* and *v.* Home, an abode; to abide.

Heeak, *v.* To loiter, to hang about with intent to eavesdrop.

Heeal, Yal, *adj.* Whole.

Heeam, Yam, *n.* Home. Also pronounced **Whoam.**

Heeat, Yat. Pronunciations of Hot.

Heed, *v.* To concern oneself, to mind, to pay proper and thoughtful attention to.

Ex.—*Ah deean't heed mich ov owt 'at he sez. Nivver heed, cum on. He nivver heeds what onnybody sez.*

Heegh. High.

Heeze, *v.* To breathe hoarsely.

Heeze, *n.* A disease incident to pigs, and when so afflicted they breathe with difficulty.

Heezy, *adj.* Wheezing, hoarse.

Heft, *v.* To fit a handle to.

Heft, *n.* 1. A handle. 2. Not all, only part.

Ex.—1. *T' knife's gitten a grand heft tul 't.* 2. *Thoo's nobbut gitten a heft on 't, sha's kept t' main on 't back.*

Heigh-how, *v.* To yawn.

Held, *v.* 1. A condition of finance. 2. Inclination.

Ex.—1. *Ah'd 'a'e lent tha t' brass leyke all that, bud Ah's badly held mysel just noo.* 2. *Ah war gretly held i' t' seeam waay,* i. e. 'I was greatly inclined the same way.'

Helm, Hellum, *n.* A rough shed or shelter away from the farm buildings.

Helter, *n.* A halter.

Helter-skelter, *n.* A wild rush of people or animals.
>Ex.—*When he seed ma he went helter-skelter doon t'*
>*lonnin' leyke a scopperil.*

Hemmel, *n.* The handrail of a wooden bridge.

Hempy, *adj.* Mischievous, even to breaking the law, malicious.

Hen-bauk, *n.* The beam for fowls to roost on.

Henkle. *Vide* **Hankle.**

Hennet=Have not. Should be written ''a'e nut.'

Henpen, *n.* The manure of fowls.

Hen-scrats, Hen-scrattings, *n.* Light, streaky, fleecy clouds, often called **Fillytails.**

Heron-sew, *n.* The heron.

Hesp, *n.* The catch which fastens gates, doors, &c.

Hessle, Hessling, Heshing, *v.* To beat, to thrash soundly.

Hide, *v.* To flog, to chastise.

Hig, *n.* Offence taken of a petty nature, to be offended for the time being.
>Ex.—*Tak neea notish, sha's nobbut ta'en t' hig.*

High-larn'd, *adj.* Highly educated.

High up, *adj.* A good position in society, rank, or office.

Hind, *n.* The head farm servant, who is hired by the year, and has a house provided rent free, with sundry other perquisites ; a sort of bailiff, in fact, but of a lower degree.

Hinder-ends, *n.* The poorer corn left after threshing.

Hing, Heng, *v.* 1. To hang. 2. To cling. 3. To continue.
>Ex.—1. *Hing thi coaat up.* 2 *He's treated her warse 'an*
>*a dog, bud sha still hings tiv him.* 3. *If t' droot hings*
>*on, to'nips 'll be ti neea good ti year.*

Hing for rain, To. A common phrase used when rain is more than probable.

Hipe, *v.* To push with the horns, to make grimaces.

Hiper, *n.* A mimic.

Hipping-steeans, *n.* Stepping-stones.

Hippings, *n.* Baby's napkins.

Hipple, *n.* A small bundle of half-dried hay.

Hiring penny, *n.* A sum of money, generally half a crown, paid as earnest money by a master on hiring his farm servant.

Hirings, *n.* A statute fair, at which servants are hired.

Hirp, Hirple, *v.* To stick the back up with cold.

Hiss. *Vide* **Siss.**

Hissel, Hissen, *pro.* Himself.

Hitch, *v.* To hop.

Hitch, strahd, an' jump or **loup.** Hop, stride, and jump.

Hoavish, *adj.* Stupid, idiotic.

Hobman. The name of an elf-man, at one time very generally believed in, doubtless akin to, if not the same as, Danish *Nisses.*

Each elf-man or hobman had his habitation, to which he gave his name, as Hob Hill, Upleatham, Hob Green, near Ripon, Hob o' t' rush Rook, on the Farndale moors, &c. There must have been both kindly natured and malicious hobmen, as stories are plentiful in proof of both.

Hobble, *v.* To move along with difficulty or from age.

Hobble, *n.* Trouble, perplexity.

Ex.—*Throw what Ah've tell'd Bob Ah've gitten mysel intiv a gret hobble. He's tell'd what Ah sed, an' sha's letten oot what he sed, an' noo wa're all iv a hobble tigither.*

Ho'd, *v.* 1. To hold. 2. To keep. 3. To maintain. 4. To keep in employment. 5. To remain with.

Ex.—1. *Thoo mun ho'd fast.* 2. *Thoo mun ho'd ti what thoo's sed. If t' daay ho'ds fair wa s'all git wer hay.* 3. *Ah ho'd 'at he's i' t' wrang.* 4. *T' job at t' chuch 'll ho'd him foor lang eneeaf.* 5. *He's laam'd foor leyfe; 't'll ho'd him ti t' end ov his daays.*

Ho'd, *n.* 1. Possession. 2. Tenure.

Ex.—1. *When he gits ho'd he'll keep ho'd.* 2. *If thoo dizn't mak thi ho'd paay thoo owt.*

Ho'd fair, *v.* To keep fair.

Ho'd off, *v.* To hold off, to keep off.

Ex.—*Ah think t' rain's gahin' ti ho'd off. If he can nobbut ho'd off fra drinkin' he'll cum roond.*

Ho'd on, *v.* 1. To retain one's grip. 2. Also used in the sense of to stop, wait a moment.

Ex.—1. *Ho'd on tiv its heead, Ah's cummin'.* 2. *Ho'd on a bit, deean't thoo slavver on seea fast,* i.e. 'Wait a moment, don't you talk so fast.'

Ho'd talk, *v.* To gossip, also as a noun.

Ex.—*Sha'll ho'd talk wi' onnybody; aye, sha's a champion at ho'ding talk.*

Ho'd teea, *v.* To agree to, to carry out, to uphold.

Ho'd up, *v.* To keep one's head up, to fight against despondency.

Ex.—*Noo deean't gi'e waay, thoo mun ho'd up; things isn't seea bad, noo ho'd up.*

Ho'd wi', *v.* To agree with.

Ex.—*Whya noo, Ah ho'd wi' t' main o' what thoo sez.*

Hoffle. *Vide* **Hobble.**

Hog, *n.* A male pig, a sheep of a year old.

Hoidle, *v.* To idle.

Hoit, *v.* To act like a fool. *n.* A fool.

Hoity-toity, *intj.* An exclamation of surprise, carrying with it slight indignation. *adj.* Somewhat ruffled in temper.

Holl, *n.* A narrow deep depression in the face of the land, varying in length, but never extensive; the dead of night.

Hollin, *n.* The holly.

Holm, *n.* Land by the side of a stream, low-lying and subject to being flooded.

Holy or **Lemmel steean,** *n.* Any water-rolled stone of small size having a hole through, once valued as a charm against witches.

Home-coming, *n.* The return home of an absent one, the festivities on such an occasion after a wedding or long absence.

Honey. A term of endearment, often preceded or followed by some other word to add greater force. Little conception can be formed of the love and tenderness which is thrown into and expressed by this word; it must be heard as coming from a mother's lips.

> Ex.—'*Oh, mah sweet honey bairn!*' said as a mother picked up a fallen child. '*Thoo little honey!*' as the baby was clasped to its mother's breast. '*Gan thi ways, honey dear; Cu' thi ways, mah honey pet,*' &c.

Honey-fall, *n.* A piece of rare luck, money left from some unexpected quarter.

Honeysouk, *n.* Honeysuckle.

Hoo, *adv.* How.

Hood-end, *n.* The flat portion found on either side of old-style fire grates, upon which a kettle or pan may be placed.

Hoos, *n.* House. *Vide* **House.**

Hooze. *Vide* **Heeze.**

Hopper, *n.* The basket or skep containing the seed corn when sowing, usually suspended by a strap over the shoulders.

Hopple, *v.* 1. To tie the legs of an animal so as to prevent its running away. 2. To hinder.

> Ex.—2. *It's neea ewse his endivering when he's hoppled wiv a weyfe leyke yon; sha's nowt bud a clog tiv his foot,* i.e. 'It is no use his striving when he is hindered or tied to a wife like that; she is nothing but a drag on him.'

Hork, *v.* To trail about.

Horry, *v.* To hurry.

Horse-gogs or **Hoss-gogs,** *n.* A common, astringent, purple brown plum.

Hoss-steean, Hoss-block, Hossin'-steps, *n.* A stone or steps used to stand upon when about to mount a horse.

Hosses together, They deean't put ther = Not friendly.

Hoss-teng, *n.* The common dragon-fly.

Hoss-trod, *n.* A bridle-road.

Hostle, *v.* To put up at an inn. 'Hostle' is only used in connexion with an inn. We 'put up' and 'hostle' at an inn, and 'lowse out' at a friend's.

Ex.—*Ah can lowse oot at thi pleeace, caan't Ah?* or *Ah'll put up at t' Black Swan. Ah hostles at t' Blew Pig.*

Ho't. Pronunciation of Hurt.

Hotch, *v.* To botch, to bungle.

Hotch, *n.* A mismanaged affair.

Hot-pots, Heeat- or **Yat-pots,** *n.* *Vide* 'Wedding Customs.'

Hotter, *v.* To jolt, to bump as in a cart over a stony road.

Hottery, *adj.* Broken, rough, uneven road.

Houe, *n.* A hill of considerable size : Houe Hill, near Ripon. A tumulus.

Houl, *n.* *Vide* **Holl.**

Hound, *v.* 1. To incite. 2. To give an opportuuity.

Ex.—1. *Them 'at hounded him on war t' fo'st ti bleeam him.* 2. *Neeabody's hounded him on mair 'an what Ah 'ev, an' yet he wadn't stick up tul him.*

House, *n.,* pron. *hoos.* With our country folk, 'hoos' is not the whole building, but the one room in which the family usually dwell ; the other rooms are spoken of as the parlour, back room, and the chambers, &c.

Ex.—*Deean't set it doon i' t' hoos, tak it inti t' parlour.*

House-fast, *adj.* Confined to the house through illness.

House or Hoos fau'k or **fooak,** *n.* The people of the house.

House-kept or **-held,** *adj.* Confined to the house owing to some preventing cause other than illness.

Housin' stuff or **sticks.** Household goods, furniture.

Hout, *intj.* Expressing incredulity or dissent.

Hover, *v.* 1. To hesitate. 2. Inclined for.

Ex.—1. *Ah hovered a larl bit afoor Ah bowt it.* 2. *Ah doot it 's hovering foor raain.*

Howk, *v.* 1. To dig. 2. To lift or push with some force.

Ex.—1. *Ah'll howk t' grund foor tha. He gat at t' back o' ma an' howk'd ma inti t' carridge afoor Ah ken'd wheear Ah war.*

Howly, *n.* A boys' game.

Howse, *v.* To bale out water, &c.

Howsomivver, Howsumivver, Hoosivver, *conj.* Howso-ever, however.

Hubble-shoo, *n.* An excited, noisy crowd.

Huckle, *n.* The hip.

Huff, *n.* Offence taken.

Ex.—*He's ta'en huff, an' sha's ta'en t' hig, an' tha've baith gitten t' hump tigither.*

Huff, *v.* To puff or swell up, as after a blow.

Huff'd, *p., a.* Offended.

Huffil, *n.* A finger-stall.

Hug, *v.* To carry, whether in the arms or on the back.

Hugger-mugger, *n.* Everything in disorder.

Huke-bone. *Vide* **Huckle.**

Huker, *v.* To barter.

Hull, *v.* To remove the pod or outer covering of peas, beans, &c.

Hulls, Hullin, *n.* The pods or outer covering of many fruits and grain.

Hummel, *v.* To break off the awns of barley.

Hummel'd, *adj.* Without horns.

Hummeller, *n.* The instrument used to hummel with.

Humped, *adj.* Sulky.

Hunger, *v.* and *n.* 1. To suffer from the pangs of hunger. 2. To withhold food, to provide insufficiently.

　　Ex.—1. *Ah war hungered past my bahdings.* 2. *He hungers ivverything aboot t' pleeace.*

Hossocks, *n.* Coarse tufts of grass.

Hutter. *Vide* **Hotter.**

I.

I', *prep.* In. ' I ' ' is used before a consonant, 'iv' before a vowel.

　　Ex.—*I' t' boddum o' t' box,* i. e. ' In the bottom of the box.' *Iv all manner o' waays.*

Ice-shoggles, Ice-shogglins, *n.* Icicles.

Ickles, *n.* Icicles.

If. Is often used for ' whether.' *Vide ex.* **Nither.**

If in case, If so be as how. Redundancies for ' if.'

If no more = If not more.

If so be that. *Vide* **If in case.**

Ill, *adj.* Bad, evil dispositioned or intentioned.

　　Ex.—*He's queer, bud sha's an ill un.*

Ill, *n.* Harm.

　　Ex.—*Thoo's warked him all t' ill 'at ivver thoo c'u'd.*

Ill-deed, *n.* Evil proceedings, ill-luck.

　　Ex.—*Ill-deed nivver thrives. He's 'ed nowt bud ill-deed fra t' startin'.*

Ill-fare, *v.* To fail through ill-luck, often used in reversed order, as **Fare-ill.**

　　Ex.—*Ah 'ed ti fetch t' meer yam agaan, Ah nobbut fared ill wi 't, ez sha brak baith her knees cumin' doon t' bank.*

Ill-favoured. *Vide* **Ill-thriven.**

Ill-gaited, *adj.* Awkward in action.

Ill-hap, *n.* Misfortune.

Illify, *v.* To speak disparagingly of, to defame.

　　Ex.—*Sha illifies onnybody an' ivverybody, sha spares nowt na neeabody.*

Ill-put-on or -putten, *adj.* Shabby, applied to clothes.

Ill-ta'en, *adv.* To take anything with bad grace.

Ex.—*It war nobbut ill-ta'en what thoo sed.*

Ill-tented, *adj.* Neglected, badly cared for or looked after.

Ill-thriven or **-throven,** *adj.* Having a weakly, ill-fed appearance, unhealthy.

Immense, *adj.* Exactly, precisely the thing required.

Imp, *n.* An extra ring, usually made of straw, used for enlarging the size, by insertion beneath the beehive.

In, Un. One. *Vide* **Un.**

Incomin', *n.* Entrance, the taking possession by a new tenant.

Inear, *n.* The kidney.

Ing, *n.* A low-lying pasture.

Ingle, *n.* 1. Fire, flame. 2. The fireside, when used with the definite article.

Ex.—*Ah tell'd my taal o' luv byv t' ingle glow.*

Ingle-neuk, *n.* The corners by the fireside within the old-fashioned open chimneys.

Inkle, *n.* A kind of tape.

Inkle, *v.* 1. To arrange plans. 2. To have a desire for.

Ex.—1. *He's awlus inklin' summat, bud it nivver cums ti nowt.* 2. *He maistly inkles efter what he can't git.*

Inkle-weavers, As thick as. In the weaving of inkle the workers were enabled to sit quite close together, the width of the fabric being so narrow; hence arose the saying, 'As thick as inkle-weavers.' The phrase also carries the idea of great friendship.

Inklin', *n.* A hint, an idea, a guess.

Ex.—*Ah've gi'en her a bit ov an inklin' o' what's gahin' on. It'll nut be lang afoor he finnds 'em oot, he's gitten an inklin'.*

In-meats, *n.* The viscera of any animal which is considered edible.

Innards, *n.* One's inside, bowels, entrails, &c.

Innerly, *adv.* More within.

Inoo, Inow, *adv.* Presently, shortly.

Insense, *v.* 1. To inform. 2. To make clear beyond all doubt.

Ex.—1. *Ah'll insense him inti 't when Ah see him.* 2. *Ah varra seean insens'd it intiv him.*

Insides, *n.* Viscera.

Intak, *n.* Land enclosed from a common or road for cultivation.

Inti, Intil, Intiv, Intul, *prep.* Into.

In wi', To be=To be on good terms with.

Ex.—*Jack's weel in wi' t' Squire.*

Iv. *Vide* **I'.**

Ivvery, *adj.* Every.

Ivvery like, *adv.* Every now and then.

D d

J.

Jab, *v.* To crush.

    Ex.—*Ak've gitten mah finger sadly jabbed wi t' yat.*

Jack, *n.* Quarter-pint measure.

Jacket, To warm one's=To beat, to chastise.

    Ex.—*If thoo gans theear onny mair, Ah'll warm thi jacket for tha,*

Jacketed, To be, *v.* To hear a charge, or bear reproof, having first been arraigned before one's superiors ; to be closeted with.

    Ex.—*He's been jacketed wi' t' gaffer i' t' parlour ower an hoor noo, Ah'll lay he's gi'en him t' lines properly.*

Jaded, *adj.* To be almost overcome with difficulties.

Jangle, *v.* To jingle.

Jannock, *adj.* Fair, honourable, just.

Jar, *v.* To quarrel.

Jar on, *v.* To be continually at variance.

Jarring, *n.* Quarrelling, squabbling.

Jaup, *v.* 1. To strike together. 2. To shake any liquid in a vessel.

    Ex.—1. *Ah'll jaup tha eggs,* i.e. boys jaup their Easter eggs by striking them one against the other ; the one succeeding in breaking the other's egg claims it as victor. 2. *If thoo jaups t' milk leyke that, thoo'll finnd butter i' t' can when thoo gits yam.*

Jaupin', Jaupen, *adj.* Gaping, wide.

Javver, *n.* Silly talk, foolish prating.

Jealous, Jillous, *adj.* Suspicious. *v.* To anticipate.

    Ex.—*Ah war a bit jillous 'at he wad splet on uz. Ah jillous'd Jim all t' tahm.*

Jert, *v.* To project a stone by catching the hand against the side.

Jill, *v.* To drink continuously but in small quantities.

    Ex.—*Neeabody ivver sees him tak a gert quantity, bud then he gans jilling aboot seea.*

Jimp, *adj.* 1. Smart in figure, slight. 2. Short measure.

    Ex.—1. *Sha's gitten ez jimp a waist ez onny lass.* 2. *It's jimp i' t' paper, an' jimp i' pot,* i.e. 'Light both as to weight and measure.'

Jin. Jane.

Jinny-spinner, *n.* The crane-fly, or any of the genus *Tipula.*

Jinny-ullot, Jenny Howlet, *n.* The tawny owl (*Syrnium stridula*).

Job, *v.* To trade in.

    Ex.—*He jobs iv ommaist owt.*

Joblijook, *n.* The name of the cock turkey, a domestic trouble or discomfort.

Jodder, Jother, *n.* A shaking, as one gets in a springless cart, a trembling.

> Ex.—*It joggled an' Ah jothered, whahl Ah felt leyke tumm'ling ti bits.*

Jodder, Jother, *v.* To shake like jelly, to tremble.

Jodderum, *n.* A trembling, shaking mass.

Joggle, *v.* To shake, to be unsteady in motion.

Joggly, *adj.* Shaky, unsteady.

Joggle-stick, *n.* The bar which secures the shafts to the body of the cart.

Jollous, *adj.* In good condition, healthy, well-fed.

Jolt-heead, *n.* A clumsy fellow.

Jorum, *n.* A pitcher-like vessel of considerable size; the whole lot, a considerable crowd of people.

Joskin, *n.* A country lad.

Joul, Jowl, *n.* The jaw; fat hanging cheeks.

Joul, Jowl, *v.* To jolt or hit against.

> Ex.—*Ah laamed mahsen sadly, Ah jowl'd my heead up agaainst t' deear.*

Jowls, *n.* A kind of hockey played by boys.

Judy-cow. *Vide* **Doody-cow.**

Jumm'lment, *n.* 1. A confusion. 2. Things of many kinds.

> Ex.—1. *Thoo's gitten things intiv a straange jumm'lment.*
> 2. *Ah nivver clapt my een on sike a jumm'lment o' trash ez he's gitten geddered tigedder.*

Jump with, To, *v.* To meet or to find.

> Ex.—*Ah jumped wi' Betty at t' lonnin' end. Efter leeaking all ower foor t' lad, Ah jumped wiv him at skeeal yat.*

June bug, *n.* The ladybird (*Coccinella punctata*). *Vide* **Doody-cow.**

Junters, *adj.* Sulks, bad temper.

K.

Kaimt, *adj.* Not straight.

Kale, Keeal, *n.* Porridge, broth. NOTE.—If for other than domestic use, it is specialized as ' Keeal for t' pigs,' 'flour keeal,' &c.

Kale-pot, Keeal-pot. An iron pot having three short iron feet, used for cooking kale in.

Kaliver, *v.* To dance about excitedly.

Kame, Keeam, *n.* A comb. Also as a *verb.*

Kane, Keean, *v.* To bring fermentation to a head.

Kave, Keeave, *v.* To rake the 'pulls and caff' from corn when thrashing.

Kavings, *n.* The short straws, &c., as above.

Kead, Ked, *n.* The sheep-tick (*Melophagus ovinus*).

Keok, Kecken, *v.* To make a noise whilst coughing, as if something was fast in the throat; to have a loathing for; fastidious.

Kecken-hearted, *adj.* Nauseated, fanciful.

Keckle, *v.* To laugh heartily.

Kedge, *n.* A glutton.

Kedge, *v.* To set the teeth on edge, to eat and drink like a glutton.

Kedging, *n.* Food.

Keeak, *n.* Cake.

Keeak, *v.* To cake, to form a hard scum. *Vide* also **Keek.**

Keeaky, *adj.* Brisk, lively.

Keeave, Kauve, *v.* To paw the ground impatiently, as a horse.

Keeaving-rake } *n.* The rake and riddle used during thrashing.
Keeaving-riddle }

Keek, Keeak, *v.* To lean towards, or tilt up.
  Ex.—*Keeak t' cart a larl bit mair.*

Keek, *v.* To pry or peep into, to observe unawares.
  Ex.—*Sha's nowt na better 'an a keyhooal keeker, sha's allus keeking.*

Keen, *adj.* Eager, energetic, desirous.
  Ex.—*Ah nivver seed neeabody sae keen afoor. He's ez keen ez a tarrier. Ah war a bit keen ti git it.*

Kegged, *adj.* Offended, inclined to be spiteful.
  Ex.—*He gat hissel sairly kegg'd ower t' job.*

Keld, Kell, Caul, *n.* The membrane enveloping the foetus in the womb, and occasionally found adhering at birth.

Kelk, *n.* Fool's parsley (*Aethusa cynapium*), a heavy blow, a single ovum of the spawn of a fish.

Kelps, *n.* The iron hooks hanging from the gally-bauk.

Kelter, *n.* Circumstances of any kind; wealth, or rather the condition of wealth as vested in property.

Kelter, *n.* To go full speed.
  Ex.—*Ah nivver cam sike a kelter i' mah leyfe.*

Keltering, *adj.* Almost beyond comparison.
  Ex.—*Mah wo'd, bud yon is a keltering good un.*

Kelterment. *Vide* **Ketterment.**

Kemps, *n.* Hairs mixed with wool.

Kempt, *pp.* Combed.

Ken, *v.* To know.

Ken, Kern, *v.* To churn. *n.* A churn.

Ken-cruddle, *n.* A churn staff.

Ken-milk, *n.* Churn-milk, i. e. butter-milk.

Kennigood, *n.* A reminder.
  Ex.—*Tak that ez a kennigood,* said a man, boxing a boy's ears.

Kenning, *n.* 1. Knowledge. 2. Recognition.

Ex.—1. *Ther's a gay bit o' kenning i' t' lad.* 2. *T' lass 'ez waxed that mich whahl ther's neea kenning her.*

Kenspak, Kenspeckle, *adj.* Easily known or recognizable, conspicuous.

Kent, *pp.* Knew.

Kep, *v.* To catch.

Ex.—*Ah'll potch an' thoo kep.*

Keslip, Keslop, *n.* Rennet.

Kessen, *part.* Cast, bent.

Kess'mas, Kess'nmas, Kessamas, *n.* Christmas.

Kess'n, *v.* To christen.

Kess'nen, *n.* A christening.

Kess'n up=To be found, to turn up.

Ex.—*Ah thowt it 'ed geean foor good, bud it's kess'n up agaain ez good ez ivver.*

Kest, *adj.* Bent, not straight, out of truth.

Kest, *v.* To cast off.

Ket, *n.* Filth, tainted meat, carrion.

Ketlook, *n.* Charlock. *Vide* **Runch.**

Ketterment, *n.* Rubbish.

Ketty, *adj.* 1. Nasty. 2. Disagreeable.

Ex.—1. *Oh, what ketty stuff! Ah caan't eat it.* 2. *It's nobbut a ketty gahin' on,* i. e. a disagreeable proceeding.

Kevel, *n.* A strong, fairly long ash handle, to which is fixed a steel hammer-head of curious shape, used as a hammer in quarry work.

Kevel, *v. and n.* Both the working of the stone and the swinging of the hammer.

Ex.—*Ah'll kevel mair flints iv a daay' an he can,* i. e. dress more flints. *He mannishes varra weel foor a new starter, an' when he's larnt t' knack o' takking a larl bit wider kevel, he'll chip all t' easier foor 't,* i. e. 'When he has learnt the trick of taking a little bit wider sweep or swing, he will chip all the easier for it.' In some way difficult to define, both the noun and verb, **Kevel,** relate to the handle and its action as well as to the head.

Kex, *n.* Dried stem of fool's parsley.

Kick, *v.* To object.

Ex.—*Ah s'all kick neea lahtle if he cums that gam on ma.*

Kicky-wicky, *adj.* Disdainful.

Kin, *n.* 1. Kind, generally of species. 2. Sort, relationship. 3. A chilblain, a chap or crack in the skin.

Ex.—1. *What a-kin is he ti Tommy?* 2. *What kin o' yan is't he's gitten?*

Kin, *v.* To chap, as one's hands in frosty weather.

Kin-cough, *n.* Whooping cough.

Kind, *adj.* On friendly terms.

> Ex.—*Tha've gitten kind agaan. Wa've been kind sen wa wur lads.*

Kindling, Kinlin', *n.* Firewood, small twigs suitable for lighting a fire.

Kink, *n.* A twist in a rope or line, stiffness of the limbs, a stiff neck.

Kink, *v.* To laugh wildly, hysterically; to laugh until one labours for breath.

Kinlin'. *Vide* **Kindling**.

Kinn'l, Kinnle, *v.* To set and light the fire; to bring forth young, applied to a rabbit.

Kipper, *adj.* Nimble, in good and lively spirits.

Kirk, *n.* A church.

Kirk-garth, *n.* Churchyard.

Kirk-warner, *n.* Churchwarden.

Kissing-bush, *n.* The mistletoe.

Kist, *n.* A chest.

Kit, *n.* A small pail with one of the staves longer than the rest, to serve as a handle.

Kite, *n.* The belly.

Kith, Kyth, *n.* Friends, acquaintances.

Kitlin', *n.* A kitten.

Kittle, Kittlish, *adj.* 1. Easily moved or upset. 2. Nice, delicate. 3. Ticklish, easily tickled.

> Ex.—1. *Keep off; it's nobbut a varra kittle consarn, varra larl'll touple all t' lot ower,* i. e. 'Stand clear; it is only a very unsteady concern, a slight shock or touch will knock it over.' 2. *Ah'd a seet reyther thoo'd tell him thisel; it's a kittlish thing foor me ti deea when Ah's gahin' ti wed his sister.* 3. *Deean't touch ma unner t' airms, Ah's that kittlish whahl Ah caan't bahd it.*

Kittle, *v.* 1. To bring forth young, said of a cat. 2. To excite, to stir up, to awaken. 3. To tickle.

> Ex.—2. *Ah'll tell him a few things 'at'll kittle him up a bit. If that weean't kittle him up a bit, Ah knaw o' nowt 'at will.* 3. *T' mair Ah scrat an' t' mair Ah kittle.*

Kitty-keis, *n.* Seeds of the ash-tree.

Kity, *adj.* Having a protuberant stomach.

Kizzen'd, *pp.* of **Kizzen**, *v.* Dried up, over-cooked, parched.

> Ex.—*Thoo's kizzen'd it whahl Ah caan't eat it.*

Knab, *v.* To gnaw as a mouse.

Knack, *n.* Adroitness, skill, aptness.

> Ex.—*Ah tried an' oor Jack tried, bud wa cu'd mak nowt on't; bud Tom teeak ho'd an' did it iv a crack, bud then he's gitten t' knack on't.*

Knack, *v.* To talk affectedly, to mince one's speech.

Knackish, *adj.* Knavish.

Knap, *v.* To give a slight tap, to knock, so as to break.

Ex.—*Ah'll knap thi knuckles foor tha. Ah've knapped a piece off t' jug spoot.*

Knappish, *adj.* Snappy.

Knapper, *v.* To talk finely. *Vide* **Knack.**

Knapper, *n.* A door-knocker.

Knappers, *n.* Leather flaps to shield the thighs when using the turf spade.

Knappery-ware, *n.* Crockery.

Knar, Knor, Knur, *n.* A ball of wood, a hard knot.

Knarl, *v.* To run in knots, as a skein of wool or twine.

Knaw, *v.* Know.

Knee-bass, *n.* A straw cushion to kneel on when washing steps, a church hassock.

Knep or **Nipe,** *v.* To bite off in small pieces.

Knodden, *pp.* Knead.

Knoll, Knowl, *n.* A stroke of a bell.

Ex.—*Whisht ! it gav six knowlls ; it'll be foor a woman, mebby Betsy Parkin.*

Knoll, *v.* To toll, generally applied to the passing bell.

Knop, *n.* A knob.

Knucks, Knacks, Knuckles, *n.* A game very commonly played in the North Riding, several holes being made in the ground some inches apart, the object being to shoot a marble from one to the other.

L.

Laan, *n.* A loan.

Labber, *v.* 1. To play with water or soft mud. 2. To struggle after falling into water. 3. To plod through wet grass or turnips.

Ex.—*T' barn labbers aboot i' yon slap hoal whahl sha's drinch'd thruff an' clarted an' labbered fra heead ti foot wi t' blathery slathery muckment.*

Labbered, *pp.* To be splashed or daubed with soft mud.

Laboursome, *adj.* Laborious, tiring.

Lace, Leeace, *v.* 1. To thrash soundly. 2. To add spirits to tea or coffee.

Ex.—1. *Ah'll lace tha soondly when Ah catch tha.*

Lacer or **Leeacer,** *n.* Any person or thing larger or taller than usual.

Lad-louper, *n.* An impudent forward lass, one who makes the first advances.

Lady-cow. *Vide* **Dundy-cow.**

Lae, Leea, *n.* A scythe.

Lae-sand, *n.* A sandstone used for sharpening scythes.

Lafter, *n.* The whole of the eggs laid before sitting, the eggs being sat upon.

Lag, *n.* A single wooden division in a cask.

Lag, *v.* To loiter, to hang behind.

Lagged, *pp.* Tired out, wearied.

Laggy, *adj.* Last. A boy shouts 'Laggy,' or 'Bags Ah laggy,' when he desires to take the last turn in any game. 'Bags Ah fuggy' is, 'I claim first, 'seggy' second, 'thoddy' third.

Lahk. *Vide* **Like.**

Lahtle, Larl, *adj.* Little.

Ex.—*Thoo's nobbut a larl un, bud if thoo nobbut wurks hard an' eats plenty o' pudden thoo'll stritch oot a gay bit.*

Laid-off, *adj.* Incapable of work through illness or other causes.

Laid out, *v.* Prepared like, got up, looked like.

Ex.—*Ah caan't saay what it war, bud it laid out leyke rice an' soapsuds; sum on 'em gulched it doon leyke all that.*

Laid out, *v.* 1. To arrange. 2. To attend to the body immediately after death. 3. To spend money.

Ex.—1. *Sha laid t' table oot varra neycely.* 2. *Hannah an' Jane's laid him oot, poor thing, an' tha're gahin' ti sahd him by o' Tho'sday.* 3. *Ah've spent all mah brass, bud Ah've laid it oot weel.*

Lairock, *n.* The lark (*Aluda arvensis*).

Lait, Late, Leeat, *v.* To seek.

Ex.—*Ah awlus 'ev ti late that lass ivvery tahm Ah want her. Ah've lated high an' low foor 't, bud Ah caan't finnd it neeawheear.*

Lake, Laak, Leyak, *v.* To play, in a modified sense often used as tease, e.g. *Tho'll lake on wi' t' dog whahl it'll bite tha.*

Lakings, *n.* Playthings.

Lalder. *Vide* **Lalling.**

Lalderish, *adj.* Lazy, listless.

Lall, *v.* To sing and shout excitedly.

Lalling, Lolling, *v.* To wander idly and aimlessly about, to lazily lean up against a wall for support.

Ex.—*He gans lolling aboot an' maks 'at he's badly; a good day's wark 'ud deea him t' maist good ov owt.*

Lallops, Lollops, *n.* A lazy lounging fellow.

Lallopy, Lollopy, *adj.* Idle, untidy, slovenly.

Lam, *v.* To beat.

Lame, Laam, *v.* 1. To hurt. 2. To injure.

Ex.—1. *Let go, thoo's laming my airm.* 2. *Whya, onny road he's lam'd t' lad foor leyfe.*

Lammace, *v.* To beat with heavy blows.

Lammaoing, *n.* A beating, a good thrashing.

Lamming, *n.* A beating.

Land, *n.* Space between two furrows.

Land, *v.* To arrive, to give a blow.

Ex.—*Ah set off efter tea an' landed a bit efter darkening. Ah'll land tha yan ower t' gob if thoo dizn't shut up.*

Landlouper, *n.* One who runs away to escape paying his debts, &c.

Lang, *adj.* Long.

Lang first, *adv.* Long before.

Lang last, *adv.* At last.

Lang length, *adv.* Full length.

Ex. —*Ah slipped, an' Ah war laid ma lang len'th on t' grund i' a crack. Ah'll gi'e tha t' lang length o' my hand.*

Lang sen, Lang sin, *adv.* Long since.

Lang settle, *n.* A long wooden seat with a high back and an arm at each end.

Langsome, *adj.* Long, tedious, troublesome.

Lang tongued, *adj.* An exaggerator.

Lang waay, *adv.* Much, certainly.

Ex.—*It's a lang waay t' best deeaing it this waay. Aye, byv a lang waay,* i.e. 'yes, certainly.'

Lang-waays, *adv.* Lengthways.

Lantern-leet, Lant'n-leet, *n.* Lantern-light, often used to denote late in the evening.

Ex.—*Ah doot Ah s'an't be wi' ya whahl efter lantern-leet.*

Lap, *v.* 1. To wrap. 2. To have done with, usually followed by 'up.'

Ex.—1. *Ah'll lap a bit o' clowt roond it, an' it'll be all reet.*
2. *Ah've nowt else ti saay; Ah s'all lap t' job up noo, an' seea ther's an end on't.*

Lap-band, *n.* Hoop-iron.

Lap-cook, *n.* A small bundle of hay twisted in the arms and laid to dry.

Lapling, *n.* A vicious fellow.

Lap up, *v.* and *n.* To wrap up, to finish; an end.

Lapwing, *n.* The plover.

Lark-heeled, *adj.* Having heels turning outward.

Larn, *v.* To teach.

Ex.—*Will ta larn me hoo ti deea't? Ah's larning mysel ti plaay t' fiddle.*

Lash oot, *v.* To kick, as a horse.

Lashin' oot, *v.* Extravagance, showing off.

Ex.—*Deean't ya think t' young doctor's lashin' oot mair 'an what he can stand teea?* i.e. 'Don't you think the young doctor is showing off (buying horses, &c.) more than he will be able to pay for?'

Lashing, *adj.* Large, either of persons or things.

Ex.—*By goa! bud he's a lashing young chap; he mun stan mair 'an six foot.*

Lasty, *adj.* Durable.

Late, *v.* To seek.

Lated, *pp.* Sought.

Lated, *adv.* Belated.

Later, *n.* A seeker.

Ex.—*Ah fan him, bud Ah's a good later.*

Latt, *n.* A lath.

Latty, *adj.* Thin.

Lawk, *intj.* Lo!

Lax, *n.* Diarrhoea.

Lay, *v.* To be certain, of that opinion, to bet or wager; also to levy a rate.

Ex.—*Thoo aims 'at he weean't, bud Ah lay 'at he will. Ah'll lay tha what thoo leykes.*

Lay on, *v.* To use extra exertion. Cattle 'lay on fat' when specially fed.

Laylac, *n.* The lilac.

Laze, *v.* To live idly.

Lead, *n.* Direction, way.

Lead, *v.* To carry goods or hay in a cart or wagon.

Lead-eater, *n.* India-rubber.

Leaf, *n.* Fat round the kidney of an animal.

Leafs, *n.* Fat along a pig's nose.

Leam, *v.* To drop or fall out when ripe, as nuts from the husks.

Leamers, *n.* Nuts quite ripe, which fall from the husks.

Leasing, *n.* The separating of differing kinds of grain.

Leather-head, *n.* A dull, stupid fellow.

Leathered, *pp.* 1. Beaten, overcome, mastered. 2. Puzzled.

Ex.—1. *Ah's leathered wi' this job hooivver,* i.e. overcome. *He's leathered him soondly,* i.e. thrashed. 2. *Ah's leathered ti knaw wheea's ti blaam,* i.e. puzzled.

Leave loose. To let go, to cease from detaining.

Leavlang, *adj.* Oblong.

Leck, *v.* To escape by drops, to leak.

Lee, *n.* The watery discharge from a wound, a lie.

Leeak for, *v.* To expect.

Ex.—*Ah s'all leeak foor ya a week cum Mondaay. Ah's glad ya've fetched it, Ah've been leeaking for it cumin' ivvery daay.*

Leeak ya, *intj.* Look you!

Leear, *n.* Learning.

Leef, Leave, Lief, *adj.* Willingly, just as soon as.

Leet, *n.* A light.

Leet, *v.* To alight, to settle upon.

Leet, I' that＝In that way, like that.
Ex.—*Ah 'grees wi' tha, when thoo puts it i' that leet. Thoo s'u'dn't tak 't i' that leet.*

Leet on, *adj.* Unbalanced.
Ex.—*Sit a bit forrad, wa're a larl bit leet on.*

Leets, Leeghts, *n.* Lungs, lights.

Leetsome, *adj.* Lightsome, cheerful.

Legs, A pair of, *n.* Stockings.
Ex.—*Sha's gitten a gran' pair o' legs foor t' wedding.*

Leg up, A, *n.* Assistance.
Ex.—*Ah'll cum an' gi'e tha a leg up mysel.*

Leister, Lyster, *n.* A three-pronged fork for striking salmon.

Lemmel-steean, *n.* A stone with a hole through it, formerly used to ward off witches.

Len, *v.* To lend.

Length, Len'th, *n.* Stature. The 'g' is always silent in *length, strength, kingdom,* and usually the final 'g' also.

Length of, The. The distance or limit of anything.
Ex.—*Ah efter it t' len'th o' t' paddock.*

Lenny, *n.* The linnet.

Let, *v.* 1. To light. 2. To alight on.
Ex.—1. *Ah let t' cann'l.* 2. *Ah tumm'ld off t' stack, bud Ah let o' mah feet.*

Let drive, *v.* To strike or kick with force.

Let on, *v.* To admit.
Ex.—*Ah didn't let on 'at Ah knew owt.*

Let on, Lite on, Leet on, *v.* To meet, usually followed by 'with.'
Ex.—*Where did ta lite on wiv him ?*

Let wit, *v.* To disclose.
Ex.—*Ah let wit 'at Ah knew summat.*

Letten, *pp.* of 'to light' and 'to let.'

Leve, *v.* To raise by leverage.

Leyke. *Vide* **Like.**

Lib, *v.* To castrate lambs.

Liberty, *n.* The parish or township.

Lick, *adj.* Swift, at a great speed.
Ex.—*He did gan wiv a lick roond t' corner.*

Lick, *v.* To thrash, to surpass. *Vide* **Leathered.**

Lick, *n.* Just a slight wipe with a damp cloth ; hence the saying, when anything is only half cleansed, *Ah've deean 't wiv a lick an' a promise.*

Lie on. *Vide* **Lay on.**

Lift, *v.* To help, to render assistance.
Ex.—*Ah aim'd ti gi'e him a bit ov a lift mysel.*

Lig, *v.* To lay down, to put down.
Ex.—*Thoo mun lig it doon a bit. Ah'll lig it doon on t' swab.*

Lig, *v. i.* To lie down, to be near to or situate.

> Ex.—*Sha ligs doon ivvery daay efter dinner. It ligs a-back o' Roseberry.*

Lig-a-bed, *n.* A sluggard.

Lig een on, *v.* To meet or see a person.

> Ex.—*Ah think he mun be deead, Ah 'evn't lig'd een on him this lang whahl.*

Lig ho'd, *v.* To take hold of.

Lig on. *Vide* **Lay on.**

Lig up, To, *v.* To store, put by.

Lightsome. *Vide* **Leetsome.**

Light, Leet, *adj.* Of little depth, applied to a furrow; weak, slight; mealy, not sodden, as applied to potatoes and bread; lacking soil.

Lightening, Leetening, *n.* Yeast (brewer's), the break of day.

Light or Leet skets, *n.* A female of doubtful morals.

Like, Leyke, *adj.* 1. Likely, highly probable. 2. In duty bound.

> Ex.—*Leyke eneeaf Ah s' be theear.* 2. *Ah s' be leyke ti show up at kess'nen.*

Like all that, *adj.* An intensive, giving greater force to some previous statement.

> Ex.—*Sha war iv a tantrum, an' flang hersel aboot leyke all that,* i.e. in a passion. *He went at it leyke all that,* i.e. with resolution. *Sha gen'd an' giggled like all that,* i.e. in a ridiculous manner. *Sha tell'd him what sha thowt leyke all that,* i.e. spoke her mind plainly.

Lile, Larl, Lahl, *adj.* Little.

Lillilow, *n.* A blaze, a flame.

Lilting, Lilty, *adj.* Jumpy, frolicsome.

Limb, *n.* A mischievous child.

Limber, *adj.* Pliant, easily bending to light pressure.

Limmers, *n.* Shafts.

Lin, Lahn, *n.* Flax (*Linum usitalissimum*).

Lin clout, *n.* A linen rag.

Linch, *v.* To flog.

Lineseed. Linseed.

Ling, *n.* Heather.

Lingberry, *n.* The seed capsule of the heather.

Ling-nail, *n.* The linch-pin of a cart-wheel.

Lingy, *adj.* Active, athletic.

Lip, *n.* Impudence, saucy talk.

Lish, *adj.* Active.

Lisk, *n.* The groin.

Lithe, *v.* To thicken with flour and water.

Lithing, *n.* Flour and water, used to thicken broth, gravy, &c.

'Liver, *v.* To deliver, to give back, usually followed by ' up.'

> Ex.—*If thoo dizn't 'livver 't up, thoo'll catch it.*

'Liverance, *n.* Liberation, freedom.
'll = Will.
Lobster-louse, *n.* The wood-louse.
Loggerheeads, To be at = To be at variance.
Loggin, *n.* A batten of threshed straw.
Lollop, *v.* To lean up against, to move about lazily.
Lone, Loan, *n.* A lane.
Long- or **Lang-strucken**, *part.* Legs too long for the body.
Loning, Loaning, Lonnin', Lo'nin', *n.* A narrow lane.
Loobily, *adj.* Foolishly.
Look a bad look
Leeak a bad leeak } **To**, *v.* To look ill.
Looking or **Leeaking for**, *v.* To expect, to desire.
Looks ta or **Leeaks ta.** Look thou or you.
Loose end, *n.* Going to the bad.
    Ex.—*He's nobbut at a loose end, sen he gat hissel henkled on wi' yon lot.*
Loose i' t' heft, *n.* Lit. loose in the handle, and hence of little use. A worthless fellow.
Lopp, *n.* A flea (*Pulex irritans*).
Loppered, *adj.* Curdled (of milk).
Lops an' tops, *n.* The small branches and tops of trees.
Lorn, *part.* Left, lost, forlorn.
Lost, *adj.* Beyond all bounds, almost helpless.
    Ex.—*Her hoos war fairly lost i' muck. He war lost i' wonder*, i. e. absolutely amazed. *Ah war lost i' 'mazement an' c'u'd deea nowt.*
Lound, *adj.* Calm, free from wind, sheltered.
Lounder, *v.* To thrash soundly.
Loundering, *n.* A thrashing.
Loundering, *adj.* Heavy, severe (of a blow).
Loup, *v.* To leap, jump, bound up.
    Ex.—*If thoo caan't loup 't, thoo mun clim 't, tumm'l ower 't, or ram thisen thruff 't.*
Low, Glow, *n.* The flame from a fire or candle, &c.
'Lowance, *n.* The forenoon drinking.
Lowse[1], *v.* To loose, to unfasten. 2. To dismiss.
    Ex.—2. *Hez t' chetch lowsed yet?* i.e. ' Has the congregation left?'
Lowse oot, Lowsen oot, *v.* To unyoke, to unpack.
Lowsing tahm, *n.* The time for unyoking after a day's work.
Lubbart, *n.* A clown.
Lucky bird or **bo'd**, *n.* The first male to cross the threshold on New Year's morn.

---

[1] The same pronunciation is often used in the sense of 'to lose.' Ex.—'Thoo'll lowse thisel,' or 'Thoo'll loss thisel;' 'It's been a lowsin' gaame fra t' fo'st ti t' last,' i.e. ' It has been a losing game,' &c.

Lucky-steean, *n.* A rounded, water-worn piece of quartz, or a stone with a natural hole through it. *Vide* **Lemmel-steean.**

Lug, *n.* The ear proper, or the handle of a pitcher or jug, &c.

Lug, *v.* To pull.
>Ex.—*Sha diz lug mah hair, when she combs it, diz mah aunt Jane.*

Lug ends, *m.* Tips of the ears.

Luke, *v.* To pull weeds from cornfields.

Lumberly, *adj.* Awkwardly.

Lurdy, *n.* A stupid fellow.

M.

Mabble, *v.* To leave the chisel-marks on stone, to rough-dress.

Mad, *adj.* 1. Very angry. 2. Wild.
>Ex.—1. *Aa bud, Ah war mad wiv her.* 2. *He seems fair mad efter t' lass.*

Maddle, *v.* 1. To bewilder, confuse. 2. To grow bewildered. 3. To conduct oneself foolishly in love affairs.
>Ex.—1. *Tha maddled ma sairly wi' ther racket an' din.* 2. *It war that pick dark 'at Ah didn't ken wheear Ah war, bud Ah maddled alang, fust yah waay an' then t' ither, whahl at last end Ah fan mysen i' Au'd Willie's pig-stee.* 3. *If thoo dizn't tak care, thoo'll gan maddlin' efter t' lass, whahl thoo'll loss thi job.*

Made oot. *Vide* **Mak** oot.

Madge, Madgipeg, *n.* The fool of the sword-dancers.

Maffle, *v.* To strive in a way quite inadequate to the success of the undertaking.
>Ex.—1. *Noo let's hear what thoo 'ez ti saay foor thisel, an' deean't maffle on i' that road.* 2. *If he maffles on wi' t' job i' yon waay he'll nivver mannish 't.*

Mafted, Mefted, *adj.* 1. Stifled. 2. Out of breath by long exertion, through fighting against a storm, generally of snow.
>Ex.—*Oppen t' winner, Ah caan't bahd; Ah's ommaist mafted i' t' pleeace.*

Mahnd, Mind, *v.* 1. To remember. 2. To pay heed to.
>Ex.—1. *Ah mahnd t' tahm,* i.e. 'I remember the circumstances.' 2. *Ah've mahnded what thoo sed,* i.e. 'I paid heed to what you said.' *Noo thoo mun mahnd all 'at Ah've tell'd tha, an' think on 'at thoo 'ezn't ti foorgit ti mahnd an' paay t' bill.*

Main, *adj.* and *adv.* 1. Largest or greatest. 2. Quite.
>Ex.—1. *T' main on 'em sez 'at it is seea,* i.e. 'The greatest number of them say that it is so.' 2. *Ah's ommaist main sartin he's in t' reet on 't,* or *Ah's main sartin,* i.e. 'I am quite certain.'

Mainswear, *v.* To take a false oath.

Mair, *adj.* More.

Maist, *adj.* Most.

Maist-hand. *Vide* **Near-hand.**

Maistly, Maistlings, Moastlings, *adv.* Mostly.

Mak, *n.* 1. Make, design, shape.

Ex.—*Ah've seen a vast o' maks i' ma tahm, bud nivver a mak leyke this. Wheeas mak's that?* i. e. 'Whose make is that?' *It 'ez a queer mak aboot it.*

Makmeeat, *v.* To make or prepare food for the household.

Mak on, *v.* To induce by kindness.

Ex.—*T' dog'll follow if thoo maks on it a bit.*

Mak oot, *v.* 1. To make, serve. 2. To succeed in an undertaking. 3. To discover, find out.

Ex.—1. *He'll 'a'e ti mak oot wi' t' bit 'at's left noo.* 3. *Ah caan't mak oot what yon chap's efter.*

Mak sharp, Be sharp, Leeak sharp = Make haste, be quick.

Mak spare = Economical, careful.

Ex.—*Noo reeach teea an' help yersels; ther's nowt ya need be neyce aboot, an' ya needn't mak spare ov owt.*

Maks an' manders, *n.* All sorts.

Ex.—*Ah've all maks an' manders on 'em.*

Man, *n.* The husband of the person speaking, or of some woman spoken of; with the addition of 'young,' it would mean the one who is courting some fair maid, e. g. *Mah man's gahin', an' thi man's gahin', an' Sally's young man mun go wiv 'em.*

Manders, *n.* All kinds, different sorts mixed.

Mang, *n.* A bran mash.

Mang, *v.* To mix various ingredients of any kind of food.

Manifold, Monifaud, *n.* The intestines. *adj.* Various.

Mannish, *v.* To manage, to conduct farming in a prosperous manner, to manure land.

Mannishment, *n.* Manure.

Mannur, *v.* and *n.* Manure.

Mar, *v.* To injure, spoil.

Mark's E'en. St. Mark's Eve.

Marrish, *n.* Low-lying ground liable to be flooded.

Marrow, Marrer, *n.* One of a pair, similar.

Marrow, *n.* To match, to produce a similar thing.

Marry, Aye, *intj.* Yes; as 'Will ta gan?' answer, 'Aye marry!'

Ex.—*Aye marry! bud sha's a beauty. Aye marry, tha're wed noo hard eneeaf.*

Mash, *v.* To draw the strength out of anything by infusion, as tea; to reduce to pulp.

Mash up, *v.* To break in small pieces.

Mask, *v.* To infuse. *Vide* **Mash.**

Mask, *n.* The face, the hunter's term for a fox's head. *Vide* **Keld.**

Master, Meeåster, Maåster, Maastther, *n.* Master; the head of the house, shop, works, or school.

Masterman, *n.* One who employs.

Matched, *pp.* Almost beyond one's ability to do; to be put to a severe test.

> Ex.—*Ah s'all be hard matched ti git t' job deean byv t' tahm 'at he wants it. He's mair 'an matched wi' yon. Ah've gitten myself sairly matched this tahm.*

Matter, *v.* To esteem. 2. To influence. 3. Information.

> Ex.—1. *Ah nivver did matter him mich.* 2. *Owt 'at he sez weean't matter mich ti onnybody.* 3. *Onny matter 'at he knaws.weean't mak onnybody neea wiser.*

Matters, *n.* Quantity, account.

> Ex.—*It maks neea gert matters owt 'at he sez. Nut onny gert matters foor me, Ah 'ed summat afoor Ah cum'd.*

Maudle, *v.* To besot.

> Ex.—*He war maudling drunk.*

Maukey, *adj.* Whimsical.

Mauls, *n.* The marsh-mallow.

Maum, Maumy, *adj.* Ripe, mellow.

Maunder, *v.* To wander, talk foolishly.

Maundering, *adj.* Grumbling, muttering.

Maunsil, *n.* A fat, slovenly female.

Maun't, Mooun't, Mun't, Munnot. Must not.

Mawk, *n.* A maggot.

Mawky. Maggoty.

Mayern, *n.* A wicken gatherer.

Mayhap, *adv.* Perhaps. **Mebbe** is most commonly used.

Maze, *v.* To bewilder.

Meadow-drake, *n.* Corn-crake.

Meal, *n.* Flour of various kind not fully dressed.

Mealy-mouthed, *adj.* Plausible.

Mean, Meean, *adj.* Bad as to character.

> Ex.—*He's aboot ez meean ez tha mak 'em. Sha's meean eneeaf ti deea onny dirty trick. Sha's meean eneeaf ti hunger t' baa'n ti deeath.*

NOTE.—'Mean' is almost always used to denote some form of badness, rarely stinginess or mediocrity.

Meat, *n.* The daily food of a workman in addition to his wages.

Meat, *v.* To provide a lodger with food as well as lodgings.

Meer, *n.* A mare.

Meg, *n.* A penny.

Mell, *n.* A wooden mallet.

Mell, *v.* To meddle, usually followed by 'on.'

> Ex.—*If thoo mells on oor larl Jimmy onny mair, Ah'll leather tha mysel. Thoo's allus melling o' t' baa'n. Will ta nivver gi'e ower?*

Mell-sheaf, *n.* The last sheaf gathered.

Mell-supper, *n.* Harvest supper. See chapter on 'Customs.'

Melt, Milt. The spawn of the milter (male fish).

Mend, *v.* To improve, to grow better.

   Ex.—*Ah's mending neycely noo, Ah s' seean be all reet agaan. He'll 'a'e ti mend his waays, or he'll end up nowt.*

Mends, *n.* Improvement.

Mennem, Mennad, *n.* The minnow.

Mense, *n.* Decency, good appearance, civility, tact.

   Ex.—*If he'd 'ed onny mense aboot him, he wadn't 'a'e sed a thing leyke that.*

Mense, *v.* 1. To add beauty or order. 2. To smooth away a misunderstanding.

   Ex.—1. *Sha seean mensed things up a bit when sha cam.* 2. *Nobbut saay thoo's sorry an' it'll mense t' matter up at yance.*

Menseful, *adj.* Becoming and decent behaviour.

Mensefully, *adv.* Becomingly, decently, civilly.

Menseless, *adj.* Untidy, useless, &c.

Merls, *n.* The game of morris.

Met, *n.* Two bushels, a five-stone weight.

Met-poke, *n.* A narrow sack, but sufficiently large to hold two bushels.

Meuse, *v.* To study, to contemplate.

   Ex.—*Ah think t' lass is lovesick, sha gans meusing aboot seea.*

Mew, *pret.* To mow. *n.* A stack.

Mew-bo'nt, *adj.* Heated or burnt in the stack.

Mew up, *v.* To be overcrowded in a heated room. 2. To huddle together.

   Ex.—1. *Ther war ower monny fau'k i' t' room; Ah war that mew'd up Ah c'u'd hardlings breeathe. Sha's gitten all her things mew'd up tigether, whahl sha'll 'a'e straange deed ti git 'em all ti reets again.*

Mich, *adj.* Much.

Middin, *n.* A manure-heap.

Middinstead, *n.* The ground or place of the midden.

Midge, *n.* A tiny fly.

Mig, *n.* The drainings from a manure-heap.

Milk-can, *n.* A milk-pail.

Milk-hoos, Milk'us, *n.* The milk dairy.

Milk-lead, *n.* A shallow leaden cistern, with a hole stopped by a wooden plug; after the milk has stood overnight, the plug is withdrawn, and the milk drained from the cream.

Mill'd in, *adj.* Shrunk, aged, withered.

Mill-e'e, *n.* The eye or hole through which the ground grain falls into the sack or bin.

Mill-gear, *n.* The machinery of a mill.

Mill-race, Mill-reeace, *n.* The cut or channel which leads to the water-wheel, the water running towards the water-wheel.

Mindful, Mahndful, *adj.* Careful.
> Ex.—*Thoo mun be mahndful hoo thoo hugs t' basket. Be mahndful what thoo sez, noo.*

Mint, *v.* To intend, purpose; to aim a blow; to pretend.

Mirak'lous, *adj.* Careless, venturesome, precocious.
> Ex.—*He's a bit mirak'lous wiv a gun. He carried on iv a straange mirak'lous waay at t' fire. He war awlus a mirak'lous kind ov a lad.*

Miscall, *v.* To give a wrong name to any person or thing, to use abusive epithets.

Misfit, *n.* Out of place, one who cannot be trusted.

Mista'en, *adj.* Mistaken.

Mistetched, *part.* Badly trained or broken in (of a horse).

Mistimed, *adj.* Put out of the regular course, especially of sleep.

Mits, Mittens, *n.* Woollen gloves covering the wrist and knitted with divisions for the fingers.

Moider, *v.* To bewilder.

Moil, *v.* To toil on when tired.

Moit, *n.* The smaller part, a small portion.
> Ex.—*Tha sed 'at tha shared it oot amang t' lot on uz, onny waay Ah nobbut gat a moit.*

Mole-rat. *Vide* **Mowdywarp.**

Moo-moo, *n.* A pet name for a cow.

Moor-titling, Moor-taalin, *n.* The meadow pipit.

Mooun't. *Vide* **Maun't.**

Moozy-feeaced, Mouzy-feeaced, *adj.* Applied to the first growth of hair on the lip or chin.

Moozy meean, *n.* A hazy moon.

Mostlings, Meeastlings, *adv.* Generally, usually.

Mouck, *v.* To creep along, to hide.

Moud, Mud, *v.* Might.

Mowdy-hill, *n.* A mole-hill.

Mowdy-rake, *n.* A rake used to level mole-hills.

Mowdywarp, *n.* The mole.

Mounge, *v.* To chew with the gums when the teeth have gone.

Muck, *n.* Dirt, excrement, manure.

Muck, *v.* To spread manure.

Muck-clout, *n.* A floor-cloth, &c.

Muck-gripe, *n.* A dung-fork.

Muck lather, *n.* In a state of excessive perspiration.

Muckments, *n.* Filthy matter.

Muck-middin, *n.* The manure- or ash-midden.

Muck out, *v.* To clean out a stable or midden.

Muck sweat. *Vide* **Muck lather.**

Mucky, *adj.* Dirty, filthy, unwashed.

Mud, *v.* Might.

Mug, *n.* Face.

Muggy, *adj.* Damp, foggy, thick and close.

Mull, Murl, *n.* Dry fine mould.

Mumm'l, *v.* To mumble.

Mump, *n.* A blow on the face with the fist. *v.* To chew without teeth.

Mun, *n.* Man.

Ex.—*Ah'll tell tha what, mun.*

Mun, *v.* Must.

Murl, *v.* and *n.* To crumble into small pieces.

Mush, *n.* Dust, rotten through decay. NOTE.—Though generally applied to anything dry, it is sometimes used to denote damp and rotten.

Ex.—*It's grund ti mush. Them to'nips is neea good, tha're all iv a mush.*

Mushy, *adj.* Dry, powdery, in a state of pulp.

Musweb, *n.* A cobweb, the white cobwebs which float about in the air.

Muther, Mudder, *n.* Mother.

My-song! *intj.* Originally **La Sangue!**

N.

Na, *conj.* Nor, than.

Naay, *adv.* Nay.

Nab, *v.* To pick up sharply, to steal.

Ex.—*Thoo mun watch him or he'll nab summat.*

Nab, *n.* A hill or rocky point, a headland.

Naekins. *Vide* **Otherkins.**

Naether, Nowther, Nowder, *conj.* Neither.

Naff, *n.* The nave of a wheel.

Naff-heead, *n.* A stupid fellow.

Naffle, *v.* To pretend, to potter about.

Naggy. *Vide* **Gnaggy.**

Nak't, *adj.* Naked.

Namby-pamby, *adj.* Affected, conceited.

Nanpie, *n.* The magpie.

Nantle. *Vide* **Naffle.**

Nap. *Vide* **Nab.**

Nap, *v.* To strike with a hammer lightly.

Nar, *adj.* Near.

Narked, *v.* Vexed beyond measure.

Nar-side, *n.* The left-hand side of a horse when leading or walking along with a team.

Nasty, *adj.* Ill-natured.

    Ex.—*He war varra nasty aboot t' job.*

Natter, *v.* To be fretful, peevish.

Nattery, *adj.* Fretful, peevish.

Nattering, *n.* Continued complaining. *Vide* **Gnatter.**

Nattle, *v.* To make a light rattling sound.

Natt'rable, *adj.* What might be expected; unassuming, kindly.

Nature, Nater, *n.* The innate good quality of things.

    Ex.—*Ther 'ez been that mich wet, whahl t' gess 'll a'e lost all t' nater oot on 't,* i. e. ' There has been that much wet, that the grass (drying for hay) will have lost all the nature (goodness) out of t.'

Naup, *v.* To give a smart tap on the head.

Naup, *n.* A tap on the head, as with a ruler.

Nauping, *n.* A thrashing.

Naw. *Vide* **Neea.**

Nay-say, *n.* The privilege of refusing.

    Ex.—*Tommy's gitten t' naay-saay on 't. Aye, Ah've bowt it, bud then Ah've hed t' naay-saay on 't foor lang eneeaf.*

Nazzed, Nazzled, *adj.* Somewhat intoxicated.

Nazzy, *adj.* Under the influence of drink.

Neaf. *Vide* **Neeaf.**

Near, *adj.* Close-fisted, very careful, greedy.

    Ex.—*Did Sammy gi'e tha owt ? Neea, he's ti near ti even wish yan weel.*

Near, *n.* A kidney.

Near-hand, *adv.* 1. Near by, close to. 2. Almost, nearly.

    Ex.—1. *Whya, sha lives near-hand Bessy.* 2. *Ah nivver wur seea near-hand gittin' putten oot o' t' road i' mah leyfe. If thoo gans near-hand yon chap, he'll smit tha.*

Nearlings, *adv.* Almost, all but.

Neavil, Nevel, *v.* To pummel with the fist.

Nevilling, *n.* A sound pummelling with the fist.

Neb, *n.* The bill of a bird, the nose, the peak of a cap.

Neb, *v.* To kiss, to peck at viciously.

    Ex.—*Did ta neb her afoor thoo let her gan ?*

Neea, Noa, Naw, Nooa, *adv.* No.

Neeaf, Neif, *n.* The fist.

Neeaf-full, *n.* A handful.

Neea matters = No great quantity, of little importance.

    Ex.—*Did he win owt at t' races ? Neea matters wo'th telling on. What sha sez is neea matters ti onnybody.*

Neeap, *v.* To raise on end, as in lifting the shafts of a cart.

Neease, Nooas, *n.* The nose.

Neease, *v.* To sneeze.

Needer, *n.* The common adder.
Needful, *adj.* Necessitous, applies to persons and things.
 Ex.—*Whya, wa mun all deea a bit; sha's varra needful, ther's a lot o' bairns. Aye, it's wivoot doot a maist need- ful case.*
Needment, *n.* Something necessary.
Ne'er-di-weel, *n.* A worthless fellow.
Neest, *adj.* Next.
Neet, *n.* Night.
Ner, *conj.* Nor.
Nervy, *adj.* Vigorous.
Nesh, *adj.* Tender, soft, weak.
Ness, *n.* A projecting headland.
Neuk, *n.* A corner, corner of a field, a hiding-place.
Never give over, With a=Without ceasing.
New-fangled, *part.* Pleased with novelties.
 Ex.—*Bairns dis git new-fangled wi' owt 'at's fresh.*
Nias, *n.* A young hawk.
Nibble, *n.* Nipple of either the breast or a gun.
Nibbs, *n.* The handles on a scythe.
Nice, Neyce, *adj.* 1. Too particular. 2. Shy. 3. Con- siderable in size and quantity. 4. Sensitive.
 Ex.—1. *Ah deean't leyke fooak 'at's sae neyce aboot what tha eat.* 2. *Noo help yersels, an' deean't be neyce aboot it.* 3. *Ah mun saay 'at ther wur a neycish few.* 4. *Ah's a bit neyce aboot what fooak saay o' ma.*
Nicker, *v.* To whinny as a foal.
Niff-naff, *n.* A trifle.
Niff-naffing, *adj.* Trifling.
Nifle, *n.* A trifle.
Nifle, *v.* To waste time. Useless occupation.
 Ex.—*Thoo nifles on, an' nivver gits nowt deean. Thoo's nifling agaan, allus at t' saam bat.*
Niggle, *v.* To deal out or give grudgingly, to be greedy in small matters.
Nigh, *adv.* Nearly, about.
Nigh at hand, *adv.* Close to, near by.
Nilder-nalder, *n.* Vacillation, hesitation.
Nim, *adj.* Quick, active.
Nim, *v.* To snatch up quickly, to steal, to be active, agile.
Ninnycocks, *n.* Young lobsters.
Nip, *v.* Run.
 Ex.—*Just nip ower ti Bob an' ass foor t' saw.*
Nip off, *v.* To run away, to move quickly.
Nip up, *v.* To snatch up quickly, to go up quickly.
 Ex.—*He nipped it up afoor Ah cu'd stop him. Nip up- stairs an' fetch mah hat doon.*

Nipper, *n.* A young child.

Nisly, *adj.* Showery.

Nit, *n.* The egg of the louse.

Nither, Nidder, *v.* To shivver.

> Ex.—*Ah nithered an' dithered an' trimm'ld all ower that mich whahl Ah c'u'dn't mak oot if sha'd been shuvved, tumm'ld, slithered, or louped inti t' beck.*

Nittering, *part.* Subdued giggling.

Nivver, *adj.* Never.

Nizy, *n.* A dunce.

Nizzled, *v.* To be under the influence of drink.

Noa ship, *n.* Clouds said to resemble the Ark. A common saying is, *T' Ark's oot, wa're in foor a spell o' bad weather.*

Nobbin, *n.* The hair on the crown of the head.

> Ex.—*He teeak her biv t' nobbin an' pulled her backkards-waay ower.*

Nobbut, *conj.* If, only. 'Only' is rarely used.

Nobby, *adj.* Handy, nice.

Nook, Nicking, *n.* A method of keeping count by cutting notches on a stick.

Nodder, *v.* To tremble.

Noggen, *adj.* Hard, rough.

Noggin, *n.* A quarter pint, a small jug.

Nominy, *n.* The name given to any doggerel rhyme.

None, Noan, Neean, *adv.* Not at all.

> Ex.—*He'll neean ho'd back, he'll deea't hard eneeaf.* 'Neean' in this case means more than 'not'; the idea conveyed is, 'He will not in any sense hold back.' *He's neean lost owt,* i.e. 'He has lost nothing at all.'

Nooatish, *v.* To notice.

Noo, *adv.* Now, well. The use of this word is most curious. *Noo, Noo, Noo! Noo,* said one man on meeting a friend. 'Noo' the first meant either 'good morning,' 'now then,' or 'well.' 'Noo' the second was addressed to the dog, and meant 'lie down.' 'Noo' the third, with a different inflection, was understood by the dog to imply, 'If you do not lie down at once, I shall hit you.' And 'Noo' the fourth clearly denoted, the dog having laid down, 'Now, then, we can talk.' This inflective power throughout the whole vocabulary lessens or adds force to words. Unfortunately it is impossible to render in print these varying tones, which are the life and soul of the dialect. When used as an interjection, it is equivalent to 'How do you do?'

Nooa. *Vide* **Neea.**

Noos an' agaains } =By chance, now and again, occasionally.
Noos an' thens }

Noration. *Vide* **Oration.**

Notified, Nooatified, *adj.* Well-known.

    Ex.—*Aye, he war a nooatified chap yance ower.*

Not ti fail. Without fail.

    Ex.—*Ah'll tell him ti cum an' not ti fail.*

Nowt, *n.* 1. Nothing. 2. Valueless. 3. Worthless person.

    Ex.—1. *Yon thing's warse 'an nowt.* 2. *It's up ti nowt neea way.* 3. *He's a nowt, an' warse 'an nowt.*

Nowt bud weel. Exceedingly good in every way.

    Ex.—*Ah can saay nowt bud weel on him.*

Nowther, Naether, Nowder, *conj.* Neither.

Noy, Noyance, Noying, *n.* Vexatious, worrying.

Nuddle, *v.* To huddle together, to squeeze.

Nullet, Nullot, *n.* An owl. Ullot is most commonly used.

Numb, *adj.* Dull, awkward, clumsy, insensible.

Nursery, *n.* A plantation of young trees.

Nut, *adv.* Not.

    Ex.—*Is ta gahin wi' ma? Neea, Ah's nut.* 'Nut' is to some extent an emphatic form of 'not.'

Nutty-crack-neet. The ninth night before Martinmas Day, on which a feast of apples and nuts is indulged in.

O.

O', *prep.* Of.

Oafing, Oafish, *adj.* Half-witted, foolish, silly.

Oaf-rocked, *adj.* More or less imbecile.

Oddments, *n.* Odds and ends.

'Od rabbits. This and other forms commencing with *'Od* is an old form of profanity, by abbreviating the name of the Deity by the omission of *G.*

Of, *prep.* By, out of.

    Ex.—*That meer he gat of t' broon meer's deean weel.*

Off. Used in the sense of 'by heart.' To be aware of, to know all about.

    Ex.—*Ah've gitten my task off. He'll nut git ower ma na mair, Ah've gitten him off noo,* i. e. 'I know all about him now.'

Offally, *adj.* Refuse. Bad, both of persons and things.

Offally maade, Offally leeaking, Offally putten tigither, *adv.* Badly or poorly made, &c.

Offalment, *n.* 1. Of little value, offal. 2. A useless, good-for-nothing fellow. 3. Intestines, &c., of animals.

Off and on, *adj.* and *adv.* 1. Vacillating, uncertain. 2. Now and again.

    Ex.—1. *He's allus off an' on, an' nivver sattles ti nowt.* 2. *He's off an' on frev yah thing tiv anuther, whahl ther's neea 'pendence on him.*

Off one's heead, *adj.* Mad, delirious.

Off on't, *adv.* 1. Poorly. 2. Disappointed.

Ex.—1. *Ah 'evn't deean nowt this week, Ah nobbut felt a larl bit off on't.* 2. *He war sadly off on 't when tha tell'd him o' Mary's trouble.*

Offen, *adv.* From off, off.

Ex.—*It tumm'l'd offen t' shelf on tiv his heead.*

Off'ns, *adv.* Often.

Ofter, *adv.* Oftener.

Okkad, *adj.* Awkward, clumsy.

Olden, *v.* To age, to show signs of age.

Ommaist, Ommost, *adv.* Though often meaning simply 'almost,' it often carries a stronger sense with it, e.g. Q. *Will ta gan wiv uz?* 'Will you go with me?' A. *Aye, Ah ommost think Ah will,* would mean, 'Aye, I certainly think I will.' The general sense, however, is that of 'almost.'

On, *adv.* 1. Here. 2. There. 3. Forward.

Ex.—1. *He's cumin' on ti-neet,* i.e. 'He is coming here to-night.' 2. *Will ta be on ti-neet?* i.e. 'Will you be there to-night.' 3. *Wa mun push t' job on or wa s'aan't git deean.*

On, *prep.* Of.

Ex.—*Sha war despert freet'n'd' at Ah war gahin' ti tell on her.*

On, To be, *v.* To assent.

Ex.—Q. *Will thoo gan wiv uz?* A. *Noa, Ah weean't be on at a gam o' that soart.*

Once ower. *Vide* **Yance ower.**

Onely sahded, *adj.* Doubtful, singular.

Ex.—*It's nobbut a onely sahded gahin' on,* i.e. 'It is only a doubtful or singular proceeding.'

Onny bit leyke, or **Owt leyke.** Fairly well, tolerably.

Ex.—*If he aim'd onny bit leyke, he mud 'd'e mannished. Wa s'all cum if t' daay be owt leyke.*

On with, To be, *v.* The act of doing, to be engaged with.

Ex.—*Ah s' be on wiv it ti morn at morn,* i.e. 'I shall be doing it to-morrow morning.' *He's dropped Sally, an' 's on wi' Jin,* i.e. 'He has jilted Sally, and is engaged to Jane.'

Oot, *adv.* Out, not within; also away, as *Git oot wi' ya,* 'Get away with you.'

Oot o' course, *adv.* Beyond comparison, beyond measure.

Oot an' away, *adv.* Undoubtedly.

Ex.—*Oot an' away t' best hoss.*

Oor, Wer, *pron.* Our.

Oorsens, Oorsels, Wersens, Wersels, *pron.* Ourselves.

Oppen, *v.* Open.

Oppen oot, *v.* 1. To bring to light, to reveal. 2. To show one's true character.

> Ex.—1. *If thoo sez mich mair, Ah'll oppen oot a bit mysen,* i.e. ' I will reveal something.' 2. *Ah think he's a varra canny chap sen he's oppen'd oot a bit.*

Oration, *n.* A commotion accompanied with much talking and shouting.

Orf, *n.* The scurf which forms under the hair of children and animals.

Orling, *n.* A mis-shapen, undersized, rickety child.

Othergates, *adj.* Otherwise.

Othersome, *adj.* Variety, of another sort.

Ought, Owt, *n.* Anything. *adv.* At all.

> Ex.—*It's all nowther owt, nowt, na summat.*

Ouse. *Vide* House.

Out, Outing, *n.* A day's pleasure.

Out with, To be = On unfriendly terms.

Out by, *adv.* Near to, in the direction of.

> Ex.—Q. *Does Mr. Jackson live near here ?* A. *Noa, he lives out by Newton.*

Outen, *adv.* Out of.

> Ex.—*Sha tumm'l'd outen t' winder i'ti t' watter-butt. Thoo caan't git thisel an' Dolly a dhriss outen that, cut it which waay thoo will. Ya mud ez weel aim ti squeeze milk outen a yat-post ez git owt outen him.*

Out-end, Out-gang, Out-gaat, *n.* An exit, a way out of.

Out o' fettle, *adj.* Unwell, needing repair.

> Ex.—*Ah s'aan't be gahin' ti-daay, Ah's a bit oot o' fettle. T' cart's gitten a bit oot o' fettle; Ah s'all 'a'e ti 'ev it leeaked teea.*

Out o' t' road, *adv.* Out of the way, out of sight, killed.

> Ex.—*Ah caan't finnd 't, sha's putten 't oot o' t' road sumwheears.*

Out-thrust, Out-thrussen, *adj.* Projecting.

Ouzel, *n.* The Bessy ducker, or ring ouzel.

Over is generally pronounced ' ower ' or ' ovver.'

Overget, Owerget, *v.* To come up with, overtake, overreach.

Oversail, *n.* The top course of masonry covering the whole width of the wall.

Over-scutch, *v.* To whip too severely.

> Ex.—*He's ower-scutched t' lad this tahm, an' Ah'll foller t' law on him an' mak him pay foor 't.*

Overwelt, *v.* To roll on the back, so as to be unable to rise again—generally applied to sheep.

Overwing, *v.* To outwit.

> Ex.—*He aims 'at he knaws a bit, bud Ah'll overwing him onny tahm iv a hoss deeal.*

Owe, Awe, *v.* To own.

Ower, *v.* 1. To last through. 2. To cease, to come to an end.

> Ex.—1. *Ah deean't think Tom 'll git here i' tahm ti see t' au'd chap, if'll tak him all his tahm to ower t' neet, let aleean t' week end.* 2. *T' meeting's owered, t' chapel's lowsed, an' t' chetch 'ez cum'd out, bud t' army's gahin' ti gan at it whahl midneet.*

Ower, *adj.* 1. Too. 2. Beyond due bounds.

> Ex.—1. *It's ower grand,* i.e. 'Too fine.' *Ower big,* i.e. 'Too large.' 2. *He's ower daft foor owt,* i.e. 'He's foolish beyond all bounds.'

Ower, *prep.* and *adv.* On the other side of, beyond.

> Ex.—*Ower t' street,* e.g. 'On the other side, across the street.' *Ower t' dale,* i.e. 'On the other side of or beyond the dale.'

Owerance, *n.* The upper hand, the mastery.

> Ex.—*He's gitten t' owerance ov all t' lot on uz. Ah ower-handed him that tahm,* i.e. 'Got the advantage of.'

Ower an' up agaan=More than once, over and again.

Ower-gaat, *n.* A stone style, the steps in a wall side.

Ower-kessen, Owercast, *v.* and *adj.* Overcast, cloudy.

Ower monny, *adj.* Too manny, too strong, beyond one's power.

> Ex.—*Ah'll nut drhive t' hoss, he's ower monny foor ma. He maay bunch t' lass, bud his weyfe's ower monny foor him.*

Ower-neyce, *adj.* Too particular, fastidious, shy, diffident. *Vide* **Nice.**

> Ex.—*Noo ya mun stritch yer elbows, an' reach teea; what's putten afoor ya's putten ti gan at; noo deean't be ower-neyce, bud set ti wark an' sahd t' lot.*

Owerset, Owersetten, *pp.* 1. Overtasked beyond one's strength. 2. Overturned.

> Ex.—1. *Ah's completely owersetten an' deean up wi' t' job. Naay what, thoo seems owersetten afoor thoo starts.* 2. *Ah owerset t' au'd lass' stall, an' t' nippers did scramm'l foor t' things.*

Owerhand. *Vide* **Owerance.**

Owt, *n.* Aught, anything.

Owther, Owder, Aether, *conj.* Either.

Ox-prod, *n.* An ox-goad.

Oxter, *n.* The armpit.

P.

Pace-eggs, Paste-eggs, *n.* Hard-boiled eggs dyed various colours, used by children on Easter Monday. *Vide* chapter on 'Customs.'

Pack, *v.* When birds at certain seasons collect together they are said to 'pack.'

Packman, *n.* A pedlar.

Pack-rag day. The day following Martinmas Day, when the servants who are changing masters pack up their belongings.

Paddle, *v.* To walk with difficulty, to wade bare-legged.

Paddy-noddy, *n.* A long wearisome tale with much repetition.

Pafty, *adj.* Pert, assuming, impudent.

Pair of stairs, *n.* A flight of stairs.

Pairt. *Vide* Part.

Pairtner, *n.* A partner, generally husband or wife.

Pally-ully, *n.* A game almost identical with hop-scotch.

Palm, Paum, *v.* To climb with the hands and legs. *Vide* Swarm.

Palm-cross day, *n.* Palm Sunday.

Palms, Paums, *n.* Catkins, 'lambs'-tails' of the hazel.

Pan, *v.* To fit into or close together.

Pankin, Pankin-pot, *n.* A large earthenware vessel.

Pankin-dish, *n.* A deep earthenware dish.

Pannel, *n.* A riding pad.

Parkin, *n.* A gingerbread cake made for the fifth of November.

Parlous, *adj.* Its general meaning carries with it a sense or state of evil. 2. Adverbially used, it always intensifies.
> Ex.—1. *Ther's been parlous deed at t' mill. Tha've locked him up at t' last, it's nobbut a parlous ending up.* 2. *He's a parlous good preeacher is yon local chap.* 3. *T' hoos is iv a parlous state, bud then it's cleeaning tahm.*

Part, Pairt, *adj.* A considerable number or quantity.
> Ex.—*Pairt fooak wur bidden ti t' funeral. Ther'll be pairt fruit ti year, nobbut Jack Frost dizn't nip t' blo afoor it sets.*

Pash, *v.* To dash to the ground, to smash into fragments.

Pash, *n.* 1. A crash. 2. A heavy fall of snow or rain. 3. The result of a smash, or of a heavy fall of rain or snow, as mud or slush. 4. Soft, rotten, pulpy matter.
> Ex.—1. *T' chim'ly cam doon wi' sikan a pash.* 2. *Wa've hed a pash o' snaw ti week.* 3. *Baith t' carts is upskell'd an' t' things ur a' iv a pash tigither.* 4. *Cum awaay fra sike pashy deed, thoo'll labber thisen all ower.*

Past, *adj.* Beyond, incapable.
> Ex.—*Past deeaing owt wi'*, i.e. 'not to be restrained or influenced.' *Past kenning*, i.e. 'grown beyond recognition.' *Past bahding*, i.e. 'beyond one's power to endure.' *Past wark*, i.e. 'incapable of working.' *He's gitten past that noo*, i.e. 'incapable of having further aid rendered.'

Past all=Beyond all bounds, generally used in a disagreeable sense; the antithesis of 'Caps all.'

Patter, *v.* To tread or beat down by many steps, as a pathway across a newly tilled field.

Patter, Pattering, *n.* The sound of quick, light footsteps.

Pause. *Vide* **Bunch.**

Paut, Pooat, *v.* 1. To paw the ground impatiently. 2. To kick lightly. 3. To walk in an affected style. 4. To walk feebly and somewhat heavily, as an aged person.

Ex.—1. *T' meer's gitting stall'd o' stannin', sitha hoo sha pauts t' grund.* 2. *Wa caan't hap t' bairn up, sha pauts aboot wiv her larl feet sae.* 3. *Sen sha's gitten long skets an' fancy stockin's on, sha diz paut alang.* 4. *Au'd Willie, Ah see, still mannishes to paut about wiv a stick.*

Pawk, *n.* **Pawky,** *adj.* Impudent, inquisitive, precocious, forward (of a child).

Pawty, *adv.* Slovenly.

Pea-hulls, Pea-swads or **-cods,** *n.* Empty pods of peas.

Peascod, *n.* Peas still in the pod.

Peffing, *adj.* Applied to short, husky, hard breathing.

Peggy-stick. *Vide* **Dolly-stick.**

Peggy wi' t' lantern. Will o' t' Wisp, Jack o' t' Lantern (*Ignis Fatuus*).

Pelt, *adv.* Speedily, swiftly.

Ex. —*He cam doon t' hill sike a pelt.*

Pelt, *n.* The skin of a flayed animal.

Pepper-cake, *n.* A kind of ginger loaf. *Vide* chapter on 'Customs.'

Perceivance, *n.* Conception, acquaintance with.

Ex.—*Neea, Ah'd na perceivance o' what he meant ti deea.*

Perishment, *n.* The outcome of a severe cold, a thorough chill.

Ex.—*Ah've gitten a perishment o' cau'd, Ah knaw that.*

Pet, To take, *v.* To be offended, to sulk, to be affronted over some petty misunderstanding.

Pick, *n.* Pitch.

Pick = Black. An intensive, or black as pitch.

Ex.—*It war pick dark.*

Pick, *v.* 1. To trip up, pitch, or push so as to bring to the ground. 2. To give birth immaturely (of an animal). 3. To find fault.

Ex.—1. *Ah shoved mah foot oot an' pickt him ower nicely.* 2. *Coo's pick'd her cauf.* 3. *Sha's nivver off mah beeans, sha's awlus picking at ma.*

Pick-fork, *n.* A pitch-fork.

Pickle, Piddle on, *v.* To play with one's food.

Pick-mark, *n.* The mark on sheep made with a hot iron stamp.

Pick up, *v.* To vomit.

Pie, *v.* To store potatoes in an earth mound for the winter, to peep, to pry.

Pie, *n.* A heap of potatoes covered by earth.

Piet, *n.* The magpie.

Piffle, *v.* To steal in small quantities.

Piffling, *v.* To do anything in a silly, half-hearted way.

Pigmeat. The refuse of the kitchen and dinner-table gathered together, and saved with other swill in a tub for pig-food.

Pig-nut, *n.* The earth-nut (*Bunium flexuosum*).

Pig-swarth, *n.* The skin of bacon.

Pike, *n.* A number of hay-cocks made into one heap.

Pinchery, *n.* Greediness, penuriousness.

Pin-faud, *n.* The pound for stray cattle.

Pinnies, *n.* Fish just hatched.

Pirl, Purl, *n.* The wooden or other winder upon which cotton or thread is wound.

Pisling, *v.* To lounge about.

Pit, *v.* 1. To match. 2. To jeer, to quarrel. 3. To mark or spot.
Ex.—1. *Ah'll pit him again thoo. Let 'em aleean, tha're well pitted.* 2. *Ther's maist o' t' street end oot, an' tha're pitting yan anither leyke all that.*

Pit, *n.* A mark left by small-pox.

Place, *n.* Service.
Ex.—*Ah isn't gahin' ti pleeace yet.*

'Plain, 'Pleean, 'Plaan, *v.* To complain, to be querulous.

Plaint, *n.* A pitiful tale.

Plash, *v.* To splash. *n.* A puddle.

Plate, *v.* To clinch a nail.

Plating, *n.* A sound thrashing.

Pleeaf. *Vide* Plough.

Pleeaf stots. Young fellows, about twelve in number, who used to go about fantastically dressed on Plough Monday, headed by music; a kind of sword-dancer.

Pleean, Plaan, *adj.* Doubtful, not handsome.
Ex.—1. *Ah wadn't trust yon, he's nobbut a plaan un.* 2. *Yon's a pleean leeaking lass, hooiveer.*

Plenish, *v.* To review, to furnish.

Plesh, Plosh, Plash, *n.* A puddle.

Plew. *Vide* Plough.

Pload, *v.* To walk with difficulty over heavy land.

Ploader, *n.* A plodding, diligent fellow.

Ploat, *v.* To pluck the feathers from a fowl.

Plodge, *v.* To wade through water.

Plook, *n.* A small pimple.

Plooky-feeaced, *adj.* Applied to a pimpled or blotched face.

Plosh, *v.* To splash, to bespatter.

Ploshy, *adj.* Splashy.

Plother, Plodder, *n.* Soft mud.

Plother, *v.* To bring into a state of soft mud.

Plothery, Ploddery, Pluthery, *adj.* Muddy, miry.

Plough, Plew, Pleeaf, Plufe, *n.* A plough.

Ploughing-day, Pleeafing-day, Plewing-day, *n.* The day

on which neighbouring farmers lend men, horses, and implements, to assist a new-comer on the land.

Ploughing iron or **airn**, *n.* The coulter.

Pluck, *n.* The heart, liver, and lungs of an animal.

Pluff, *n.* A tube to pluff with.

Pluff, *v.* To force anything through a tube by blowing.

Plug, *v.* To load a cart with manure.

Plugger, *n.* Anything larger than usual.

Pluke. *Vide* **Plook**.

Plum, *adj.* Perpendicular.

> Ex.—*That's nut plum byv a lang waay.*

Plump, *v.* To come straight down, hence to accuse openly.

> Ex.—1. *It cam plump doon i' t' frunt o' ma.* 2. *Ah plump'd him wi' 't tiv his feeace,* i.e. 'I accused him to his face.'

Plump, *adj.* Straightforwardly, exactly.

> Ex.—*Ah tell'd him plump oot what Ah thowt.*

Plunder, *n.* The legitimate profit made out of any business transaction.

Pluther. *Vide* **Plother**.

Plutherment, *n.* Slush, water and mud, or snow and mud mixed ; any liquid filth.

Pook-arr, *n.* The scar left by small-pox.

Podge, *n.* A short fat man.

Podgy, *adj.* Little and fat.

Poke, Pooak, *n.* A sack or bag.

Poringer, *n.* A mug which widens toward the base.

Porrets, *n.* Small onions.

Porriwiggle, *n.* The tadpole.

Posh, *n.* Slush, mud.

Posh, Poss, *v.* To pound with a possing-stick whilst washing clothes. *Vide* **Dolly-stick**.

Poshing-stick, Possing-stick, *n.* The stick used to poss or beat with, something like a heavy club.

Poskit, Peggy-tub. A large oaken tub used to poss clothes in, often called a **Possing-tub.**

Posy, *n.* A bunch of flowers to carry in the hand.

Pot-blossoms, *n.* Blotches on the face caused by excessive drinking.

Potherment, *n.* Petty annoyance.

Pot-lug, *n.* The handle of a jug.

Pot-sitten, *adj.* Burnt whilst cooking, especially in the case of milk or porridge. Almost universally styled now **Setten on.**

Potch, *n.* To throw.

> Ex.—*Gi'e ower potching steeans.*

Potter, *v.* To attempt in a feeble way, often followed by 'about.'

> Ex.—*Hoo he diz potter aboot ! Diz he ivver get owt deean ?*

Pottering, *adj.* Slow, feeble, awkward.

Preachment, *n.* A wearying discourse.

Présent, *v.* To present.

Ex.—*Tha've presented her wiv a clock an' a silken pess wi' twenty pund in 't.*

Pretty warm, *adj.* Comfortably off, well-to-do.

Prickle, *v.* 1. To have a pricking sensation. 2. To prick.

Ex.—1. *Ah prickle all ower.* 2. *Ah've prickled my han's all ower wi' gethering bumm'l-kites.*

Pricky-back otch'n, *n.* The hedgehog.

Prod, *n.* Usually a hazel stick with a sharp point.

Prod, *v.* To prick or push with a prod.

Proddle, *v.* To poke about, to prick, to poke about under stones, &c.

Proffer, *v.* To make an offer.

Ex.—*Ah proffered ti gan ower an' give him a lift.*

Prood, *adj.* Proud.

Propped up, *adj.* Kept alive owing to the observance of certain rules and other advantages.

Ex.—*Tha've propped him up foor a bit, but it weean't be foor lang, he fails ivvery daay.*

Pross, *n.* A friendly gossip.

Providence, *n.* Food, &c., provided for any kind of feast.

Ex.—*A mirical wadn't a'e maad yon providence last.*

Pubble, *adj.* Plump, soft and round.

Puddings, *n.* Entrails.

Pull, *v.* To pick.

Ex.—*Wa mun pull t' currants ti morn.*

Pulls, *n.* The shells of ripe turnip seeds, &c.

Pulsey, *n.* A poultice.

Pum, Pumm'l, *v.* To beat with the fists.

Purlings, *n.* Ribs upon which the spars of the roof of a house rest.

Push, *n.* 1. Moment. 2. Energy.

Ex.—1. *He awlus leeaves ivvery thing ti t' last push.* 2. *Ther's neea push i' yon youth.*

Pushed, *adj.* Hurried, inconvenienced.

Ex.—*Ah war varra mich pushed for tahm.*

Put about, *v.* To be incommoded, put out of one's ordinary course, disgusted.

Ex.—*Ah nivver war seea grieved an' vexed an' putten about iv all mah leyfe.*

Put off, Put away. To kill, to remove one's outer garments.

Putten, *pp.* of 'Put.'

Putten by, *v.* To put away, to bury.

Putten ti reets, *v.* 1. To put in order. 2. To correct.

Ex.—1. *Ah'll git things putten ti reets a bit.* 2. *Thoo'll git thisen putten ti reets if thoo dizn't tak care.*

Puzzon, *n.* A poison.
Puzzon, *v.* To poison.

Q.

Quality, *n.* Gentry.
Quart, *v.* 1. To cross transversely, as in ploughing. 2. To disagree, to quarrel.
    Ex.—2. *Ah aim 'at oor Tom wad quart wiv a stuffed monkey.*
Queery, *n.* Any circumstance of an extraordinary character.
Quick-sticks, *adv.* Sharply, at once.
    Ex.—*If thoo dizn't git it deean i' quick-sticks, Ah'll wahrm thi jacket foor tha.*
Quirk, *n.* A trick, deception.
Quite better = Quite recovered.

R.

Rabate, *v.* To return something, in consideration of.
    Ex.—*Thoo gav him fahve pund foor 't, an' 'ed ti gan foor 't thisen, what rabate did ta git?*
Rabble, *v.* To read or speak so hastily as to be indistinct.
Rabblement, *n.* Indistinct, confused talk; a mob of low scoundrels.
Race. *Vide* **Mill-race.**
Rack, *n.* Fleecy clouds driven by wind.
Rackapelt, *n.* A worthless fellow.
Rackit, *n.* A turbulent, boisterous noise.
Raddle, *v.* To beat or thrash soundly.
Raddling, *n.* A sound thrashing.
Radged, *adj.* Furious, mad.
Raff, *n.* 1. A confused heap. 2. A disreputable person.
    Ex.—1. *Thoo's gitten things all iv a raff.*
Raff, After, *n.* A second mowing, generally of clover.
Raffle, *adj.* Idle or foolish.
Raffle, *v.* and *n.* 1. To become confused, to wander. 2. To entangle. 3. To lead a wild, irregular life.
    Ex.—1. *He raffles on seea whahl yan dizn't knaw what he meeans.* 2. *What a raffle sha's gitten t' wool inteea!* 3. *He'll raffle on whahl he'll gan thruff t' bit o' brass t' au'd chap left him.*
Raffle-pack, *adj.* Of loose, irregular lives.
Raffling, *adj.* Riotous, dissolute.
Raffly, *adj.* Applied to a confusion of ideas or weakened mental powers.
    Ex.—*He gits a larl bit raffly at tahms.*
Rag, *v.* To enrage, to vex.
    Ex.—*Ah did rag him aboot Polly.*
Ragabash, *n.* A bad character.

Ragally, *adj.* Loose, unseemly, unprincipled.

Rageous, *adj.* Furious.

Ragged, *pp.* To be enraged.

Ragged, *adj.* Borne down with fruit.

Raggel, *n.* A worthless vagabond.

Rag out, *n.* Passion, temper.

Ex.—*Deean't git his rag oot,* i. e. 'Don't vex him.' *Wa gat his rag oot,* i. e. 'We got him into a passion.'

Rag-river, *n.* A tomboy.

Raitch, *n.* The white line down a horse's face.

Raited, *pp.* Applied to hay or straw injured by wet or damp; peeled off after soaking.

Rain. *Vide* **Rein.**

Rakapelt, *n.* A low, dissolute fellow.

Raking, *v.* To wander about with a doubtful purpose.

Ram, *adj.* Possessing a fetid smell.

Ram, *v.* To push forward, to work hard.

Ex.—*Ah ram'd at it, an' seean gat it deean.*

Raments, *n.* Shavings, odd bits.

Rammack. *Vide* **Rannack.**

Ramm'l, *v.* To idle about.

Ex.—*Noo off thoo gans; thoo's awlus ramm'ling about t' pleeace.*

Ramp, *n.* A series of steps or drops on the upper part of a wall; the name given to garlic.

Rampageous, *adj.* Furious, boisterous, wild.

Ramp and Rave, To, *v.* To be mad with passion.

Ramper, *n.* The sloping side of a raised footpath.

Ramscallion, *n.* A filthy, loathsome person.

Ramshackle, *adj.* Disjointed, unsteady, needing repair.

Ranch, *adj.* Acid.

Ranch, *v.* To sprain.

Ranch, Rinch, *n.* A sprain.

Rand, *n.* A piece cut out of or off.

Rands, Reeands, *n.* The unploughed edges round a field.

Randy, *adv.* Madly, wildly, riotous. *adj.* Mad.

Rannack, *n.* A dissolute spendthrift.

Rann'l- or **Randle-bauk,** *n.* The bar upon which the reckons hang.

Rantipole, *n.* A romping child.

Ranty, *adj.* Much excited, angry.

Rap, *n.* A friendly chat.

Ex.—*Cu' thi waays, an' lets 'ev a pipe an' a bit o' rap.*

Rap-off, *v.* To speak on the spur of the moment.

Raps, *n.* Gossip, news.

Rapterous, *adj.* Ecstatic.

Rase, *pret.* of 'Rise.'

F f

Rase, *v.* To raise, to cause to move.
  Ex.—*Ah rase a rabbit i' that coorner last neet. Ah rase
  't up mysen.*
Raspin, *adj.* Excellent.
Rasps, *n.* Raspberries.
Rasselled, *adj.* Applied to withered fruit.
Ratten, *n.* A rat. **Rattener,** *n.* A catcher of rats.
Ratten-trap, *n.* A rat-trap.
Rattle-beeans (bones), *n.* A very thin man.
Rattle-cap, *n.* A lively, somewhat wild person.
Rattle-doon, *adj.* Tumble-down.
  Ex.—*It's nobbut a rattle-doon spot at t' best.*
Raum, Reeam, *v.* To bawl at the top of one's voice.
Raun, *n.* Fish roe.
Rave. *Vide* **Rive.**
Rawk, *n.* *Vide* **Roke.**
Rawp, *n.* Rape (*Brassica napus*).
Rax, *v.* To strain to the utmost.
Rax, *n.* A strain, a twist of limb or muscle.
Razzle, *v.* To roast on the outside before the fire, to hurriedly
  cook over a flame.
Reach, *v.* To hand or fetch anything.
  Ex.—*Reeach ma t' breead. Reeach ma yon mug o' milk.*
Reach to, *v.* To help oneself.
  Ex.—*Ya're all on ya varra welcum ti t' best o' owt Ah've
  gitten, sae reach to, and mak yersels at heeam.*
Reap up, *v.* To refer to some past misdeed.
Rear, *v.* To raise up, to raise into a perpendicular position.
Rear, *adj.* Applied to meat underdone.
Reckan-bauk. *Vide* **Gally-bauk.**
Recklin. *Vide* **Wrecklin.**
Reckon, *n.* The bar suspended from the rann'l-bauk.
Reckon, *v.* To imagine, to suppose.
  Ex.—*Ah reckon you'll be him. Ah reckon I knaw summat
  aboot it.*
Reckon-crook, *n.* The hook of the reckon.
Red up. *Vide* **Reet up.**
Reead-yat, *adj.* Red-hot.
Reeak, *n.* A rook.
Reeasty, *adj.* Rancid, e.g. 'reeasty bacon.'
Reeasty-cropt, *adj.* Hoarse.
Reek, *n.* Smoke. *v.* To smoke.
Reet, *adj., adv.,* and *n.* Right.
Reet up, To, *v.* To put things in order, to tidy up.
  Ex.—*Ah'll reet things up a bit, an' then Ah'll cum.*
Reft, *n.* A chink, a slit.
Rein, *n.* The sides of a field overgrown with brushwood.

Reist, *n.* A horse which refuses to move is said to have taken the ' reist.'

Rench, *v.* To rinse.

Ex.—*Ah'll gi'e it a rench oot.*

Render, *v.* To convert the fat of pigs to a liquid state by heat.

Renky, *adj.* Tall, but too thin, as trees when grown too close together.

Reshes, Reashes, *n.* The rush (*Juncus glaucus*).

Rezzil, *n.* The weasel (*Mustela* or *Putorius vulgaris*). **Wezzil** and **Wuzzil** are equally common.

Rick, *n.* A quantity of hay larger than a pike.

Rickle, *n.* A small heap of peat set to dry.

Ride, *v.* To travel on horseback, or in any kind of vehicle.

Ex.—*Ah s'all rahde t' meer theear, bud rahde back i' t' cart wi' Billy.*

Ride rough-shod ower, To, *v.* To obtain our own ends careless of other people's rights.

Ex.—*Ah'll nut let him rahde rough-shod ower me when Ah've gitten t' reet o' mah sahd.*

Riding, Ridding, *n.* The space made by felling trees, generally within a wood.

Riddle, *n.* A sieve.

Rife, *adj.* Inclined. ready.

Ex.—*He's rife foor onny rackit. He war rife foor t' job.*

Riff-raff, *n.* A low mob, scum.

Ex.—*He'll gan wi' onny sike leyke riff-raff.*

Rift, *v.* To belch.

Rig, *v.* To dress oneself.

Rigg, *n.* The back of a man or beast, the rows in which turnips grow. Hence ' rigg and furr,' the latter being the raised part running between each rigg.

Rigged, *v.* To be laid on the back unable to rise, applied to sheep ; to tidy oneself, to put on one's best.

Rigging, *n.* The framework of a roof.

Rigging tree, *n.* The top spar of a house.

Right, Reet, *adj.* True, correct.

Ex.—*It's reet what Ah's telling on ya.*

Right on end, *adv.* Direct as to direction, in a straight-forward manner.

Right up, *v.* To put things in order.

Ex.—*Ah've setten Janey ti reet things up a bit.*

Ring-shaken, *adj.* That part of timber which cannot be used owing to its being diseased.

Rise, *n.* A steep ascent.

Rive, Rahve, *v.* 1. To tear in two. 2. To pull with force. 3. To split.

Ex.—1. *He gave it a snip wi' t' sithers, an' then rahve it reet across.* 2. *Ah rakve it up, it war deead.* 3. *Ah s'all rive t' maist o' yon wood up.*

Rist, *n.* Rust.

Rist, *v.* To rest.

Road, Oot o' t' = Out of the way, killed.

Rods, *n.* Pea-rods, used to support peas when growing.

Roil, *v.* To be noisy, turbulent.

Roist, *adj.* Wild, dissolute.

Roistering, *adj.* Wild, noisy, or dissolute.

Roke, Rawk, *n.* A thick fog.

Roky, Rauky, Roaky, *adj.* Foggy, damp.

Roll, *n.* The pad of cloth worn on the head by potter women and others who carry a basket in that position.

Roll-egg day, Troll-egg day. Easter Monday. *Vide* chapter on ' Customs.'

Roo, Roo on, *v.* To work hard amidst confusion.

    Ex.—*If thoo'd nobbut sahd a few things by ez thoo went on, thoo wadn't 'a'e ti roo on i' this fashion. Sha awlus 'ez ti roo on at t' finish.*

Rooar, *v.* To make a loud noise when crying.

Rook, *n.* A cock of clover set up to dry.

Rook, *v.* To set up in small heaps.

Rossil, *n.* Resin.

Rostle, Rossel, *v.* To disturb, to shake.

Rouk, *v.* To snore loudly, as pigs.

    Ex.—*Ah weean't sleep wi' him na mair, he rouks warse 'an a pig.*

Roughen, *v.* To make rough.

Round, To get, *v.* To cajole, to assuage.

Roundy, *adj.* Of fairly good size, as compared with another sample containing much dust and small pieces ; applied to a good sample of coal.

Rouped up, To be, *v.* To be hoarse.

Roupy, *adj.* Hoarse from cold.

Rout, Rowt, *v.* To wander, to stray ; to bellow loudly, as cattle.

Rout about, *v.* To turn every place out.

Routering tahm. Cleaning time, house-cleaning.

Roving, *adj.* Of an unsettled nature.

Rovven, *pp.* Riven.

Row, *v.* To form ridges in the land for setting potatoes, &c.

Rowan-tree, *n.* The mountain ash (*Pyrus Aucuparia*). *Vide* chapter on 'Witchcraft.'

Rownd. *Vide* **Raun.**

Rowty, *adj.* Rank.

Roy, Roy on, *v.* To lead a fast life.

    Ex.—*If he roys on leyke yon, he'll seean 'a'e ti spell want.*

Royously, *adv.* Extravagantly.

Rud, *n.* Red ochre, also ruddle.

Rud-stake, *n.* The post to which a cow or ox is fastened when in its stall.

Rue, *v.* To alter one's mind after making a bargain.

Rue-bargain, *n.* A sum of money paid to cancel a bargain.

Ruffle, *v.* To rub or raise the skin.

Rumbustical, *adj.* Noisy, rough in play.

Runch, *n.* The charlock (*Sinapis arvensis*).

Rung, *n.* The step of a ladder.

Runnel, *v.* A small stream of water, the channel it runs in, a funnel.

Run out, *adj.* Exhausted, impoverished.

Runty, *n.* Short, thick-set.

Rush, *n.* A large concourse of people.

Russelled. *Vide* **Rasselled.**

Rutterkin, *n.* A sly old fellow.

Rutting, *n.* The sound made by deer during the pairing season.

Ruttle, *v.* and *n.* To breathe with a rattling, gurgling sound, as when suffering from bronchitis, or when dying. Hence *t' deeath ruttle's seetten in, it'll seean be owered wiv him noo.*

Rutty, *adj.* A road deeply furrowed by cart-ruts.

S.

'S. Is, has, or as.

S', *v.* Shall.

Sa. *Vide* **Seea.**

S'aan't, *v.* Shall not.

Sack, To get the, *v.* To be turned out of or lose a situation, to be dismissed.

Sackless, *adj.* Lacking common sense, foolish.

Sad, *adj.* Heavy, as badly-risen bread, damp.

Sadden, *v.* To make firm by stamping, treading, &c.
   Ex.—*Sae monny fooak tramping on t' land sairly saddens 't.*

Sadly, *adv.* Very much.
   Ex.—*It sadly wants deeaing,* i.e. 'It wants doing very much.' *Ah sadly wanted her ti stop a bit langer.*

Sadly begone, *adj.* Surprised and distressed at the same time.

Sadly ta'en in, *adv.* Very much deceived.
   Ex.—*Ah've been sadly ta'en in wiv 'em.*

Sae. *Vide* **Seea.**

Safe, Seeaf, *adj.* and *adv.* Certain, without doubt.
   Ex.—*Ah's seeaf ti cum,* i.e. 'I am certain to come.' *Safe eneeaf he did it,* i.e. 'Without doubt he did it.'

Sag, *v.* To hang lower in the middle than at either end, as a rope.

Sahded by, Sided by, *pp.* Buried.
   Ex.—*It's owered wiv him noo, wa've gitten him sahded by.*

Saim, Saam, *n.* Lard.

Sair, *adj.* Sore, in all its senses.

> Ex.—*Wa've 'ed a sair tahm,* i. e. 'a sad time.' *It's varra sair news,* i. e. 'sorrowful.' *T' lad's gitten a naisty sair spot,* i. e. 'sore.'

Sair, Sairly, *adv.* Sorely, greatly, extremely; used as an intensive.

> Ex.—*Sha'll be sairly missed, will Jane. It war a sair mannish'd job. Sha sairly wanted ti git yam.*

Sam, *v.* 1. To cause milk to curdle, to coagulate. 2. To gather in a hurry. 3. To pack things carelessly.

> Ex.—2. *Ah samm'd all t' lot tigither iv a twinklin'.* 3. *Sam 'em in onnyhoo.*

Sammer, *adj.* Larger than usual.

Santer, *v.* To loiter, to walk slowly.

Sappy, *adj.* Heavy, sodden.

Sap-tree, *n.* The rowan-tree.

Sark, *n.* A shirt or chemise.

Sarten, *adj.* Certain.

Sarve, *v.* 1. To feed cattle. 2. To pay back revengefully.

> Ex.—1. *Thoo mun sarve t' pigs.* 2. *Ah'll sarve him oot foor't.*

Sattle, *v.* To settle; usually followed by ' down'; to feel at home.

> Ex.—*Ah s' sattle efter a bit. Oha, he's sattled doon neycely.*

Sattle one's hash, To. To completely discomfit.

> Ex.—*If sha sez owt ti me Ah'll seean sattle her hash, an' tell her her neeam fur nowt an' all; sha'd best leeak oot.*

Sauce, *n.* and *v.* An impudent answer.

> Ex.—*Ah tell'd her what Ah thowt, an' sha sauced ma back ageean leyke all that.*

Sau't, *n.* Salt.

Sau't-kit, *n.* Salt-box.

Sauve, *n.* Ointment.

Sauve, *v.* 1. To cajole. 2. To apply ointment.

> Ex.—1. *Thoo mun sauve him ower byv talking neycely.*

Savelicks, *n.* Canker of the dog-rose.

Saw-cum, -com, or **-coom,** *n.* Sawdust.

Saw-hoss, *n.* A saw-pit, or the arrangement of two tressels upon which the wood to be sawn is rested.

Say, *n.* 1. Power, influence. 2. Opinion.

> Ex.—1. *T' parson 'ez t' maist say ov onnybody hereabouts.* 2. *Noo let me saay mah saay noo,* i. e. 'Now let me express my opinion now.'

Say, *v.* To control or influence.

> Ex.—*Ther's neea saying onny o' Martha's bairns. Ah caan't saay t' dog.*

Scacelings, *adv.* Scarcely.

Scaldered, To be, *v.* To have an unhealthy skin, so that the surface comes off in scales. Children's heads are often said to be scaldered when suffering from dandruff.

Scalderings, *n.* Nodules of half-burnt lime.

Scale, Scaling, *v.* To scatter or spread, as manure ; to cause the milk to be absorbed in the female breast.

Scale-dish, *n.* A shallow metal pan used to skim milk.

Scallibrat, *n.* A passionate, noisy child.

Scamp, *v.* To execute work in a dishonest manner, not paying attention to details which are hidden from view.

Scar, *n.* The face of a precipitous rock, or the rock itself.

Scart, *v.* Frightened.

Scaud, *n.* and *v.* A scold, a vixenish woman.

Scaud-heead, *n.* · Applied both to dandruff and ringworm.

Scau'p, *n.* The head, the skull, the bare spots of rock and stones on a hillside.

Sconce, *n.* 1. A screen, usually lined with tin, which is kept very bright so as to reflect ; this is placed in front of any joint roasting before the fire. 2. Hence the usage of the word in the sense of a 'ruse,' 'deception,' i. e. a screen to hide one's real intentions.

> Ex.—2. *He aim'd at wa s'u'd think 'at he'd cum'd ti see t' au'd chap, bud it war nowt bud a sconce ti finnd oot what wa'd gitten i' t' hoos.* The word is also used in the sense of 'tale-bearing' in such a way as either to hide one's own fault or to obtain one's own ends.

Scopperil, *n.* A teetotum, a pierced bone button with a wooden peg through it.

Scourging top, Scurgy, *n.* A whipping-top.

Scow, *n.* Confusion, hurried and somewhat disorganized preparation for an expected event, bustle with confusion.

Scowder, Scowderment, *n.* Confusion.

Scraffle, *v.* To struggle, to strive.

> Ex.—*Ah mannished ti scraffle thruff't, bud Ah s'all tak t' hedge t' next tahm. Sha's deean mair 'an weel ti scraffle on wi' a family leyke yon.*

Scrag-cauf, *n.* A name applied to females whose legs are very thin.

Scraggy, *adj.* Lean.

Scran, *n.* Food.

Scranky, *adj.* Very lank.

Scrannel, *adj.* Poor, worthless.

Scrap, *v.* and *n.* To quarrel.

Scrape, *n.* Misfortune, trouble.

Scrape the tongue, To, *v.* To speak affectedly.

Scrat, *v.* and *n.* 1. To scratch. 2. A scraping together of one's belongings by hard toil.

> Ex.—2. *Yan gits yan's things scratted tigither oddly by*

tahms. Neeaboddy's made a harder scrat foor what tha've gitten 'an Liza Jane.

Scrat, *n.* A miser, the itch.

Scrat, Au'd, *n.* The devil.

Scrawm, *v.* To scratch irregular marks on any surface, to grope about in the dark.

Scrawmy, *adj.* Straggly, irregular, unshapely.

Scrawmy cauf, *n.* A badly shaped leg. *adj.* **Scrawmy-cauf'd.**

Ex.—*Mah wo'd, bud Polly war sairly flowter'd when Ah dropped on her shauming, an' Ah seeaa sha'd neea call ti be, fer sha's owt bud a scrawmy-cauf'd un.*

Screed, *v.* To run a line or border on the edge of anything.

Screed, *n.* A shred, the border or edge of any material.

Screeve, *v.* To mark with a screever.

Screever, *n.* A small pointed steel tool used to mark metal, &c.; the sound produced by such marking.

Scriggle, *v.* To twist about.

Scrimp, *adj.* 1. Niggardly. 2. Scant. 3. Short.

Ex.—1. *It war nobbut a scrimpy do.* 2. *It war a varra scrimpy set oot.* 3. *Did ta run sho't o' stuff? T' sket nobbut seems scrimpy an' sho'tish at t' back.*

Scrogs, *n.* Stunted bushes or shrubs.

Scrout, *v.* To lengthen, as the days.

Scrow and Scrowing. *Vide* **Scoow.**

Scruff, *n.* Scurf, either on the skin or head; scum, hence 'the rabble.'

Scruffle, Scruffling, *v.* 1. To push, strive, to put on one side by force, as pushing through a crowd. 2. To weed turnips.

Ex.—1. *Ah'd a despert scruffle afoor Ah gat inti t' tent. Neeabody teeak na notish o' neeabody, bud iveryboddy scruffled t' best waay tha c'u'd, whahl wa war all scruffling tigither.*

Scruffle, *n.* A quarrel accompanied with a struggle, an unruly crowd.

Scruffler, *n.* A hoe for weeding turnip rows. Formerly it was fashioned from an old horse-shoe fixed to a long handle.

Scuff, *n.* The nape of the neck.

Scuff, *v.* To seize or shake by holding the neck.

Scumfish, *v.* To oppress with either heat, smoke, or foul air.

Scut or Scud, *v.* To run away.

Scutter, *v.* To run away quickly.

Scutters, *n.* Diarrhoea.

Scuttle, *n.* An open rough-made basket considerably narrowing towards the bottom, and used to gather potatoes in, &c.

Sea-fret, *n.* Fine rain, usually commencing with the rise of the tide.

Seagling, *part.* Sauntering.

Sea-tang, *n.* Sea-weed or wrack (*Laminaria digitata*).

Seddle, *n.* The wrist-bone.

Seea, Sae, Sa, Soa, Sooa, *adv.* So.

Seear, Shower, *adj.* and *adv.* Sure.

Seed. *pf. part.* of ' Saw.'

Seed-lip, *n.* The basket from which the seed corn is cast when thrown on the land.

Seeing-glass, *n.* A looking-glass.

Seeve, Seeave, *n.* The common rushes (*Juncus effusus* and *conglomeratus*).

Seet, *adj.* Considerable, many.

> Ex.—*Ther war a seet mair fooak theear 'an what Ah thowt ther'd be. He's a seet better 'an what Ah leeak'd foor.*

Segged, *v.* To be distended, swollen, accompanied by hardness.

Seggrums, *n.* Common ragwort.

Seggy, *adj.* Second.

> Ex.—*Bags Ah seggy,* i. e. ' Second turn.'

Segs, *n.* A name applied somewhat loosely to several rushes and flags.

Sen, Sin, *adv.* Since.

Servers, *n.* Females, generally two in number, who hand the cake, biscuits, and wine to mourners and others at a burial.

Set, *v.* To accompany any one either the whole or a short way on a journey.

> Ex.—*Tommy set ma ivver sae fur. He put t' meer in an' set ma all t' waay. Ah've setten her ti t' deearstan.*

Set, *v.* To arrange or settle a price.

> Ex.—*Setten at that price, he'd nivver git his awn ageean. Ah've setten it at less na what Ah aimed ti git.*

Set a day, To, *v.* To fix a definite appointment.

Set agate, *v.* To set in motion, to start work, to put into action. *Vide* **Agate.**

Set in, *adj.* Applied to dirt on the clothes or skin of long standing; commenced and likely to continue.

Set on, Setten on, *v.* To burn in the pan when cooking, especially when milk is used. *adj.* Small, stunted in growth.

Set on knees, *v.* To kneel.

Set-pot, *n.* A large iron cauldron fixed in brickwork.

Set-teea, *n.* A fight.

> Ex.—*Let 'em 'ev a set-teea, an' then tha'll git it sattled. Bob's 'ed a set-teea wi' Billy.*

Set teea, Set on, *v.* To begin or cause to begin.

> Ex.—*Thoo mun set teea at yance, an' Ah'll set Tom on ti morn at morn.*

Setter, *n.* A seton. Also *v.* To insert, &c.

Settle, *n.* *Vide* **Lang settle.**

Settled, *v.* To be decided, satisfied, contented. *Vide* **Sattle.**

    Ex.—*Ah've sattled that point lang sen. Ah's nobbut hauf sattled wi' t' waay things is gahin' on, an' Ah s'aan't feel sattled whahl Ah've been ti see foor mysen.*

Set up, *v.* To greatly delight.

Sez, *v.* Says.

    Ex.—*If sha sez 'at thoo sez what thoo sez sha sez, sha sez what's wrang.*

Shabby, *adj.* Disagreeable, unpleasant as to weather.

    Ex.—*Wa nobbut 'ed a shabby hay-tahm ti year.*

Shackle, *n.* The wrist.

Shade, *n.* A wooden or lightly constructed building, a shed.

Shades, *n.* Lace curtains.

Shaff, *n.* Sheaf.

Shaffle, *v.* To shuffle in walking, to evade by subterfuge, to be undecided.

Shaft, *n.* A handle, as of a fork, rake, hoe, axe.

Shaft, *v.* To fix a handle to anything.

Shak, *v.* To shake.

Shak-bag or **-back,** *n.* An untrustworthy fellow.

Shake, *n.* A split or crack in furniture.

Shak-fork, *n.* The fork used for lifting and shaking the thrashed straw.

Shak-ripe, *adj.* So ripe that shaking will cause the fruit to fall. Anything likely to fall either from a shake or wind.

Shanks' nag, Shanks' pony, *n.* One's own legs as a means of going from place to place.

    Ex.—*Ah s'all 'a'e ti gan on Shanks' pony,* i.e. ' I shall have to walk.'

Shap, Shaape, *v.* 1. To show good judgement. 2. To give promise.

    Ex.—1. *He shaps weel ti deea 't, diz t' lad.* 2. *It shaps ti mak a good un.*

Sharp, *v.* To insert nails or screws in a horse's shoe during frosty weather.

Sharp, *adj.* Quick, smart, intelligent.

    Ex.—1. *Noo gan ez sharp ez thoo can,* i.e. 'quick.' 2. *Noo that war a sharp trick ti deea,* i.e. ' smart.' 3. *He's a sharp lad that,* i.e. ' intelligent.'

Sharps, *n.* Flour with the admixture of bran.

Shaum, *v.* To warm the legs and knees by sitting close to the fire; in the case of females, with the skirts, &c., pulled above the knees.

Shear, *v.* To cut corn with a sickle.

Shearling, *n.* A sheep of the first year from the time of shearing.

Sheep-ked or **-keead,** *n.* A sheep-tick.

Shell, *n.* A slide. *v.* To slide.

Shelvings, *n.* Wooden frames fixed on either side of a cart to increase the size.

Shift, *v.* To remove from one house to another, to change one's clothes, to move.

Shift, *n.* A chemise.

Shifty, *adj.* Deceitful, crafty.

Shill, *n.* Scum of anything left to stand.

Shill, *v.* 1. To shell, as peas, &c. 2. To cause to curdle so that the whey and curds separate. 3. To make a noise something between a howl and a whistle.

> Ex.—3. *Mah wo'd, bud t' wind did shill roond t' chetch last neet. It's nobbut a feeal 'at trimm'ls when t' wind shills.*

Shills, *n.* Shafts of a cart.

Shine, *n.* The pupil of the eye; a disturbance, a quarrel.

Shinnop, *v.* To play at hockey.

Shinny, *n.* Hockey.

Shippy, or **Ship starnel,** *n.* The starling.

Shiv, *n.* A husk of corn.

Shive, *n.* A slice.

Shoe, *n.* The drag applied to the wagon or cart wheel when descending a hill.

Shog, *v.* To shake, to be slowly driven along with a jolting motion.

Shoggle, *v.* To shake with unsteady motion.

Shogglin, *n.* An icicle.

Sholl, *n.* Slide. *v.* To idle.

Shool, *n.* A shovel.

Shoon, *n.* Pl. of 'Shoe.'

Shoot, *v.* 1. To shout. Often implies to call without raising the voice. 2. To break into ear (of corn).

> Ex.—1. *Shoot on him, he's i' t' next room.*

Shot, Shut, *v.* To be freed from, rid, clear of.

> Ex.—*Hez ta gitten shut on him?* i. e. 'Have you got rid of him?' *Ah've gitten shot o' that claim,* i. e. 'I have got clear of that claim.'

Sho't, *adj.* Short, hasty.

> Ex.—*Saay neea mair, leeave that sho't,* i. e. 'Don't tell or explain the whole.' *Ah thowt 'at he war a bit sho't wi' ma,* i. e. 'a trifle hasty.'

Shot-ice, *n.* Sheets of ice.

Shovven-string, *n.* Boot-lace.

Shrag, *v.* To lop, to trim.

Shrift, *n.* The condition of an animal's coat after having been kept on soft food in the open during winter; on beginning to better its condition it sheds its coat.

Shudder, Shuther, *v.* To shake, to tremble.

   Ex.— *Yah crack o' thunner made all shuther ageean.*

Shut, *v.* To shoot with a gun, to put out or shoot out, to quit.

Shuttance, *n.* Riddance.

   Ex.— *Tha've gane, an' good shuttance tiv 'em,* i. e. 'They have gone, and good riddance to them.'

Shutters, *n.* A shooting party.

Shy, *adj.* Bitter and piercing (of the wind).

Sich, *adv.* So.

Side-lang, *v.* To fasten the fore and hind foot of a sheep together to prevent its straying.

Side up, *v.* To put in order, to tidy.

Side-wipe, *n.* Censure, conveyed by innuendo.

Sidling, *adj.* Fawning, servile.

   Ex.—*He awlus sidles an' maks up ti fresh fooak, bud he's a sidling sooart ov a chap.*

Sie, *n.* A fine sieve to strain milk, a spot, a stain left by anything falling in drops.

Sie, *v.* To strain milk.

Sike, *adj.* Such.

Sikan, *adj.* Such (used before a vowel).

Sike-like, *adj.* Such-like, so forth, similar.

Sile, *n.* A strainer.

Sile-brigg, *n.* The wooden frame upon which the sile rests when used.

Sill-horse, *n.* The shaft horse.

Sin, *adv.* Since.

Sink-hoal, *n.* A dug-out or other hollow place in which the drainage from a midden-stead collects, or water from the sink.

Sinter-santer, *v.* To idle, to dawdle.

Sipe, *v.* To soak through, to drain away slowly, to sink away.

Sippel, *n.* A thin slice of anything.

Sipper-sauces, *n.* Dainty dishes.

Siss, *v.* To hiss, as water dropping on the fire ; to spit (of a cat) ; to hiss like a goose.

Sitfast, *n.* The hard cyst of a wound or boil.

Sitha, pronounced *Si-tha.* Calls attention to. It is a corruption of 'seest thou.' **Sutha** originally was 'saw thou.' 'Sitha' 'and 'sutha' are equally common.

Sit up on end, To, *v.* To sit up.

   Ex.— *He's mending grandly ; whya, he's sitting up on end i' bed.*

Sizzapur, *n.* A heavy blow. As an *adj.* Large of its kind.

Skaff, Skeeaf, *n.* A rough, steep, broken bank.

Skare on, *v.* To overlap or splice.

Skate, *v.* To turn sharp round.

Skaum. *Vide* **Skime.**

Skeeal, *n.* School.

Skeel, *n.* A large wooden milk-pail.

Skeg, *n.* A glance, a cast of the eye.

Skel-beast, *n.* Wooden partitions in the cow byre.

Skell, *v.* To tilt, to raise up one end of anything, to shriek out.

Skell up, Skell ower, *v.* To upset, by the lifting of one end or side too high.

Skeller, *v.* To squint.

Skellered, *adj.* Bent by heat, as the covers of a book held too near the fire.

Skelly, *n.* A squint.

Skelp, Skelping, *n.* A thrashing. *adj.* Quickly, with great speed.

> Ex.—1. *Ah gav' him a skelp.* 2. *He did gan wiv a skelp.*

Skelp, *v.* 1. To strike with the open palm. 2. To move quickly.

> Ex.—1. *Noo Ah'll skelp tha.* 2. *He skelp'd off yam t' min.t he seed ma.*

Skelper, *n.* **Skelping,** *adj.* Huge.

Skep, *n.* A basket made from either flags or willows.

Sket, *n.* A skirt.

Skew, *v.* To twist round or about, to wrench.

> Ex.—*Sha skews hersen aboot warse 'an nowt. Skew 't off if t' weean't pull oot.*

Skid, *n.* The iron shoe used as a break.

Skid, *v.* To fix the iron shoe to the wheel.

Skill, *v.* To understand, to unravel.

> Ex.—*It's putten tigither queerly, it's a bit of a rum un ti skill. It's a queer taal, can ta skill 't ?*

Skillet, Skellit, *n.* A small pot for the fire with a long handle.

Skime, Skaum, *v.* To droop the eyelids, to scowl.

> Ex.—*Oppen thi e'es, an' deean't gan skauming aboot leyke that. Noo leeak pleasant, an' dean't skaum.*

Skimmering, *adj.* Bright, sparkling, brilliant. *v.* Shining brightly.

Skiny, *adj.* Greedy.

Skirl, *v.* To scream.

Skirtling, *n.* The lower and dressed part of a haystack.

Skirts, A pair of, *n.* Petticoat.

Skite, To take one's, *v.* To leave quickly.

> Ex.—*Ah heeard what he'd gitten ti saay, an' then Ah teeak my skite.*

Skit, *v.* To sneer at, to make fun of.

Skit, *n.* A remark, or printed matter of a personal character.

Skivvers, *n.* Wooden skewers.

Skrike, *v.* To screech.

Skrimp. *Vide* **Scrimp.**

Slabby. *Vide* **Sleazy.**

Slack, *adj.* Slow, lacking go or briskness.

    Ex.—*It war nobbut slack deed. T' market war varra slack.*

Slack, *n.* A small valley.

Slafter, *n.* Slaughter.

Slafter-hoos, *n.* Slaughter-house.

Slain, Sleean, *n.* The smut blight of wheat (*Ustilago segetum*).

Slair, *v.* To idle away one's time.

Slairy, *adj.* Untidy, sluttish.

Slaister, *v.* To do anything in an idle, slovenly manner ; to scamp work ; to flog with a whip or cane.

Slaisterer, *n.* An idle, slovenly fellow.

Slake, *v.* To lick ; to cleanse imperfectly by just wetting and rubbing, as licking a slate.

Slake, *n.* A lick, a pretence of cleaning.

    Ex.—*Ah just gav' things a slake ower.*

Slap, *v.* To spill.

    Ex.—*Thoo'll slap 't if thoo hugs it leyke that, an' if thoo diz slap 't Ah'll slap tha foor slapping 't.*

Slap, *v.* To go or do anything quickly, to be energetic.

    Ex.—*He went slap at it ez if he meant it. Ah'll run slap ower at yance.*

Slape, *adj.* Slippery ; smooth, as applied to even or polished surfaces ; untrustworthy, crafty.

Slape-feeaced, *adj.* Applied to a hypocrite.

Slape-fingered, *adj.* Butter-fingered.

Slapen, *v.* To make slippery, to open the bowels by laxatives.

Slape-scalp or **-scaup.** A hypocrite.

Slape-shod, *adj.* Shoes, especially of horses, are said to be 'slape-shod' when much worn and smooth.

    Ex.—*Is ta slape-shod? Neea, Ah've just gitten sharp'd.*

Slape-t'unged, *adj.* Plausible.

Slappy, *adj.* Sloppy, puddly, wet.

Slaps, *n.* Slops.

Slap-stone or **-steean,** *n.* The kitchen sink.

Slap up, *v.* To eat or drink in a hurry.

Slap-up, *adj.* First-class, exceedingly good.

    Ex.—*He's gitten a slap-up t'on-oot. Noo that's a slap-upper if ya leyke.*

Slathery, *adj.* Continued, as applied to wet weather ; puddly, of the roads. The word as used often embodies both ideas.

Slating, *n.* Scolding.

    Ex.—*Ah gat sike a slating foor brecking t' winder.*

Slattery, *adj.* Slovenly.

Slaup, *v.* To eat and drink with the mouth too full.

Slaverment, *n.* Insincerity, fawning, hypocrisy.

Sleave, *v.* To twist. To 'sleave' a lass is to put one's arm round her waist.

Sleaved, *part.* Twisted.

Sleazy, *adj.* Badly made, slight, unsubstantial.

Sleck, *v.* To quench one's thirst, to quench fire by pouring water on it, to remove the caustic element from lime.

Sleck, *n.* Drink.

> Ex.—*That's all reet foor them 'at can deea wi' 't, bud Ah leyke a sup o' beer foor a sleck.*

Sled, *n.* A sledge.

Slem, *adj.* Bad, applied to work put together badly.

Slem, *v.* To do work imperfectly, to slur over, to hide work by an outer covering. Its usage is a trifle loose.

> Ex.—*Ah slemm'd it ower wi' pent.*

Slew, *v.* To swerve, to turn or twist round. In the passive, to be intoxicated.

Slidder } *v.* 1. To slide. 2. To disappear unobserved.
Slither }

> Ex.—1. *He set hissel on t' top ov a larl bit of a sled, an' went slithering doon t' hill leyke all that.*

Sliddery } *adj.* Slippery.
Slithery }

Slinky, *adj.* Inclined to act evasively.

Slip, *v.* 1. To forget. 2. To go, to come.

> Ex.—1. *It slipt my mahnd ez cleean ez nowt.* 2. *Slip ower ti Bob an' tell him ti slip ower ti me,* i. e. 'Go to Robert's and tell him to come to me.'

Slip, *n.* A pinafore.

Slipe, *v.* To strip off an outer covering, as bark, with a rapid action.

Slirt, *v.* To squirt water.

Sloke, *n.* Slime on the surface of stagnant water.

Slope, *v.* To dishonestly evade payment, to defraud; to abscond, leaving one's debts unpaid.

Slosh, *n.* Melted snow or mud.

Sloshy, *adj.* Applied to a condition of general thaw.

Slot, *n.* A slit in a garment for a tape to be run through.

Slot, *v.* To slam.

> Ex.—*Ah sed nowt, bud just slotted t' deear iv his feeace.*

Slough, Sluff, *n.* The outer skin, especially of fruit, as the gooseberry.

Slowdy, *adj.* Flabby, soft; applied to fish out of condition and season.

Sluddery, Sluthery, *adj.* Applied to melted snow and mud.

Slummer, *v.* To sleep almost in a comatose state.

Slush. *Vide* **Slosh.**

Slutherment, *n.* Any slimy, viscid matter.

Sluthery, *adj.* .Having to the touch a feeling of slime or viscid matter.

Sly-cakes, *n.* Ordinary looking cakes, but filled with fruits.

Smally, *adj.* Puny, thin, undergrown.

Smatch, *n.* A savour, a trifle, a small portion.

Smeark, *v.* To half smile.

Smere, *n.* The membrane covering the nostrils of a foal at birth.

Smiddy, *n.* A blacksmith's shop.

Smiddy-oom, *n.* The sweepings of a blacksmith's bench and floor.

Smit, *n.* Infection.

Smit, Smitch, *n.* Fine particles of soot which fall from the smoke of the chimney.

Smitting, *adj.* Infectious.

Smittle, *v.* To infect.

Smock, *n.* A chemise.

Smoor, Smurr, *v.* To smother, suffocate.

Smoot, *v.* To partially hide the face.

Smooth, *v.* To iron clothes.

Smooth-feeaoed, *adj.* Bashful.

Smoot-hoal, Smoot-hole, *n.* A hole, varying in size, in a hedge or wall; e. g. a rabbit smoot, a sheep smoot.

Smoot-steean, *n.* A slab or stone used to stop a smoot-hole.

Smudge, *v.* To smear; to emit smoke, but without any flames visible.

Snaffling, *v.* To speak through the nose.

Snag, *v.* To cut the branches from felled trees, to top and tail turnips.

Snahl, *n.* Snail.

Snake-steean, *n.* An ammonite.

Snarly, *adj.* Biting, chilling (of the wind).

Snavvie. *Vide* **Snaffling.**

Sneb, *v.* To rebuke.

Sneck, *n.* The fastening of a gate or door.

Sneck, *v.* To fasten, to latch.

   Ex.—*Noo think on an' sneck all t' yats.*

Sneeap, *v.* To check, to put down.

   Ex.—*Ya caan't sneeap 'em, an' they weean't be snebbed, an' neeabody's gitten neea saay ower 'em at all, an' if yan diz call 'em, tha deea nowt bud snifter, snitter, an' gen at yan.*

Snicker. *Vide* **Snitter.**

Snickle, *v.* A slip-noose of wire used as a snare.

Snifter, *n.* A sniff, a smell of short duration.

   Ex.—*Noo it's varra neyce, just tak a snifter on 't.*

Snifter, *v.* To snuff up.

    Ex.—*Wipe thi snoot; deean't snifter.*

Snig, *v.* To drag timber from the wood.

Snig-cut, *n.* A short cut, a by-path.

Sniggle, *v.* To laugh behind one's back, to laugh derisively.

Snite, *v.* To blow the nose, not necessarily with a handkerchief.

Snitter, *v.* To sneer, to giggle with ill-nature and derisively.

    Ex.—*Ah'll gi'e tha summut ti snitter at if thoo dizn't shift thisen.*

Snook-smarls, *n.* The knotty entanglements of thread, string, &c.

Snod, *adj.* Smooth, neat-looking, trim.

Snoke, *v.* To smell with a deep inspiration.

Snow-flag, *n.* A snow-flake.

Snubbits, *n.* The projecting pieces of wood at the end of a cart, on which it rests when tilted up.

Snubby, *adj.* Knotted (of wood).

Snudge, Snuggle, Snowzel, *v.* To lie close together.

Soa. *Vide* **Seea.**

Soamy, *adj.* Close, oppressive (of the weather).

Sob, *v.* To sigh as the wind does on the approach of calmer weather.

Sock, *n.* The ploughshare.

Sod, *n.* An opprobrious epithet = Ass, fool.

Sodden, *v.* To soften by soaking in water.

Sods, *n.* 1. Square parings of grass and earth. 2. A lump of earth and grass.

    Ex.—1. *Ah'll hev hauf o' t' garden laid wi' sods.* 2. *Ah'll chuck a sod at tha.*

Soft, *adj.* 1. Inclined to wet weather. 2. Silly, half-witted.

    Ex.—1. *Ah's feeard wa's gahin'. ti 'ev a softish back-end.* 2. *Poor bairn! is sha a larl bit soft?*

Somerset, *n.* Somersault.

Sooa. *Vide* **Seea.**

Sooart, *n.* Sort, kind, quality.

Soond, *v.* To faint, to sound. Also *n.*

Soonest, *adj.* Quickest, nearest, shortest.

    Ex.—*Ah's gan by t' foot brigg; it's seeanest road. It'll be t' seeanest deean i' that waay.*

Sore. *Vide* **Sair.**

So so = That will do, enough, cease.

Soss, *v.* and *n.* To fall with force into the water; to lap water, as a dog.

Sough, Soo, *v.* To sob, to sigh (of the wind).

Soup, *v.* To soak, to drench with water.

    Ex.—*Ah's fairly souped ti t' skin.*

Sour-dooken, *n.* The wild sorrel (*Rumex acetosa*).

Sowl, *v.* To give a thorough rinsing in water, to chastise.

G g

Sowse, *v.* 1. To cause to be wet all over. 2. To throw into water.
> Ex.—1. *He sowsed a bucket o' mucky watter cleean ower ma.* 2. *Ah sowsed t' beggar i' t' beck.*

Spade- or **Speead-graft,** *n.* A spade depth.

Spane, Speean, *v.* To wean.

Spang. *Vide* **Spanker.**

Spank, *v.* To strike with the open hand.

Spanker, *n.* One who takes long strides; large of its kind; hence **Spang,** *n.* A leap.

Spanking, *adj.* Tall and broad, rapid.

Span-new, *adj.* Quite new.

Sparrow-feathers, *n.* The chaff of oats is so called when used for beds in the place of feathers.

Spattle, *n.* Spittle.

Speak, *v.* Even yet the usage in an active sense of 'to address' is often heard in the dales.
> Ex.—*Ah seed him, bud wa didn't speeak yan anuther. What didn't ta speeak her foor?*

Speeak, Spooak, *n.* The spoke of a wheel.

Speean, *n.* A spoon.

Spelk, *n.* A long thin slip of wood, a splint.

Spell, *n.* A splinter of wood, the cross-bar of a ladder; a spill, either of wood or paper; a turn at work, not necessarily of long duration; the trap upon which the ball rests in the game of spell and knorr.

Spic an' span, *adv.* New, clean, tidy; lit. new, from 'spike to span' of a knight's lance. Another form is 'Bran spander new.'
> Ex.—*Es thoo's gahin' ti see t' lass foor t' fo'st tahm, thoo mun mak thisen leeak es spic an' span es a new-maad pin. Mr. Henry war gitten up spic an' span.*

Spice, *n.* Raisins, currants, &c.

Spice-bread, *n.* A cheaper form of plum-cake.

Spice-cake or **-keeak,** *n.* Plum-cake.

Spink, *n.* The chaffinch, often named **Bull-spink.**

Spinner, *n.* A spider's web. Also **Spinner-web.** The latter, however, is generally confined to the gossamer threads so commonly found floating in the air on a summer's evening.

Spit, *n.* A long narrow spade used for draining.

Spittle, *n.* A small spade.

Splatter, *v.* To splash about, to make splashes.

Splatter-dash, *n.* and *v.* 1. A showing-off. 2. Commotion. 3. To brag, to make a foolish display of wealth.
> Ex.—1. *Ah caan't bahd sike splatter-dash gahins on. It's nowt bud a lot o' splatter-dash.* 2. *Ah, what a splatter-dash ther is i' t' pleeace.*

Splatterer, *n.* One who splashes.

Splauder, *v.* 1. To sprawl, to spread out one's limbs. 2. To display, to be vulgarly ostentatious. Hence **Splaudered, Splauderment.**

> Ex.—1. *Hoo yon lass diz splauder her feet oot. Talk aboot a splauder o' stuff, ther war mair ti eat na wa c'u'd 'a'e mannish'd if wa'd 'ed tweea goes apiece.*

Splaudy, *adj.* Wide-spreading.

Splaws, *n.* Pen-nibs.

Splet, Split, *v.* To tell of one's doings, to break confidence.

Splutter, *n.* Bustle, excitement, nervousness.

> Ex.—*Deean't git i' sike a splutter, wa've endless o' tahm. Didn't sha git intiv a splutter when sha heeard what Jin Ann 'ed sed aboot her!*

Sponge, *n.* Leaven, a portion of leavened dough saved from each baking to raise the next week's kneading with.

Sponge, *v.* To swell and froth as a dead body.

Spool, *n.* The wooden reel upon which thread is wound.

Spout, *n.* A small waterfall.

Spraggy, *adj.* Thin, bony, having many sharp projections.

Spraints, *n.* Otter's dung.

Spreead, *v.* Spread.

Spreead, *n.* Abundance of food and of extra quality.

> Ex.—*Ah nivver war at sikan a spreead afoor, ther war ommaist ivverything ya c'u'd think on* (imagine).

Sprent, Sprint, *v.* To sprinkle, to spurt, to cause water to fly about by compression or striking the surface sharply.

> Ex.—*Mary Jin's slapt t' slap-hoal wiv her battledooar, an' 's sprented ma all ower wi' blash an' sluthery muckment.*

Sprent, *n.* A spot or mark left by a splash.

Spring, *v.* 'To spring' is applied to cows when near calving.

Sprunt, *n.* 1. Short, stiff, lively. 2. A steep road, a hill.

> Ex.—1. *Ya'll mannish ti trunn'l yersen t' best hauf o' t' waay, bud efter that ya'll finnd it a bit sprunt* (said to a cyclist).

Spurrings, *n.* The banns.

Squab, *n.* A rude long settle with cushions, usually with only one arm.

Square up, To, *v.* To settle an account or dispute.

Squary, *adj.* Compact, both as to size and shape.

> Ex.—*It's a neyce squary kitchen. It's just sich an* (sikan) *a squary bit ez Ah want.*

Stack-bar, *n.* A hurdle.

Stack-garth, Stagg'ath, *n.* The stack-yard.

Stack-prod, *n.* A stick used in thatching, being pointed and thrust into the stack. The string is wound round it in such a way, from prod to prod, as to hold the *thack-bands* secure.

Staddle, *n.* The foundation of cross-beams upon which a stack is built, the stain left after washing out the producing cause.

Staddling, *n.* A foundation of brushwood, brackens, &c., to build the stack upon.

Stag, *n.* A gelding over a year old.

Stagnated, *part.* Much bewildered, astonished.

> Ex.—*T' whoal lot on uz wur stagnated.*

Staith, *n.* and *v.* An embankment; to protect land from overflowing of water by an embankment.

Staithe, Steeath; Steers, *n.* A landing-place.

Stakker, *v.* To stagger.

Stall, *v.* To eat until satiated, to tire out, to weary.

Stan', Stand, *v.* 1. To stand. 2. To be responsible for; to agree to maintain, uphold. 3. To stop, as a clock. 4. Remains. 5. Holds.

> Ex.—2. *Ah'll stand tiv all he diz. Thoo said thoo wad, an' thoo'll 'a'e ti stan' ti 't noo.* 4. *That'll stand good*, i. e. 'That is settled.' 5. *It stands a good chance ti win.*

Stand again, *v.* To withstand, oppose.

> Ex.—*Thoo maun't aim ti stan' agaan what's deean.*

Stand for, *v.* To act as sponsor.

Standing, *n.* The stall for a horse or cow.

Stand-ups, *n.* God-parents.

Stane, Steean, *n.* A stone.

Stang, *n.* A pole or stake.

Stang, To ride the. *Vide* chapter on 'Customs.'

Stape, *v.* To slope, to incline.

Stapple, *n.* A staple.

Stark, *adj.* Stiff, unyielding, powerful. The Danish word *stærk* means being strong, possessing strength. Hence 'Stark mad' is quite correct.

> Ex.—*Thoo's starched t' things whahl they're ez stark ez a booard.* A very common redundancy is *Stiff stark steean deead.*

Starken, *v.* To become stiff. *adv.* **Starkly.**

Star-slubber or **-blubber**, *n.* Frog-spawn.

Start, *n.* Work, employment.

> Ex.—*He sez 'at he'll gi'e tha a start. Ah've gitten a start at a pund a week.*

Start, *v.* 1. To begin. 2. To set going.

> Ex.—1. *Ah'll start wi' t' job ti morn. He started off a gay bit sen. Tha've started a pianner, 'ez t' fooak next doour.* 2. *Ah'll start it fur tha.*

Starvatious, *adj.* Cold, very chilly.

> Ex.—*No'thallerton station's t' maist starvatious spot onny-wheear.*

Starve, *v.* In the passive voice, to suffer from cold ; in the active voice, to cause hunger.

Staup, *v.* To walk about clumsily.

Ex.—*Sha staups aboot that okkad whahl sha'll tumm'l ower her shadder sum daay.*

Stead, Steead, *n.* Common as a suffix, denoting the exact place, as home-stead, yat-stead, middin-stead, deear- or dooar-steead, &c.

Steck, *v.* To close and fasten a door or gate.

Stee, Stey, Stegh, *n.* A ladder, a style with steps like a ladder.

Steead, *pp.* Stood.

Steeal, *n.* Stool.

Steean, *n.* Stone.

Steer, *n.* An ox under two years.

Steer-tree, *n.* The left handle of a plough.

Steg, *n.* A gander, a fool.

Stegly, *adj.* 1. Shaky. 2. Unsymmetrical, unsuitable.

Ex.—2. *It's a gret stegly hoos* (said of Faucet Vicarage).

Stell, *n.* An open ditch varying in width and depth.

Stent, *v.* To abstain, to deny oneself.

Step, *n.* An undefined distance.

Ex.—*Ah went a good step wiv him.*

Step, A langish = Quite a long way off.

Steven, *v.* To bawl out, to shout at the top of the voice ; to howl and bluster, as the wind. NOTE.—Rarely heard now.

Stick, *v.* To kill an animal by stabbing, as a butcher.

Stickle, *v.* To hesitate, to object.

Stickle-haired }
Stickly } *adj.* Bristly.

Stickler, *n.* A difficulty, a poser.

Sticks, *n.* Furniture, belongings.

Stick up, To, *v.* To boldly maintain one's right.

Stiddy, *n.* An anvil.

Stiddy, *v.* To be steady, attentive to business.

Stife, Stify, *adj.* Close, foul, as to air.

Stiff, *adj.* 1. Steep, difficult. 2. Firm, obstinate.

Ex.—1. *Ah'll tell ya what, it's a stiffish clim'. Ah've gitten a stiff job this tahm.*

Stifler, *n.* A bad odour ; a heavy blow, such as to cause insensibility.

Stint. *Vide* Stent.

Stir on, Plenty to = Rich, well-to-do.

Ex.—*He's gi'en ten pund, bud then he's gitten plenty ti stir on.*

Stirk, *n.* A heifer.

Stirrings, *n.* An unusual excitement, gaiety.

Ex.—*Ya'll be 'eving sthraange stirrings when t' young chap cums at age.*

Stitch, *n.* A sharp pain in the side.

Stithe, *v.* To taint, to give a taste of smoke, &c.

Ex.—*What 'a'e ya putten on t' fire? it's stithed all 'at's i' yewn thruff t' crack i' t' boddum.*

Stob, *n.* Usually a short pointed stick or stake; the stump of a tree, a small splinter.

Stob, *v.* To mark out land with short stakes, to dig up a fence, to strengthen with stobs.

Stob off, *v.* To lop off branches of a tree or the top half of a hedge.

Stock, *n.* A beam of wood, generally applied to the frame of a bedstead, e. g. bed-stock.

Stock, *adv.* Quite, absolutely.

Ex.—*He steead stock still.*

Stodge, *v.* To satiate with over-eating; to make anything too thick, as the admixture of too much meal with water.

Ex.—*Ah caan't eat it, it's nowt bud stodge.*

Stone-naked, *adj.* Absolutely naked.

Stonies, *n.* Common stone taws.

Stooden, *pp.* of 'Stand,' but the usage is somewhat peculiar.

Ex.—*Things wad 'a'e stooden different if t' bobby 'ed catched him,* i. e. been. *Ah've stooden Bedale market ivver sen Ah wur a larl nipper,* i. e. attended.

Stook, *n.* Twelve sheaves of corn set up against each other in the harvest field.

Stook, *v.* To set up stooks, and bind the same.

Stooth, *v.* To apply plaster on laths instead of to the wall itself, or to make in a room a false wall of battens, laths, and plaster.

Stor, Sturr, *v.* and *n.* To stir; a stir, excitement.

Storm, *n.* A continuance of frost and snow, with or without wind.

Stortioners, *n.* The common nasturtium.

Stot, *n.* A young ox.

Stoup, *n.* A measure of ale.

Stour, *v.* To blow in clouds, whether of dust, rain, hail, or snow; also the action of smoke as it comes from a chimney on fire.

Stour, *n.* Dust, &c.

Stour, Stower, *n.* A stake, the middle bars of a cattle rack, the cross-bars of a ladder.

Stout, *adj.* Convalescent, healthy looking.

Ex.—*Sha leeaks weel an' stoot agaan.*

Stoven, *n.* The old stump of a tree not yet quite dead.

Stowp, *n.* An upright post.

Stra, Streah, *n.* Straw.

Stracklin', *n.* A worthless fellow, a waster.

Straighten, *v.* Often followed by 'up.' To put in order, to punish, to settle accounts.

> Ex.—*Ah mun straighten things up a bit afoor t' parson's missus drops in. If thoo dizn't drop it, Ah'll straighten thi jacket foor tha. When thoo's deean, fetch thi bill in, an' wa'll straighten up.*

Strand, *n.* The beach.

Strapping, *adj.* Strong, tall, big.

Strather, *n.* Haste, excitement.

Streah. *Vide* **Stra.**

Streamers, *n.* Minnows during spawning.

Streean, Strain, *n.* Descent, breed.

Streean, *v.* To do one's utmost.

Strength, Stren'th, *n.* 1. Security. 2. Belief.

> Ex.—1. *He 'ezn't t' stren'th o' fifty pund,* i. e. 'Could not find security for that sum.' 2. *On t' stren'th o' what thoo sez,* i. e. 'Acting on the belief,' &c.

Strickle, *n.* The stone or other contrivance used to sharpen a scythe.

Stride-whallops, *n.* A lanky, long-legged lass. An older word, now fallen into disuse, was **Stridykirk.**

Stridlings, *adv.* Astride.

Strike, *v.* To kick with the hind leg (of a horse), to fly-blow meat, to balance an account, to make a line with string and chalk.

Strik'-stick, *n.* The stick used to scrape off the superfluous corn when measuring.

String-halt, *n.* A twitching of the hind leg of a horse.

Strip, *v.* To drain the udder dry.

Stritch-stick, *n.* The bar which keeps the trace chains apart. Also **Stretcher.**

Stroke, Stroak, *n.* A single bat, a commencement.

> Ex.—*Ah 'evn't deean a stroak o' wark ti-daay.*

Strong, *adj.* 1. Hard, severe. 2. Heavy, bulky. 3. Stiff, clayey.

> Ex.—1. *Wa s' 'ev a strangish frost efter this.* 2. *It's a strangish leead foor t' au'd meer.* 3. *T' land's varra strong hereaboots.*

Strother. *Vide* **Strather.**

Strucken, *pp.* of 'Strike.'

Strunt, *n.* The tail.

Strunt, *v.* To cut the tail short.

Struts, *n.* The posts used in the roof-frame of a house.

Stuck up, *adj.* Proud.

Stuff, *n.* Of very loose application, e. g. material, furniture, chattels, produce, &c.

> Ex.—*Thoo's gitten stuff eneeaf ti mak tweea coats. Thoo's gitten stuff i' t' chaamer eneeaf foor tweea rooms. Thoo's gitten mair stuff on t' land na ivver Tommy 'ed.*

Stunning, *adj.* First-class.

Stunt, *adj.* Short, stumpy; stiff, unyielding.

Stunt, *adv.* and *n.* Sulky, obstinate.

    Ex.—*Tak neea notish, he taks t' stunt at nowt.*

Sturdy, Stoddy, *n.* A disease, i. e. hydatids in the brain.

Stut, *v.* To stutter.

S'u'd, *v.* Should.

Summat, *n.* Something.

Summer-bink, *n.* A seat shaded by leaves in summer-time.

Summer-oolt, *n.* Undulating vapour near the ground.

Sump, *n.* A bog or marsh.

Sumpy, *adj.* Wet, boggy.

Sunder, *v.* To dry in the sun.

Sundown, *n.* Sunset.

Sup, *n.* A small quantity of any liquid.

    Ex.—*Ah wants a sup o' milk. It leeaks nowt bud leyke a sup o' wet.*

Sup, *v.* To drink either by sips or with a spoon.

Sup off, *v.* To drain one's glass.

Surance, *n.* Surety.

    Ex.—*Bud what tha 'a'e gi'en, tha 'ez surance for 't?*

Surfeit o' cold, *n.* A very severe cold.

Swab, *n.* A drunken sot.

Swad, *n.* A peascod, and the like.

Swag, *v.* 1. To swing about. 2. To lean towards.

    Ex.—2. *Ya'll 'a'e ti put summat at yon sahd ti balance 't, it swags gertly ti this sahd.*

Swage, *v.* To soften, to quiet down.

Swaimish, *adj.* Bashful.

Swale, Sweeal, *v.* 1. To waste by burning unevenly, as a candle in a draught. 2. To squander.

    Ex.—1. *Shut t' doour, t' cann'l's sweealing.* 2. *Yon chap 'ud sweeal a ransom awaay.*

Swang, *n.* A boggy stretch of land.

Swangy, *adj.* Boggy.

Swanky, Swanking, *adj.* Great of its kind.

Swap, *v.* To exchange.

Swape, *n.* An oar of peculiar shape, a pump handle.

Swappy, *adj.* Plump.

Swarm, *v.* To climb by clasping a pole or tree with both arms, knees, and legs.

Swart, *adj.* Black looking.

Swarth, Swa'th, *n.* The outer skin, rind; the quality and quantity of grass upon the land.

Swarve, *v.* To swerve.

Swash, *v.* To dash about in waves.

Swatch, *n.* Fit, size, the precise thing required.

Ex.—*This yan'll deea, it's just mah swatch. It's just t'
swatch foor ma.* NOTE.—Swatch was originally a wooden
tally or other means by which any person might prove
their claim to cloth which had been left to dye—cloth, by-
the-way, which was home-spun.

Swathe, *n.* The full reach of the scythe when cutting.

Swathe-bauk, *n.* The grass left uncut by the blade at the end
of its sweep.

Swatter, *v.* 1. To play and splash with water. 2. To squander.
Ex.—1. *Tho'll sprent thisen all ower, swattering on i' that
waay.* 2. *He'll swatter t' bit o' brass awaay.*

Swelt, *v.* To faint, to swoon; to overpower, as with heat.

Swelter, *v.* To burn, to bear or suffer heat, to perspire pro-
fusely.

Swidden, *n.* Any place on a moor which has been cleared by
burning.

Swidden, Swithen, *v.* To singe or burn off superficially.

Swidge, *v.* To tingle, burn (of inflammation).
Ex.—*It war nobbut a bleb at t' fu'st, bud it swidged an'
throbbed an' then started ti kittle, an' Ah think that wur
t' warst ov all.*

Swig, *v.* To drink at one draught.

Swill, *n.* Pigmeat.

Swill, *v.* To cleanse by throwing water out of a pail, as on
flags, &c.

Swingle-tree, *n.* *Vide* **Stritch-stick.**

Swip, *n.* A marrow, the image of.
Ex.—*He's fair t' swip ov t' au'd chap.*

Swipple, *n.* That part of a flail which beats out the corn.

Swirrel, *n.* Squirrel.

Switch, *v.* To throw, to dash.
Ex.—*Sha teeak t' paail o' mucky watter, an' switched t' lot
all ower ma.*

Switched, *adj.* Drunk.

Switcher, *n.* Good, better than ordinary.

Switching, *adj.* Grand, noted, extensive.

Swither, *v.* 1. To tingle and smart with pain. 2. To dis-
sipate by slow degrees, a little at a time.
Ex.—2. *If he gans on i' that road, he'll swither all t' brass
he hez awaay.*

Swittle, *n.* A heated iron rod used to bore holes in wood.

Swizzen, *v.* To singe. *Vide* **Swidden.**
Ex.—*It'll swizzen t' clothes, t' iron's ti hot.*

Sword-dancers. *Vide* chapter on 'Customs.'

Syke, *n.* A small streamlet, a gutter, a small rill draining from
a boggy place.

T.

'T, *pron.* It.

T', *def. art.* The.

Ta, *per. pron.* Thou, you.

Taal, *v.* To settle, to accommodate oneself to a new condition of habits, &c.

Taoket, *n.* A tack.

Ta'en, Takken, *pp.* of 'Take.'

Ta'en agaan or **ageean,** *v.* To take a dislike to.

    Ex.—*Ah've ta'en agaan her, an' Ah s' nivver tak up wiv her na mair.*

Ta'en tiv, *v.* To take to, to like.

Tag, *n.* A twist of long grass or rushes, a wisp.

Tag, *v.* To flog with a tag.

Tahm, *n.* 1. Time. 2. Life.

    Ex.—2. *Ah've seen a vast i' mah tahm.*

Tahm by ohanoe, *adv.* Occasionally.

Taistrel, *n.* A peevish character.

Tak, *n.* 1. A flavour somewhat pronounced. 2. Land which has been taken at a fixed rent. 3. Piecework.

    Ex.—2. *If he's letten tha 't at nowt na mair 'an what thoo sez, it's a varra cheeap tak.* 3. Q. *Hes ta ta'en 'em byv t' yackker or by t' week?* A. *Neea, he wadn't be on byv t' week, seea Ah've ta'en 'em byv t' tak this go.*

Tak, *v.* 1. To take. 2. To rise to bite, as a fish. 3. To attract. 4. To gain one's esteem or regard.

    Ex.—2. *Are tha takkin' onny?* i.e. biting. 3. *Wa mun 'ev a bisittle race, hooivver; tha tak t' best ov owt noo.* 4. *Ah tak tiv him at yance,* i.e. 'He gained my esteem at once.'

Tak ho'd, *v.* To undertake to do, or fill a position.

    Ex.—*Ah wanted him ti preeach i' t' pleeace o' Tommy, bud he wadn't be on, he's shy o' takkin ho'd.*

Tak in, To, *v.* 1. To understand. 2. To deceive.

    Ex.—1. *Gan on, Ah's takkin 't all in.* 2. *Noo if thoo taks ma in, Ah'll traade wi' tha na mair.*

Takken ti heart=Giving way to any affliction.

Takkin, *n.* 1. The actual result of labour. 2. A condition, a bad temper.

    Ex.—1. *Thoo's gitten a rare takkin; wheear did ta catch 'em?* 2. *Sha's iv a despert ill takkin.*

Tak off, *v.* 1. To make fun of, to ridicule, to imitate, mimic. 2. To leave without due notice.

    Ex.—2. *He niver sed nowt, bud just teeak off.*

Tak on, *v.* 1. To retake. 2. To re-engage. 3. To get excited.

    Ex.—1. *Ah've ta'en t' farm on agaan.* 2. *He ga' ma t' sack, bud he's ta'en ma on agaan.* 3. *He did tak on when he gat ti knaw.*

Tak on wi', *v.* To engage oneself to another.

Tak tent, *v.* To engage oneself to look after, e. g. as a boy keeping crows off the land.

Tak t' hig, To, *v.* To take offence.

Takt, *adj.* Acid, sharp to the taste.

Ex.—*It's a lahtle bit ower takt ti mah liking.*

Tak up, *v.* 1. To become fair. 2. To reform one's character.

Ex.—1. *If 't dizn't tak up seean, t' hay'll be nut wo'th leading.* 2. *If he'll nobbut drop drinking an' tak up, ther's a seet o' good iv him.*

Tak up wi', *v.* 1. To make friends with another. 2. To become engaged to.

Ex.—1. *He's neean ower neyce whaw he gans wi', he'll tak up wi' onny lass.*

Tale, *n.* The number agreed upon.

Ex.—*Ther dizn't leeak owt leyke a full tale, Ah s'all coont 'em afoor Ah paay tha.*

Talk, *n.* Report, gossip.

Taller-cake, *n.* Any cake made with the fat from about the kidney of a sheep or beast.

Taller-craps. *Vide* **Craps.**

T' ane, T' yan = The one of two or more followed or replied to by **T' other** or **T'ither.**

Ex.—*Tha wur all feighting t' ane amang t' ither.*

Tang, *n.* The tongue of a buckle.

Tangle, *n.* An entanglement, the long fibre of a root, sea-wrack.

Tangle, *v.* To entangle.

Tangly, *adj.* Slatternly, slovenly. Applied to a slut.

Tantle, *v.* 1. To waste time. 2. To play on with.

Ex.—1. *Noo set ti wark ez if thoo meant it, an' deean't tantle on leyke that.*

Tappy-lappy, *adv.* Anyhow.

Tatchy, *adj.* Sticky, viscous, adhesive.

Tattling, *n.* The necessary tackle or equipment of things for carrying out any purpose.

Ex.—*He hezn't gitten onny tattling foor a job o' yon size,* i. e. neither ladders, ropes, nor scaffolding poles.

Taum, *n.* The twisted hair to which the fish-hook is attached.

Taum ower, To, *v.* To faint.

Taws, *n.* Boys' marbles.

Team, Teem, *v.* and *n.* 1. To pour from any vessel. 2. To rain heavily. 3. To empty.

Ex.—1. *Team all t' cau'd tea oot.* 2. *It teem'd doon,* i. e. of rain. 3. *Teeam t' coals oot at t' backside.*

Tea-party, *n.* A tea meeting given in the village school or barn to raise money for some object.

Teave. *Vide* **Tew**.

Teea, *prep.* To. *Vide* **Till**.

Teeagle, *v.* To raise timber from the ground by means of a tripod of strong poles and a pulley.

Teeak, *v.* Took.

Teeals, *n.* Tools.

Tell, *v.* 1. To recognize. 2. To know. 3. To number, to reckon up, to judge.

> Ex.—1. *Ah c'u'd tell wheea 't wur ez seean ez Ah clap't mah een on ya.* 2. *'Twur good eneeaf ti tell what he wur gahin' ti saay.* 3. *Gan ti t' gaate an' tell t' sheep ez tha cum thruff.*

Telly-pye-tit, or **Tell-pyet,** *n.* A tale-bearer.

Tempesty, *adj.* Thunderous, blustery, or having the appearance of stormy weather.

Teng, *v.* To sting.

Tenged, *pp.* Stung.

Tengs, *n.* Tongs.

Tent, *n.* Attention, care.

> Ex.—*Tak tent o' what he saays, noo.*

Tent, *v.* To look after, to keep watch over.

> Ex.—*Yan's tenting craws fur Billy, an' t' other's tenting wur awn coos i' t' lonnin'.*

Tetchy, *adj.* Cross, peevish.

Teufit, Teeafit, Tewit, *n.* The pewit, plover, or lapwing (*Vanellus cristatus*).

Teugh, Teeaf, *adj.* Tough.

Tew, *v.* 1. To toil. 2. To tire and grow weary. 3. To tire by restlessness. 4. To crumple and crease by rough or unskilful handling.

> Ex.—1. *Ah've tewed all t' daay,* i.e. 'toiled.' 2. *Ah've gitten 't deean, bud it's sadly tewed ma.* 3. *Sha's tired noo, bud then sha's tewed on all t' neet.* 4. *Put 'em doon, thoo's tewing 'em, whahl tha weean't be fit ti put on.*

Tha, *per. pron.* They, thou, and thee.

Thabble, *n.* The plug which fits the hole in the milk trough.

Thack, Theeak, Theeaking, *n.* Thatch.

Thack, Theeak, Theeaking, *v.* To thatch.

Thacker, Theeaker, *n.* A thatcher.

Thack-bands, Theeak-bands, Theeaking-bands, *n.* Bands of straw for thatching.

Thack-prods, Theeak-prods, Theeaking-prods. *Vide* **Stack-prod**.

Thah, *per. pron.* Thy.

Tharf, Tharfish, *adj.* **Tharfly,** *adv.* Backward, reluctant, shy, bashful, unwilling.

Thauvel, Thivel, *n.* A stick used for stirring or pushing down the contents of a pan likely to boil over.

Thee, *n.* Thigh.

Theet, *adj.* Water-tight.

Them, *pron.* Those.

Thick, *adj.* Very friendly, intimate.

Thills, *n.* Shafts of a waggon.

Think long of, To, *v.* To be long expectant, weary of waiting.

Think on, *v.* To bear in mind, to remember.

As an example of redundancy, I heard a woman say, *Noo mahnd an' think on, an' deean't forget ti beear i' mahnd 'at thoo'ez ti fetch a pund o' treacle.*

Think up, *v.* To originate, to arrange.

Ex.—*Noo it'll 'a'e ta'en a lot o' thinking up, will a do leyke yon.*

Tho, Thoo, *per. pron.* Thou.

Thoff, *conj.* Though.

Thrave, *v.* To thrive.

Thrave, Trave, Treeav, *n.* A stook of corn, or twelve battens of straw.

Thraw. *Vide* **Throw.**

Threead, *n.* Thread.

Threeap, *n.* A contentious fellow.

Threeap, *v.* To maintain pertinaciously, to argue positively.

Threeap down, *v.* To overpower by argument.

Threeap up, *v.* To refer to bygone mistakes or misunderstandings in an unkindly manner.

Threeten. Threaten.

Three-thrums, *n.* The purring of a cat.

Thribble, *adj.* Treble.

Thriver, *n.* Healthy, strong, likely to improve.

Thro. *Vide* **Thruff.**

Throng, *adj.* 1. More than usually busy or crowded. 2. Engaged in.

Ex.—2. *T' bairn's thrang gitting its teeth.*

Throng, Thrang, *n.* Bustle, a great crowd, confusion, excitement.

Throng deed, *n.* Excitement over some event, the bustle and confusion attendant on any celebration, tea party, wedding, &c.

Thropple, *n.* The windpipe.

Thropple, *v.* To strangle.

Throstle, Throssel, *n.* The thrush.

Through, *n.* A lathe.

Through, Thruff, *prep.* At some time, at intervals.

Ex.—*Ah'll mebbe deea't thruff t' morning. It teeam'd doon thruff t' neet.*

Through or **Thruff with,** *adv.* Finished, complete. N.B. 'Through' is also pronounced 'throwgh' and 'thro.'
  Ex.—*Ah s'all be thruff wi' t job by ti morn.*
Throughly, *adv.* Completely, fully.
Through time= In time, gradually, by-and-by.
  Ex.—*Ah s'all git better through time. If t weather ho'ds thoo'll git deean through time.*
Through, To get, *v.* To dispose of.
  Ex.—*Ah've fetched t coo yam ageean, bud Ah gat thruff t sheep.*
Throvven, *pp.* To thrive.
Throw, *v.* To vomit.
Throw back, *v.* To have a relapse.
  Ex.—*He's warse ti-daay, he's gitten thrown back a lump sen last neet.*
Throw over, *v.* To turn over, to upset, to be overturned.
Thruff, Throw, *prep.* Through.
Thrumble, Thrumm'l, *v.* To examine the quality of anything by the touch or rubbing action of the finger and thumb.
Thrumm'l, *n.* A rope firmly bound round a grooved iron ring.
Thrummy, *adj.* Bulky, plump.
Thrust, *v.* To push with some force.
Thrust out, Thrussen oot, *pp.* Projecting forward, bulging, turned out.
Thumping, *adj.* Big, large of its kind.
Thunner, *n.* Thunder.
Thwack, *v.* To administer a sharp blow.
  Ex.—*Gi'e it a good thwacking wiv a hezzel stick, thaf'll fetch t' dust oot on 't.*
Thysen or **Thysel, Thisen** or **Thisel,** *pron.* Thyself or yourself.
Ti, *prep.* To.
'Tice, *v.* To allure, induce.
  Ex.—*A young widow knows hoo ti 'tice a chap.*
'Ticing, *adj.* Alluring, seductive, winning
'Tick. *Vide* **Cade.**
'Tick, *v.* To mark off goods or other items, as in an invoice, by placing a small mark against each when called.
Tiddle, *v.* To fondle, to finick.
Tiddy, *adj.* Small, puny.
Tidy-betty, *n.* A guard to prevent the ashes dirtying the hearth.
Tie, Tee, Tah, *n.* A hair band to secure the legs of a cow whilst being milked.
Tie, *n.* 1. Obligation. 2. Necessity. 3. Burden. 4. Care.
  Ex.—1. *Ah's unner neea tie tiv him.* 2. *Ther's neea tie fur thoo ti gan.* 3. *Thoo'll finnd her a despert tie, sen sha lost t' ewse ov her legs.*

Tied, Tahd, *v.* Obliged, constrained, compelled.

> Ex.—*If sha's leyke ti dee, Ah s' be tied ti gan. He'll be tied ti drop a bit ower t' meer. Ak's nut tied ti deea 't acoz thoo tells ma.*

Tied, It's = It must, no doubt exists.

> Ex.—*It's tied ti be ez he sez. It's tied ti tumm'l doon wi' t' fo'st gust o' wind.*

Tiffany, *n.* Strong, fine-meshed gauze.

Tift, *n.* A quarrel, generally of words only.

Tift, *v.* To contend.

Tig, *n.* A light tap.

> Ex.—*Ah didn't hit, Ah nobbut tigg'd him.*

Tiggings, *n.* A game played by children, the object being to tap each other; the one so touched must then chase the rest until he or she gently taps some other.

Tightish, *adv.* and *adj.* 1. Somewhat fast or close-fitting. 2. Lacking means. 3. Difficult.

> Ex.—1. *It's varra well putten tigither, bud a larl bit tightish i' t' lid.* 2. *Ah caan't len' tha ten pund, Ak's a bit tightish held mysel just noo.* 3. *It's a tightish fix thoo's gitten thisen intul.*

Till, Tull, Ti, *prep.* To. **Tiv** before a vowel.

Tim'ered, Weell, *adj.* Well built.

Tim'er-toed, *adj.* A man wearing a wooden leg is said to be timber-toed.

Timersome, *adj.* Nervous, apprehensive of danger.

Ti morn, *n.* To-morrow.

Ti morn at morn = To-morrow in the morning. Hence **Ti morn at neean,** 'noon'; **Ti morn at neet,** 'night.'

Tinkler, *n.* A tinker.

Tip-trap, *n.* An arrangement which closes the door, owing to the weight of the animal releasing a lever as it passes in.

Tipe, *v.* To turn over, or fall over.

Tipple over, *v.* To fall over.

Tipple-tail-over, *n.* Somersault.

Tit up, *v.* To pay one's share.

Tite. *Vide* **As tite.**

Titter, *adv.* and *adj.* Sooner, first, willingly.

Titterly, *adj.* Early, forward in growth.

Titty, *n.* The mother's milk.

Tiv. *Vide* **Till.**

Tivvy, *v.* To roam about.

To, *prep.* Often used instead of 'for.'

> Ex.—*We're gahin' ti 'ev dumplings ti dinner.* Common in old writers and the Bible.

Toft, *n.* A small grove of trees.

Tommy-loach, *n.* The stone-loach.

To'n, *n.* A good turn = a kindness.

> Ex.—*They'll deea onnyboddy a good to'n, will John an' Annie.*

To'n, *v.* To turn.

Toon, *n.* A village.

Toon street, *n.* The village street.

Top-dressin', *n.* Manure thrown on, not ploughed in.

Topping, *n.* A natural standing-up roll or curl on the forehead, the hair of the head.

> Ex.—*Sha teeak him byv t' topping an' shuvved him inti t' hollin bush.*

Topping, **Topper**, *adj.* First-class, very fine.

Tottering, *adj.* Unsettled as to weather and life.

> Ex.—*It's been nobbut a tottering tahm fur hay. He's nobbut 'eving a tottering tahm on 't; Ah doot he's nut lang fur here.*

Tottle, *v.* To toddle, as a child or an infirm person.

Tottling, *pp.* Falling.

Touchous ⎱ *adj.* Irritable, resentful.
Touchy ⎰

Touple, *v.* Another form of **Tottle**. To sway or totter and then fall over. **Whemm'l** carries the same double meaning, but is rarely heard now. To fall.

Trail, *v.* To drag along the ground. 2. To move with difficulty, or lazily.

> Ex.—*Hoo that lass dis trail aboot. Ah can hardlin's trail yah leg efter t' other.*

Trailtengs, *n.* A gossiping woman.

Trailtripes, *n.* A slatternly woman.

Trallops, *n.* A slatternly woman.

Tramp, *n.* and *v.* A beggar ; to go on foot.

Tramping, *part.* Trampling.

Trap, *v.* To be severely nipped, as by a box-lid falling on one's finger, and the like.

Trapes, *n.* A dirty, untidy woman.

Trapes or **Trapus**, *v.* To walk aimlessly about hither and thither.

Traps, *n.* Belongings.

> Ex.—*Pack thi traps up an' cum alang.*

Trash, *n.* Good for nothing, either of persons or things.

Travel, *v.* To walk, to move along.

> Ex.—*Theease steeans mak it bad travelling.*

Trig, *v.* To fill. As a *noun*, a stone to stop a wheel.

Trigger, *n.* One who feeds the cattle. NOTE.—Only used in the east of the North Riding.

Trim, *v.* To cut a hedge, to apply the finishing touch.

Trimmer, *adj.* Really good, first-class. *n.* A sharp fellow.

Trimm'ling-gess, *n.* Trembling grass.

Trod, *n.* A footpath.

Troll, *v.* To roll.

Troll-egg day. *Vide* chapter on 'Customs.'

Trollibobs, *n.* Entrails.

Trunking, *n.* The business of lobster and crab catching.

Tu'n. *Vide* **To'n.**

Tundish, *n.* A funnel.

Tup, *n.* A ram.

Turve, *n.* A block of turf to be used as fuel.

Turve-cake, *n.* A cake baked in a pan having a tightly fitting lid, which is covered over with burning turves until sufficiently baked.

Twadgers, *n.* A ginger-bread cake.

Twangy, *adj.* and *adv.* Affected, applied to intonation.

Twank, *v.* To administer a sharp smack, to whip.

Twattle, *n.* Gossip.

Twattle, *v.* To stroke, to pet.

> Ex.—*Thoo twattles on wi' t' pup ez if 'twar a bairn.*

Tweea, *num. adj.* Two.

Twill, *n.* A quill, as 'twill pen.'

Twilt, *n.* A bed-quilt.

Twilt, *v.* To beat, to flog.

Twilting, *v.* Cross-stitching two thicknesses together.

Twine, *v.* 1. To twist or turn from a direct course. 2. To be fretful.

> Ex.—1. *He twisted an' twin'd uz aboot whahl Ah didn't knaw wheear wa war.*

Twiny, *adj.* Peevish.

Twisty, *adj.* Cross, fretful.

Twitch-bell, *n.* The earwig (*Forficula auricularia*).

Twitters, *n.* A state of nervousness.

Tyaak. *Vide* **Teeak.**

Tyke, *n.* A disreputable fellow; the name given to a Yorkshireman.

U.

'Ud. Would.

Udge, *v.* To urge.

Un. One.

> Ex.—*Sha's a good un,* i. e. 'She is a good one.

Unbated, *adj.* Not repressed.

Unbeknown, *adj.* Not known.

Unbethink, *v.* To call to mind.

Uncomeatable, *adj.* and *adv.* Difficult to approach or get at.

H h

Underdraw, *v.* To cover with lath and plaster.
Underhanded, *adj.* Undersized, poorly developed.
Underling, *n.* A stunted, weakly child.
Undermind, *v.* To undermine.
Ungain, *adj.* Distant, difficult of access, awkward.
  Ex.—*It's sik an ungain spot ti finnd, is yours.*
Unmenseful, *adj.* Unbecoming, unseemly, ill-mannered.
Unreave, *v.* To unwind.
Unsayable, *adj.* Not amenable to advice, self-willed.
Unslot, *v.* To unfasten by pulling back the slot or bolt.
Unsteck, *v.* To unfasten and push open.
Up, To speak, *v.* To speak aloud, to defend oneself against an unjust charge.
Up with=The matter with.
  Ex.—*What's up wi' t' bairn?*
Upbray, *v.* To upbraid.
Upend, *v.* To set on end, to stand upright.
Upgang, *n.* A pathway up a hill or mountain.
Upgrown, *adj.* Adult.
Uphold, Upho'd, *v.* 1. To maintain, to give one's unqualified support. 2. To provide those things necessary for a person's welfare, to sustain.
  Ex.—1. *Thee gan on wi' 't, Ah'll upho'd tha iv all thoo d`z, 'coz thoo's i' t' reet on 't.* 2. *It'll tak summat ti uphold t' waay 'at he's gahin' on,* i.e. living.
Upset-price, *n.* The marked price at which an article is offered for sale.
Upset wiv, *adj.* Put out, disconcerted, worried.
  Ex.—*Ah nivver war sae upsetten wiv owt ez Ah war when t' au'd meer deed.*
Upshot, *n.* Final issue, the conclusion of anything.
  Ex.—*An' t' upshot on 't war 'at he gat hissel weel bunched.*
Use, To no=Useless, unprofitable, worthless.
Use ti o'u'd=Once was able.
Us, *adv.* and *conj.* As. *Vide* **Es.**

V.

Varra, *adv.* Very. *Vide* **Very.**
Vast, *n.* and *adj.* A large number.
  Ex.—*A vast o' fooak cam ti t' feeast. Ther wur a vast mair hosses 'an Ah aim'd ti see.*
Verser, *n.* A rhymster.
Very, *adj.* An intensive.
  Ex.—*Thoo maay slavver on, varra few 'll pay onny heed ti what thoo sez. Aye, a varra deeal o' what he sez is o' varra larl matter tiv onnybody.*

Vessel cups=Wassail cups.
Viewly, Viewsome, *adj.* Pleasing to look at, handsome, neatly and well put together.
Ex.—*It's a varra viewly cauf. Sha's a varra viewly lass.*
Volumous, *adj.* Large, bulky.
Ex.—*It's a maist volumous consarn, yon is. Ah deean't tak ti sike volumous things.*

W.

Wa, *pron.* We.
Wad, *v.* Would.
Wade, *v.* To glimmer, as the sun does when rising if the atmosphere is charged with moisture.
Ex.—*It'll rain afoor neet, t' sun waded sadly ez sha peeped ower Rosberry.*
Waff, *n.* 1. A slight puff of wind. 2. The slightest scent.
Ex.—1. *It's despert clooase, ther hezn't been a waff o' wind ti-daay.* 2. *Noo Ah've 'ed yah waff o' thi silidge, an' Ah want na mair on 't.*
Waff, *v.* To bark as a little dog.
Waffle, *v.* To hesitate, waver, to be undecided.
Waffly, *adj.* 1. Undecided, wavering, vacillating. 2. Shaky, insecure. 3. Weak, dizzy, from illness. 4. Given to foolish talk, chatter, &c.
Ex.—1. *T' wind's all roads, it'll nobbut be a waffly sooart ov a daay. It's a varra waffly gahin' on.* 2. *Thoo'd best prop it up wi' summat, it leeaks a bit waffly.* 3. *Liggin' i' bed sae lang maks yan feel a bit waffly.* 4. *Ah reckon nowt ov her waffly waays.*
Waffy. *Vide* **Wauf.**
Waft, *n.* A slight puff of wind; a wraith, the appearance in the spirit form of some known one whose death is imminent.
Wag, *v.* To beckon with the finger or hand.
Ex.—*Ah wagg'd on him, bud he w'u'dn't cum.*
Wage, *v.* To induce by promise of payment.
Ex.—*Ah c'u'dn't wage him ti staay efter he'd seen Mally's waft.*
Wahnt=Was not, were not.
Wain, *n.* A wagon.
Wain hoos, *n.* Wagon shed.
Wait of } *v.* To wait for.
Wait on }
Wake, Waak, *adj.* Weak.
Wakken, *v.* To awake, *active* and *neuter.*
Wakkensome, *adj.* Easily roused.

Wale, Weeal, Wheeal, *v.* To flog with a stick.

Waling, Weealing, *n.* Planks so fixed as to strengthen the bank of a river.

Walk with, *v.* To court, to be engaged.

Ex.—*Sha's gi'en Tom t' go-by, an' walks wi' t' young gardener noo.*

Walsh, *adj.* Watery, without flavour.

Wame, Wheeam, *n.* The stomach.

Wan, *v.* Won.

Wangle, Wankle, *v.* To totter preparatory to falling, or to totter so as to have the appearance of falling.

Ex.—*Leeak oot! cum back! sha's startin' ti wang'l.*

Wangle, Wankle, Wankly, *adj.* Tottering.

Ex.—*T' larl brigg's a wankly consarn.*

Want, *v.* Its use is somewhat curious, e.g. *Does this book want changing?* i.e. 'Is this book to be changed?' *I want my coat brushing,* i.e. 'I wish my coat to be brushed.' *Thoo wants a good thrashing,* i.e. 'You deserve,' &c. *He hezn't gitten mair 'an he wanted,* i.e. 'He has not got more than he deserved.'

Wap-cloth, *n.* Coarse cloth for pilot coats.

War, Waur, Wor, Wur, Wuz, *imp. tense* of 'to be.' Was or were.

Warbels, *n.* Swellings on the back of a beast, caused by the larvae of the gad-fly (*Oestrus bovis*).

War-days, *n.* Any day save Sunday.

Wards. A common suffix signifying direction.

Ex.—*He war cumin' fra Newton-wards.*

'Ware, *v.* Beware.

Ware, *v.* To lay out one's money, to spend.

Ex.—*He awlus wares his brass ez if he meant ti git fowr penno'th o' stuff fur a threpenny bit.*

Wark, *v.* and *n.* Work. Its use is manifold, see below.

Wark, *v.* To ache, also as a *noun.*

Ex.—*Mah back warks past bahding. Thoo mun wark it* (arrange it) *seea ez he 'ez ti deea a day's wark* (a day's labour). *That'll gi'e him t' back-wark* (ache). *'At'll wark* (remove) *all t' warks* (pains) *'at's warking* (aching) *oot on him.*

Warm, *adj.* In easy circumstances, well-off.

Warm, *v.* To chastise, to flog.

Warn, *v.* To summon, to call together, to warn or swear in.

Warp, *v.* To flood land with water, either by artificial means or naturally by overflowing during heavy rains, in order that a deposit may be left upon the surface when the water recedes.

Warridge, *n.* The withers of a horse.

Warse, Wuss, Wess, *adj.* Worse.

Warsen, Warsening, *v.* To gradually grow worse.

Ex.—*T' crop warsens ivvery year. Tommy warsens; he's gahin' ti pop off if he dizn't pick up a bit.*

Warzle, Wezzle, *v.* To gain by craft, to cajole, to flatter, to wheedle.

Ex.—*Sha's a queer un, sha can wezzle owt oot o' ma. He can warzle tha inti believing owt.*

Wastrell, *n.* An extravagant spendthrift.

Water-bleb. *Vide* **Bleb.**

Water-brash, Water-springs, *n.* Acidity, heartburn.

Water-heck, *n.* A rail or swing gate hung across the stream to prevent cattle from straying.

Wath, *n.* A ford.

Watter. The common pronunciation of 'Water.'

Wauf, Waufish, *adj.* Faint, weak, insipid.

Wax, *v.* To grow.

Ex.—*He's a waxing lad that.*

Wax kernel, *n.* Swellings in the neck and hollow of the jaw.

Way-corn, *n.* Oats or barley.

Way-wards. *Vide* **Wards.**

Ways, *n.* Way. Used in such sentences as *Gan thi ways heeam. Noo git thi ways in. Cu' thi ways, honey.*

Wean, Weean, *n.* A female. An opprobrious epithet.

Weather-fast, *adj.* Kept in or prevented from carrying out one's plans owing to stress of weather.

Weather-gaul, *n.* The incomplete arc of a rainbow, only half being visible, the sure sign of a coming shower, if not of a bad spell of weather.

Ex.—*A dyer's neeaf an' a weather-gaul*
Sheppards warn 'at rain 'll fall.

Weazand, Wizzan, *n.* The windpipe.

Ex.—*He did shut his tung oot when Ah nipped his wizzan foor him.*

Wed, *v.* To marry. 'Marry' is rarely used in any tense or mood.

Weearish, *adv.* Irritable.

Weeks, *n.* Corners. I give the word because I know a few old people on whose lips it still lingers, but it is rarely heard now. I heard an old dame not so long ago say to a well-known gossip, *If thoo hed t' weeks o' thi mooth stitchen, an' t' weeks o' thi een slitten, thoo'd be yabble ti see t' muck i' t' weeks o' thi awn hoos, an' saay less aboot uther fowk.*

Weetless, *adj.* Lacking knowledge.

Wefted, To be, *v.* To be closely associated with.

Weight, Wite, *n.* Quantity, &c.

Ex.—*There warn't a gret weight o' taaties ti year. Neea gret weight o' rain fell thruff t' neet.*

Welt. *Vide* **Rigged.**

Welting, *n.* A sound thrashing.

War, Wern, *poss. pron.* Our, our own.

Werrick, *n.* and *v.* A half-smothered laugh ; to laugh, to chuckle.

Wersells} *pron.* Ourselves.
Wersens}

Wet, To, *v.* To rain lightly.

Wet-shod, *adj.* Wet as to feet, boots and stockings soaked.

Weyfe, Wahfe, *n.* Wife.

Wezzel. *Vide* **Rezzel.**

Wezzle. *Vide* **Warzle.**

Whack, *v.* To flog.

Whacker, *adj.* Larger than ordinary.

Whahl, *adv.* Until. *Until,* however, is never heard amongst the country people, *whahl* or *while* being general.

Whallack, *v.* To flog with a stick or strap.

Whallacker, *adj. Vide* **Whacker.**

Whallacking, *adj.* Very large.

Whallop, *v.* To whip soundly.

Whang, Wheeang, *n.* A thong.

Whang, *n.* A sudden and heavy drop, or a blow ; a thick slice. Also as a *verb,* to strike a heavy blow.

Whanging, *adj. Vide* **Whallacking.**

Whap, *n.* A sudden movement, a jerk.

    Ex.—*He went by wiv a whap.*

Whap, *v.* To close with a bang ; to give a smart tap on the knuckles ; to flap, as a wing.

Whapper, Whopper, *adj.* Huge.

What for, What for not, *adv.* Why, why not.

What mud be deean = No matter what precaution may have been taken.

    Ex.—*Ah shuv'd wi' my back, an' Billy thrust his hardest w.v a powl, but doon it cam, what mud be deean.*

What one could, or **'Ativver he, Ah,** or **yan could** = One's very best efforts.

    Ex.—*Ah pull'd 'ativver Ah could pull, bud it war ti neea ewse. Yan did what yan could, bud it war ti larl good.*

Whatten, *pron.* What.

    Ex.—*Whatten a tahm o' daay is 't ? Whatten a sooart ov a thing diz ti call that ?*

Whau, Wheea, *pron.* Who.

Wheea s' ow' 't ? lit. who shall owe or own it, i.e. To whom does it belong ? Who owns it ?

    Ex.—*Wheea s' ow' 't bairn ?*

Whemmel, *v.* To rock to and fro and then fall over.

Whewling, *adj.* Dizzy.

Whewtle, *v.* To whistle, to squeak.

Whidder, Wither, *n.* 1. A rush. 2. A sharp and swinging blow.

    Ex.—1. *He did gan by wiv a wither.* 2. *Ah'll catch thee sike a wither aback o' t' lug if thoo dizn't mahnd.*

Whiff, *v.* To puff in short blasts, as smoke sometimes puffs downwards and into the room.

Whiffle-whaffle, *n.* Idle talk.

Whiffley, *v.* To trifle, to vacillate.

Whimly, *adv.* Quietly, softly. *Vide* **Whisht**.

Whimsey, *adj.* Changeable, unstable.

Whins, *n.* The gorse.

Whipster, *n.* A doubtful character.

Whip-stitch, *n.* A useless fellow.

Whirken, *v.* To choke.

Whisht, *adv.* Noiselessly, quietly.

    Ex.—*Them bisittles gans varra whisht.*

Whisht, *adj.* Silent, noiseless.

Whisht, *intj.* Be quiet! Hush!

Whittle, *n.* A knife.

Whittle, *v.* To shave or slice off with a knife.

Whizzle. *Vide* **Warzle**.

Whoats, Whots, *n.* Oats.

Whya, *intj.* Well. If used at the end of a remark = Very well.

    Ex.—Q. *Thoo'll cum on o' Sundaay?* A. *Whya.*

Wi', *prep.* With. **Wiv** before a vowel.

Wick, *adj.* Living, lively, vigorous.

    Ex.—*Ah want yan 'at's wick, nut a deead un. By goa, sha's a wick un, is yon young miss.*

Wick, *n.* Life.

    Ex.—*This bangs all 'at Ah've seean i' mah wick.*

Wicken, *v.* To gather wickens.

Wickens, Wicks, *n.* Couch grass.

Wicken-wood, *n.* The mountain ash, the rowan-tree.

Wicker, *v.* To neigh, whinny.

Wicks, *n.* Seedlings of the whitethorn.

Wicksilver, *n.* Quicksilver.

Widdle-waddling, *v.* To waddle.

Widdy, *n.* A young willow shoot.

Wikes, *n.* The corners of the mouth.

Wildfire, *n.* Erysipelas.

Win, *v.* To attain one's object by considerable effort.

Wind, *n.* Information, a hint.

    Ex.—*Ah gat wind o' what he war efter. If he gets wind o' what thoo's deean, thoo'll drop in for 't.*

Wind, To lose one's = To die. 'Wind' is often used for 'breath.'

Winder, Winn'l, *v.* To winnow.

Winder or **Winn'ling machine,** *n.* A winnowing machine.

Windle straw or **Winn'l streah,** *n.* A dead stalk of straw or grass.

Winge, *v.* To threaten to kick (of a horse), to cry peevishly.

Winter-hedge, *n.* A clothes-horse.

Wipe, *n.* A sharp slap, a hurried rub.   Also a *verb.*
> Ex.—*Ah'll wipe tha across t' feeace.*

Wire-ling, *n.* The crowberry plant.

Wire-rush, *n.* The hard rush (*Juncus glaucus*).

Wit, *n.* Knowledge.
> Ex.—*He hezn't wit ti deea a job o' that sooart. He show'd mair wit 'an what Ah aim'd foor.*

Wiv, *prep.* With.

Wivoot, Widoot, *prep.* Without, unless.

Wizen, *v.* and *adj.* To shrivel, to dry up.
> Ex.—*Sha's gitten an au'd wizen'd feeace.*

Woomle, *n.* An auger.

Wor. *Vide* **War.**

Worral-hole, *n.* A draught-hole let into the wall through a drain-pipe at the back of the fire, used to burn sea-coal.

Worn, *adj.* Exhausted, used up.
> Ex.—*Ah's fairly woorn oot wi' t' job. Ah gat weary an' worn afoor t' daay war spent.*

Worry, *v.* To kill.
> Ex.—*Sha's nobbut a young un, bud sha's worried a ratten alriddy.*

Worsen, Warsen, *v.* 1. To make worse. 2. To gain the advantage of. *Vide* **Warsen.**
> Ex.—1. *Thoo worsens owt 'at thoo puts thi han' teeea.*
> 2. *Ah worsen'd him all t' waay thruff t' bargain.*

Wostler, *n.* Hostler.

Wrang, *adj.* Wrong.

Wrecklin, *n.* The last and smallest of a litter or brood.

Wringe, *v.* To whine like a dog, to cry out in pain. Often **Winge.**

Wrizzled. *Vide* **Rasselled.**

Wrong with, To get, *v.* To quarrel, to have a misunderstanding.

Wrought, Wrowt, *v.* To work, to strive.
> Ex.—*Neea chap's wrowt harder 'an what he hez. Ah've wrowt an' tew'd all t' daay whahl Ah's worn oot.*

Wummely, *v.* To move in a sinuous manner.

Wur. *Vide* **War.**

Wurk. *Vide* **Wark.**

Wus. *Vide* **War.**

Wye, *n.* A heifer under three years of age.

Wyke, Week, *n.* A small bay on the sea-coast.

Y.

Yabble, Yabblins. 1. Able. 2. Maybe, perhaps.

    Ex.—1. *Thoo'll be yabble ti deea 't.* 2. Q. *Will ta leeak in ez thoo passes?* A. *Yabblins* (or *Ablins*) *Ah will.*

Yaccorn, Yakron, *n.* The acorn.

Yacker, *n.* Acre.

Yaffle, *v.* To mumble, to speak indistinctly.

Yah, *num. adj.* One. N.B. **Yah,** unlike **Yan,** is never used singly, but is always followed by a word agreeing with it, e. g. ' Yah chap,' ' Yah tahm.'

    Ex.—*Yah daay Ah went wi' yan on 'em. Yah tahm yan o' your lads bunched ma. Yan's shooting yah thing,* &c.

Yak, *n.* Oak.

Yal, *n.* Ale.

Yalhoos. Alehouse.

Yam, *n.* Home. *Vide* **Heeam.**

Yam, *v. Vide* **Aim.**

Yan, *num. adj.* and *indf. pron.* One. *Vide* **Yah.**

Yance, *adv.* Once.

Yance ower. Once, at that time.

Yank, *v.* To thrash, to flog.

Yap, *v.* To bark at one's heels, to talk foolishly.

Yark, *v.* 1. To strike with a switch. 2. To pull out with a jerk.

    Ex.—2. *Thi float's blobb'd unner, yark 't oot.*

Yarker, *n.* The best of a sample.

    Ex.—*Tak that un, mun, it's a yarker.*

Yarking, *n.* A whipping with a switch.

Yarp, *v.* To shout, to speak loudly. *Vide* **Yowp.**

Yat, *adj.* Hot.

    Ex.—*It wur that yat, Ah c'u'dn't ho'd it.*

Yat, *n.* A gate.

Yat-steead, *n.* The ground covered by the sweep of the gate.

Yat-stoop, Yat-stoup, *n.* A gate-post.

Yaud, *n.* A horse or mare, usually on its last legs.

Yearn, *v.* To curdle milk.

Yearning, *n.* Rennet.

Yed, *v.* To make runs underground, as a rabbit, mole, &c.

Yedder, Yether, *n.* A young shoot in a hedge, which, being half cut, is utilized to strengthen some weaker part.

Yeead, Heead. Head.

Yer-nut, *n.* The earth-nut (*Bunium flexuosum*).

Yet, *adv.* Still.

    Ex.—*Is t' wagon here yet?* would not imply ' Has the wagon arrived ? ' but ' Is it still here ? '

Yeth, *n.* Earth.

Yethwurm, *n.* The earthworm.

Yewn. *Vide* **Yown.**

Yooken, *v.* To swallow greedily.

Yoke, *n.* The shoulder-bar by which two pails can be carried with ease.

Yoke, *v.* To buckle the harness on the horse to the shafts.

Yon, *adj.* and *adv.* That, over there. Used demonstratively of persons and things.

Yotten. *Vide* **Yooken.**

Youst, *pp.* Used.

Yow, *n.* A female sheep.

Yowl, *n.* A plaintive howl.

Yowl, *v.* To howl, to cry plaintively.

Yown, Yewn, Yuen, *n.* An oven.
  Ex.—*Now 'i's neyce, t' yuen's nivver been yat.*

Yowp, Yope, *v.* To cry as a young dog when first kennelled, to speak in a shrill voice.

Yuck. A curious usage is attached to this word. At any social gathering in the Cleveland dales, when those assembled have grown excited, some one will shout, *Yuck foor oor deeal,* to which another will instantly reply, *Yuck foor Castleton,* or *Yuck foor* ——, mentioning his own locality. I fancy in days past it would be given as a challenge; it now carries with it the sense of 'To cheer,' or 'Here's to our dale.'

Yuer, Ur, *n.* The udder of a cow.

Yuk, *v.* To beat.

Yuking, *n.* A beating.

Yule-cake, *n.* A rich plum-cake made for Christmastide, and cut into on Christmas Eve.

Yule-candle, -cann'l, *n.* A large wax candle lighted on Christmas Eve.

Yule-log or **-olog,** *n.* The log burnt on the fire on Christmas Eve.

CONCLUDING REMARKS

IT is a fact, and one worthy of all commendation, that every Yorkshireman considers the dialect spoken in the immediate locality wherein he was reared, as being not only the best, but the purest. Doubtless in some cases this is quite correct, but not in all. Contiguity to other counties has a deteriorating influence, which naturally extends across both borders, and is sometimes very far-reaching in its effect. Owing to this and other causes, many of my readers will find the pronunciation of some words, as given both in the Glossary and throughout the work, not quite in tune with the sound in which they daily hear such words uttered. This difficulty presented itself at the very commencement of the work. A rule had to be adopted to obtain something approaching uniformity and conciseness. To accomplish this, area has been chosen; i. e. in all cases in which a word has several pronunciations, those given in the Glossary and elsewhere, so far as the writer knows, are the pronunciations most generally in use throughout the riding. It may be noted, as we approach the West Riding and South Lancashire, that the vowel sounds of *a*, *e*, and *o* have a growing tendency to broaden in sound, often becoming *u*.

This, however, should be carefully guarded against in writing the dialect of the North Riding[1], as there is ample proof that over a very wide area the original sound of eighty years ago was the same as now used in Cleveland. These gradual local alterations form in time what botanists call sports.

Many words in such places are to-day passing through a transitional stage. E. g. let us compare a few words as spoken eighty years ago in two places I well know, viz. Bedale and Great Ayton. The former is much nearer the West Riding than the latter, and very forcibly shows the gradual alteration in pronunciation some words have undergone since 1800.

PRONUNCIATION.

As used in the North Riding, 1898.	As given in a Glossary published at Bedale, 1800.	As pronounced in Bedale, 1898.	As pronounced in the West Riding, 1898.	Meaning.
Chetch		Chŭch		Church
Deear		Doour		Door
To'n		Tŭ'n		Turn
Stor		Sturr		Stir
Fo'st		Fust		First
Ez		Uz		As
Fau'k		Fooak		Folk
Neeaze		Nooaz		Nose
Cleease		Clooase		Close
Ken *or* Kern		Chen *or* Chun		Churn
Diz		Duz		Does

[1] In several instances this rule has been broken, but only to give a correct rendering of the pronunciation as spoken in a particular district to-day.

As used in the North Riding, 1898.	As given in a Glossary published at Bedale, 1800.	As pronounced in Bedale, 1898.	As pronounced in the West Riding, 1898.	Meaning.
Wark		Wurrk		Work
War *or* Wor		Wuz		Was *or* were
Ax'd		Ast, Assed		Asked
Clais, Cleeas		Clooaz		Clothes
Deean't		Dooan't		Don't
Fleear		Flooar		Floor
Gahin' *or* ganning		Bown	Bahn	Going

The Glossary contains many words common to other dialects[1], especially the folk-speech of North Lincolnshire, Cumberland, Westmoreland, North Lancashire, and East Anglia.

It may be of interest to note over what a wide area the dialect of the North Riding is understood and in the main spoken. As an entertainer, I come in touch with the country people of many places, and I have often been surprised at the quickness with which the various points in my dialect sketches have been seized by those of other counties. Naturally I am able to indulge much more freely, both in dialect and idiom, in some places than in others.

The North and West Riding dialects widely differ not only as to vocabulary, but in drawl and intonation; e. g. take the following sentences :—

NORTH RIDING. Noo, mun, wheear's ta gahin' teea? Ah's gahin' doon t' toon.

WEST RIDING. Nah, lad, whor's ta bahn tew? Ah w' bahn dahn t' tahn.

[1] The term 'dialect' is used throughout this work for want of a better word, and to avoid tautology. Our folk-speech is not a dialect, it is a language.

Hear each sentence uttered by men of their respective ridings, and my readers will better understand my meaning than from pages of written explanation. There is also another difference. Whilst many titled people, and members of the best families in the North and East Ridings, can, when they have a mind to, speak the dialect fluently, of only a few of the leading families in the West Riding whom I have met am I able to say the same thing. There seems to be a feeling that in some way it would be *infra dig.* to admit ability to speak a word of their own folk-speech.

Referring to the wide area over which the dialect of the North and East Ridings is spoken, granting without questioning slight variation in pronunciation, the addition of new words, and the loss of familiar ones as we pass along, we find that practically the same dialect exists amongst the country folk inside the following rough boundary line. Draw right-lines commencing at Boston Spa, Lincolnshire, and connecting the following places, Doncaster, Harrogate, Lancaster, along the coast-line to Carlisle, thence to Darlington, Stockton, Middlesborough[1], and along the north-east coast. By so doing you wall in what may be aptly termed, 'the north-east folk-speech.' But far over this imaginary line, in certain directions, the dialect is understood and appreciated. This is not surprising when we remember the same races overran and peopled the whole of the country from the Wash to the Tyne and thence north-westward.

[1] The map issued with the North-Eastern 1*d.* Time-table answers well for the purpose.

They may be easily traced by their place-names—the by's, thorpes, cliffs, wicks, dales, &c.

But if we compare the folk-speech of the district so walled in, with that of the Danes and their kinfolk, then its Norse origin is seen at a glance. E. g. take the few following words—scores of the like could have been given :—

North and East Riding.	Cumberland and West-moreland.	Danish.	Scotch.	Standard English.
Mowdy-warp	Mowdy-warp	Muldvarp	Moudie	Mole
Beck	Beck	Bæk	...	A small stream
Lake	Lake	Lege	...	Play
Beeal	Beel	Bjæle	...	Bellow
Bield	Bield	Bylja (Swedish)	...	A shelter
Gah, gan	Ga, gang	Gaae	Ga	Go
Neeaf	Neif	Næve	Neive	Fist
Bink	Bink	Bænk	Bink	Bench
Gliff	Gliff	Glippe	Gliff	Quick glance
Gesling	Gezling	Gjæsling	Gesling	Gosling
Gloor	Glower	Glo	Glower	Stare
Skrike	Skrike	Skrige	Skreich	Scream
Teeam	Teem	Toomme	Toom (to empty)	Pour out
Feck, n. ability				
Feckless, adj.	Feckless	Fik is the past tense of faa, to get[1], imp. tense, feck	Feckless	Incapable of providing for one-self

[1] Our dialect word *Fick*, which is the *Fik* given, has three distinct meanings : (1) to struggle under some form of restraint ; (2) to strive to obtain ; (3) to succeed, to get.

Ex.—1. 'T' pig ficked that hard whahl Ah c'u'dn't git it inti t' cart.' 2. 'He made a poor fick on 't,' i.e. he made a feeble attempt. 'He weean't mak a fick for 't,' he won't strive to do, obtain, or get. 3. 'He ficked it at t' finish,' he got it in the end.

The Danish, Norwegian, Lowland Scotch, and north-east folk-speech are closely allied. We must not, however, compare the spelling, but the general sound of the words. Take the two first lines of the Danish national song—

DANISH. Kong Christian stod ved hoien mast.
NORTH RIDING. King Christian steead byv t' heegh mast.
DANISH. I' Rog[1] og damp.
NORTH RIDING. I' roke an' reek.

Again, take two lines from a poem in Modern Friesic published in 1834. The centre lines are from the poem, with the modern North Riding dialect above and standard English below.

NORTH RIDING. What be'st thoo, leyfe?
FRIESIC. Hwat bist dhow, libben?
STANDARD ENGLISH. What art thou, life?

NORTH RIDING. Fra t' scepter'd king ti t' slaave.
FRIESIC. Fen de scepterde kening ta da slave.
STANDARD ENGLISH. From the sceptred king to the slave.

For a list of words common to the English, Dutch, and Scandinavian languages, see *Trans. Phil. Soc.* part i. 1858.

Much that is written and spoken at the present day is quite over the heads of our country people. Take the following, from one of our best authors:—' He who performs every part of his business in due course and season, suffers no part of time to escape without profit. And it is well always to regard the quality rather than the quantity of your work, and bear in mind, if you delay till to-morrow what ought to be

---

[1] 'Roke' is the common dialectic word for mist or fog. 'Reek' is the North Riding word for smoke. 'Rog' is the Danish.

done to-day, you overcharge to-morrow with a burden which belongs not to it.' Our country folk would fully grasp the above if put to them something like the following :—' Him 'at diz a daay's wark iv a daay, dizn't waste his tahm, an' mannishes ti git a bit foor hissel. An' yan awlus owt ti aim ti deea t' bit 'at yan diz deea fo'st-class, mair 'an aiming ti clash thruff a seet o' wark onny road ; an' think on, if ya lig o' yah sahd whahl ti morn what ya owt ti-deea ti daay, ya saddle ti morn wiv a boddun 'at it's neea call ti bear.'

Hah am the rose o' Sharon and the lily o' the valley.

In a work kindly lent me by my friend Dr. Johnson of Lancaster, and published some years ago for the Philological Society, the author, quoting from *Latham on the English Language*, gives the above as a specimen of North Riding dialect—nay, more, of Cleveland itself. Surely the writer can never have spent a day in any part of Cleveland, for the sentence given contains but twelve words, seven of which are distinctly not Clevelandic.

The country people, when speaking *naturally*, rarely use the aspirate, except as an intensive. Otherwise they have little use for it. And when ' H ' is preceded by the definite article, they do not drop it in the sense generally understood ; the fact is they cannot well sound it, for this reason—the definite article is ' t',' ' the[1] ' being but rarely used. They could not say ' t' horse,' ' t' house, ' t' hamper,' &c. ; with them it is, ' t' hoss,' ' t' hoos,' ' t' hamper,' pronounced ' toss,' ' toos,' ' tamper.'

[1] ' The' is always used before the name of the Deity, and often in conversation of a grave and sorrowful nature.

'The horse is yoked,' 'the hamper is in the wagon,' and 'the whip is under the wheels,' as spoken, would sound to unfamiliar ears as if the speaker had said 'toss is yoked,' 'tamper's i' twagon,' and 'twip's unner tweels.'

The definite article, to those unaccustomed to our folk-speech, seems to be entirely wanting. Certainly before *b*, *m*, and *n* it is only very slightly sounded, and it becomes the merest touch of the tongue against the palate when preceding words commencing with *d* or *t*. 'Shut the door, the bacon and the beans are on the table,' would sound to a stranger as though the speaker said, 'Shut deear, bacon an' beeans is on table'; the speaker having in reality said, 'Shut t' deear, t' bacon an' t' beeans is on t' table.'

To return, however, to the line from Solomon's Song, given as a specimen of Cleveland dialect. Let us see what the rendering should have been.

Hah am the rose o' Sharon and the lily o' the valley.
Ah's t' roase o' Sharon an' t' lily o' t' valley.

The lower line is North Yorkshire and pure Cleveland, the upper line is said to be so.

It has been remarked that the aspirate is almost unknown—so it is as a letter, but not as an intensive. The aspirate, when misplaced by those speaking naturally, is only used to add greater force. 'He's mah henemy foor hivver,' leaves no doubt that the injury sustained is of an unbridgeable character. Such a sentence, however, holds quite a different place in grammar, too. 'Hi hallers taike shagar i' my tea.' The first example is Yorkshire intensified, minus any adjectives, the first

'H' expressing or suggesting some such feeling as implacable, and the 'hever' meaning for ever and ever. The latter is the vile and affected speech of the upper circles of Yorkshire flunkeys and maids, who try to improve upon their mother tongue. It holds no place in our folk-speech. It is hateful, and is only indulged in by those of whom the old people say, ' When they start ti knack an' scrape ther tungs, what they saay's nowther nowt na summat,' i. e. 'When they begin to talk affectedly, what they say is neither one thing nor another.'

There is one other peculiarity which must be noticed —the possessive case. I should imagine a hundred years ago its disuse was universal in both ridings. My reason for so thinking lies in the fact that in any old books wherein the owners have inscribed their names —and they usually did (books were valued in those days)—the names are never written in the possessive case. It is always 'Tom Smith book,' 'Ann Scott book.' Even to-day in many places, when speaking, the observance of the case is conspicuous by its absence. E. g. in the Boroughbridge and other districts they would not say ' Jack Wilson's dog bit Smith's calf,' and 'Peggy's cat flew through Nanny's window,' but ' Jack Wilson dog bit Smith cauf,' and 'Peggy cat flew throw Nanny window.' Such sentences as 'Ho'd t' hoss heead,' 'Pull t' pig lug,' and 'Twist t' coo tail,' &c., are still universal in both ridings. The instances in which the possessive is used, and vice versa, are now about equal in the North Riding. The peculiar forms of redundancy are many and curious. 'Ah nivver at neea tahm sed nowt aboot nowt ti neea-

body,' simply means, 'I never said anything to any one.
I think the following example, which I overheard
one Yorkshireman say to another just before the
train moved out of Guisborough station, is the finest
on record. 'Whya,' said he, 'thoo mun saay what
thoo 'ez a mahnd teea, bud think on, thoo knaws,
'at Ah knaw 'at he knaws, 'at thoo knaws 'at Ah
knaw, all aboot ivverything 'at's ivver been deean
an' 'at's ivver ta'en pleeace.' I heard a man say
a short time ago, 'Ah s' be agate ti git agate ti
set agate Tom fo'st thing ti morn at morn'; i.e.
'Ah s' be agate,' I shall be about; 'ti git agate,'
to commence work; 'ti set agate,' to set Tom
to work; 'fo'st thing ti morn at morn,' first thing
in the morning. Said one to another, 'Noo Ah'll
tell ya what, hard eneeaf, he war neean ower-suited
when he fan oot 'at he'd 'ev ti 'ev 't ower wi' ma
owther thruff or by. An' noo when Ah've fetched
him up ti t' scrat, he sez 'at he's putten t' dog oot
'o' t' road; bud Ah's satisfied o' yah thing, t' dog
rave mah britches, an' Ah s'all leeak ti him ti mak
'em good agaan, foor he 'ez a reet ti owther deea
that or 'livver summat up i' lieu on 't; bud Ah reckon
nowt o' what he sez, an' that's t' len'th on 't.' I.e.
'Noo Ah'll tell ya what,' now I assure you; 'hard
eneeaf,' without doubt; 'he war neean ower-suited,'
he was not over-pleased; 'when he fan oot,' when he
discovered; ''at he'd 'ev ti 'ev it ower wi' ma,' that
he would have to talk it over with me; 'owther thruff
or by,' either one way or the other; 'an' noo when
Ah've fetched him up ti t' scrat,' and now when I
have made him toe the mark; 'he sez 'at he's putten

t' dog oot o' t' road,' he says that he has killed the dog; 'bud Ah's satisfied o' yah thing,' but I am certain of one thing; 't' dog rave mah britches,' the dog tore my trousers; 'an' Ah s'all leeak ti him ti mak 'em good agaan,' and I shall expect him to replace them; 'foor he 'ez a reet ti,' for he ought to; 'owther deea that or 'livver summat up,' either do that or give something; 'i' lieu on 't,' in place of it (them); 'bud Ah reckon nowt o' what he sez,' but I place no confidence in anything he says; 'an' that's t' len'th on 't,' and that is the extent of it.

If the reader masters the abbreviations and elisions facing page 1, the *pons asinorum* will have been crossed, and the reading of our folk-speech found to be a thing easy of accomplishment and a delightful acquisition.

It will be well to remember, when reading aloud, that a consonant with an elided vowel must be joined either to the word preceding or following, as 't' hoss.' 't' hens,' 't' wax,' the horse, the hens, the wax, which would be pronounced 'toss,' 'tens,' 'twax.' Again, 'Sha's i' t' sulks' would be 'shas it sulks,' and 'Oot wi' 't, put tane ti t' ither,' would be rendered as 'oot wit, put tane ti tither.' 'Ah've deean noo, t' ink's ommaist dhry i' mah pen, seea this'll 'a'e ti be

T' LAP UP ON 'T.'

PUBLIC AND PRIVATE

HUMOROUS RECITALS

OF HIS

Original Character Sketches in the Yorkshire Dialect

(AS SPOKEN IN THE NORTH RIDING)

ARE GIVEN BY THE AUTHOR

AT

DRAWING-ROOMS IN TOWN OR THE PROVINCES
AT HOMES, HOUSE PARTIES,
RECEPTIONS, PRIMROSE LEAGUES,
LITERARY SOCIETIES, CONCERTS & BAZAARS, &c.

---

*Secretaries of Literary Societies will oblige by booking their
dates as early as possible for a Lecture entitled,*
'**Customs and Folklore of the North Riding.**'

——➤•◄——

*TERMS, VACANT DATES, TESTIMONIALS AND SYLLABUS
FORWARDED ON APPLICATION.*

——➤•◄——

NOTE.—*A reduced fee is offered to Clergymen of small parishes booking
a date during the months of September, October, or November.*

Address—

R. BLAKEBOROUGH, Society Humorist,

24 Trent Street, Stockton-on-Tees.

CPSIA information can be obtained at www.ICGtesting.com
Printed in the USA
BVOW03s2321121214

379084BV00019B/206/P